This is a volume in the Arno Press Series

NATIONAL BUREAU
OF
ECONOMIC RESEARCH
PUBLICATIONS
IN REPRINT

*See last pages of this volume
for a complete list of titles.*

The Frontiers
of Economic Knowledge

ESSAYS BY

ARTHUR F. BURNS

ARNO PRESS
A New York Times Company
New York — 1975

Editorial Supervision: Eve Nelson
Reprint Edition 1975 by Arno Press Inc.

NATIONAL BUREAU OF ECONOMIC RESEARCH
PUBLICATIONS IN REPRINT
ISBN for complete set: 0-405-07572-3
See last pages of this volume for titles.

Manufactured in the United States of America

Publisher's Note: The list of Publications
of the National Bureau of Economic Research
Since 1945 on pages 359-364 has been deleted
from this edition.

—◆—

Library of Congress Cataloging in Publication Data

Burns, Arthur Frank, 1904-
    The frontiers of economic knowledge.

    (National Bureau of Economic Research publications in
reprint)
    Reprint of the ed. published for the National Bureau
of Economic Research by Princeton University Press,
Princeton, N. J., which was issued as no. 57 of the
Bureau's General series.
    Includes bibliographical references.
    1. Economics--Addresses, essays, lectures. I. Title.
II. Series. III. Series: National Bureau of Economic
Research. General series ; no. 57.
[HB171.B87 1975]   330   75-19695
ISBN 0-405-07576-6

The Frontiers
of Economic Knowledge

NATIONAL BUREAU OF ECONOMIC RESEARCH

NUMBER 57, GENERAL SERIES

The Frontiers
of Economic Knowledge

ESSAYS BY

ARTHUR F. BURNS

PUBLISHED FOR THE
NATIONAL BUREAU OF ECONOMIC RESEARCH, NEW YORK

BY PRINCETON UNIVERSITY PRESS, PRINCETON
1954

Printed in the United States of America
by Princeton University Press, Princeton, New Jersey

Foreword

The five qualities required of an economist, Alfred Marshall said in his *Principles of Economics*, are perception, imagination, reason, sympathy, and caution. It is against this standard that the reader will judge the volume now spread before him.

Here are Mr. Burns' reports, as Director of Research, on the work of the National Bureau of Economic Research, and related short pieces written by him during the past two decades. Because it includes papers prepared by him in his private capacity, the volume is not a National Bureau study in the usual sense. Nevertheless, it is a volume that we think will further the Bureau's object, "to ascertain and to present to the public important economic facts and their interpretation in a scientific and impartial manner."

The collection is not a miscellany to which only the professional economist will turn now and then for some particular piece. When a scientist has wholeheartedly devoted himself to his subject, even the essays he has written over a period of years and for a variety of occasions are bound to form a connected whole. When his focus is the course of economic change, which lies at the heart of the major economic problems of our day, and his pen is skillful, his audience will be wide. When he has cultivated the qualities of which Marshall spoke, and is armed with the support of a corps of coworkers, what is said in his essays will command attention. This is, therefore, a book for every intelligent reader who seeks a stimulating discussion of what we know—and do not know—about the origins and consequences of change in our economy.

The problem of economic instability is approached along the road solidly laid down by Wesley C. Mitchell, Director of Research at the National Bureau during its first twenty-five years. Drawing on and adding to the work of Mitchell and other colleagues, Burns paints a vivid picture of business cycles. Anyone reading his essays will find a realistic, yet comprehensible, portrayal of the round of prosperity and depression. Compared with the canvas thus created by wide observation, patient sifting of facts, careful analysis, and repeated testing of hypotheses, other and perhaps more popular portraits will seem oversimplified and incomplete.

While Burns deals most fully with the type of economic change called business cycles, this is by no means his only concern. The long cycles that characterize residential construction engaged his attention almost at the outset of his career. The species of change economists know as 'secular trends' has been a major subject of investigation by the National Bureau throughout its existence. Change in the distribution of income, new habits of saving, alterations in economic organization, and productivity trends are among the many topics informatively discussed in the essays. When the reader has pursued these topics through the present volume, he will not wish to overlook the analysis of the process of economic growth in Burns' volume on *Production Trends in the United States since 1870.*

Burns emphasizes what we know about economic behavior, and the role played by systematic scientific work in the cumulation of economic knowledge. In his reports on the National Bureau's program of work and in his review of the work of others, he rightly points also to what we do not know. There are many reasons why our ignorance is great. "The development of a body of tested knowledge, adequate for coping with society's economic ills is bound to be a slow process."[1] Reaching for "warranted statements about the world in which men have to live—statements that can be tested by others, cumulatively improved, and applied to practice,"[2] is laborious; the success of any particular effort is unpredictable. Economic research encounters surprises, unpleasant as well as pleasant. The economic investigator will frequently be forced to detour, or even to return to his base camp to prepare for another try.

The reader will find himself sharing in the high adventure of working at the frontier of economic knowledge as he reads Burns' successive reports on the National Bureau's activities. The fact that the reports—like the rest of the essays—are reprinted virtually as they originally appeared, with all their questions and hopes and promises as well as their records of accomplishment, helps to convey this quality of adventure. The reader will sense also the camaraderie that from the National Bureau's very beginning has enriched the lives of those fortunate enough to participate in its activities; the analogy to an organized party of mountain climbers is not misplaced.

The reports recount the most recent chapter of the National Bureau's efforts at impartial and organized research in economics, a chapter that began when Burns succeeded Mitchell as Director of Research in 1945 and ended when Burns was granted a leave of

[1] A. F. Burns, preface to *Economic Research and the Development of Economic Science and Public Policy* (Twelve Papers Presented at the Twenty-fifth Anniversary Meeting of the National Bureau of Economic Research, 1946), p. viii.
[2] W. C. Mitchell, in the volume cited above, p. 11.

absence to enter the public service in 1953. This chapter is linked to those that came before. The National Bureau is a venture into the unknown on which a few bold and far-seeing men embarked over a generation ago. Wesley Mitchell, who mapped out the general course which the National Bureau has steadily followed, has described its character: "Those who assisted the launching of our experiment were prompted by public spirit. They could expect no personal advantage, for the National Bureau began its researches with a study of national income, in which all citizens have a common interest. It published its findings for the benefit of contributors and noncontributors alike. It expressed no moral judgments such as might give comfort to special groups, and it offered no practical advice on how to deal with current issues. Its function was solely to ascertain the ever changing state of affairs as precisely as possible, and put its findings at the disposal of anyone and everyone who cared to use them. Only those who believed that 'the truth shall make you free' had reason to lend a hand."[3]

This, then, is a book about the National Bureau, about what we know and do not know about the nature and causes of economic change. It is a book about the adventure of economic research, and particularly about one organized expedition's explorations in economics. Being these, it is a book also about Wesley Mitchell—and Arthur Burns.

S. F.
G. H. M.

June 1953

[3] W. C. Mitchell, "The National Bureau's First Quarter Century," *Twenty-fifth Annual Report of the National Bureau of Economic Research* (May 1945), p. 11.

ix

Contents

PART ONE

Reports on the National Bureau's Work

Economic Research and the Keynesian Thinking of Our Times

I. THE LESSON OF RICARDIANISM

It is now almost a century since John Stuart Mill's great work on the *Principles of Political Economy* appeared. In this treatise Mill rounded out and summed up the classical system of which Ricardo had been the leading architect. Mill wrote with dignity, assurance, and authority. His mind was not beset by doubts concerning the true principles of political economy. "The most important proposition in political economy," he proclaimed, "is the law of production from the land, that in any given state of agricultural skill and knowledge, by increasing the labour, the produce is not increased in an equal degree." In Mill's world, diminishing returns defined the production function in agriculture and thus set the stage within which economic progress could unfold. Population and technology were the dynamic factors in economic life, but population was considered the more potent variable. As population increased, the land already being farmed would need to be cultivated more intensively or inferior land brought under the plow; costs on the margin of cultivation consequently would rise, and serve ultimately to enrich the landlords and injure the capitalists and workers. "It is vain to say," Mill lamented, "that all mouths which the increase of mankind calls into existence, bring with them hands. The new mouths require as much food as the old ones, and the hands do not produce as much."[1]

If these doctrines of the classical school make curious reading today, it is well to note that our perspective has been altered by the emergence of new problems and a century of experience with the old ones. From the vantage point of history, we know that the Ricardians vastly overestimated the dynamic pressure of population and underestimated the power of technology. We know that the static tendency of land to yield a diminishing return to successive increments of labor has been swamped by the historical tendency towards improvement in the industrial arts. Between 1870 and 1940 we have tolerably reliable measurements, and they show

Reprinted from *Twenty-sixth Annual Report of the National Bureau of Economic Research* (June 1946), pp. 3-29. A subsequent and more detailed critical examination of Keynesian economics appears in Part Two of the present volume, in the essay "Keynesian Economics Once Again." See also the essays below on "The Instability of Consumer Spending" and "Hicks and the Real Cycle."

[1] J. S. Mill, *Principles of Political Economy*, ed. Ashley, pp. 177, 191.

that the output of American agriculture increased much faster than employment, decade after decade. At the end of the seventy-year period employment was only 34 per cent higher than at the beginning, while output was 279 per cent higher.[2] Today many are troubled by the mechanization of agriculture and the slow growth of population, few are concerned over the 'law of diminishing returns.' In their study of American agriculture, published by the National Bureau in 1942, Barger and Landsberg do not even mention the law.

I have taken this excursion into history because we are living in a time of bold and vigorous theoretical speculation, the only close parallel of which is the Ricardian age. The principal practical problem of Ricardo's generation was whether the state should foster the economic power of the landlords or of the rising manufacturing class. The heated discussions of this question stimulated Ricardo to take the distribution of incomes as the principal problem of economic theory, and he thereby set the pattern of classical economics. The principal practical problem of our own generation is the maintenance of employment, and it has now become—as it long should have been—the principal problem of economic theory. This transformation of economic theory is due in large part to the writings of John Maynard Keynes, which are exercising a great influence on the thinking of economists and the shaping of public policies in our own and other countries. But although Keynes and his followers are concerned with a range of problems that the classical economists shunned, by and large they still seek to arrive at economic truth in the manner of Ricardo and his followers. Broadly speaking, the Keynesians investigate the volume of employment and income of a country on much the same plane as the Ricardians investigated the distribution of incomes. If the fate of the Ricardian system carries a moral, it has not been clearly impressed on this original and able group of economists of our generation.

II. Keynes' Theory of Underemployment Equilibrium

I have said enough to set the theme of my report, which is to relate the work of the National Bureau to the Keynesian thinking of our times. The opinion is widespread that Keynes has explained what determines the volume of employment at any given time, and that our knowledge of the causes of variations in employment

2 Harold Barger and Hans H. Landsberg, *American Agriculture, 1899-1939*, p. 253. Of course, these figures exaggerate the disparity, since they take no account of the shift from direct labor on farms to indirect labor in factories.

is now sufficient to enable government to maintain a stable and high level of national income and employment within the framework of our traditional economic organization. If this opinion is valid, the solution of the basic problem of democratic societies is in sight, and the National Bureau would do well to reconsider its research program. Unhappily, this opinion reflects a pleasant but dangerous illusion.

The basis for the Keynesians' confidence is Keynes' theory of underemployment equilibrium, which attempts to show that a free enterprise economy, unless stimulated by governmental policies, may sink into a condition of permanent mass unemployment. The crux of this theory is that the volume of investment and the 'propensity to consume' determine between them a unique level of income and employment. The theory can be put simply without misrepresenting its essence. Assume that business firms in the aggregate decide to add during a given period $2 billion worth of goods to their stockpiles, using this convenient term to include new plant and equipment as well as inventories. This then is the planned investment. Assume, next, that business firms do not plan to retain any part of their income;[3] so that if they pay out, say, $18 billion to the public, they expect to recover $16 billion through the sale of consumer goods, the difference being paid out on account of the expected addition to their stockpiles. Assume, finally, that the 'consumption function' has a certain definite shape; that if income payments are, say, $18 billion, the public will spend $17 billion on consumer goods and save $1 billion, and that one-half of every additional billion dollars of income will be devoted to consumption and one-half to savings. Under these conditions, the national income per 'period' should settle at a level of $20 billion.

The reason is as follows. If income payments were $18 billion, the public would spend $17 billion on consumer goods. But the firms that made these payments expected to sell $16 billion worth to the public and to add $2 billion worth to their stockpiles; the actual expenditure of $17 billion on consumer goods would therefore exceed sellers' expectations by $1 billion, and stimulate expansion in the consumer goods trades. On the other hand, if income payments were $22 billion, the public would spend $19 billion on consumer goods; this would fall short of sellers' expecta-

---

[3] This assumption is not essential to the Keynesian system; I make it here in order to simplify the exposition. The figures used throughout are merely illustrative. Further, the exposition is restricted to the proximate determinants of employment in Keynes' system; this simplification does not affect the argument that follows.

tions by $1 billion, and set off a contraction in the output of consumer goods. In general, if income payments fell below $20 billion, the sales expectations of business firms would be exceeded; while if income payments rose above $20 billion, the expectations of business firms would be disappointed. In either case, forces would be released that would push the system in the direction of the $20 billion mark. Hence, in the given circumstances, $20 billion is the equilibrium income, and it may be concluded that the basic data—that is, the volume of investment and the consumption function—determine a national income of unique size. If we assume, now, a unique correlation between income and employment, it follows that the basic data determine also a unique volume of employment—which may turn out to be well below 'full' employment.

This is the theoretical skeleton that underlies the Keynesian system. The theory implies that when unemployment exists, an increase in consumer spending out of a given income will expand employment; so too will an increase in private home investment or in exports, and so again will governmental loan expenditure, its effect on employment being in a sense similar to that of private investment expenditure. The theory implies also that the magnitude of the expansion in employment by any of these routes is a precisely calculable quantity, since the determinants of employment are alleged to have been isolated. To get more out of the theory, more specific assumptions must be made.

At this vital juncture the Keynesians differ somewhat among themselves, but two institutional assumptions dominate the thinking of the school. The first is that consumer outlay is linked fairly rigidly to national income and is unlikely to expand unless income expands; in other words, there is little reason to expect, at least in the short run, that a condition of unemployment will be corrected through a reduction in individual savings. The second assumption is that investment opportunities are limited in a 'mature' economy such as our own; consequently, private investment may continue, year in and year out, at a level that falls considerably short of what the community would save if 'full employment' existed. If neither an upward shift in the consumption function, nor an expansion of private investment at home, nor an increase in net exports can be confidently counted on, it follows that our lot may be persistent mass unemployment. We may escape the fate of secular stagnation, however, if the effective demand for employment is supplemented by governmental spending. Furthermore, this remedy for secular stagnation is also the remedy for business cycles, since the most that can be expected of private investment is that it may rise sufficiently to generate 'full employment' during a fleeting boom.

Of late this theory has been refined and elaborated, so that 'deficit financing' need no longer be the key instrument for coping with unemployment, and I shall refer to one of these refinements at a later point. But the practical significance of the modifications of the theory is problematical, and in any event the theory as I have sketched it still dominates the thinking of the Keynesians when they look beyond the transition from war to peace. The similarity of this theory to the Ricardian model is unmistakable. The most important proposition in Ricardian economics is that the production function in agriculture has a certain shape, that is, the marginal product diminishes as the input of labor increases. The most important proposition in Keynesian economics is that the consumption function has a certain shape, that is, consumer outlay increases with national income but by less than the increment of income. The Ricardians treated the production function as fixed, and deduced the effects on income distribution of an increase or decrease in population, or of a tax or bounty on the production of corn. The Keynesians treat the consumption function as fixed, and deduce the effects on the size of the national income of an increase or decrease in private investment, or of an increase or decrease in governmental loan expenditure. The Ricardians believed that population was the key dynamic variable, and they drew a gloomy picture of the course of events if that exuberant variable was not counteracted. The Keynesians believe that investment is the key dynamic variable, and they draw a gloomy picture of the course of events if that timid variable is not fortified by governmental loan expenditure. To be sure, the Ricardians recognized that the production function in agriculture was subject to change, and they frequently inserted qualifications to their main conclusions. The Keynesians likewise recognize that the consumption function is not absolutely rigid, and they frequently insert qualifications to their main conclusions. But I have formed the definite impression that the Keynesians—except when they discuss changes in personal taxation—attach even less importance to their qualifications than did the Ricardians; all of which may merely reflect the fact that the Ricardians were concerned largely with secular changes, while the Keynesians are mainly concerned,

7

despite their anxiety over secular stagnation, with comparatively short-run changes.

There is, of course, nothing unscientific about Ricardianism as such. But *ceteris paribus* is a slippery tool, and may lead to serious error if the premises accepted for purposes of reasoning are contrary to fact, or if the impounded data are correlated in experience with factors that the theorist allows to vary, or if the very process of adjustment induces changes in the impounded data. Let us go back to the theoretical skeleton of the Keynesian system and examine it more carefully. Suppose that the volume of intended investment is $2 billion, income payments $20 billion, and consumers' outlay at this level of income $18 billion. On the basis of these data, the economic system is alleged to be in equilibrium. But the equilibrium is aggregative, and this is a mere arithmetic fiction. Business firms do not have a common pocketbook. True, they receive in the aggregate precisely the sum they had expected, but that need not mean that even a single firm receives precisely what it had expected. Since windfall profits and losses are virtually bound to be dispersed through the system, each firm will adjust to its own sales experience, and within a firm the adjustment will vary from one product to another. Under the circumstances the intended investment cannot—quite apart from 'autonomous' changes —very well remain at $2 billion, and the propensity to consume is also likely to change. Our data therefore do not determine a unique size of national income; what they rather determine is a movement away from a unique figure. Of course, we cannot tell the direction or magnitude of the movement, but that is because the basic data on which the Keynesian analysis rests are not sufficiently detailed for the purpose.

I have imagined that Keynes' aggregative equilibrium is realized from the start. But suppose that this does not happen; suppose that, in the initial period, the intended investment is $2 billion, income payments $16 billion, and that savings at this level of income. are zero. Will income now gravitate towards the $20 billion mark, as the theory claims it should? There is little reason to expect this will happen. In the first place, windfall profits will be unevenly distributed, and the adjustment of individual firms to their widely varying sales experiences will induce a change in the aggregate of their intended investment. In the second place, unemployed resources will exercise some pressure on the prices of the factors of production, and here and there tend to stimulate investment. In the third place, if an expansion in the output of consumer goods does get under way, it will induce additions to inventories for purely technical reasons; further, the change in the business outlook is apt to stimulate the formation of new firms, and to induce existing firms to embark on investment undertakings of a type that have no close relation to recent sales experience. In the fourth place, as income expands, its distribution is practically certain to be modified; this will affect the propensity to consume, as will also the emergence of capital gains, the willingness of consumers to increase purchases on credit, and the difficulty faced by consumers in adjusting many of their expenditures to increasing incomes in the short run. These reactions, and I have listed only the more obvious ones, are essential parts of the adjustment mechanism of a free enterprise economy. Under their impact the data with which we started—namely, the amount of intended investment and the consumption function—are bound to change, perhaps slightly, perhaps enormously. It is wrong, therefore, to conclude that these data imply or determine, even in the sense of a rough approximation, a unique level at which the income and employment of a nation will tend to settle. In strict logic, the data determine, if anything, some complex cumulative movement, not a movement towards some fixed position.

If this analysis is sound, the imposing schemes for governmental action that are being bottomed on Keynes' equilibrium theory must be viewed with skepticism. It does not follow, of course, that these schemes could not be convincingly defended on other grounds. But it does follow that the Keynesians lack a clear analytic foundation for judging how a given fiscal policy will affect the size of the national income or the volume of employment. Fiscal policy is now the fashion among economists, and three fiscal paths to 'full employment' have recently been delineated. The first is to increase expenditure but not taxes. The second is to increase taxes as much as expenditure. The third is to reduce taxes but leave expenditure unchanged. The first of these methods—that is, loan expenditure—avoids, we are told, the excessively large expenditures of the second method, and the excessive deficits of the third. This is a highly suggestive conclusion, and may have much to recommend it on practical grounds. But to accept it as an approximation to scientific truth we must be willing to make assumptions of the following type: (1) the consumption function is so shaped that the dollar volume of savings increases as income increases, (2) the consumption function is practically invariant except in response to personal taxation, (3) an increase in taxes will lower the consumption function considerably but by less than the addition to taxes, (4) a reduction in taxes will raise the consumption function but by considerably less than the tax reduction, (5) the planned savings of business enterprises are correlated simply and uniquely with income payments, (6) monopolistic practices of business firms can safely be neglected, (7) private investment will not be influenced appreciably by the character of the fiscal policy pursued by government. Although assumptions such as these may be extremely helpful at a stage in our thinking about an exceedingly complicated problem, it seems plain that the inferences to which they lead cannot be regarded as a scientific guide to governmental policies.

III. Issues of Fact Raised by the Keynesian Doctrine

During the last decade the world has moved swiftly in a Keynesian direction. Keynes' *General Theory* crystallized the despondency of the thirties and gave it brilliant intellectual expression. Then came the war, and with it unprecedented government expenditures. The public debt followed suit; but the curse of unemployment was lifted. This experience has convinced many that democratic governments can, if they only have the will, readily subdue business depressions. While the war was still raging, the British government made the epoch-making announcement that it deemed the maintenance of a stable and high level of employment a fundamental responsibility, which it would seek to discharge by varying its own rate of spending and by such other devices as may keep total national expenditure steady. Similar policies have been proclaimed in Canada and Australia. In our own country this policy is being actively debated.[4] The immediate outcome of the controversy is uncertain; but it is reasonable to expect that the gap between our thinking and the British will narrow quickly when extensive unemployment again develops, and that at least in the near-term future we shall seek a solution within the framework of an individualistic capitalism. For both reasons the need for authentic knowledge of the causes of unemployment in modern commercial nations is now greater than ever.

The problem of unemployment facing our generation calls for realistic, thorough, and unceasing investigation. The great and obvious virtue of the remedies proposed by the Keynesians is that they seek to relieve mass unemployment; their weakness is that they lean heavily on a speculative analysis of uncertain value. This

4 [This was written before the passage of the Employment Act of 1946.]

weakness attaches also to my critical remarks on the theory of under-employment equilibrium. Granted that the simple determinism of Keynesian doctrine is an illusion, it does not follow that secular stagnation is another, or that the consumption function may not be sufficiently stable in experience to enable public officials to forecast reliably some consequences of their policies. These questions raise factual issues of the highest importance, which should be faced objectively: they are closely related to investigations that we have carried out in the past and to investigations that we now have under way.

In 1938, under a liberal grant from the Falk Foundation, we undertook a detailed historical study of production and employment in the United States. This investigation has pushed statistical measures of output back to 1870 or 1880 for some major industries, back to about 1900 for others. Whatever the time range covered, the leading industries of the country show notable advances, decade after decade, until we reach the thirties. There is nothing in this statistical record to suggest 'secular stagnation' before that fateful decade. The story appears dramatically in the statistics of manufacturing production. Output rose 58 per cent from 1899 to 1909, 41 per cent from 1909 to 1919, 64 per cent from 1919 to 1929. In the next decade these remarkable advances came to an abrupt stop; output increased a mere 3 per cent, whereas population rose 7.5 per cent.[5] Estimates of the flow of goods, which Kuznets and Shaw have traced back to about 1870, repeat Fabricant's story for manufacturing: substantial growth decade after decade, then virtual standstill in the thirties. Data on employment and unemployment are less reliable and do not go back as far as data on output. But they too give no hint of stagnation until the thirties, when everything seemed to change: unemployment, which amounted to 1.5 million in 1929, reached nearly 9 million in 1939.

All this, of course, is generally known, as is also the chasm in economic activity between 1929 and 1937 and the valley between 1937 and 1939. The significant question raised by the thirties is not what happened to aggregate activity, but why economic progress suffered its severest setback of recent times. This question has evoked lively debates in which many economists have participated. One group, largely of the Keynesian persuasion, holds the view that profound changes have been occurring for some time in the dynamic factors of our economic life, but that their full impact was delayed by the outbreak of World War I and other special

[5] For the sources of the figures cited in this section, see Appendix One.

circumstances until the 1930's. This group stresses the declining rate of population growth, the disappearance of the frontier, and the capital-saving character of many modern technological innovations—all of which, it is argued, is tending to check investment outlets severely. Another group traces the stagnation of the thirties to ill-judged policies of government, particularly with respect to labor, industrial combinations, public utilities, and the public debt. A third group rationalizes the thirties in terms of a peculiar conjuncture of short and long cycles, or in terms of a haphazard succession of business cycles. Each group has defended its position with persuasive logic and reassuring statistics, but no one has as yet presented an interpretation of the thirties that weighs carefully and dispassionately the many conflicting pieces of evidence.

That is by no means an easy task, as an examination of Table 1 will quickly demonstrate. Stagnation—once we have learned how to use this term—may perhaps describe adequately the aggregate output and employment of the thirties, but it describes little else. The period was anything but stagnant, even if the violent cyclical movements are put out of sight, as they are roughly in Table 1. It was a period of turbulence, of swift and momentous change in nearly every department of economic life. Let us stand back in 1929 and look ten years forward in our table. What do we see? A growth in population but a drop in the rate of growth; some decline in the number of active corporations and a severe slump in the formation of new ones; consumer outlay in constant prices up 11 per cent, gross capital formation down 27 per cent; consumer outlay on perishable goods up 29 per cent, on durable goods down 20 per cent; public construction unchanged, residential construction down 24 per cent, business construction down 67 per cent; the flow of income payments reduced but the inequality of personal incomes apparently lessened; technological progress making rapid strides over a wide range of industries; the cost of living down 19 per cent, the average hourly earnings of factory workers up 12 per cent, their hours worked per week down 18 per cent, and the number of them employed down 6 per cent; a still greater improvement in the real hourly earnings of coal miners but not in their employment; a sharp deterioration of farm wages; a vast growth of trade unionism and industrial strife; wholesale commodity prices in general down 19 per cent, but prices of 'finished' products down only 15 per cent, of building materials 5 per cent, and of business capital goods 1 per cent; corporate profits much reduced and new security issues down to a trickle; the stock mar-

TABLE 1

Conspectus of Economic Changes, United States, 1923-1939

(All figures are expressed as relatives on a 1929 base. Sources are given in Appendix One.)

Series number	Series	1923	1929	1937	1939
	POPULATION				
1.	Total	92	100	106	107
2.	Annual increment	158	100	69	83
	GROSS NATIONAL PRODUCT[a]				
3.	Total	81	100	97	103
	Consumer outlay				
4.	Total	81	100	103	111
5.	Perishable goods	84	100	122	129
6.	Semidurable goods	83	100	84	95
7.	Durable goods	75	100	83	80
8.	Services	79	100	99	111
	Gross capital formation				
9.	Total	82	100	71	73
10.	Producer durable goods	77	100	88	81
11.	Residential construction	103	100	51	76
12.	Private nonresidential construction	69	100	40	33
13.	Public construction	58	100	88	100
	LABOR FORCE[b]				
14.	Total	90	100	110	112
	Number employed				
15.	Total	90	100	98	97
16.	Civil nonagricultural	86	100	97	95
17.	Number unemployed	175	100	485	590
	OUTPUT AND EMPLOYMENT IN MAJOR INDUSTRIES				
	Agriculture				
18.	Output	92	100	106	111
19.	Number employed	105	100	91	89
20.	Output per worker	87	100	116	124
	Coal mining				
21.	Output	111	100	80	73
22.	Number employed	132	100	90	82
23.	Hours per worker	88	100	76	70
24.	Output per man-hour	96	100	116	126
	Manufacturing				
25.	Output	77	100	103	103
26.	Number employed	98	100	102	94
27.	Hours per worker	104	100	84	82
28.	Output per man-hour	76	100	121	133
	Steam railroads				
29.	Output	98	100	81	75
30.	Number employed	112	100	68	60
31.	Hours per worker	103	100	94	94
32.	Output per man-hour	85	100	127	132
	Electric light and power				
33.	Output	50	100	136	152
34.	Number employed	67	100	96	93
35.	Hours per worker	98	100	86	85
36.	Output per man-hour	72	100	164	192

(continued on page 14)

TABLE 1 (continued)

Series number	Series	1923	1929	1937	1939
	INCOME OF INDIVIDUALS				
	Income payments				
37.	Total	82	100	86	85
38.	Wages and salaries	83	100	91	90
39.	Entrepreneurial withdrawals	84	100	84	85
40.	Dividends, interest, and rent	79	100	73	69
	Relative share going to highest				
41.	1% of income recipients	85	100	90	82
42.	5% of income recipients	88	100	92	90
	Net income after federal income tax, for incomes of				
43.	$ 5,000	99	100	99	99
44.	10,000	97	100	97	97
45.	25,000	96	100	94	94
46.	100,000	91	100	80	80
47.	500,000	78	100	50	50
48.	1,000,000	76	100	42	42
	LABOR MARKET				
	Average hourly earnings				
49.	Manufacturing	92	100	110	112
50.	Coal mining	116	100	120	125
51.	Steam railroads	92	100	106	112
	Average daily wage				
52.	Farm laborers	100	100	72	69
53.	Trade union membership	106	100	195	239
54.	Number of workers on strike	262	100	644	405
	COMMODITY PRICES				
	Wholesale				
55.	"All" commodities	106	100	91	81
56.	Raw materials	101	100	87	72
57.	Semimanufactured goods	126	100	91	82
58.	Finished goods	105	100	92	85
59.	Building materials	114	100	100	95
60.	Business capital goods	104	100	99	99
61.	Cost of living	100	100	84	81
	STATUS OF CORPORATIONS				
62.	Number active	78	100	99	97
63.	New incorporations	...	100	63	57
	Profits				
64.	Total	62	100	48	62
65.	Dividends paid	61	100	82	67
66.	Income retained	65	100	−93	43
67.	Depreciation and depletion	61	100	85	86
	SECURITIES MARKET				
	Prices of common stocks				
68.	"All"	36	100	58	47
69.	Industrial	35	100	69	55
70.	Public utility	31	100	40	36
71.	Railroad	49	100	33	19
72.	Shares traded	21	100	36	23
73.	Corporate security issues	32	100	24	22

TABLE 1 (concluded)

Series number	Series	1923	1929	1937	1939
	INTEREST RATES				
74.	Commercial paper rate	86	100	16	12
	Customers' rate				
75.	New York City	88	100	41	39c
76.	Southern and western cities	97	100	68	67c
77.	Spread: (No. 76) — (No. 75)	288	100	669	685c
	Corporate bond yields				
78.	Moody's *Aaa* bonds	108	100	69	64
79.	Moody's *Baa* bonds	123	100	85	84
80.	Spread: (No. 79) — (No. 78)	181	100	151	167
	SUPPLY AND TURNOVER OF MONEY				
81.	Currency in public circulation	103	100	155	168
82.	Deposits	75	100	99	106
83.	Turnover of deposits	70	100	54	45
	Bank debits				
84.	Total	54	100	51	46
85.	New York City	39	100	33	28
86.	Outside New York City	72	100	74	69
	FOREIGN TRADE				
87.	Imports	86	100	70	53
88.	Exports	80	100	64	61
	FEDERAL FINANCE				
89.	Receiptsb	97	100	141	120
90.	Expendituresb	97	100	242	277
91.	Total debt	132	100	211	238

a Adjusted for changes in prices.
b Relatives for 1923 are not strictly comparable with those for 1937 and 1939. See Appendix.
c Computed from data for 1938. See Appendix, notes 75-76.

ket in a bad slump, particularly the prices of railroad and public utility stocks; interest rates on the highest grade loans sharply down but the spread among different types of interest rates very much widened; bank deposits up 6 per cent but their rate of turnover much reduced; currency in the hands of individuals and firms up 68 per cent; foreign trade a shadow of its former self; the federal income tax pressing much harder, especially on the upper brackets, yet the federal debt sharply up; the output of agriculture up 11 per cent, of coal down 27 per cent, of manufacturing up 3 per cent, of railroads down 25 per cent, of electric light and power up 52 per cent.

This bare recital might be elaborated to advantage, and a contrast drawn between the 'new era' of the twenties and the 'stagnation' of the thirties—both being represented in our table. But the recital suffices for my present purpose, which is merely to show that for a period as complicated and turbulent as the thirties it is not difficult to find particular facts that agreeably support any one of several simple hypotheses. To some extent that is always a danger in historical interpretation, and the only real safeguard against it is thorough scholarship. For some time we have planned a volume that would sum up and interpret the massive information developed in our studies of production, employment, and productivity. The most important problem to be faced in that final volume is the setback to economic progress in the thirties: whether that decade defines a new trend of stagnation or a passing historical episode. To serve this purpose it will be necessary to cover the secular changes in the output and employment of American industry at least since the Civil War. Also, the depression of the thirties should be compared with the severe depressions that followed the crises of 1837, 1873, and 1893, and some analysis of foreign experience made. The investigation will start from our findings on employment and production, and as it proceeds draw heavily on results reached in our historical studies of national income, agriculture, transportation, construction, mechanization, trade unionism, migration, wages, prices, interest rates, security markets, and banking. Doubtless, a great deal of new and difficult research will still be necessary, especially in connection with foreign countries and the period before 1900 in this country. But an objective interpretation of the thirties is of vital significance; and if our resources prove adequate, we should not be deterred by the prospect that the capstone of our studies in production and employment may develop into a series of monographs instead of a single volume.

A study that comes to grips with the doctrine of secular stagnation must deal not only with the hypothesis of declining or inadequate investment opportunity, but also with the second main pillar of the Keynesian edifice—namely, the assumption that the consumption function is highly stable. This assumption raises important questions of economic fact, quite apart from its bearing on the stagnation thesis. A tentative exploration of the existing statistics indicates that the consumer outlay corresponding to a national income of a given size varies appreciably with the month of the year, the stage of the business cycle, and with time generally; in other words, that the consumption function is subject to seasonal, cyclical, and secular shifts. Furthermore, random shifts seem so considerable in any one group of statistics, and to differ so much from one group to another, that our ability to forecast what increment of consumer outlay will accompany a specified increment of income, to say nothing of a specified increment of governmental loan expenditure, is as yet very limited. These results should be tested, converted into quantitative statements if possible, and pushed in a constructive direction; in other words, a statistical test of the Keynesian assumption concerning the relative stability of the consumption function should become an incident in a positive analysis of the influences that play on consumer spending over time. Numerous studies already made by the National Bureau or now in process will contribute materially to this undertaking—especially the investigation by Ruth Mack of the shoe market and other aspects of the purchasing and prices of consumer goods, the studies on national income and consumer outlay by Kuznets, Shaw, and Barger, on consumer debt by the Financial Research Program, on capital gains and losses by Seltzer, and on the inequality of personal incomes by Friedman, Kuznets, and Mendershausen.

The study of consumer spending links up with the study of secular stagnation when interest turns to the secular shifts in the spending-savings pattern. Common observation and some existing statistics suggest that, for the population as a whole, thrift has been declining over the decades in the sense that the average saving at a given level of family income has been shrinking. If such a trend has continued into the present, there is less reason to fear secular stagnation than if the trend has been arrested. The data necessary to develop adequately the secular aspects of consumption and saving will not be easy to find or to interpret when found, but the importance of the question may justify our taking the risk.

IV. THE NEED FOR TESTED KNOWLEGE OF BUSINESS CYCLES

The investigations I have sketched deal with certain of the institutional assumptions of the Keynesian economists. If these investigations prosper they should help materially to clarify public thinking about the problem of maintaining a stable and high level of employment in the years ahead. But these investigations cannot be more than pieces in the solution of the great puzzle of business cycles.

From its inception the National Bureau has recognized the need of thorough study of economic fluctuations. A program of research in business cycles was authorized by the Executive Committee in 1921, and has led to substantial publications on different aspects of the subject by King, Thorp, Jerome, Mitchell, Wolman, Macaulay, Clark, Schmidt, Gayer, Mills, and Haberler. A volume on

Measuring Business Cycles will be off the press in a matter of weeks, and other reports will follow shortly. Not a few of our studies abound in subtle theoretical analysis, but they stress especially those observable phenomena of cyclical behavior which in common parlance pass as 'facts.' This feature of our work reflects a cool scientific judgment: viz., if business cycles are to be explained reliably, we should have precise and tested knowledge of what the business cycles of actual life have been like. Unless such knowledge is attained, any explanation is bound to bear an uncertain relation to the experiences we seek to understand or to guard against.

The consequences that may flow from a disregard of this elementary precaution are exemplified in Keynes' sketch of business cycles at the end of his long treatise on underemployment equilibrium. Keynes starts by saying that a theory of business cycles should account for a certain regularity in the duration and sequence of cyclical phases—that the duration of contractions, for example, is about three to five years. Second, the theory should account for the sharp and sudden transition from expansion to contraction, in contrast to the gradual and hesitant shift from contraction to expansion. These starting points for a theoretical inquiry suggest preoccupation with a single dramatic case—the collapse from 1929 to 1933. In the United States at least, business cycle contractions have not run typically from three to five years; the typical duration is much shorter. Nor is there any such systematic difference between the upper and lower turning points as Keynes supposes. The upturn of 1933 in this country conforms to his rule, the upturns of 1924 and 1938 do not, nor do the downturns of 1926 and 1937—to mention only a few recent cases. Since Keynes works with an artificially simplified business cycle, it is not surprising that his explanation collides with the facts of experience. His theory is that a collapse of investment brings prosperity to a close; that this in turn is caused by a collapse of confidence regarding the profitability of durable assets; and that the contraction which follows is bound to last, say, three to five years, since recovery is possible only after stocks have been worked off and, more important still, after the 'fixed' capital of business firms has been reduced sufficiently to restore its profitability. But can this theory be easily reconciled with the fact that orders for machinery, orders for other durable equipment, and contracts for different categories of construction often reach cyclical maxima at widely scattered dates? Or with the fact that even a sharp decline in investment orders is ordinarily converted into a fairly gradual decline in investment expenditure, which moreover starts several months later? Or with the fact that the stock of durable goods in a growing country is virtually free from any trace of business cycles, increasing as a rule during contractions of business activity as well as during expansions?

Keynes' adventure in business cycle theory is by no means exceptional. My reason for singling it out is merely that the *General Theory* has become for many, contrary to Keynes' own wishes, a sourcebook of established knowledge. Fanciful ideas about business cycles are widely entertained both by men of affairs and by academic economists. That is inevitable as long as the problem is attacked on a speculative level, or if statistics serve merely as a casual check on speculation. To develop a reliable picture of the business cycles of actual life it is necessary to study with fine discrimination the historical records of numerous economic activities—not merely investment, or employment, or public finances, or banking operations, but all these and many others. Statistical data, preferably by months or quarters, must be marshaled with care; wherever possible these records must be pushed back well into the nineteenth century, checks on each series must be devised, contradictions among series sifted, new data developed and old data recombined as needed, the relation of each series to the process it purports to represent investigated, and a scientific method for measuring the cyclical features of time series developed. Work on this plan is costly and time-consuming; it means much turning back, revising, rethinking, redoing; it often leads to disappointments and taxes patience. But there is no reliable short cut to tested knowledge. Public thinking about business cycles can be confused by hurried and ill-digested statistical inquiries, no less than by speculative excursions from the dreamland of equilibrium or from the caprices of common sense.

It is tempting for statistical investigators, as it is for speculative writers, to analyze business cycles on the basis of comprehensive aggregates. But although broad index numbers or aggregates give useful summaries, they tell nothing of the processes by which they are fashioned. The conception of a business cycle as a synchronous expansion of all economic activities followed by a synchronous contraction, which theorists so often hold, is not drawn from life. Expansions and contractions occur together, side by side, at every stage of the business cycle. If that fact sometimes escapes our notice, it is only because we are in the habit of watching aggregates. Pulsating movements go on steadily within the aggregates, and they often have no close relation to the cyclical tide of the aggregates. A community, an industry, an individual firm experiences a rise here and a fall there; each faces some pressure or opportunity of its own—finding an outlet for its wares, adjusting to a competitor's improved technology, financing an expansion of output, replacing an exhausted source of raw materials, starting a new business, converting to a new kind of production, adjusting to new governmental regulations, and so on. These divergencies in economic fortune are no less important for the understanding of business cycles than is the dominance of expansion during some periods and of contraction during others.

The character of the employment problem is not brought out adequately by existing statistics, and it will not be until statistical agencies publish three figures instead of one for each industry and all industries combined; that is, the number of employees in 'firms' experiencing a rise in employment, the number in 'firms' experiencing a decline in employment, as well as the total number employed. A rough equivalent of this type of information, however, is the breakdown of some aggregate figure, such as factory employment, into industrial components. Our Business Cycle Unit has analyzed the behavior of many of the published subdivisions as well as of the broad composites. Table 2 shows the distribution of changes in direction of twenty-one independent series on factory employment, from stage to stage of the four business cycles in this country from 1921 to 1938. We find that expansions are imperfectly diffused during a cyclical upswing in aggregate activity, and that contractions are imperfectly diffused during a cyclical downswing. But the diffusion is much greater during a vigorous cyclical movement such as that from 1929 to 1933 than during a mild cyclical movement such as that from 1926 to 1927. There is also some tendency for the diffusion to be greater during the middle stages of a cyclical upswing or downswing in aggregate activity than during the transitional stages from one phase to the other. If our table covered 210 series instead of 21 it would doubtless show smaller diffusion throughout. That would also be true if we examined shorter periods than our stage-to-stage intervals, which is a matter of some importance in a long cyclical phase such as that of 1929-1933. On the other hand, it seems likely that if the table showed the actual volume of employment gained by industries experiencing a rise and the actual volume lost by industries experiencing a decline, the diffusion would appear greater than it

TABLE 2

Directions of Change from Stage to Stage of Business Cycles
Index of Factory Employment and Twenty-one of Its Components
United States, 1921-1938

Cycle and interval	Direction of change of index of factory employment	NUMBER OF COMPONENTS THAT		
		Rise	Fall	Show no change
Cycle of Sept. 1921 to July 1924				
Stage I to stage II	+	11	9	1
Stage II to stage III	+	13	8	...
Stage III to stage IV	+	18	3	...
Stage IV to stage V	+	16	4	1
Stage V to stage VI	−	11	10	...
Stage VI to stage VII	−	3	18	...
Stage VII to stage VIII	−	3	18	...
Stage VIII to stage IX	−	2	19	...
Cycle of July 1924 to Dec. 1927				
Stage I to stage II	+	15	6	...
Stage II to stage III	+	16	5	...
Stage III to stage IV	+	13	8	...
Stage IV to stage V	+	11	10	...
Stage V to stage VI	−	9	12	...
Stage VI to stage VII	−	12	9	...
Stage VII to stage VIII	−	9	12	...
Stage VIII to stage IX	−	5	16	...
Cycle of Dec. 1927 to March 1933				
Stage I to stage II	+	8	12	1
Stage II to stage III	+	11	10	...
Stage III to stage IV	+	17	4	...
Stage IV to stage V	+	15	6	...
Stage V to stage VI	−	2	19	...
Stage VI to stage VII	−	...	21	...
Stage VII to stage VIII	−	...	21	...
Stage VIII to stage IX	−	5	16	...
Cycle of March 1933 to May 1938				
Stage I to stage II	+	21	...	...
Stage II to stage III	+	19	2	...
Stage III to stage IV	+	18	3	...
Stage IV to stage V	+	20	1	...
Stage V to stage VI	−	6	15	...
Stage VI to stage VII	−	...	21	...
Stage VII to stage VIII	−	2	19	...
Stage VIII to stage IX	−	6	15	...
Average of 4 cycles, 1921-1938				
Stage I to stage II	+	13.8	6.8	0.5
Stage II to stage III	+	14.8	6.2	...
Stage III to stage IV	+	16.5	4.5	...
Stage IV to stage V	+	15.5	5.2	0.2
Stage V to stage VI	−	7.0	14.0	...
Stage VI to stage VII	−	3.8	17.2	...
Stage VII to stage VIII	−	3.5	17.5	...
Stage VIII to stage IX	−	4.5	16.5	...

Stage I represents the initial trough of a business cycle, stages II-IV successive thirds of expansion, stage V the peak, stages VI-VIII successive thirds of contraction, and stage IX the terminal trough. For explanations of the chronology of business cycles and their division into stages, see A. F. Burns and W. C. Mitchell, *Measuring Business Cycles* (National Bureau, 1946), Chap. 4, Secs. III-V; Chap. 5, Sec. VII; and Appendix A. The employment series are indexes by the Bureau of Labor Statistics, adjusted for seasonal variations. The twenty-one components are the maximum number of subdivisions available in our business cycle collection. They include flour, baking, cane sugar refining, slaughtering and meat packing, tobacco manufactures, cotton goods, silk and rayon goods, dyeing and finishing textiles, men's clothing, shirts and collars, women's clothing, millinery, leather, boots and shoes, paper and printing, iron and steel products, furniture, glass, transportation equipment, machinery, building materials. These series represent 67 per cent of total factory employment in 1923-1925.

does in the present table. But even as the figures stand, they bring out a vital feature of business cycles. They suggest that the mere maintenance of aggregate expenditure by governmental action may give slight aid to the declining sectors of the economy just after a peak in aggregate activity has been passed; further, since no two contractions are strictly alike, a governmental policy aiming at 'full employment' will need to rely on measures that are adjusted from case to case.

The breakdown of aggregates not only helps to define the nature of the business cycle problem; it often also gives a clue to the processes that link different business factors together. Suppose, for example, that 'investment' goes up. This may be a sign that business will soon improve materially, as when extensive new construction gets under way; or it may be a sign that business will soon get worse, as when goods pile up beyond dealers' intentions. The ambiguity can be cleared up a little by examining investment in inventories apart from investment in structures and equipment. But the cyclical behavior of inventories, or of net changes in inventories, is itself a resultant of highly diverse patterns. For example, the stocks held by manufacturers tend to lag about nine months on the average at the cyclical turns in production; this lag covers up the tendency of goods in process to move synchronously with production, of raw material stocks to lag about two months at cyclical turns, and of stocks of finished manufactured staples to lag more than a year. These findings set a problem. Why, for example, is the adjustment of stocks of finished staples retarded so long? This question naturally impels an investigator to examine the behavior of production, shipments, and prices.

Again, broad composites on construction contracts and building permits show that commitments for new structures as a rule begin to decline while industrial production, employment, and national income are still expanding; further, commitments for new structures as a rule turn upward months before general business activity revives. It is tempting to suggest an explanation of the cyclical lead in terms of broad market forces. But such an explanation cannot be entertained seriously unless the cyclical leads that appear in the aggregates of construction work are repeated in minor subdivisions. To this question the statistics give, on the whole, an affirmative answer, but the breakdown also discloses systematic discrepancies in the movements of different parts of construction. For example, public and institutional projects tend to move irregularly in relation to business cycles while private projects conform closely; residential projects tend to lead industrial projects both at recoveries and recessions; contracts for new factories in industries organized into many small units seem to lead contracts of industries characterized by relatively few but large units; new railroad projects led cyclical recoveries in the 1870's and 1880's by a substantial interval, but the lead shrank with the passage of time and has now disappeared. These and similar findings incite a realistic investigator to examine the changing pace of new investment undertakings in relation to the circumstances peculiar to different classes of investors, as well as in relation to factors—such as the movement of national income, construction costs, interest rates, and the policies of lenders—which may be expected to influence investors generally. Further, just as the investigator must work backward from contracts to the factors that shape investment decisions, so he must work forward and analyze the timing of construction expenditures and of completed projects. As long as production periods are short, as is true of the great bulk of manufactured commodities, it is sufficient ordinarily to speak of the production of an industry during a certain month or year without specifying whether 'production' refers to the volume started, or the volume executed, or the volume completed. These distinctions can be neglected in the case of the construction industry only at the risk of confusion and error. For example, contracts for factory construction typically reach a peak about two months before general business activity turns down, but it appears that the crop of newly completed factories reaches its maximum when contraction is well under way—or just in time to intensify the competitive struggle then in process.

I have stressed the importance of breaking down aggregates because this matter, so slighted by the Keynesian economists, is a central feature of our own work on business cycles. It explains better than anything else why our investigations extend over years. Happily, we have reached a point where a substantial part of our results will soon be made available to the public. Several of our monographs on special topics are close to the stage of publication. Most important of all, we expect to publish this year Wesley Mitchell's progress report on *What Happens during Business Cycles.* This volume will be the first instalment of a grand synthesis of our cyclical measurements, which even in their present unfinished state cover a very wide range of economic activities. Mitchell's progress report will render obsolete his California treatise, which—although published thirty-three years ago—has remained to this day the best theoretical account of how the economic organization of the Western world generates business cycles.

We hope that our quest of the lessons of experience will aid other students, as well as laymen who must wrestle practically with business cycles. Whether a cyclical downturn can be recognized promptly enough to permit immediate governmental intervention, whether cost-price relations are of slight consequence in the termination of a boom, whether inflationary tendencies become important only as 'full employment' is approached, whether the volume of the circulating medium rises and falls in close sympathy with aggregate activity, whether minor cycles mainly reflect inventory fluctuations, whether the volume of investment is materially affected over periods of business cycle length by the rate of change in consumer spending—these and similar matters are, after all, not metaphysical questions. True, the most painstaking studies of experience will not always lead to conclusive answers; but they should at least narrow the margins of uncertainty, and thus furnish a better basis than now exists for dealing with grave issues of business cycle theory and policy.

V. THE RANGE AND CONTINUITY OF THE BUREAU'S RESEARCH PROGRAM

If I am right in believing that the Keynesian thinking of our times makes realistic investigation of business cycles more necessary than ever, we should seek to intensify our work on that subject. The obvious method of promoting this objective is to expand the Business Cycle Unit well beyond its present size, but such a policy would be shortsighted. The 'material' of speculative investigations of business cycles consists largely of concepts and models, which often have no obvious use in any other branch of economics. Realistic investigations, on the other hand, draw their material from records of experience. In such inquiries the subject of business cycles can never be put in a box by itself. Any record that makes a contribution to knowledge of how our economic organization works becomes automatically a datum in business cycle analysis. That is clearly true of records that come in the shape of time series, and is no less true of cross-section studies which indicate the order of magnitude of economic quantities.

The main reason why we are able to conduct the far-reaching studies of business fluctuations that I have sketched in this report is that throughout our history we have done basic statistical research on national income, production, employment, prices, wages, and finance. These inquiries have developed factual information of the highest importance, have stimulated work by other students, and led to improvements in the work of official agencies. Their work in turn has stimulated ours, and this process must continue. The study of national income is our oldest enterprise, and one that has proved especially useful to economists, businessmen, and public officials. Nevertheless, vital differences of concept and fact still divide estimators of national income. Employment estimates have been much improved and extended in recent years, but it is uncertain whether they can meet the strain that may soon be put on them. Measures of the cost of living and price indexes of other types still require careful attention, especially in comparisons of distant periods and different countries. We are therefore not only continuing, but expanding, our work in these directions. Meanwhile we are engaged in new statistical explorations of the flow of money payments, urban real estate finance, and agricultural finance. We expect that beside making a direct contribution to knowledge, these explorations will lead to substantial improvements in current statistics.

The usefulness of our various studies extends beyond their value in business cycle analysis. Although the issue of 'full employment' justly dominates economic thinking today, we must not allow our concern with that problem to blind us to other matters of genuine significance. Apart from the ravages of unemployment the standard of living is still appallingly low for the great masses of mankind, and different groups of society—within and across national boundaries—have special and changing problems of their own. In the years ahead we must continue to shape our research program with an eye to these requirements for economic knowledge, as well as the problem of business cycles. We must continue to focus attention on the large issues concerning the 'production, exchange, and distribution of wealth,' substitute as far as possible facts for speculations, remain critical of our work, strive steadily to improve it, and cooperate with others. If our zeal and industry remain strong, we shall not fail to render a definite service to our own generation and to the generations that will come after us.

I am grateful to several friends for reading and criticizing this report. My chief debt is to Geoffrey H. Moore, who did the great bulk of the work on the tabular matter presented. Mr. Moore was assisted by Virginia Buckner, Millard Hastay, Hanna Stern, and other members of the National Bureau staff.

Stepping Stones towards the Future

I. Forecasting as a Goal of Research

The forecasting of economic affairs has fascinated successive generations. Once economists began to think of 'crises' as a phase of a recurring movement, explorations of periodicity in business fluctuations followed naturally. Imaginative men reasoned that since business activity was wavelike, the time span of the waves might well be uniform, and in that event it should be possible to predict the coming of booms and depressions just as confidently as the hour of sunrise or sunset. In 1829 an American writer noted the opinion "entertained by many that every fourteen years or thereabouts, there is a sort of revolution in property—that real estate, especially, undergoes a speculative rise and fall, and that consequently wealth becomes transferred from one individual to another, by the mere operation of time." In 1844 J. B. Turner, another American, declared that "revulsions in commerce have become a sort of . . . epidemic . . . whose periods and returns can be safely affirmed by all, while the shrewd financier is tolerably aware of their precise times."[1] When Jevons published his famous papers on crises and sunspots, a considerable English literature already existed on the periodic hypothesis, the most interesting of the early writers being Hyde Clark, who a century ago speculated on the existence of two economic cycles—one decennial, the other a full Kondratieff wave of fifty-four years.

With the increasing application of mathematical methods to economic data, hypotheses of periodic fluctuations proliferated in later years. Periodicities of forty months, seven years, eight years, ten years, and many others were repeatedly suggested. The failure of the simple periodic hypothesis to stand up under close factual scrutiny led to refinements. For example, Samuel Benner allowed cycles to vary in length, but insisted that they come in sets that are themselves repeated. In 1878, the year in which Jevons first announced his sunspot theory to the English public, Benner had the first opportunity to see that his own periodic scheme, which for a while worked marvelously and brought him great renown, could yield false as well as true prophecies of the price of iron. Nevertheless, the line of thinking followed by Benner appealed

Reprinted from *Twenty-seventh Annual Report of the National Bureau of Economic Research* (March 1947), pp. 3-27.

[1] This and the preceding quotation are from Harry E. Miller, *Banking Theories in the United States before 1860* (Harvard University Press, 1927), pp. 192, 193.

to some economists, while others speculated, as had Hyde Clark before them, on the existence of several or many cycles running a simultaneous course. As the scope of economic statistics expanded and the irregularity of successive business cycles impressed itself on observers, interest shifted increasingly to the study of sequences —that is, to a search for repetitive leads or lags among different activities. More recently still, the Keynesian consumption function, tied to estimates of private investment and the governmental deficit, has become the pillar of forecasting techniques.

Practically every forecasting device ever suggested has occasionally proved successful. But it does not appear that any method has as yet yielded, for any long period, consistently good predictions of changes in business activity. This unsatisfactory record is not peculiar to business cycle forecasting. Werner Sombart begins the last chapter of his *Hochkapitalismus* with these words: "The prediction of the future is always a hazardous affair. And in the sphere of economic and social history it seems to be especially dangerous. It is precisely the most gifted men who have made the most fundamental mistakes." With this warning to the reader behind him, Sombart at once plunges into an account of what economic organization will be like in the future. He is not deterred by the experience of his great predecessors—Ricardo, Mill, Marx, Schmoller, and many others. And, of course, Sombart does merely what every one of us is always doing. If forecasts go awry, we do not stop forecasting. We merely try to profit by our own and others' mistakes, or as we commonly put it—'to learn by experience.' And there is little else that we can do. Prediction is inseparable from life. All human activity—whether within or outside the economic sphere—inevitably reflects forecasts of the future, mingled with current pressures and past commitments. The forecasts are sometimes bold, definite, and comprehensive; more often they are hesitant, amorphous, uttered instinctively—if at all. The choice before man is not whether to engage in forecasting or to abstain from it, but whether to base expectations on 'hunches' or on lessons carefully distilled from experience.

Systematic analysis of actual economic experience has been the principal objective of the National Bureau and other research organizations. Investigators affiliated with a center of economic research can draw on a large and growing body of factual data; they may count on clerical and computing assistance in developing new information; most important of all, they find colleagues working on cognate problems and possessing skills that complement their own. Investigators thus equipped are in a better position to cross-examine history effectively than the scholar who relies entirely on his own strength. If they use their opportunities properly, they should offer increasingly sound testimony not only on the regular and repetitive features of experience, but also on history's disconcerting habit of springing surprises. In this report I shall illustrate the contribution that the National Bureau is making to this great purpose, by commenting briefly on our recent investigations.

II. THE STRUCTURE OF NATIONAL INCOME

For my first illustration I draw on Simon Kuznets' work on income distribution. In *National Income: A Summary of Findings*, published last year, Kuznets shows succinctly how our national income during the twenty years between the two world wars was divided among the factors of production, among individuals, among different industries, and among different uses. About two-thirds of the nation's income accrued to employees, another sixth to proprietors; the remaining sixth was paid out as rent, interest, and dividends, in roughly similar proportions. The top 1 per cent of the income recipients enjoyed about an eighth, and the top 5 per cent about a fourth, of the nation's income. Manufacturing accounted for about a fifth of the total, mining for a fiftieth, agriculture a tenth, government an eighth. About 93 per cent of the nation's net product, which is equivalent to its income, passed into the hands of the public as consumption goods; only about 7 per cent was added to the stock of capital goods or to claims against foreign countries. Of the goods flowing to consumers the preponderant part—approximately 75 per cent—consisted of services and perishable commodities.

These remarkable data on the disposition of the net product of our economic activity substitute quantitative approximations for the vague conjectures with which earlier generations had to do their economic thinking. They fix our ideas about the order of magnitude of different branches of production, of the incomes accruing to the fortunate few and to the masses, of the goods consumed quickly and those consumed slowly, of the incomes received by workers and men of property. In these various ways, and as far as they go, the proportions I have cited delineate the structure of our economy. But how dependable are the proportions? What guide do they offer to the years ahead, once wartime dislocations have been largely overcome? The figures for individual years help to answer these questions. They show that the compensation of employees has been a fairly steady proportion of the nation's income. This proportion has not varied from, say, 20 per cent in one year to 90 per cent in another, but has moved within a comparatively narrow range, never falling below 59 or rising above 74 per cent between 1922 and 1938. Other components of national income likewise show rough stability in their order of magnitude. For example, dividends are a consistently small fraction of the national income, at no time exceeding 8 per cent; the share of the top 1 per cent bracket of the population is about one-eighth of the total in every year covered; the share of agriculture in no year exceeds a tenth, and the share of manufacturing stays within the limits of 15 and 23 per cent. Capital formation is notoriously unstable, but is nevertheless a consistently small element in national income: year in and year out the dominant part of our output has moved into the hands of the public, in no year has this part fallen below 88 per cent, and in some years the nation at large has even dipped into its accumulated stockpile.[2]

This rough stability in the relations among different parts of the national income during 1922-1938 is the more impressive because I have made no distinction between years occupying different stages of the business cycle, or even between the placid twenties and the turbulent thirties. In view of the comparatively narrow range within which the figures move, it seems reasonable to expect that once reconversion is fully accomplished, the broad divisions of our national income will not be very different from the prewar averages. For many purposes of economic analysis, this rough and confident projection of prewar averages will suffice. No student who accepts the figures as substantially accurate is likely to think otherwise, unless he expects a revolutionary change in our institutions, or is concerned with specific problems of economic organization rather than its broad and abiding features.

III. Forecasting Business Conditions

The projection of national income in the years ahead or even in the next twelve months poses a much more difficult problem than the projection of the proportions in which national income is divided. Past experience fails to furnish the forecaster with any rule that is at once simple, objective, and trustworthy. Business

[2] Pertinent figures for individual years are given in Kuznets' *National Income and Its Composition, 1919-1938* (National Bureau, 1941), Vol. I, Tables 12, 22, and in his *National Product since 1869* (National Bureau, 1946), Table I-18. Data on the distribution by size are published in Kuznets' *Shares of Upper Income Groups in Income and Savings* (National Bureau, 1952).

conditions not only alternate between prosperity and depression, but each cycle in business activity differs significantly from all its predecessors. Between 1885 and 1914 there was some approach to a 40-month cycle in the United States; this rough rule vanishes as we move forward or backward. The shortest business cycle of which we have a definite record lasted 17 months, the longest 101 months. Factory employment declined 5 per cent in one business cycle contraction, 42 per cent in another; the range of cyclical declines in factory payrolls runs from 5 to 65 per cent, in pig iron production from 17 to 86 per cent, in industrial stock prices from 12 to 86 per cent. Exports parallel the movement of aggregate activity in one business cycle, move inversely in another, haphazardly in still another. Bank deposits rise during some business cycle contractions, decline in others. The like is true of bank loans and investments. Trading in corporate shares recovered 19 months earlier than general business activity in one instance, slumped 23 months earlier in another instance, recovered 7 months later in a third, and slumped 4 months later in a fourth. At the peak of 1929 wholesale commodity prices reached a maximum 10 months before industrial production; at the trough of 1938 their minimum point came 14 months later.

At first glance it may seem impossible to extract any order whatever from such highly variable phenomena. Yet the studies by Wesley Mitchell and his collaborators demonstrate that although business cycles are decidedly less regular than theorists are prone to assume, they are far more regular than observers preoccupied with individual episodes commonly suppose. I may illustrate this broad conclusion, which I think is basic to a true perspective, by summarizing an experiment reported in *Measuring Business Cycles*, another of last year's publications. The experiment was performed on seven highly significant series, extending back to the 1870's or earlier. Two series represented the production of durable goods, two the money market, two the stock market, and one the aggregate volume of transactions. When these series were examined individually, very wide differences appeared in their behavior from one business cycle to the next. The result was similar when the behavior of the seven series during one business cycle was compared with their behavior during other business cycles. But when the measures of each series were averaged for small groups of cycles, whether on a chronological or some analytic plan, the idiosyncrasies of the individual case tended to vanish. The average behavior of the same series in one group of cycles as a rule turned out to be very similar to its behavior in another group, the average patterns of the several series became sharply differentiated within each group, and the relations among the various series persisted with great regularity from one group of cycles to the next; in other words, a strong tendency towards repetition in the sequence of different activities at revivals and recessions, and in the direction and amplitude of their response to business cycles, came clearly to the surface.

This experiment suggests an important conclusion: namely, that although every business cycle is a unique historical episode, the characteristic features of business cycles have been substantially uniform in the long run. The experiment gives little or no support to the widely held view that depressions are becoming progressively more severe, or to the hypothesis that business cycles succeed one another in a repetitive order that generates long waves. Of course, findings based on a small group of series, however important they may be, cannot be regarded as conclusive. But the present findings have already been tested informally on numerous series; and while methodical testing is still necessary and may turn up surprises, it can be said definitely that if, as seems plausible a priori, business cycles actually have undergone secular or structural or rhythmical changes, such changes have not impressed themselves very clearly on statistical records and must be small in comparison with the rather haphazard variation of successive business cycles.

The monograph on *Measuring Business Cycles* foreshadows other findings that may prove significant to economists and men of affairs. I shall single out four that seem to me especially important. (1) The volume of activity at the peak of a business cycle has as a rule exceeded the level reached at the preceding peak. The outstanding exception occurred in 1937 when activity fell short of the 1929 peak; another exception apparently occurred in 1895. (2) The amplitude of a business cycle expansion gives little or no clue to the amplitude of the following contraction. On the other hand, there is some tendency for the amplitude of a business cycle expansion to be correlated positively with the amplitude of the preceding contraction. The difference in the two relations reflects the fact that the volume of activity has been decidedly more uneven at successive troughs than at successive peaks of business cycles. (3) While there is a broad tendency for economic activities to fluctuate in unison, expansions and contractions run side by side at every stage of a business cycle. The degree to which individual processes resist a cyclical movement in aggregate activity depends largely on its amplitude. In a mild business cycle expansion or contraction, countercyclical movements are relatively numerous. In a vigorous cyclical phase, on the other hand, few processes run counter to the general tide. (4) During an expansion in aggregate activity the number of expanding processes tends to increase for a time, then diminish; in other words, the number of expanding processes tends to reach a maximum before the expansion in aggregate activity itself culminates. Likewise, once a business cycle contraction gets under way, it engulfs a wider and wider range of activities; but in every stage of a general contraction some processes keep expanding, and their number typically passes through a minimum before aggregate activity itself turns up again.

These broad generalizations provide some clues to the maze of irregularities in the actual course of events, and may prove helpful in anticipating changes in the direction of aggregate activity. But they also carry a warning against oversimplification of the problem of forecasting business conditions. Possessing as it does an exceptionally full record of cyclical fluctuations, the National Bureau may render a valuable service by hunting for regularities where there seems the best chance of finding them—not in the relations between pairs or small groups of time series, or within the last few years, but in the relations among numerous and varied activities over decades. Early in 1938 we published a bulletin on statistical indicators of cyclical revivals, which began by listing the attributes of an 'ideal' indicator. Not one of the hundreds of time series examined met all the specifications; but since a carefully selected group of series can be more reliable than any single series, we segregated the series that had proved most trustworthy in the past, and presented the list in the hope that it might aid men of judgment to interpret the general drift of current conditions. In view of later experience with the list, the gains in knowledge since it was drawn up, and the heavy responsibilities of government under the Employment Act of 1946, it has seemed our duty to undertake a thorough revision of the earlier study and this time investigate recessions as fully as revivals. The results of the new study are approaching completion and will be published as promptly as possible.

In the meantime our exploration of the fundamentals of business fluctuations is being pushed energetically. The first fruits of Mills' study, which is unmasking the underlying features of the cycles in prices, production, and sellers' receipts, were harvested last year under the title *Price-Quantity Interactions in Business Cycles*. Another valuable study is Mendershausen's *Changes in Income Distribution during the Great Depression*. Several additional publications on business cycles may be expected this year or next: Hultgren's analysis of costs, prices, and profits in the railroad industry; Moore's report on the interrelations between crop fluctuations and business cycles; Ruth Mack's analysis of the processes by which shifts in the demand for shoes are transmitted to earlier productive and distributive stages; Evans' study of the ebb and flow of business incorporations since the early days of the nineteenth century; Abramovitz' analysis of the processes whereby inventories are built up and drawn down; Mills' full evidence on the relations between the cyclical movements of prices and production; Wolman's investigation of the behavior of wage rates at recoveries and recessions; and Mitchell's progress report on what typically happens in all leading economic activities during a business cycle.

IV. Trends in Spending and Saving

I suggested earlier that the proportions in which national income is divided can be projected more reliably than the curve of national income itself. It may be objected that the contrast rests on a simplification that for some purposes is intolerable. Surely, the trade union strategist concerned with labor's precise share in national income in the years ahead cannot rest content with a projection of prewar averages, nor can the farm specialist pondering the role of agriculture in the national economy, or the fiscal expert mapping the revenue needed to sustain the expanded sector of governmental enterprise. Men faced with problems of this nature will seek to take account of the slowly evolving changes in economic organization that are concealed by averages for the interwar period. They will want to analyze secular trends over a still longer time if possible, and give due weight to the changes wrought by the war itself. Investigators who embark on such speculations concerning future trends will find their task facilitated by Kuznets' two volumes published last year—*National Income: A Summary of Findings* and *National Product since 1869*.

The latter monograph is devoted to a statistical analysis of the growth of the American economy. In broad summary, aggregate real income in the 1920's was almost eight times as large as in the 1870's, and per capita real income was almost three times as large. The rate of growth was uneven, but every decade up to the 1930's registered substantial improvement. During that decade per capita income fell appreciably below the level of the 1920's; nevertheless it was higher than in any other decade, and about two and a half times as large as in the 1870's. What this amazing performance has meant to the American people is suggested by Kuznets' division of total output into the part that passed into the hands of consumers and the part that was added to the nation's capital. Between 1869 and 1938 the output of the American economy amounted to about $2,800 billion in 1929 prices. Of this huge total, the flow of commodities and services to consumers accounted for fully 90 per cent, and this figure would be raised 2 points if residential buildings were classified as consumer goods. The remaining 8 per cent includes new industrial plants, business structures, public improvements, additions to inventories, and additions to claims against foreign countries.

If these figures fail to excite the reader, the reason may well be that Kuznets' findings concerning capital formation in the interwar period are now common knowledge. Before Kuznets' original results were published, most economists had extremely vague notions about the relative magnitude of capital formation, and some actually believed that a great if not dominant part of our rapidly expanding industrial power was diverted to the building of new houses, factories, roads, machinery, equipment, and other capital goods. Kuznets demonstrated that there was no foundation for this opinion even in the experience of the 1920's, and he has now extended the demonstration back to the Civil War.

It also appears from his new study that savings were a nearly constant fraction of the national income, decade after decade, before the 1930's. This result, if broadly valid, throws new light on processes of spending and saving in a progressive economy. A typical speculative analysis of the savings problem starts with the observation that the percentage of income going into savings tends to rise as family income increases, then notes that the incomes of families have risen generally and substantially over the years, and ends by inferring that savings have been a steadily rising fraction of national income. But according to Kuznets, that has not happened. Apart from possible complications on the side of business savings, the reason must be that the static tendency of the savings-income ratio to rise as family income increases has been counteracted historically by the tendency of the 'propensity to save' to decline; that is, the average American family with a real income of any given size has tended over the decades to save a progressively smaller fraction of its income. Many influences have surely worked in this direction. The most important seem to have been, first, the shift of population from rural to urban areas, second, the relative decline of independent proprietors in the general scheme of entrepreneurship, third, the increasing range of commodities and services considered necessary for acceptable living standards.

The secular decline in the 'propensity to save,' so strongly suggested although not directly demonstrated by Kuznets' calculations, has an obvious bearing on the long-run prospects of the American economy. If the decline should continue, as seems not unlikely, the prospect that our economy may be able to maintain a generally high level of employment without prodigious private investment or government spending is by no means so dark as appears from some recent mathematical projections of national income, which blink the secular element in the savings-income relation.

V. THE LONG-TERM ECONOMIC OUTLOOK

But secular trends can change on short notice, and the forecaster's inescapable ordeal is to distinguish, somehow, the short-run movements that release new trends from others, no less prominent, that soon fade away. Ricardo saw the problem clearly. He warned his contemporaries at the end of the Napoleonic War not to confuse a temporary "revulsion of trade" with a "retrograde state of society," but at the same time honestly added that "it would perhaps be difficult to point out any marks by which they may be accurately distinguished."[3] That difficulty, unhappily, has not been erased by time. During the 1920's some economists thought they had escaped from it by embracing a 'law of growth,' and some today believe they can do so by embracing a 'stable consumption function.' But the signs are multiplying that, although the latter conception may prove even more fruitful than has the former, the forecasts yielded by the one can be just as misleading as those stemming from the other.

The economic catastrophe of the 1930's continues to weigh heavily in speculations about the future, but the simple fact is that no one can tell today with any great confidence whether that experience defines a new trend of stagnation or a passing historical episode. Kuznets' findings concerning the long-run trends of savings and consumption are reassuring. But once the present boom has run its course, if the volume of investment should revert to

[3] *Principles of Political Economy*, ed. Gonner, p. 250.

the level of the 1930's, may not even a substantial decline in the 'propensity to save' prove insufficient to sustain the high level of income that seems physically within our reach? The intense activity of recent times has thinned the ranks of those who accept the doctrine of secular stagnation. So too has the widespread realization that a huge backlog of replacements has accumulated in industry, that years must pass before the housing shortage is eliminated, that vast opportunities for exporting capital may soon become available, and that immeasurable investment outlets may be opened up by aviation, radar, atomic energy, and other technological wonders. Nevertheless, the spectre of secular stagnation still haunts the minds of some sensitive men as they look beyond the next five or ten years. And while their dark forebodings are based on an untested hypothesis of economic development, they cannot be dismissed outright, as some believe possible, merely by citing the investment opportunities afforded by foreign countries and by technological innovations. For, on the one hand, foreign investment on a considerable scale is impossible in an atmosphere of international distrust and, on the other hand, technological progress can go on at a rapid rate and investment still remain at an unsatisfactory level.

The experience of the thirties abundantly illustrates both of these statements, but I shall confine myself to the latter. Jacob Gould's monograph on *Output and Productivity in the Electric and Gas Utilities*, still another of our publications last year, shows that between 1929 and 1939 the output per unit of labor increased 92 per cent in the electric light and power industry, and 20 per cent in the manufactured gas industry. Other studies by Fabricant, Barger, and their associates show gains of 24 per cent in agriculture, 26 per cent in coal mining, 33 per cent in manufacturing, and 32 per cent in steam railroads.[4] Plainly, technological progress made rapid strides on a wide industrial front. In fact, as Gould demonstrates, the reduction in unit labor requirements effected by American industry during the 1930's was not very different from the reductions achieved in preceding decades, at least since 1900. But before 1929 increasing efficiency in the use of labor was generally accompanied by a rising trend in the aggregate number of men employed, while in the following decade the ability of private enterprise to create new jobs was drastically impaired and the increase in technical power dissipated in mass unemployment.

[4] See "Economic Research and the Keynesian Thinking of Our Times," Table 1, above.

The causes of this extraordinary setback to progress have been extensively debated, but not thoroughly investigated. What part did the decline in the rate of growth of population play? Did a significant shift take place from capital-using to capital-saving innovations? Is there any validity in the hypothesis of an unfavorable conjuncture of economic cycles with different wave lengths? In what degree may monopolistic practices of business firms and labor unions be held responsible? What part did the policies of the New Deal play—with respect to taxation, borrowing, labor, public utilities, the security markets? Were foreign developments responsible in any significant degree for our economic plight? And if so, in what measure did we export economic trouble before we in turn imported it? Some of these questions are now being explored by Wolman in his studies of the labor market. The Conference on Research in Fiscal Policy will consider others in a new investigation of the influence of different types and levels of taxes on business enterprise. But if I am right in thinking that a fuller understanding of what happened in the 1930's may contribute vastly to the shaping of wise economic policies in the future, there is room in our program for a study which, while drawing extensively on research now in process, is devoted specifically to the problems and events of that period.

To accomplish its purpose the study should rest on a broad inductive foundation, and this must be sought in a comparative analysis of earlier periods and other countries. As the research work of the Bureau has taken shape, we have found it necessary time and again to carry measurements back into the past. But the economic experiences of foreign countries in recent years may prove no less instructive than our own economic fortunes in a remote past. And neither recent nor distant American experience can be understood apart from foreign events. The importance of these methodological principles was fully recognized at the beginning of our work on business cycles, and has not been neglected in other parts of the Bureau's program. At present our 'foreign' research includes Morgenstern's investigation of the financial relations among different countries during business cycles, Smit's study of the phenomena connected with the international gold standard during 1816-1914, Hultgren's study of transportation and Moore's of crops in relation to the business cycles of Western Europe, Maxwell's survey of the development of fiscal relations between the Dominion of Canada and its provinces, Higgins' study of British banking and finance during the war, Long's study of the labor force in several countries, Bry's study of wages in Germany, and Copeland's measurements of the flow of payments between the United States and the rest of the world. Wide-ranging though these studies are, they can provide only a small part of the materials needed to interpret what happened in the United States during the 1930's, to say nothing of the larger problem of America's changing role in the world economy. If we are to realize these objectives, we must give more attention to foreign economies and the links that tie us to them than we have in the past.

VI. Economic Penetration of the Service Industries

One of the deepest trends in a country undergoing rapid industrialization is the relative shrinkage of the commodity-producing industries taken as a whole. This trend appears clearly in Kuznets' industrial breakdown of the national income in the United States, and stands out still more prominently in the longer series on the labor force. In 1870 agriculture, forestry, fishing, manufacturing, mining, and construction together accounted for 76 per cent of the labor force; their combined percentage fell to 68 in 1900, to 61 in 1920, and to 48 in 1940. If the miscellaneous category that mars statistical tables on the labor force is counted with the commodity-producing group, obviously a doubtful statistical expedient, the percentage in 1940 rises from 48 only to 55. If transportation and public utilities are also lumped in their entirety with the commodity group, another doubtful expedient, the percentage is still only 62.[5] The remaining 38 per cent of the labor force in 1940 was scattered in trading and financial establishments, a great variety of private services, and in government work. During the war the commodity-producing sector expanded sharply, but the services now seem to be reasserting their secular force.

These facts have not as yet been fully assimilated in our thinking. Treatises on economic theory continue to be written as if manufacturing and the extractive industries were the only ones of any consequence. With important exceptions much the same emphasis is found in journalistic writings, governmental policies, and even official statistics. But if technological progress in the commodity-producing industries continues at anything like the pace felt during the past half century, will not the service industries soon become the primary source of employment? May we expect the services to expand sufficiently to fill the 'gap' between those

[5] Based on estimates by Daniel Carson in a paper presented at the National Bureau's Conference on Research in Income and Wealth, November 1946.

needed in the commodity-producing industries and the total labor force? To what extent is technological progress likely in merchandising establishments, financial businesses, personal service industries, the private professions, and government work? What are the implications of the growth of the service industries for the problem of monopoly? What are the implications for the problem of business cycles? What is the cultural incidence of the changing character of the labor force? Are our institutions flexible enough to prevent a hierarchy of special privileges from being amassed by aggressive sections of the commodity-producing group?

To cope with these and related questions, factual information on the service sector of the economy is essential. But the service industries are a vast conglomerate, including activities as diverse as specialized medicine, on the one hand, and street sweeping, on the other. Neither the social significance of the penetration of the service industries, nor their capacity for further expansion, can be accurately gauged from broad aggregates. For example, the number of physicians was 157 per 100,000 persons in 1900, and only 133 in 1940. In 1900 there were 1,980 servants per 100,000 persons, in 1940 only 1,590. On the other hand, the number of public school teachers increased faster than population, yet not so fast as the entire class of government workers. According to Fabricant's estimates, government employees constituted 4.5 per cent of the labor force in 1900; this percentage doubled by 1940 and on July 1, 1946 one out of every ten workers was on some governmental payroll.

These illustrative data emphasize both the importance of analyzing trends in the service industries, and the need of examining them individually. Among our recent publications is the highly original monograph on *Income from Independent Professional Practice* by Friedman and Kuznets. Initiated by Kuznets, who in the course of work on national income had felt keenly the lack of data on the services, this study was executed mainly by Friedman. A second publication on the service industries is last year's *Occasional Paper* by Stigler, which presents some very useful information on the number, incomes, and working conditions of domestic servants—a class of workers hitherto neglected by professional economists, although before the war they were as numerous as the employees of railroads, coal mines, and automobile factories combined. Other monographs now being prepared will deal in detail with education, trade, and government, as well as the service industries in their entirety.

VII. THE CHANGING FINANCIAL STRUCTURE

Financial institutions rank low among the service industries as employers of labor, but they exercise great influence on the economy by their activities of lending, investing, and providing the community with means of payment. In 1900 a typical commercial bank might still have been described as performing the classical functions of deposit, discount, and note issue. At present that description can only excite historical interest. The power of note issue, barred for all practical purposes to state banks since the Civil War, is no longer exercised even by national banks. The place once occupied by short-term commercial loans in the portfolio of a commercial bank has been preempted by federal securities. Total loans and discounts of commercial banks in 1946 were considerably below the level reached in 1929, despite the great increase in production and the rise in prices. Investments in federal obligations, on the other hand, have soared in recent years. At the end of June 1946 they accounted for over 90 per cent of the investments held by commercial banks, and investments in their turn were more than three times as large as loans.

The enormous volume of securities now tucked away in the vaults of commercial banks represents largely a monetization of the federal debt. But in looking to the future, it is important to bear in mind that the recent war accentuated a trend long in the making. Government securities first became a considerable factor in commercial bank assets during World War I. In the 1920's commercial banks did not increase their holdings of federal obligations materially; however, the holdings of other securities expanded much faster than loans, and as a consequence loans diminished relative to investments. During the Great Depression loans were sharply deflated; but government obligations offset the shrinkage in other securities, and investments as a whole changed little. In 1934 investments of commercial banks outstripped loans for the first time. Banks added heavily to their federal securities between 1934 and 1939, and by the end of the latter year investments exceeded loans by 36 per cent. During the next six years both loans and investments increased, but the growth of investments was much faster. Last year investments declined appreciably, but the drop is of slight significance, since the Treasury merely used its swollen deposits in commercial banks to retire a sizable block of its securities.

The momentous changes in the functions of commercial banks since 1900 are analyzed by Jacoby and Saulnier in their monograph on *Business Finance and Banking,* which has just been published. The authors of this scholarly study focus attention on the changing relations between business concerns and commercial banks. In exploring the causes of the relative decline of 'commercial lending' since the 1920's, they analyze, first, the changes in the industrial composition of the economy to which I referred earlier in this report; next, changes in the size of business enterprises, in the types of assets held by business concerns, and in the competitive framework within which commercial banks have functioned. The study makes an important contribution to the understanding of how business, as well as banking, practices have developed in recent decades.

The provision of means of payment is the one function that commercial banks today discharge much as they did in 1900. It is a curious fact that despite the widespread and persistent interest of economists in the supply of money, current monthly measures of the aggregate supply of means of payment have become available only in the last few years. A historical background for interpreting the new official compilations on the public's currency holdings is provided by the recently published *Technical Paper* by Anna Schwartz and Elma Oliver, which presents monthly estimates of currency held by the public since 1917. We hope that this statistical record may soon be supplemented by another showing, month by month, the public's holdings of deposits.

However important statistics on the supply of money may be, it is difficult to interpret them apart from measures of the turnover of money. The common impression that the supply of money fluctuates in close harmony with aggregate economic activity is not supported by a long view of history. That much seems firmly established by our investigation of business cycles, as is also the great sensitivity of the turnover of money to fluctuations in aggregate activity. In our studies of business cycles we have hitherto relied heavily on approximations of the aggregate supply of money, its average rate of use, and the aggregate volume of payments. We have been unable to differentiate sufficiently the stocks of money held or the payments made by leading groups of transactors in the economy. This gap in statistical information has been a barrier to scientific progress, but there is a prospect that Copeland's experiments in tracing the flow of money may soon improve matters. The Board of Governors of the Federal Reserve System has recognized the high importance of his undertaking and will attempt, in collaboration with the National Bureau, to develop statistics on the flow of money on a current basis.

In tracing money flows Copeland presents information on the debt and credit position, as well as the amounts paid and received, for each of various groups of transactors. For one category of debt, corporate bonds, the National Bureau has for some time sheltered in its files a virtual census, starting in 1900. Analysis of this extraordinary body of information was begun last year under Hickman's direction. One of the principal aims of the new project is to develop investment experience tables that may serve as a guide for evaluating securities and establishing loss reserves. Related studies of risk experience with mortgages are being conducted by Saulnier and his associates. If these investigations prosper, the fickleness of individual securities may be no obstacle in the future to tolerable forecasts of security experience in the mass.

VIII. THE GROWTH OF GOVERNMENT

One reason for the decline of 'the commercial loan' in bank portfolios is the expansion of government and its heavy reliance in recent years on borrowing. Indeed, the outstanding trend in the service sector of our economy has been the growth of government. The figures on employment that I cited earlier are merely important symptoms. They include regular civilian employees of government, but omit the employment afforded by private industry on account of governmental purchases. They do not even include military personnel or workers on emergency public projects. And, of course, no employment figure, however comprehensive, can give any inkling of the influence of interest on the public debt, or of payments to veterans, or of financial aid to foreign countries, to say nothing of the influence exercised by government on the economic life of the nation through nonfiscal devices.

The colossal wartime expenditures of government have now abated. Also, the pervasive controls of private industry are being lifted, and free markets reestablished. But a very large part of the nation's income continues to flow through government channels. The ratio of government expenditures (inclusive of so-called transfer payments) to the gross national product, which was 20 per cent in 1939 and rose to 52 per cent in 1944, was still about 35 per cent in 1946. A further reduction may reasonably be expected during the next few years, but the figure is likely to remain above the prewar level. However loudly the public may grumble about taxes, there is no easy escape from the fiscal problem facing the nation. In a careful analysis of the federal budget, now nearing completion, Crum and Kendrick have reached the conclusion that federal expenditures during the first postwar decade may well average $32 billion per year [in 1947 prices]. If state and local outlays are added in, government expenditures may approach the $45 billion mark.

The recent shift of the political tide in this country may check the government's part in the economy of the nation, but it seems unlikely that the reduction will be large or permanent. The size of the public debt and the obligation to veterans work strongly against curtailment of governmental activity; so too do the assumption of responsibility for a high level of employment, the growing awareness of the needs of underprivileged groups, the continuance of international rivalry and friction, the spread of collectivism abroad, and our own tradition of governmental intervention. The practical question is not whether the government need play an important part in the nation's economic life, but how that part will be played. Under the circumstances, the National Bureau can make a useful contribution to public policy by subjecting large governmental activities to objective study. The investigations now being conducted by Crum, Seltzer, Smith, and their associates of the Conference on Research in Fiscal Policy are a step in this direction. So also is Fabricant's investigation of trends in government employment, as well as Colean's study of the influence of government on urban real estate finance.

The novel statement of federal finances devised by Copeland in the course of his experimental tracings of the flow of money is a welcome addition to our inadequate kit of tools for analyzing fiscal policies. This statement makes available for the first time a clear and comprehensive record of federal fiscal operations, and will be published promptly as a *Technical Paper*. The statement combines transactions of public service enterprises, credit agencies, and insurance funds with general federal operations. It shows dealings with the public, not interagency transactions; in short, it gives the sort of information needed to trace the impact of fiscal operations on the economy. If plans for developing the data on a current basis materialize, as now seems likely, economists will gain a new weapon in their struggle with 'the shape of things to come.'

IX. Forecasting and Economic Policy

Economists are now engaged in a lively discussion of the business outlook. At no time since the 1920's have forecasters been so outspoken, insistent, and self-confident. Strong in faith, they address their predictions—sometimes in ordinary prose, sometimes in esoteric symbols—not only to business executives and the stock-buying public, but also and preeminently to government itself. Today's forecasters have enormous advantages over their predecessors: keener analytic tools, longer and better statistical records, sounder analyses of past experience. These stepping stones towards the future will become firmer with time, but two serious difficulties are likely to remain in the forecaster's path: first, the imperfect tendency of history to repeat itself; second, the forecaster's own hopes and fears about the future, which tend to insinuate themselves into his predictions, no matter how elaborate their statistical or mathematical scaffolding.

The recent outburst of articulate forecasting will bear careful watching. A scientific investigator can learn nothing from the intuitive prophet, whether his forecasts prove true or false. On the other hand, the forecasters who are now devising ingenious theoretical models may contribute significantly to economic science, even if many of their forecasts prove wrong. The economist who values truth must discriminate conscientiously among false prophets, but it is also his duty to warn men of affairs that they cannot safely practice similar tolerance. At our Twenty-fifth Anniversary celebration last June, Joseph S. Davis stressed the need for wider recognition of the nature of economic forecasts. His sage remarks deserve repetition: "In economics . . . really scientific predictions are usually impossible except as statements of what can be expected under a certain combination of assumptions. Such specialized predictions have their place, but they are too easily confused with outright prophecies. The assumptions underlying the forecasts, and the margin of error in them, typically deserve as much weight as the forecasts themselves, if the users and indeed the authors are not to be misled. But there is greater need of warning that certain forecasts cannot be made within a margin of error small enough to warrant serious reliance upon them. This is true of many forecasts—of crops, of food supply and demand, of labor force and unemployment, and even of population some decades ahead. Policies cannot soundly be based upon *specific forecasts* of this type, or an average of them, but ought to take account of a considerable range of possibilities."[6]

The question now agitating many people is when the next down-

6 *Economic Research and the Development of Economic Science and Public Policy* (National Bureau, 1946), pp. 187-188. The italics are mine.

turn in business will come, and how far it will take us. Men in high stations have made reassuring statements on these matters, and they are likely to multiply in coming months, especially if the downturn occurs. Unfortunately, the benevolent pronouncements rarely rest on firm knowledge. The paramount lesson of experience is that the only perfectly regular feature of business cycles is the recurrence of the phenomenon itself. For well over a century business cycles have run an unceasing round. They have persisted through vast economic and social changes; they have withstood countless experiments in industry, agriculture, banking, industrial relations, and public policy; they have confounded forecasters without number, belied repeated prophecies of a 'new era of prosperity,' and outlived repeated forebodings of 'chronic depression.' Men who wish to serve democracy faithfully must recognize that the roots of business cycles go deep in our economic organization, that the ability of government to control depressions adequately is not yet assured, that our power of forecasting is limited, and that true foresight requires policies for coping with numerous contingencies.

The Cumulation of Economic Knowledge

I. Recent Changes in Economics

Economic knowledge is so obviously inadequate for coping with society's ills that we sometimes lose sight of the progress that has been made in recent decades. Thirty or forty years ago the typical economist was a college teacher, who devoted himself primarily to speculations on the theory of value, or to the practical problems receiving public attention—such as the tariff, the property tax, labor organizations, the state of the currency, or the devious ways of monopoly. The Marshallian synthesis of economic theory was broadly accepted, and with it the reassuring principle of continuity. Most economists, deploring poverty and monopoly, felt that the state could alleviate their harsher features; but it was taken for granted that social change was and must remain gradual, and that it was not the function of economists to participate in the political processes of change. The outstanding tool of economic investigation was marginal analysis, which Ricardo had been the first to put to effective use. Economic statistics hardly extended beyond commodity prices, foreign trade, immigration, banking, and the security markets. In any event, technical specialists alone were supposed to dabble in such matters. Statistical theory was in a primitive state, little known, and little used. The warnings of a Marx, a Veblen, or a Mitchell that economists were neglecting changes in the world gathering around them, that preoccupation with states of equilibrium led to tragic neglect of principles of cumulative change, went unheeded. Even Henry L. Moore's plea for a statistical complement to pure economics was received with faint enthusiasm.

Nevertheless, the limited equipment of economists seemed reasonably adequate, as long as events moved in fairly familiar grooves and instruction of college youth was the main task of the profession. Even the outbreak of war in 1914 had slight influence on the pattern of economic thinking or responsibility until our own country entered the struggle three years later. But the war was only the first of a series of portentous developments, the last of which is not yet in sight. A single generation has already witnessed two world-wide armed conflicts, countless revolutions, the rise and fall of great empires, vast upheavals of population and

Reprinted from *Twenty-eighth Annual Report of the National Bureau of Economic Research* (May 1948), pp. 3-17.

trade, marvelous advances in technology, a train of astronomic inflations, revolutionary changes in public finance, the severest business depression of which we have a definite record, and the spectre of secular stagnation. In many parts of the world independent trade unions virtually disappeared. Here they flourished despite internal strife; social insurance emerged and developed rapidly, and the hourly wage of labor moved upward in the face of grave unemployment. Still more momentous developments of our time are the rise and spread of the communist state in continental Europe, the systematic restriction of free enterprise in the land of its birth, and the vast expansion of governmental activity in our own country and elsewhere. Now, a conflict between the rival ideologies of Russia and the United States is rapidly gathering momentum, and whatever its outcome the world seems likely to remain in turmoil for many years to come.

This swift rush of events has flung economics into a position of prominence which it neither sought, nor was adequately prepared to assume. In a complex and growing civilization intricate division of labor is unavoidable. To be sure, economists were not regarded as proven experts by the community at large. But as economic problems requiring urgent attention kept coming up, a distraught citizenry turned increasingly to men who were supposed to be specialists for precise facts concerning what was going on, for explanations of the course of events, for forecasts of the shape of things to be, and for aid in devising acceptable solutions.

The most obvious effect of the upsurge in thinking about changing conditions appears in the economist's tool chest, which now bulges with devices such as index numbers, sampling theory, correlation techniques, time-series analysis, reference cycles, factor analysis, income analysis, multiplier technique, statements of sources and uses of funds, national income accounts, economic budgets, and econometric models—devices that were unknown or little used or comparatively crude a mere thirty years ago. Some of these instruments are still imperfectly conceived, and all need further testing. But the significant thing is that both the old and the new instruments are being focused on the workings of our economic organization. True, the substantive achievements have hardly begun to meet the hopes or needs of mankind. That they are, nevertheless, considerable will, I think, be clear to anyone who would compare what the best-informed economists knew before World War I with what they know today about national income and its distribution, or about the rate of growth of employment and output whether in individual industries or industry as a whole, or about the nature and forms of competition and monopoly, or overhead costs, or the behavior of wages and prices in principal markets, or consumer and business debt, or the income-generating effects of investment, and so on over a list that can be appreciably expanded. And while deepening concern with actual conditions has not yet yielded a dependable theory of the workings of the economy as a whole, that concern and nothing else explains why economic theory broke loose from its Marshallian moorings; why it moved first in the direction of monopoly and later in the direction of employment and income flows; and why the fences that previously separated public finance, money and banking, labor problems, international trade, and business cycles, both from one another and from general economic theory, have crumpled.

II. THE NEED FOR EMPIRICAL RESEARCH

These, in broad compass, seem to me to be the major changes that have swept over economics in our generation. Economists are still of many schools and clash heatedly on a thousand issues. Scientific craftsmanship is still a relatively rare skill. Notable advances towards realistic thinking and towards definite knowledge have nevertheless been made. The turbulence of life has driven the economist out of his den and forced him to reckon with the changing economic scene—with mobilization for war, reparations, foreign lending or relief, inflation, depression. Urgent problems of this character cannot be handled by introspection alone, and they can be tackled in a spirit of casual empiricism only at the nation's peril.

The mounting requirements for exact economic knowledge have given a great impetus to empirical research, and the National Bureau has participated in this development. The National Bureau was established in 1920. Some of its founders were men of affairs; others were unusual scholars who had learned their economics from life as well as print. The group as a whole included men with widely dissimilar views on economic and political issues. They had, however, one aim in common: to substitute as far as possible fact for conjecture and tested theory for plausible hypothesis, in order that the world might have a sounder basis for choosing among the conflicting policies that are constantly being urged. We have clung firmly to this purpose through the years. Our publications have not urged this or that policy on the nation, but have put steadily before the public the results of objective analyses of fundamentals that underlie the ever shifting issues of the day.

This concern with the workings of economic organization has characterized the major economic theorists. To Adam Smith the basic problem was the size of the national income, to Ricardo its distribution, to Marshall the interaction of demand and supply, to Walras the interdependence of prices, to Fisher the level of prices, to Keynes the level of employment. In the main, the theorists have explored these questions from the point of view of the economy as a whole, rather than of a particular region or industry or class. This has also been the characteristic approach of the National Bureau, although the parts that make the whole meaningful receive close attention in our studies. Like the theorists, too, the National Bureau has sought to separate the persistent or repetitive from the haphazard elements of experience; that is, to establish regularities of sequence and covariation among economic phenomena. But whereas the theorists have ordinarily speculated on the basis of only vague knowledge about economic quantities and relations, the National Bureau has sought to determine the magnitude of the leading economic variables, their characteristic movements over time, and their actual relations to one another. The ground covered has been smaller, but the findings have been better supported by evidence.

Of course, this difference in method reflects, in part at least, a difference in scientific opportunity. Every major theorist from Adam Smith to Keynes had a lively interest in the conditions of his time. Some, like Smith or Marshall, had great historical knowledge. Others—like Jevons, Keynes, and Fisher—had a good eye for statistical methods. Every one of them had some familiarity with statistical data, made some use of them in his work, and stimulated others to examine facts. If they did not do so in greater degree, the reason is partly that the data needed often did not exist, or were not to be trusted unless subjected to laborious and time-consuming tests or revisions—a task the single-handed investigator could rarely undertake. Adam Smith's famous declaration that he had "no great faith in political arithmetic" was not a hostile or flippant utterance, but a confession by a good scholar that he could not "warrant the exactness" of the "computations" at his disposal.

Seldom have the statistical data available to the economist been gathered to serve a purely scientific purpose. To a very considerable degree, they are by-products of administrative operations by government or private enterprises of different sorts. Some branches of activity are not covered by statistical data at all, either because they have not yet become matters of social concern or because they present unusual problems of measurement. Statistical data often do not become available until a problem—whether it be unemployment, the length of the working day, or the rate of formation of new firms—is generally recognized as pressing. This means that many problems regarded as sufficiently urgent to call for action must be dealt with on an inadequate basis of fact. What data are available are often hard to compare or combine, and even when homogeneous may not be available as frequently as is desirable for scientific purposes. Finally, the statistical data with which the economist must work commonly stop at the surface of economic life. They record the results of mass activities, but do not penetrate to the motives that twist and drive the consuming and producing units of society.

These difficulties have been reduced by the vast extension and improvement of economic statistics in recent years, but they have not been swept away. Nor will they ever be in a complex and rapidly changing world. As a consequence, fruitful empirical research calls for a combination of qualities that is not yet widespread in economics. Like the formal theorist, the realistic investigator must have the ability to formulate economic concepts and to think through economic relations precisely. He must put definite questions to statistical data, yet be ever ready to reformulate his questions in the light of accumulating evidence. He must have the patience to examine with meticulous care the economic coverage and representativeness of the statistics that lie at hand; the enterprise to seek out remote and inaccessible bodies of information; the imagination and technical skill to devise appropriate methods of relating, combining, reducing, or decomposing statistical observations; the personal industry or the clerical assistance to carry through these laborious operations; the common sense to make full use of nonquantitative information about commercial markets and processes; the conscience to test results repeatedly against fresh observations; the character to scrap results if error or unconscious bias is spotted; the fortitude to expose his materials and methods to the public's gaze; the wisdom to seek the help of others who might make his own best efforts obsolete. This process of constructing an analytical framework, seeking out observations, processing them, reshaping the framework, seeking out new observations, and so on, is the continuous and well-tried method of science. If it is followed persistently in economics, the results will be cumulative and a body of scientfic knowledge will gradually take shape.

III. How Knowledge Cumulates

That this expression of faith has some basis in experience I think I can make clear by an illustration. One of the perennial problems of economic analysis centers around the formation of capital—or, as it is now usually called, investment. Different aspects of capital formation have attracted attention at different times. Without capital, division of labor is virtually impossible. With it, round-about processes of production can be started and industrial efficiency increased. This is the aspect of the problem on which the classical economists concentrated. They realized that incomes were generated by investing; that a 'revulsion of trade' ordinarily meant a shrinkage of investment, and that employment suffered as a consequence. But they paid little attention to these matters, considering them of minor and temporary importance. Modern economists, on the other hand, characteristically take for granted the role of capital in economic progress, and concentrate on the influence of investment on current employment and income.

Many proposals for mitigating the fluctuations of investment or raising its level have been advanced in our time, and they have rested on different hypotheses concerning the underlying process. Economists have tried to explain the behavior of investment in terms of variations in construction costs, in terms of expectations concerning the rate of profit relative to the going rate of interest, in terms of the demand for consumer goods or its rate of change, in terms of changes in the money supply, in terms of technological progress and innovations, in terms of the rate of change in population or national income, in terms of policies of government or of the banking system or of trade unions. Baffled by these diverse explanations and impressed by the instability of investment, some economists have taken refuge in the hypothesis that investment as a whole, or at least a very substantial portion of it, is an 'autonomous' or 'spontaneous' variable in the economic system. This and other hypotheses have been able to thrive because our factual knowledge of investment has been scanty.

The early publications of the National Bureau recognized the instability of investment, and its great influence on economic conditions at large. But the "fragmentary and ambiguous" character of the statistics, as Oswald Knauth summed up the situation in the early twenties, severely limited analysis. The only branch of investment that received systematic attention was construction work. At first, this was a technical consequence of preparing estimates of national income by industrial divisions. But there was also a great deal of discussion during the twenties of the possible use of public works as a balancing factor in the economy. After the stock market crash of 1929 interest in public works was intensified, and there was a demand for accurate information on the investment goods industries in general. Our publications of that period reflect the great concern over investment, but they reflect also the inadequate information that existed. In 1929 King estimated the volume of construction in the United States during 1928 at $7.8 billion. Next year Wolman raised the figure to $9.9 billion. A little later Gayer came out with a figure of $13.0 billion and Kuznets with $15.9 billion. I do not think it a great exaggeration to say that up to the thirties our knowledge about the volume of investment in the United States was hardly more secure than was knowledge about the earth's population at the close of the seventeenth century, when the learned priest Riccioli estimated the "true number of mankind" to be 1,000 million and the political arithmetician Petty put the number at no more than 320 million.

The amount of investment is, of course, a more elusive quantity than the number of mankind. The latter is mainly a question of fact, the former involves also difficult questions of concept. An important step toward clarifying the problem was taken by Wesley Mitchell in *Business Cycles: The Problem and Its Setting*. Mitchell observed that consumption in any given year was not limited rigidly by that year's income, since a nation could draw on its accumulation from past efforts. But how large was this accumulation? And what portion of a year's income was typically added to it? To answer the second question Mitchell used the fragile but instructive estimates by King and Ingalls. To answer the first question he turned to estimates of wealth by the Bureau of the Census for 1922. After omitting the value of land, he got a total for man-made appliances that was three to four times as large as the year's national income. This total, it turned out, included inventories with a value almost as large as all movable industrial equipment, and 'furniture and personal effects' of still larger value. Mitchell therefore concluded that students of business cycles who wish to follow realistically the investment process cannot confine attention to buildings, machinery, and public utility equipment; they must take account also of consumer durable goods and the additions to or drafts upon the nation's vast reservoir of inventories of raw materials, semifinished products, and finished goods.

Mitchell's analysis was a brief excursion, incidental to another and larger theme. The same was true of Mills' interesting measurements of the aggregate output of finished durable goods, and of other more limited efforts by our staff. However, these side explorations yielded valuable insights into the problem of investment, uncovered new materials, and suggested new approaches to measurement. In combination they indicated that knowledge might be advanced rapidly by a new project concerned exclusively with investment. When the Social Science Research Council proposed late in 1932 "a statistical study of the formation of capital during the 1920's in terms of commodities and services," the National Bureau eagerly accepted the invitation and help of the Council. The investigation was started in January 1933, with Simon Kuznets in charge. To this study Kuznets brought, beside his own invaluable experience in measuring national income, a full knowledge of the Bureau's earlier work.

What Kuznets sought to do I can convey best, perhaps, by a paradigm. Imagine a huge vacant lot on which every member of the gainfully occupied population plies his trade. When a tangible product flows from economic activity it shows up on the lot; otherwise, let us say, some token is deposited there. During the course of a year each of us tears down the pile on the lot as well as builds it up; we build up the pile by placing there our product, we tear it down by withdrawing this or that for consumption. At the end of the year what is left on the lot represents the year's accumulation by the nation, or its investment. If every item on the lot has a valid price tag attached to it, the amount of investment can be ascertained by straight addition. What does the investment consist of? It includes, first, all residential buildings, factories, waterworks, roads, bridges, and so on—that is, construction of 'permanent improvements.' It includes, next, tools and machinery, trucks, tractors, railroad cars, and so on—that is, producers' equipment in the way of movable durable goods. It includes, third, raw materials, semifinished goods, and products ready for final use—that is, inventories of all sorts. These three categories comprise everything on the lot. The sum of their values, nevertheless, will not measure investment under conditions differing from those I have envisaged. For if a portion of the stuff produced on the lot was shipped abroad and no compensating product received in return, a claim has been acquired against foreign countries and its amount must be counted in the year's investment. Any addition to the stockpiles within households should likewise be included, and anything that smacks of a capital gain excluded. Finally, I have assumed that the 'lot' is empty at the beginning of the year, whereas in fact it is piled high with the accumulations of generations; hence the value of the pile at the year's start must be deducted to get the net investment of the year. The magnitude of net investment is, of course, vital in judging the economic prospects of a nation in the long run. But to gauge the current activity associated with the building up of capital, it is desirable to combine the replacements of structures and equipment with the net additions. The resulting quantity is the gross investment or, in Kuznets' phrase, gross capital formation.

I hope this brief sketch has at least identified Kuznets' broad objective. By the middle of 1934 he had completed a preliminary investigation, which was published as *Bulletin 52*. The bulletin presented annual estimates of gross investment in the United States from 1919 to 1933. Changes in consumer stockpiles were omitted, except for gross additions of durable consumer goods. Otherwise, the totals were complete in principle. They included construction, the flow of durable equipment to enterprises, the flow of durable commodities to consumers, net changes in business inventories, and net changes in claims against foreign countries— each expressed both in current and in constant prices. The new series, especially the data on inventories, were highly suggestive, and the results as a whole seemed promising enough to justify expanding the investigation.

One particularly dark corner of the investment problem was the consumption of capital—more precisely, the value of durable goods used up in the course of producing commodities and services. Solomon Fabricant began work on this baffling subject. A little later David Wickens joined the staff to try his hand at developing basic estimates for residential real estate—a great segment of the nation's wealth largely neglected by economists. In the meantime Gayer continued his research on public works. Each of these studies eventuated in an important publication: Gayer's *Public Works in Prosperity and Depression* appeared in 1935, Fabricant's *Capital Consumption and Adjustment* in 1938, and Wickens' *Residential Real Estate* in 1941. Long before these volumes saw daylight, some of the leading results were published in our *Bulletin*. Of course, the results were available at all times to the staff, and Kuznets was in a position to profit continuously by the work of his colleagues. He made constructive use of the opportunity. By adopting Fabricant's measures of capital consumption, he was able to pass from gross to net investment. By adopting Wickens' data on nonfarm residential building and Gayer's on public works, he was able to improve his own treatment of construction. But Kuznets did not confine revision to these matters. On the contrary, he bolstered the authority of his earlier work by testing and revising every part of his preliminary investigation. A summary was published in 1937 in *National Income and Capital Formation.* The following year, in his monumental volume *Commodity Flow and Capital Formation,* Kuznets demonstrated at length how a skilled investigator can transform a nondescript mass of fragmentary data, scattered over hundreds of sources, into a coherent account of aggregate investment and its major components.

The new measures quickly attracted attention, and they have greatly influenced both economists and men of affairs. It is easy to see why that happened. Thinking men were much exercised about the low volume of investment in the 1930's; but they had only vague and conflicting notions about the actual volume of investment, or the importance of its leading parts, or the drop of different categories of investment from the level of the 1920's. Kuznets supplied the essential information in a well-considered analytical setting. He found, for example, that out of every $100 of national income during 1919-1935, only $2.40 was devoted to expanding business plant and equipment. All channels of investment together absorbed $8.30; the remaining $91.70 was spent on consumer goods. These remarkable figures, however, give no inkling of the expenditure on replacing capital goods. Since the provision of replacements is a vital part of the activity of the capital goods industries, Kuznets set forth also the record of gross investment—which includes replacements of durable goods as well as the additions. On a gross basis, investment during 1919-1935 was 19.2 per cent of the gross national product (which exceeds national income by the amount that gross investment exceeds net investment). The results can be put this way: out of every $100 of gross national product, $80.80 was expended on ordinary consumer goods, $3.60 on residential construction; $10.40 on business plant and equipment, $1.00 on additional business inventories; $3.60 on governmental plant and monetary stock; $.60 on the foreign balance. But $9.50 of the $80.80 spent by households went into durable consumer goods. If these too are counted as investment purchases, gross investment comes out 29 per cent of gross national product.

The new findings by Kuznets and Fabricant inevitably raised questions about the part played by investment in earlier stages of the nation's history. If investment averaged only some 8 per cent of national income after 1919, what was it in the boisterous past? Was the increase in the government's share of investment after 1919 a new development or merely a continuation of a trend deeply rooted in social evolution? Was the marked instability of investment a recent phenomenon or an abiding characteristic of the capitalist process? These questions, and others like them, are obviously of first-rate theoretical interest. Being hotly debated in the late thirties, they were of practical importance as well. But before specific problems of secular change could be tackled with any confidence, new information had to be acquired, and this was bound to prove increasingly difficult as the statistical clock was turned further back.

William Shaw undertook the task with full knowledge of the risks, having served previously as Kuznets' associate. After several years of unremitting labor, he attained what seemed to be good estimates of the flow of perishable, semidurable, and durable commodities to consumers, of durable equipment to producers, and of building materials to construction sites—all expressed in producers' prices for every year since 1889 and decennially since 1869. Some of Shaw's results were released in 1941 in *Occasional Paper 3*, and the fully documented final report was published last year under the title *Value of Commodity Output since 1869*. Perhaps the most important result of this study is the demonstration of the increasing role of consumer durable goods in the nation's economy. According to Shaw's measurements, the physical flow of all finished commodities into domestic consumption increased at an average annual rate of 3.2 per cent between 1879 and 1939. The rate of growth of consumer durable goods was half again as large, 4.7 per cent. As a consequence the share of consumer durables rose from 9.6 per cent of the value of finished commodities in 1879 to 18.1 per cent in 1939. The increase before World War I was slight. The big jump occurred after 1914, and it exceeds any change in the nation's habits of consumption previously experienced, at least since the 1870's.

Just as Shaw's research grew out of Kuznets' original study of capital formation, so Kuznets' later research grew out of Shaw's work. The estimates prepared by Shaw did not of themselves reveal what portion of national income consisted of investment. Before that could be ascertained, the estimates had to be transformed and amplified. Kuznets' efforts in this direction are recorded in *Occasional Paper 6* and *National Product since 1869*. It appears from the new study that about 91 per cent of the output of the American economy from 1869 to 1938 can be traced to the doors of consumers. The remaining 9 per cent is the net investment of the period by government and private enterprise. The government's share has been increasing for many years, but more rapidly since 1919. During the 1930's investment as a whole diminished to a mere trickle. In the preceding sixty years it had been very considerable by comparison, averaging 12 per cent of the national income. Not only that, but the fraction of national income added to capital was nearly constant, decade after decade. It is common knowledge that family incomes have generally risen over the decades, and that in any one year the proportion of income saved is higher for families with large incomes than for families with small incomes. In view of these facts, the nearly constant ratio of investment to national income almost certainly implies that the American public accommodated itself in the past to progressively higher incomes by spending a progressively larger amount out of income of any given size.

The studies I have just sketched were designed primarily to determine the characteristic magnitude of investment, its division into major components, and broad secular changes. But the investigators concerned with these questions were in continuous touch with our Business Cycle Unit, and made important contributions to its work. Although the great instability of investment had long been familiar from sample data, the comprehensive summaries by Kuznets and Fabricant provided a check on existing knowledge and added to its definiteness. Their records demonstrated that net investment is even more volatile than gross investment. This was to be expected from ordinary practices of charging depreciation; but before the results were finally assembled, I do not see how anyone could have argued with much force that net investment is positive in years of depression as well as years of prosperity. Yet, except for the catastrophe of the early 1930's, that is what the Kuznets-Fabricant figures show. Another basic finding relates to inventory investment, which according to Kuznets' data regularly alternates between substantial plus values in prosperity and minus values in depression. Not only has this segment of investment conformed with great sensitivity to business cycles, but its fluctuations have been so enormous that they account for about half of the amplitude of the cyclical swings in gross investment between the two wars, and for more than a fifth of the amplitude of the cyclical swings in gross national product.

The arresting fluctuations of inventory investment became the starting point of a special investigation of inventories by Abramovitz. His study of inventory holdings by manufacturers during business cycles is virtually completed, and a summary will be published promptly as *Occasional Paper 26*. Abramovitz' first task was to supplement Kuznets' comprehensive annual aggregates by monthly records of inventories held at many different points in the system. The evidence indicated that although new inventory investment by manufacturers tended to move coincidently with the business cycle, actual holdings of inventories lagged by about six to nine months; in other words, inventories continued to rise some months after production had begun to decline, and continued to fall some months after production had begun to rise. This systematic lag is a net resultant of widely different circumstances surrounding the holding of distinct classes of inventories—raw materials, goods in process, and finished goods. Goods in process, for example, rise and fall in almost perfect unison with output. This is a technical corollary of the production process itself, as is the similar behavior of inventories of finished goods made to order. Inventories of raw materials, on the other hand, lag behind cycles in output by about four months; the lag is usually shorter when the materials are secured from domestic manufacturers or dealers, and again longer when secured from distant sources or on long-term contracts. Much the longest lag characterizes inventories of finished staples sold from stock. When sales decline, manufacturers as a rule reduce their output promptly; but the reduction is not sufficient to overtake the decline in shipments, and inventories therefore pile up for a year or even longer. Clearly, the movements of inventories can be understood only by observing the technical processes and marketing arrangements that impede here and facilitate there the efforts of businessmen to adjust their inventories to changing requirements. Abramovitz' great contribution consists in demonstrating that inventories are not a homogeneous mass, that their behavior does not lend itself to aggregative analysis; but that economic law nevertheless governs the process of inventory accumulation and decumulation.

IV. THE PATH AHEAD

Every investigator whose work on investment I have touched in these hurried pages has consolidated knowledge at some point, and broken new scientific ground at another. In this group belong, of course, many scholars outside the National Bureau, notably the economists working on capital formation at the Department of Commerce. Each investigator has made progress by building on the work of his colleagues or predecessors—adding new facts, mending old series, often clarifying concepts, and always trying to see how the pieces at hand fit together. If so much has been accomplished in a bare twenty years, is it too much to claim that economics is already assuming, however hesitantly and gradually, the shape of a body of knowledge cumulating in the spirit of science? Everything I have said of the National Bureau's studies of investment seems to point to this moral and to justify this faith. And the illustration I have developed is by no means an isolated one. I could equally well have taken Stigler's recent essay on *Trends in Output and Employment* as a point of departure to illustrate the cumulation of knowledge of industrial productivity, or the new *Technical Paper* on bond yields by Durand and Winn to illustrate the cumulation of knowledge of interest rates, or the *Technical Paper* on a federal financial statement by Copeland to illustrate the beginnings of what I trust will be a cumulative process of expanding realistic knowledge of money flows. And if I followed any one illustration far enough I would surely encompass before long all the others, as well as much of the extensive research of other economists on which our own work so largely rests. For the economic process is one whole, and so in the course of time must become our knowledge of it.

But before this goal can be attained, there is much fundamental work to be done on limited sectors of the economy—construction expenditures, consumer outlays, farming, finance, foreign trade, and the like. Economics is still in its infancy, and must not overreach its strength. Preliminary attempts at integration of knowledge won from stubborn facts must nevertheless go on, both for their own sake and to guide specialized inquiry. Wesley Mitchell's essay summarizing the findings of our business cycle studies, which I hope will be published fairly soon, is a significant step in this direction, and other large efforts at integration and interpretation of results will follow.

As economics moves forward, many contradictory movements

are visible on its surface. But the habit of insisting upon evidence is spreading, and today evidence less often means deduction from untested premises. Economic models continue to receive hopeful attention; but mere logical consistency or aesthetic appeal now counts for less, and performance under test for more, than a generation ago. Ever widening circles of men are recognizing that a piece of research whose reliability can be accepted is a great economizer of human energy. The path ahead of the National Bureau is clear: We must continue to insist on thorough and realistic scholarship as we press our closely related investigations of the workings of economic organization, for we are traveling a road along which economic knowledge will cumulate.

Wesley Mitchell and the
National Bureau

Wesley Mitchell died in the early hours of Friday, October 29, 1948. He was then at work on his favorite subject—business cycles. A year earlier he had suffered a heart attack, but after a few weeks was again working at full efficiency on a manuscript he liked to think of as a progress report on What Happens during Business Cycles. A second attack in late August left little hope for recovery, though the end did not come promptly. With courageous tenacity he stayed at his desk, completing the penultimate chapter of the first volume of his report. He managed also to put his papers in order, to render an account of the precise state of his scientific enterprises, and to draft a letter to a friend who had expressed a practical interest in the National Bureau's future. That much accomplished, he finally yielded to the insistent plea of his physician to put his manuscript aside. Idleness of even a limited sort can spell only hardship to an energetic man accustomed to good health over a lifetime, but it was no part of Wesley Mitchell's character to complain. As his physical strength gave way, the exquisite gentleness and courtesy that always marked his dealings with others continued to govern. These traits ran deep in Mitchell's character, and they flowed on unchanged until the end. So too did the steady play of his keen and eager mind. Work, especially of an analytical type, was a permanent part of the man. It could not be suppressed by family solicitude or medical exhortation. It went on relentlessly, triumphing over a fading consciousness, and ceased only with life.

While Wesley Mitchell's incredible will to work was testing his impaired constitution, Herbert Hoover—a friend since California days—wrote him: "I hear that you are laid up. This is not in the national interest." His illness was indeed against the interest of the nation, and his death brings great sorrow. Few men of our times contributed as much or as quietly to the still small voice of reason in adjusting men's conflicts. None added more to the 'reasoned history of man,' to which all social science aspires. None

Reprinted (with minor revisions) from *Twenty-ninth Annual Report of the National Bureau of Economic Research* (May 1949), pp. 3-55. The present text is taken from *Wesley Clair Mitchell: The Economic Scientist*, ed. Arthur F. Burns (National Bureau, 1952).

added as much to knowledge of the boisterous money economy in which we move and dwell.

It is not to honor Wesley Mitchell—his works alone can do that—but to gain perspective on our responsibilities and opportunities that I invite you to join in an hour of remembrance.

I

Let us go back thirty years. The precise date is December 27, 1918, the place—Richmond, Virginia. With the war at an end the entire nation has been rejoicing and squabbling. A return to 'normalcy' can already be felt in this ancient city as elsewhere. Here the American Statistical Association is holding its Eightieth Annual Meeting. Its membership has grown rapidly in number and self-confidence during the year. Young men are conspicuous in the assembled throng. Many know at first hand the vital part that statistics played, and the still greater part it could have played, in the economic mobilization for war. Among this group is Wesley Clair Mitchell, a Columbia professor who became Chief of the Price Section of the War Industries Board after being pressed into emergency work.

Wesley Mitchell, not yet forty-five, is President of the Association, and is now addressing his colleagues on the subject "Statistics and Government." He minces no words on the incapacity of the established statistical agencies to cope with the problems of war, or on the hurried improvisations of the new statistical units set up by the war boards. The economists who flocked to Washington "worked with passionate intensity. They were appalled by no obstacles. Where they could not get definite data, they did not hesitate to estimate." Nevertheless, there was great confusion and waste. No one was able "to put before the responsible authorities promptly the data they needed concerning men and commodities, ships and factories." Not until the armistice was signed were we "in a fair way to develop for the first time a systematic organization of federal statistics." But the war boards were being rapidly demobilized, and the considerable gains in extending and organizing federal statistics were in jeopardy.

For some fifteen minutes Mitchell has been speaking in this vein. He is about to turn to tasks of the future. Let us join the audience at this point and follow his precise words:

In physical science and in industrial technique . . . we have emancipated ourselves . . . from the savage dependence upon catastrophes for progress. . . . In science and in industry we are radicals—radicals relying on a tested method. But in matters of social organization we retain a large part of the conservatism characteristic of the savage mind. . . .

The 'social reformer' we have always with us, it is true. Or rather most of us are 'social reformers' of some kind. . . . Yet the story of the past in matters of social organization is not a story that we should like to have continued for a thousand and one years. Reform by agitation or class struggle is a jerky way of moving forward, uncomfortable and wasteful of energy. Are we not intelligent enough to devise a steadier and a more certain method of progress?

Most certainly, we could not keep social organization what it is even if we wanted to. We are not emerging from the hazards of war into a safe world. On the contrary, the world is a very dangerous place for a society framed as ours is, and I for one am glad of it. . . .

Taking us all together as one people in a group of mighty peoples, our first and foremost concern is to develop some way of carrying on the infinitely complicated processes of modern industry and interchange day by day, despite all tedium and fatigue, and yet to keep ourselves interested in our work and contented with the division of the product. . . . What is lacking to achieve that end . . . is not so much good will as it is knowledge—above all, knowledge of human behavior.

Our best hope for the future lies in the extension to social organization of the methods that we already employ in our most progressive fields of effort. In science and in industry . . . we do not wait for catastrophes to force new ways upon us. . . . We rely, and with success, upon quantitative analysis to point the way; and we advance because we are constantly improving and applying such analysis.

While I think that the development of social science offers more hope for solving our social problems than any other line of endeavor, I do not claim that these sciences in their present state are very serviceable. They are immature, speculative, filled with controversies. . . . Nor have we any certain assurance that they will ever grow into robust manhood, no matter what care we lavish upon them. . . . Those of us who are concerned with the social sciences . . . are engaged in an uncertain enterprise; perhaps we shall win no great treasures for mankind. But certainly it is our task to work out this lead with all the intelligence and the energy we possess until its richness or sterility be demonstrated.[1]

This, in essence, was Mitchell's scientific creed. He chose the proper time and place to proclaim his faith in a quantitative social science. Statistics had gained new prestige during the war. Many economists who had never before worked with observational records learned to do so in their Washington posts, and they were not likely to lose the habit upon returning to their academic jobs. In the new era of peace there would be time for fundamental quanti-

---

[1] Mitchell, "Statistics and Government," in his *The Backward Art of Spending Money and Other Essays* (McGraw-Hill, 1937), pp. 45, 47, 48-51. Originally appeared in *Quarterly Publications of the American Statistical Association*, March 1919.

tative studies of economic organization, in contrast to the rushed memoranda of war days. The American Statistical Association linked together in some degree the different branches of the study of man. As its President, Mitchell could address himself to social scientists at large. He was known to the members of the Association as an authority on index numbers. Many knew him also through his work on money and banking, and as the author of the massive treatise *Business Cycles*, which, by its skilful blending of economic theory with statistical and historical fact, was a symbol of what the new social science might become. Now, as Mitchell spoke of the role that statistics might play in building a useful social science, the lustre of his office added force to his considerable personal authority.

But only a few who heard Mitchell's address could know that he was stirred by a vision of a new scientific adventure, in which he might soon take an intimate part. Early in 1917 Mitchell had joined Malcolm Rorty, Edwin Gay, and N. I. Stone in a committee that was being organized "to meet a growing demand for a scientific determination of the distribution of national income."[2] The committee expected its second project to be Business Cycles. But the war intervened, and all plans were temporarily put aside. Now the war was over. And Mitchell spoke freely the thoughts he had long cherished, as his mind's eye glimpsed the organization that might soon concern itself with factual studies of national income, business cycles, and related matters.

One year later the National Bureau of Economic Research became this organization, and Wesley Mitchell its Director of Research. To Mitchell the National Bureau was the fulfillment of a dream that had its dim beginnings in his youth. I must now take another leap backward and mark a few steps in his moral and intellectual development before he assumed direction of the Bureau.

II

Wesley Mitchell once related that his family claimed to be descended from an Experience Mitchell, said to have come over on the Mayflower, adding dryly that he could not vouch for the justice of the claim. However that may be, it is known that Mitchell's forebears hailed from New England. His father, John Wesley Mitchell, was born on a farm in Avon, Maine, December 30, 1837. In time he became a physician, saw service in the Civil

[2] *Twenty-fifth Annual Report of the National Bureau of Economic Research* (May 1945), p. 8.

War as an army surgeon, leaving with the rank of brevet colonel. He married Lucy Medora McClellan, the daughter of a Middle Western farmer, whose ancestors can be traced to Massachusetts. Wesley Clair was their second child, born on August 5, 1874 in Rushville, Illinois. Soon the number of children grew to seven. They were devoted to one another, and loved and admired their parents.

Young Clair matured rapidly. The family's means were scant, and his father repeatedly ill from a wound received during the war. Clair had the opportunity to learn at first hand about economic struggle, and its moral concomitants in sturdy folk. In a letter to Lucy Sprague, shortly before their marriage, he wrote of his parents:

Such strength of character as they possess I've never found elsewhere. But they could not help resting a part of family responsibilities on me, as the eldest son, far too early. I had to think about money matters, to learn the hard side of life, when most children are free from care. No doubt this fact strengthened my bent for reading and the world of imagination which reading helps to enlarge.[3]

Clair found another refuge in spinning logical exercises and relating them to facts. Often he engaged in theological discussions with his grand aunt, who "was the best of Baptists, and knew exactly how the Lord had planned the world." Mitchell liked to tell of his "impish delight in dressing up logical difficulties" for her. Unable to dispose of them, she "always slipped back into the logical scheme, and blinked the facts in which" he "came to take a proprietary interest."[4]

Despite the straitened circumstances of his family, Clair managed to go off to Chicago, where he studied under the remarkable faculty assembled by President Harper at the new university. In the summers he worked on the family farm, and in the winters he knew how to live on next to nothing. To a boy of his "experience and temperament college was a shining opportunity, not a dull duty."[5] Years later he drew a lively sketch of his college days:

I began studying philosophy and economics about the same time. The similarity of the two disciplines struck me at once. I found no difficulty in grasping the differences between the great philosophical systems as they were presented by our textbooks and our teachers. Economic theory was easier still. Indeed, I thought the successive systems

[3] Letter to Lucy Sprague, October 18, 1911.
[4] Letter to John Maurice Clark, August 9, 1928. See Clark, *Preface to Social Economics*, pp. 410ff. Originally printed in *Methods in Social Science*, ed. Stuart Rice.
[5] See note 3.

of economics were rather crude affairs compared with the subtleties of the metaphysicians. Having run the gamut from Plato to T. H. Green (as undergraduates do) I felt the gamut from Quesnay to Marshall was a minor theme. The technical part of the theory was easy. Give me premises and I could spin speculations by the yard. Also I knew that my 'deductions' were futile. . . .

Meanwhile I was finding something really interesting in philosophy and in economics. John Dewey was giving courses under all sorts of titles and every one of them dealt with the same problem—how we think. . . . And, if one wanted to try his own hand at constructive theorizing, Dewey's notion pointed the way. It is a misconception to suppose that consumers guide their course by ratiocination—they don't think except under stress. There is no way of deducing from certain principles what they will do, just because their behavior is not itself rational. One has to find out what they do. That is a matter of observation, which the economic theorists had taken all too lightly. Economic theory became a fascinating subject—the orthodox types particularly —when one began to take the mental operations of the theorists as the problem. . . .

Of course Veblen fitted perfectly into this set of notions. What drew me to him was his artistic side. . . . There was a man who really could play with ideas! If one wanted to indulge in the game of spinning theories who could match his skill and humor? But if anything were needed to convince me that the standard procedure of orthodox economics could meet no scientific tests, it was that Veblen got nothing more certain by his dazzling performances with another set of premises. . . .

William Hill set me a course paper on 'Wool Growing and the Tariff.' I read a lot of the tariff speeches and got a new sidelight on the uses to which economic theory is adapted, and the ease with which it is brushed aside on occasion. Also I wanted to find out what really had happened to wool growers as a result of protection. The obvious thing to do was to collect and analyze the statistical data. . . . That was my first 'investigation'. . . .[6]

By the time he graduated from college, Mitchell knew he should devote himself to economic research. Laughlin and Dewey busied themselves on his account, and helped him find the material path to the doctorate, which he attained in 1899 *summa cum laude*. Mitchell embraced a university career eagerly. He began teaching at the University of Chicago in the autumn of 1900. In January 1903 he followed Adolph Miller, one of his former teachers, to the University of California. Mitchell liked teaching and always attended conscientiously to his classes, but he was the investigator

[6] See note 4. Mitchell warned Clark that he might be rationalizing. In his diary he noted on August 8, 1928: "Wrote more about myself to Maurice Clark, getting more doubtful about validity of what I was saying." Mitchell consented to the publication of the letter with considerable reluctance.

first and the teacher second. He valued the career of a university professor primarily because it enabled him to engage in creative investigation. From a year spent with the Census Office, he had learned that he could not be happy except as his own master. For a while he was an editorial writer for the *Chicago Tribune*, but newspaper work involved too many compromises with his sense of craftsmanship. He had a sample of executive work at Red Cross Headquarters in San Francisco after the earthquake, and as the superintendent of field work for the Immigration Commission while it was being organized. But he did not deem any of these tasks as significant as those he had found for himself.[7]

III

The 1890's were an exciting period for a young man entering the study of economics. Agrarian discontent was widespread, and labor disputes ominous. Tariffs, trusts, railroads, and the income tax were much discussed, but the fate of the nation's monetary system dominated every other issue. The price of silver was declining, and the proponents of 'easy money' campaigned actively for its 'free and unlimited' coinage. Their cause was measurably advanced by an act of 1890 requiring sharply increased purchases of silver by the Treasury. Fear for the safety of the gold standard and the established economic order spread. The Senate's passage of a free-coinage measure in 1892 intensified the anxiety of reputable circles. Foreign capitalists sought safety by dumping securities on the New York market, and withdrawing their balances in gold. Domestic hoarders added to the drain on bank reserves and on the Treasury's gold stocks. In May 1893 an old-fashioned panic broke loose, banks suspended or limited payments, and a severe depression of economic activity developed. Grave uncertainty about the nation's money continued until Bryan's decisive defeat at the polls in 1896 practically closed the issue for a generation.[8]

These stirring events imparted a monetary slant to Wesley Mitchell's economic thinking, which deepened with the years. In the realistic atmosphere of Chicago's economics department, the subject of money was steadily and vigorously threshed out. To Professor J. Laurence Laughlin it was a plain duty to enlist the interest of students in the unsolved problem of the monetary standard. An apostle of 'sound money,' he fought heresy with unfailing en-

[7] See note 3.

[8] See the dramatic sketch of this period drawn years later by Wesley Mitchell in his *Business Cycles* (University of California Press, 1913), pp. 48-62.

ergy. But he was as honest as he was orthodox, and did more to stimulate students to think for themselves than his more original colleagues.[9] Laughlin warmly encouraged able youth. In March 1896 the *Journal of Political Economy*, of which he was editor, featured an article on "The Quantity Theory of the Value of Money." The author was Wesley C. Mitchell, a senior at college.

This essay played a role in the polemical literature of its day, and makes interesting reading still, despite its youthful crudities. Some of the traits that made Mitchell a strong constructive force in economics—a concern with basic issues, analytical skill, lucidity, and predilection for statistical testing—are already in evidence. In taking up the relation between the quantity of money and the level of prices, Mitchell went straight to the scientific issue underlying the currency debates of the day. He displayed skill both in breaking the problem down into simple elements and in clothing his reasoning in a clear and orderly prose. Most revealing of all is his emphasis on the complexity of the forces at work and the need for empirical testing. Let me quote a passage:

Deductive reasoning . . . is proverbially likely to lead the inquirer astray, unless its results are checked and corrected by inductive investigation. Such a theoretical examination as the above might well be complemented by applying the test of fact to the theory. If it were found to offer a satisfactory explanation of the price phenomena of actual life, a strong presumption would be created against the criticisms suggested. If, on the other hand, the theory failed to account for observed facts, the case against it would be more complete.[10]

And having given his first public sermon on methodology, Mitchell proceeded to practice what he had preached. This college youth took it as a matter of course that a "workman who wanted to become a scientific worker" had a responsibility to check his speculative reasoning.[11]

During the next several years Mitchell contributed regularly to the *Journal of Political Economy*. Several of his articles dealt with the greenback issues of the Civil War—the subject of his doctoral dissertation. If Laughlin expected from Mitchell a learned monograph on the folly of paper issues, he was doomed to partial disap-

[9] In his letter of August 9, 1928 to Clark, cited above, Mitchell referred only incidentally to Laughlin. A year later, on the occasion of the dedication of the Social Science Research Building at the University of Chicago, Mitchell made good the omission. See his paper "Research in the Social Sciences," reprinted in *The Backward Art of Spending Money*; and especially his article "J. Laurence Laughlin," *Journal of Political Economy*, December 1941.

[10] *Journal of Political Economy*, March 1896, pp. 157-158.

[11] See note 4.

pointment. "To stand apart and distribute praise or blame from an academic retreat some forty years later" struck Mitchell as "a failure to understand the real problem." He quickly saw significance in "the long chain of events which constrained the federal government to develop a policy which no one had planned." He got interested in the economic consequences of the greenbacks and, not being content with a qualitative analysis, "had to invent ways of measuring their effects."[12] The result was the substantial volume *History of the Greenbacks*, which has served as a standard authority on the Civil War inflation since its publication in 1903.[13]

In this work Mitchell analyzed the fiscal embarrassments of the federal government that led to the greenbacks, but he put the main emphasis on their broad consequences—the confusion in the monetary circulation, the premium on gold, the rise of commodity prices at wholesale and retail, and the intricate and painful readjustments of the earnings of the people. He did not explicitly raise any important questions about the theory of value and distribution, but his quantitative and historical approach forced to the surface various features of economic organization which had not received much attention in the theoretical literature. The usual explanations of the value of money stressed the quantity in circulation; yet Mitchell noticed that the premium on gold shifted regularly with the fortunes of the Northern armies. This fact among others led him to attribute the variations in the premium to the "varying estimates which the community was all the time making" of the government's ability to redeem its notes.[14] His studies indicated that during the Civil War the recipients of profits gained at the expense of the rest of the community, especially of persons who lent capital at interest. But why did the high rate of profit not lift the rate of interest? Here Mitchell found a place for uncertainty—that is, the inability to foresee changes in the price level. Again, Mitchell observed that the revolution in prices left some commodities behind, that wages lagged behind prices, and that the lag was not the same in all industries. These facts led him to examine the obstacles to "readjustment in the scale of money payments"[15]—contracts, convention, and the push and pull of the bargaining process. At a time when most economic theorists were busy reformulating the essentials of Ricardo's theory of competitive

---

[12] See note 3.
[13] Its full title is *A History of the Greenbacks, with Special Reference to the Economic Consequences of Their Issue: 1862-65* (University of Chicago Press, 1903).
[14] *ibid.*, p. 199. [15] *ibid.*, p. 139.

price or Cournot's theory of monopoly price, Mitchell was beginning to hammer out a new problem in price theory—the relations that bound prices together in a system of responses through time.

This problem came to his attention in the course of work with factual records. Mitchell's prodigious industry was revealed for the first time in his *History*, as was his superb skill in organizing a great mass of factual material and extracting from it significant generalizations. He made extensive new calculations, set out the statistical records in full, explained their derivation, and noted their shortcomings. An experimental mind was obviously at work, carefully checking one piece of evidence against another, yet stopping short of pedantry. So gracefully did Mitchell move back and forth between theoretical reasoning and factual documentation that the need for whatever statistical detail he presented was hardly ever left in doubt. These traits became more prominent still in Mitchell's later work.

Let me illustrate some of these generalities by showing how Mitchell handled the problem of the price level. Having taken on the task of measuring the effects of the paper issues, the need to ascertain variations in the price level was obvious. For that purpose Mitchell could have used Falkner's index of wholesale prices. He decided against this convenient procedure, first, because Falkner's index was annual and did not permit close comparison with the highly oscillatory price of gold; second, because Falkner's price quotations referred to different dates of the year—which may distort the actual variations in the value of money in a period of rapid change. In view of these difficulties, Mitchell embarked upon the laborious job of constructing a new index of wholesale prices by quarters. He refined it by adjusting the effective weight of certain commodities such as cotton, and supplemented arithmetic means of price relatives with medians. Then he checked the results by constructing another index from independent observations, viz., records of prices paid for numerous commodities by various federal agencies. But to trace the course of events, indexes of retail prices and of the cost of living were also needed. Since measures of this type did not exist, Mitchell proceeded to devise them. The indexes were computed on different plans, and compared with one another and the wholesale price index. When Mitchell needed some specific classification, he did not hesitate to make it. For example, he believed that the rise in the cost of living was the main factor in driving wages upward. This hypothesis he tested by constructing separate indexes of retail prices in the East and West, and comparing their movements with those of corresponding indexes of wages.

The extensive experience with statistical records which Mitchell gained in writing the *History of the Greenbacks* led him to more discriminating views on the quantity theory of the value of money than he had expressed in his early essay. He now observed that statistical attempts to deal with the quantity theory "must always be inconclusive so long as there are no accurate data regarding the volume of exchanges to be performed by the use of money and the rapidity of circulation." Since even the quantity of money during the Civil War was shrouded in obscurity, "a rigorous comparison between the quantity and the gold value of the currency or between quantity and prices" was "out of the question." Mitchell nevertheless remained critical of the quantity theory, and advanced the hypothesis that "the quantity of the greenbacks influenced their specie value rather by affecting the credit of the government than by altering the volume of the circulating medium."[16] In an article published shortly after the *History of the Greenbacks*, Mitchell took a more constructive approach to the quantity theory, pointing out that the participants in the continuing debate failed to define basic concepts precisely or to measure the importance of variations in the money supply relative to other factors. Repeating the self-criticism already made in the *History*, he noted also that his youthful essay on the subject was by no means blameless.[17] Forthrightness was one of Mitchell's outstanding traits, and is no less responsible than his scientific craftsmanship for the moral authority he later exercised over his colleagues and, for that matter, over the entire profession of economics.

IV

The California decade was decisive for Mitchell's personal and scientific life. Here he discovered Lucy Sprague, the gifted Dean of Women who in 1912 became his wife. Here he glimpsed the vision of an expanding money economy, and expressed its fundamental rhythm in his unforgettable *Business Cycles*. Here also he learned to get on with the two conflicting sides of his nature, each becoming more insistent: one driving him furiously to hypotheses of ever wider scope, the other holding him down to the facts needed to support or refute the generalizations.

16 *ibid.*, pp. 207-208.
17 "The Real Issues in the Quantity Theory Controversy," *Journal of Political Economy*, June 1904, p. 405; and *History of the Greenbacks*, p. 208.

Mitchell was a lonely man in these years of intellectual struggle, despite tennis and billiards, dining out and dancing parties. The last few years at California he withdrew more and more into himself, and worked hard even by his own standards. To Lucy Sprague he wrote before their marriage:

Outwardly I live in the accredited academic fashion, and doubtless I have insensibly acquired through long association pedantic modes of expression. But spiritually I acknowledge no kinship with these passive folk. My world is the world of thought; but the world of thought has a realm of action and I live there. It is a place where one has to depend upon himself—his own initiative, his own sustaining faith. My danger in this realm is not from lack of vigor, but from lack of caution.[18]

While working on the monetary upheaval of the Civil War, Mitchell gave much of his leisure to the history of economic institutions and ideas. These studies led him into ethnology and psychology, which soon consumed an increasing part of his energies. At California he had the opportunity to teach whatever subjects he liked and to experiment as he would. Mitchell flourished in this atmosphere of freedom. Promptly he settled on a course in primitive culture, exploring the "origin and early development of fundamental economic customs and institutions." This course in Economic Origins he supplemented with several on current organization—Principles of Economics, Money, Banking, and Problems of Labor. The experiment brought out in sharp relief the peculiar sway of pecuniary forces in modern society. Soon Mitchell was at work on a course in the Theory and History of Banking, trying to forge links between man's remote past and the current scheme of pecuniary institutions. At the same time he busied himself with technicalities of international finance, which he felt he needed to round out his knowledge of money. In the academic year 1905-1906 he gave for the first time a course on the relation between the money economy and business fluctuations. Thus, his offering that year included Economic Origins, the Theory and History of Banking, and Economic Crises and Depressions in the fall semester; and Money, International Exchanges, and Problems of Labor in the spring. Two years later he began reaping the harvest of this extraordinary preparation for constructive work in economic theory. The courses on Economic Origins, Labor, and International Exchanges had served their purpose, and he supplanted them with the History of Economic Thought and Economic Psychology.

[18] See note 3.

Mitchell has described succinctly this period of storm and stress:

When I came to California I still had the proofs of the *History of the Greenbacks* to read and the plan of a continuation from the close of the war to the resumption of specie payments to execute. While I was working on the latter, the ferment of philosophy and ethnology was gradually widening my notions of what economics ought to be. I held to my old tasks long enough to complete the statistical apparatus for the second volume on the greenbacks and to publish it as *Gold, Prices, and Wages under the Greenback Standard.* But I wanted to be at something larger in its scope and more penetrating in its interest than this detailed work with a passing episode in monetary history. My rather vague notions gradually crystallized into the idea that the important matter to understand about money is the money economy— that is, the cultural significance of the highly organized group of pecuniary institutions, how they have developed since the middle ages, how they have gained a quasi-independence, and how they have reacted upon the activity and the minds of their makers.[19]

Gold, Prices, and Wages was published in 1908. It satisfied Mitchell even less than the *History*. To a mind bent on large generalizations but willing to accept only what is rooted in experience, it was natural to think of *Gold, Prices, and Wages* as the "statistical apparatus of a book still to be written," just as it was natural to regard the *History* as a mere fragment.[20] The *History* was a monograph of a "fragmentary character" because it stopped short of the downward revolution in prices that followed the Civil War; also because it failed to compare the Civil War inflation with similar episodes across the centuries in this country and abroad. *Gold, Prices, and Wages* was the "statistical apparatus of a book still to be written" because it remedied only in part the first of these deficiencies of the *History*. But Mitchell's contemporaries shared neither his imperial conceptions nor his misgivings. The formidable companion piece of the *History* was quickly recognized as a great work of scholarship, and remains an authoritative source on the period from 1862 to 1878.

In this volume[21] Mitchell carried forward, extended, and refined the laborious measurements first presented in the *History*. His statistical experiments set a new standard in economics for analyzing mass observations over time, and his charts and tables set a new standard for presenting results. Unwilling to allow averages of price changes to bury the variety of movements they summed up, he hit upon the device of deciles—a technique that

---

[19] See note 3.   [20] See the prefaces to both volumes.
[21] The preparation of the statistical material was aided by a grant from the Carnegie Institution.

has since been widely used.[22] The style, lucid always, became more dignified, and itself a symbol of elegant organization of an enormous range of materials. But *Gold, Prices, and Wages* was a good deal more than a technical tour de force. Economic analysis lives through its pages, and the final chapter is devoted to nothing else. The causal links between the premium on gold and the level of wholesale prices, which were left uncomfortably vague in the *History*, are here developed with masterly care. Another theoretical contribution is the generalization of lagged response—wholesale prices behind gold, retail prices behind wholesale, the cost of living behind retail prices, wages behind the cost of living—and the attempt to bring the system of responses under a unified explanation.

The statistical materials for the greenback period gave Mitchell a lively impression of the magnitude and diversity of economic fluctuations. During 1862-1878 the country experienced two price revolutions, a major boom, a crisis, a great depression, and sundry minor fluctuations. These movements stood out in time series, clamoring for attention. At the close of the book Mitchell noted that his tables "suggest more problems than they solve." Let me quote from his concluding section on the "economic significance of the price revolutions of the greenback period":

Writers upon money usually state that it performs three functions, serving as a common denominator of value, a medium of exchange, and a standard of deferred payments. To enumerate the functions of money in this fashion, however, is very far from suggesting the importance of the role which money plays in economic life. To understand this role attention must be fixed upon the complex mechanism of prices, rather than upon money itself. . . . Men who make use of the system of prices in their economic activity are constrained to obey its logic and to adapt themselves as best they may to its technical exigencies. . . .

Perhaps the clearest conception of the price revolutions is gained by regarding them as changes made by the business community in its effort to adapt itself to the monetary conditions created by an inconvertible paper currency. . . . An economic theorist, accustomed to imagine immediate and accurately gauged changes of prices occurring in a frictionless hypothetical market under the stimulus of some 'disturbing factor,' might perhaps regard this lagging of one class of prices behind another as an important deviation from the 'natural' course of events. But a student of prices in less highly organized business communities, or an economic historian familiar with earlier price

[22] See Mitchell's earlier paper on this subject, "Methods of Presenting Statistics of Wages," *Quarterly Publications of the American Statistical Association*, December 1905.

revolutions, would be much more impressed by the rapidity and system with which prices of different classes of goods were changed, than by the lack of completeness in the adjustment.[23]

The "economic theorist" and "economic historian" of this quotation are, of course, none other than Wesley Mitchell himself. He had arrived at the conception of an interdependent system of prices, as had Walras and Marshall before him; and now, pondering the results of his statistical inquiries, he was feeling his way to the theory that this interdependent system, shot through as it was with lagged responses, generated business cycles instead of equilibrium.

V

Monetary theory before 1914 was concerned mainly, if not exclusively, with the causes of variations in the value of money. This problem attracted Mitchell at the start of his scientific career, but before a dozen years elapsed he broke through to a new conception. From the quantity theory of money he passed first to the analysis of a particular monetary inflation, next to the evolution of the price system and its impact on human behavior, later to the "recurring readjustments of prices,"[24] which led him into business cycles.

In December 1905, while working out a syllabus for a course on Money, Mitchell spanned in one vision the unexplored realm between the quantity theory of money and business cycles. To quote from a letter of that date:

I am trying to work out an account of the variations in the general price level by a rather novel method. The traditional method of attack is to apply the theory of value to the special case of money prices, and the traditional result is either a reaffirmation of the quantity theory, or a denial of its adequacy. In neither case does one learn *how* changes in the price level are brought about. . . . Another method of attack is to apply the microscope to the case of particular articles. . . . I am trying to steer a crooked course between these two methods, by dealing with conditions of demand and supply abstractly considered, but with the businessman's apprehension of these conditions as price factors; and on the other hand to take the businessman's point of view also in considering not a single article but all the articles that he buys and sells. The result is that I am involved in an analysis of an exceedingly complex set of business considerations. . . . I have begun with the influence of consumers on the level of retail prices and

[23] *Gold, Prices, and Wages under the Greenback Standard* (University Press, Berkeley, 1908), pp. 279, 281-283.
[24] See note 4.

then taken up the retailer's position as a price maker. This morning I came to a tentative close with the retailer and now face the wholesaler. After him will come the manufacturer, the wage earner, the dealer in raw materials, the farmer, the speculator, the investor, the promoter and the gold miner.

When I have worked out the peculiarities in the positions of each of these gentry in turn with reference to the making of prices, then I shall have to give an account of the way in which important changes in the economic situation—like marked alterations in the harvests, increases in the gold supply, changes in the standard, credit difficulties, changes in productive processes, etc.—affect prices, and how the price disturbances are propagated from one group to another. Finally, I may become very ambitious and attempt to interpret the movement of prices, wages, interest, etc., since 1890 by way of illustrating the interactions of the various factors. Of course I am not fond enough to fancy that I shall get more than a skeleton of all this drawn up before next semester, but I am very anxious to have such a skeleton in order to know what to do next. If I succeed I may be able to evolve some flesh during the next few years with which to drape the bones.[25]

When Mitchell wrote these lines he was still at work on the second volume on the greenbacks. The task for which he soon set aside this investigation was a theoretical treatise on money—a study in which he at first saw no place for statistics.

Mitchell's interest at this time centered on the evolution of the price system, its current institutions and their interactions. Ethnological studies had shown him that money was far more than the mere "contrivance for sparing time and labor"[26] the classical economists had supposed it to be. The fact most suggestive of its part in economic development was that society has gradually evolved an economic organization based on the making and spending of money incomes. Between men's activities as producers of goods and their activities as consumers, a vast network of financial machinery and prices has intervened. "Monetary and banking systems, practices regarding mercantile credits, the pecuniary organization of business enterprises, the financial policies of governments, the interadjustments of the system of prices, the machinery of security markets, all are features of the money economy which man has made only to fall under their power."[27] The interrelations of prices, not industrial capacity or men's desire for useful commodities, determine what is now produced, how much is produced, and the

[25] Letter to a friend, December 20, 1905.

[26] The phrase is J. S. Mill's. For the context, see his *Principles of Political Economy*, ed. Ashley, p. 488.

[27] Mitchell, "The Rationality of Economic Activity," *Journal of Political Economy*, March 1910, p. 209.

shares of the final product accruing to participants in the productive process. Since money is the key to the understanding of economic life, it must be the root of economic science. Mitchell turned to this grand theme, and started writing a "Theory of the Money Economy."

The manuscript of *Gold, Prices, and Wages* was completed toward the end of June 1907. Several weeks earlier Mitchell had begun drafting the first chapter of the "Theory of the Money Economy." He stayed with this manuscript until March 1908, when he shifted to work he had agreed to do for the Immigration Commission. From the end of April through the summer he was fully occupied with this activity. The following academic year he lectured at Harvard on money and business cycles. Although his academic duties left little time for the "Theory of the Money Economy," he managed to go through a considerable amount of historical literature and to look into statistical records, especially such as bore on the crisis of 1907. Meanwhile he had become uneasy about his manuscript, and began modifying plans in a fateful direction. In his own words:

I was working away from any solid foundation—having a good time, but sliding gayly over abysses I had not explored. One of the most formidable was the recurring readjustments of prices, which economists treated apart from their general theories of value, under the caption 'Crises.' I had to look into the problem.[28]

When Mitchell returned to California in the autumn of 1909, he brought with him a firm resolve to work out promptly "the subject of 'Business Cycles' as a *Vorarbeit* of the 'Money Economy.' "[29]

He lost no time getting started. On September 3 he began sketching an outline. On September 15 he hired an assistant, at his own expense, to prepare tables of interest rates—a subject he had omitted in *Gold, Prices, and Wages*, and to which he had paid only slight attention in the *History*. In December he was ready to turn to security prices, another subject he had neglected in earlier studies. Mitchell was working from a definite plan, starting with the subjects he knew least well, and determined to carry out a comprehensive study of the "recurring readjustments of prices," which seemed to drive and shape the industrial activities of the money economy. He worked at a feverish pace, undeterred by the vast magnitude of his enterprise, seeking to embrace every significant aspect of economic activity, to reach back statistically to 1890, and to cover the four countries in which the money economy had

[28] See note 4.　　　　　　　　[29] See note 3.

reached its fullest expression—the United States, Great Britain, Germany, and France. Not finding the statistics he needed on commodity prices, wages, stock prices, bond prices, bond yields, or the money supply, he made extensive calculations, pioneering boldly in each field. Much of the clerical work he did himself, and he supervised and checked all of it. How vast was the range of factual information he tapped, and of the theoretical and monographic literature he embraced, a casual inspection of his *Business Cycles* will indicate. The work prospered. In April 1911 Mitchell wrote exultantly: "The various difficulties of explanation seem to dissolve of themselves as I approach."[30] There were occasional setbacks: "Now that I've come to the point of discussing crises themselves I am temporarily at a loss. Everything happens all at once, and to arrange an orderly exposition is more difficult than I had supposed."[31] But the setback was momentary; within a fortnight the chapter on "Crises" was drafted. Mitchell was pleased as he stopped to look back: "My own impression is that the chapters are rather good—particularly the crucial one on the breeding of crises."[32] Months of recasting and revision followed. Finally, on October 15, 1912 he sent the last of the manuscript off to the printer. Except for the proofs, *Business Cycles*, a 600-page quarto, was completed. In the amazingly short time of three years, Mitchell had worked out and written one of the masterpieces in the world's economic literature. And this burst of creative activity carried with it other outstanding achievements. Beside attending to his duties at the university during this period,[33] Mitchell managed to compose the famous articles on "The Rationality of Economic Activity" and "The Backward Art of Spending Money," to write a half dozen technical papers growing out of the work on business cycles, to review the voluminous publications of the National Monetary Commission,[34] to woo and win Lucy Sprague, and to spend several months in Europe with his bride.

Business Cycles is a beautifully organized and closely reasoned treatise. More than that, it is a landmark in the development of economics. No other work between Marshall's *Principles* and Keynes' *General Theory* has had as big an influence on the economic thought of the Western world. The simplest way to make clear the novelty and scientific force of Mitchell's work is to com-

[30] Letter to a friend, April 3, 1911.   [31] Letter to a friend, April 17, 1911.
[32] Letter to a friend, May 2, 1911.
[33] During the academic year 1910-1911 Mitchell was on leave, at two-thirds salary.
[34] In the *Quarterly Journal of Economics*, May 1911, pp. 563-593.

pare his approach to business cycles with that of earlier investigators.

The traditional method of accounting for business cycles was to start from simple assumptions, based on common sense, concerning the state of business in equilibrium or in 'late' prosperity or depression; then call attention to some new factor arising from within or outside the business situation; finally, show how the adaptations of the business community to the new factor generated a cyclical movement. Since imaginative thinkers had no difficulty in assigning a critical role to one factor after another, plausible theories of business cycles multiplied abundantly. Occasionally a theorist would use statistical data, but as a rule their function, when called upon at all, was merely to support or illustrate a particular stage of an argument. Mitchell broke with this tradition. Instead of starting theoretical analysis with assumptions concerning the state of business in late depression, such as might be suggested by common sense, he started with assumptions derived from systematic observations of experience. Again, instead of passing from these assumptions, reinforced by others about the arts and human motives, to supposedly tight inferences concerning the condition of business in the next stage of the cycle and stopping there, Mitchell checked his reasoning by consulting systematic observations of experience. This plan of working had two revolutionary consequences. First, business cycle theory became, or at least approached, a tested explanation of experience instead of an exercise in logic. Second, in the process of observing economic life in its many ramifications, the theory of business cycles broadened into a theory of how our economic organization works.

Mitchell began with a review of current theories of business cycles, then paused to outline his method of investigation:

One seeking to understand the recurrent ebb and flow of economic activity characteristic of the present day finds these numerous explanations both suggestive and perplexing. All are plausible, but which is valid? None necessarily excludes all the others, but which is the most important? . . .

There is slight hope of getting answers to these questions by a logical process of proving and criticizing the theories. For whatever merits of ingenuity and consistency they may possess, these theories have slight value except as they give keener insight into the phenomena of business cycles. It is by study of the facts which they purport to interpret that the theories must be tested.

But the perspective of the investigation would be distorted if we set out to test each theory in turn. . . . For the point of interest is not the validity of any writer's views, but clear comprehension of the facts. To observe, analyze, and systematize the phenomena of prosperity, crisis, and depression is the chief task.[35]

Before passing to this task, Mitchell developed his theoretical orientation in a chapter on the organization of the money economy, so that the statistical facts could be seen as "details of a larger system." The "system" rests on the proposition that the ebb and flow of activity depends on the prospects of profits, except in times of crisis when a quest for solvency supplants profits as the main driving force of business enterprise. Mitchell used current theories of business cycles as suggestions concerning the processes that were worth examining, and his sketch of the money economy as the analytical framework into which the statistical chapters of Part II were fitted. Every one of these chapters "bears upon the crucial problem of business profits, either by dealing with factors which determine profits, like prices and the volume of trade; or by dealing with necessary conditions for the successful quest of profits, like the currency, banking, and investment; or by offering direct gauges of business success and failure, like the statistics of profits themselves and of bankruptcies." And just as Mitchell's theoretical sketch of the "controlling factors" in a money economy provided a framework for the statistical analysis in Part II, so also it provided a framework for the theoretical analysis of "The Rhythm of Business Activity" in Part III.[36]

Mitchell's theory is cast in a mould of evolutionary concepts. Business cycles are not merely fluctuations in aggregate activity, but fluctuations that are widely diffused through the economy. They are therefore a product of culture, and arise only when economic activities have become largely organized on the basis of making and spending money incomes. Again, business cycles are not minor or accidental disruptions of equilibrium, but fluctuations systematically generated by economic organization itself. As prosperity cumulates, costs in many lines of activity encroach upon selling prices, money markets become strained, and numerous investment projects are set aside until costs of financing seem more favorable; these accumulating stresses within the system of business enterprise lead to a recession of activity, which spreads over the economy and for a time gathers force; but the realignment of costs and prices, reduction of inventories, improvement of bank

[35] *Business Cycles*, pp. 19-20. Part III of this volume was reprinted in 1941 by the original publisher, the University of California Press, under the title *Business Cycles and Their Causes*.
[36] *Business Cycles*, pp. 20, 91, 92.

reserves, and other developments of depression gradually pave the way for a renewed expansion of activity. In this theoretical scheme "the recurring readjustments of prices," which first attracted Mitchell's curiosity, play a crucial role, but so too do a host of interrelated industrial and financial changes. Each phase of the business cycle evolves into its successor, while economic organization itself gradually undergoes cumulative changes. Hence, Mitchell believed, "it is probable that the economists of each generation will see reason to recast the theory of business cycles which they learned in their youth."[37]

"The case for the present theory," Mitchell concluded, "and also the case against it, is to be found ... in an independent effort to use it in interpreting the ceaseless ebb and flow of economic activity." In the years that have elapsed since the publication of Mitchell's classic, knowledge of business fluctuations has been appreciably extended. Yet I know of no theoretical work that, taken as a whole, has met as well as Mitchell's old book "the practical test of accounting for actual business experience."[38] No one else has succeeded in tracing with comparable skill or knowledge the interlacing and readjustment of economic activities in the course of a business cycle, or developed as fully or as faithfully the typical process by which one stage of the business cycle gradually evolves into the next. I venture the prophecy that if Mitchell's homely work of 1913 were translated into the picturesque vocabulary of 'propensities,' 'multipliers,' 'acceleration coefficients,' and the like, it would create a sensation in the theoretical world, especially if the translator were mindful enough to shift passages here and there from the indicative to the conditional mood.[39] However that may be, it is worth noting and remembering that much of the special vocabulary of today's theorizing centers around economic fluctuations, and that this was already Mitchell's central theoretical problem before World War I.

VI

Indeed, the basic design of Mitchell's economic thinking was laid down before he reached his thirty-fifth year. He had found his problem in the workings of the money economy—its evolution, present status, and impact on men's minds and activities. To this

[37] *ibid.*, p. 583.   [38] *ibid.*, p. 570.
[39] In this connection see the third section of Professor Friedman's paper in *Wesley Clair Mitchell: The Economic Scientist*, ed. Arthur F. Burns (National Bureau, 1952).

problem he brought theoretical insight, historical knowledge, and the profound generalization that "during the long centuries that men have been gaining their mastery over the use of money, pecuniary concepts have been gaining a subtler mastery over men."[40] Had Mitchell pursued his ideas on the money economy in the speculative manner fashionable among economic theorists, he might have added a brilliant treatise to the active inventory of economic theory and stopped there. Instead, he sought to develop a theory that would enable men to come to grips scientifically with social problems, and therefore worked out first the "most technical phase" of the money economy—that is, the phenomena of business cycles. He thought of *Business Cycles* as part of "the necessary pioneer work toward the construction of useful economic theory."[41]

Mitchell put the finishing touches on the manuscript of *Business Cycles* in London during October 1912. Upon his return in December he took up residence in New York, wishing to observe the nerve center of the money economy at close range. He joined the Columbia faculty in 1913, and soon achieved outstanding success as a teacher. Between the completion of *Business Cycles* and the inception of his researches at the National Bureau, Mitchell largely devoted his time to empirical studies of prices and critical and historical studies of economic theory. During this period he wrote a masterly paper on Wieser's *Social Economics*, then unknown to English-speaking readers, and the famous essays "The Role of Money in Economic Theory" and "Bentham's Felicific Calculus."[42] The latter was originally intended as a chapter of a book on Types of Economic Theory which Mitchell began writing in 1916. Upon entering government service early in 1918, he had to lay this manuscript aside. He returned to it briefly after the war and looked forward to completing it when he retired from the National Bureau. Then his arduous labors on business cycles would be at an end and his mental muscles still nimble enough for the lighter task of literary scholarship! He was not privileged to realize this dream, nor are we to share its fruit. Some notion of the intellectual flavor of Mitchell's manuscript—its social vision, theoretical power, and literary distinction—may be gained from the papers[43] collected in

[40] Mitchell, "The Rationality of Economic Activity," *Journal of Political Economy*, March 1910, p. 208.

[41] See note 3.

[42] All three are reprinted in *The Backward Art of Spending Money*.

[43] Besides the one on Bentham, the paper on "Postulates and Preconceptions of Ricardian Economics," published in 1929, was adapted from his manuscript, which

1937 by Professor Joseph Dorfman under the title *The Backward Art of Spending Money and Other Essays*. But this volume gives hardly an inkling of the historical range of Mitchell's uncompleted manuscript, or of his brilliant analysis of the social conditions out of which classical political economy and its offshoots developed.

In 1914 Royal Meeker invited Mitchell to write an introduction to a bulletin by the Bureau of Labor Statistics on index numbers of wholesale prices. Mitchell responded with "The Making and Using of Index Numbers"[44]—a monograph in which he extended his earlier experiments in measurement, and discussed at length the practical problems involved in constructing and using index numbers. This study has had an enormous influence on statistical understanding and practice, both in this country and elsewhere. As late as 1938 the Bureau of Labor Statistics reissued the monograph to meet the "continuing demand, particularly in colleges and universities."[45] After completing the work on indexes of wholesale prices, Mitchell turned to a companion piece on stock prices, in which he analyzed methods in relation to uses, and carried out many experiments beyond those reported in *Business Cycles*. The results were published in the *Journal of Political Economy* for July 1916, under the title "A Critique of Index Numbers of the Prices of Stocks." Mitchell's six articles on security prices, published between 1910 and 1916 in the *Journal*, became the foundation for much of the later research and practice in this field.

Another of Mitchell's achievements just before the National Bureau got under way was the preparation of the *History of Prices during the War* under the auspices of the War Industries Board. Mitchell edited the publication and wrote two of its fifty-seven bulletins—*International Price Comparisons* and the *Summary*. This scholarly venture was due largely to Mitchell's initiative and organizing skill—traits that later proved invaluable to the National Bureau. After the armistice, when the dominant mood in Washington was to demobilize promptly, Mitchell did as much as anyone to preserve the statistical work accomplished and to continue

was the foundation also of some of his lectures at Columbia on Types of Economic Theory. A mimeographed edition of the lectures, taken down stenographically by a student on his own responsibility, has circulated fairly widely, and has recently been reissued by Augustus M. Kelley, New York. See the review of these lectures by T. W. Hutchison in *Wesley Clair Mitchell: The Economic Scientist*, cited above.

[44] *Index Numbers of Wholesale Prices in the United States and Foreign Countries*, Bulletin of the U.S. Bureau of Labor Statistics, No. 173, July 1915.

[45] Bulletin No. 656 of the Bureau of Labor Statistics, p. iii.

the new work started during the war. Three days after the armistice was signed, he boldly requested authority not only to retain his staff in the Price Section, but to add a dozen men, so that the knowledge newly gained about price movements could be made available to economists and businessmen. Edwin Gay liked the idea and won Bernard Baruch over. The project itself was completed in a few months. Despite its hurried execution, the *History of Prices* proved to be a valuable reference source. One scientific novelty of Mitchell's *Summary* is a production index contructed so as to be precisely comparable with a price index. As far as I know, no one had ever carried out this obvious but significant step before. Indeed, Mitchell was the first investigator to attack systematically the technical problems of weighting and industry grouping in the construction of a production index. It seems that there was hardly a thing to which he ever turned, large or small, on which he did not leave some imprint of his originality and enterprise.

VII

At heart Wesley Mitchell was a reformer. Ever since taking up residence in New York he had participated in social causes—settlement work, woman suffrage, better schooling, adult education. For a while he taught carpentry to a class of youngsters. A year before the war's end he preached a lay sermon in All Souls Church, White Plains, on The Worlds We Make. In 1918 he joined James Harvey Robinson, Charles A. Beard, and Alvin Johnson in organizing the New School for Social Research "to take its position on the firing line" of new ideas. These activities were dear to Mitchell, yet he had no great faith in the improvisations of reformers. The reliable path to social reform, he felt, was through scientific investigation of social processes.

While still working on *Business Cycles* and unknown to fame, he wrote Lucy Sprague:[46]

Ethnological studies have given me a peculiarly strong impression of the practical value of theoretical knowledge in human affairs. But to be of use theory must take hold of phenomena by their handles. Much the most effective handles are found in causal interconnections. . . . We putter with philanthropy and coquette with reform . . . and try to do what little we may to alleviate at retail the suffering and deprivation which our social organization creates at wholesale. What we need

46 See note 3. Before the publication of *Business Cycles*, Mitchell's reputation was restricted to a relatively small professional circle.

as a guide for all this expenditure of energy is sure knowledge of the causal interconnections between social phenomena. . . .

Whether there is good prospect of accomplishing any results in economic theory within the present generation I am not sure. But . . . this task is more important and more vital, as well as more difficult, than the tasks of the people who are running the existing social machine or of the people who are trying to patch it.

But I also know that few men could be found with more than a smile for my pretensions. . . . There is no use in proclaiming aloud a program of critical research, when you are not sure that any of the leads will repay working. Here the prospector must go off quietly by himself and develop his claims before he can get recognition. And if the claims don't pan out well, he'll have to find his reward within himself—or go without.

Mitchell had gone off quietly by himself and demonstrated that broad economic generalizations based on empirical observation were possible. Hence, economic theory could make headway without such restrictive assumptions as a constant value of money or a full-employment level of income. The course of events tested and favored Mitchell's approach to economics. The threatening rise in prices was turning men's minds to the problem of business cycles. The war experience with economic mobilization emphasized the need for accurate quantitative information on national income, inventories, prices, the labor supply, and other basic factors in the economy. An increasing number of men now shared a sense of urgency about empirical research, if not faith in an empirical science of economics. In this atmosphere of social thinking the National Bureau was formed "to encourage, in the broadest and most liberal manner, investigation, research and discovery, and the application of knowledge to the well-being of mankind; and in particular to conduct, or assist in the making of, exact and impartial investigations in the field of economic, social and industrial science."[47]

Mitchell was forty-five when he assumed direction of the National Bureau. He brought rich personal gifts to the venture: character, a judicial temperament, self-assurance mellowed by wisdom, exacting scientific standards, a kind and understanding nature. More than that, he was a tireless scientific explorer, committed to social improvement through science and reason. He regarded the Bureau as an experiment which, if successful, might

[47] National Bureau, *Charter and By-Laws.* The by-laws were adopted by the Board of Directors on December 29, 1919; the certificate of incorporation was approved January 23, 1920; the first Annual Meeting of the Board, at which Mitchell was elected Director of Research, was held February 2, 1920.

lead to similar work by others, the joint effort becoming in time a powerful instrumentality of progress. The Bureau meant also personal fulfillment. Here "a program of critical research" might actually be carried out, not just proclaimed "aloud." Here empirical investigations might be undertaken, broader and more fundamental than any yet attempted by economists. Here complementary technical skills could be pooled, and the process of developing new knowledge made more efficient. Here an investigator could subject his methods and results to the steady and searching scrutiny of skilled colleagues. Here hypotheses could be checked by statistical data, statistical data stimulate new hypotheses, and hypotheses new data. Here tested findings could cumulate, reinforce one another, and open up new problems, as was routine in the established sciences. Most important of all, here was an experiment in democratic action, men of many shades of political opinion joining in the undramatic enterprise of reviewing the factual findings of a technical staff. If a group so constituted as the National Bureau's Board of Directors could work harmoniously and accept staff investigations of a controversial question such as the proportion of the national income paid out in wages or accruing as profits, might not reason triumph over passion in an ever widening circle of men? Stirred by this vision, Mitchell put his great energies to the Bureau's task at once. His faith never wavered.

The subject selected by the Board of Directors for its first study was the size of the national income and its distribution. Nothing could have been more congenial to Mitchell. If modern economic life is organized on the basis of making and spending money incomes, economic analysis should start from that fact. To measure the magnitude of the national income and its principal components is to set out the framework of a moving economic system. This was the sort of problem on which Mitchell could work with enthusiasm. Willford I. King, Oswald Knauth, and Frederick R. Macaulay soon joined the staff, and the research of the National Bureau was launched. At the first meeting of the group, held May 17, 1920, Mitchell urged the importance of both "spontaneity and system," sketched the preliminary work done on national income, and blocked out several methods of estimation. After further canvass of the problem, he and his colleagues decided that the hazards in estimating national income made it necessary to subject the operation to definite statistical controls. King then undertook to calculate the national income from the product side; while

Knauth sought to determine the incomes received by the public, to which he would add the undistributed income of business enterprises. The concept of income was, of course, the same for both, but the sources of information were entirely different. Mitchell reported the scientific design to the Directors:

The plan of making two separate estimates of the National Income, quite independently of each other, set up a hard test of the work done by Mr. King and Mr. Knauth. We felt not a little nervous when the day came on which we first cast up the totals by Sources of Production and by Incomes Received. . . . When the largest discrepancy in any one year proved to be only 7 per cent we felt a marked increase of confidence in our work.[48]

This pioneering investigation was completed in less than two years and published in two volumes, a small book summarizing the findings, and a substantial volume giving detailed results, together with the sources and methods used.[49] Mitchell was largely responsible for writing the summary volume, which may justly serve as a model of exposition. It would be difficult to name another publication that has had comparable success in making 'irreducible and stubborn' facts tell a vivid and pertinent tale without stooping to oversimplification. The role of this volume in winning public and professional support for the National Bureau in its early years of struggle cannot be overestimated.

The last project planned by Mitchell was the study that Morris Copeland has recently brought to completion. Mitchell leaped at the opportunity offered by the interest of the Committee for Economic Development in money flows. The volume of monetary transactions is, of course, much larger than the national income, since it includes financial beside industrial transactions, as well as all intermediate stages of the latter. How much money do business enterprises pay out to the public? to government? to financial institutions? to one another? What of the payments by consumers, the government, financial institutions? How much money moves against commodities? services? securities? financial claims? In the late spring of 1944 Mitchell spent several weeks compiling figures and ransacking sources, testing the feasibility of a quantitative study of the volume of monetary transactions and its subdivisions. These weeks of exploration were pure joy to Mitchell, whose special concern with business cycles never obscured an older and

---

[48] *A Bold Experiment: The Story of the National Bureau of Economic Research* (Second Annual Report of the Director of Research, February 6, 1922), pp. 7-8.
[49] *Income in the United States: Its Amount and Distribution, 1909-1919* (Vol. I, Harcourt Brace, 1921; Vol. II, National Bureau, 1922).

larger interest in the money economy. Reporting to the Board, he sketched the projected inquiry on money flows, then reflected prophetically: "It may be that this pioneering job will in time yield results comparable with those attained in national income, eventually to get incorporated into the statistical routine of a governmental bureau, and the thinking of all economists."[50] This report was Mitchell's 'swan song.' He had served twenty-five years as Director of Research, and requested relief so that he could have more time for his own work on business cycles.

The quarter century separating the first investigation of national income and the start of the study of money flows is almost the full span of the National Bureau's history. From its original focus of national income, the Bureau's research program moved outward, not according to a rigid plan, but on a principle enunciated by Mitchell at the beginning. Let me quote from his First Annual Report to the Board:[51]

I should like to submit a general suggestion, regarding the principle upon which future topics should be chosen. I think we should plan to complete our studies of the National Income, and work outward from that central field. It may be desirable to take up a few incidental inquiries . . . which we can manage without serious derangement of our main program; but it would be poor policy to scatter our energy over a considerable number of unrelated topics, however fascinating.

If you approve of the general policy I am suggesting, it would probably mean that after the current report is finished, we should take up for careful study the shares of wages, rent, interest and profits, and the subject of savings versus current consumption. . . . It is quite possible that still other investigations supplementing our first report may seem to be desirable by the time that report is finished.

May I also suggest one topic on which we shall come as soon as we move outward from our central field? Our preliminary figures indicate that the National Income can scarcely be large enough to secure what we consider a decent standard of living for all American families. If the final figures are not much larger than we anticipate, they will lend new emphasis to the call for a greater output of staple commodities. But while all the producing interests may admit the desirability of having more and better food, clothing, and housing for our people, they also point out the difficulty of finding profitable markets for the current output. Here lies, indeed, the great economic problem of the future. . . .

Mitchell's suggestion of a basis for choosing new topics guided

[50] "The National Bureau's First Quarter-Century," in the Bureau's *Twenty-fifth Annual Report*, May 1945, p. 39. [Copeland's volume, *A Study of Moneyflows in the United States*, was published in 1952.]

[51] Presented February 7, 1921, not published.

the National Bureau's development over the years. First, the subject of business cycles was added to the program, then the labor market, commodity prices, industrial productivity, financial operations, fiscal problems, and, recently, international economic relations. From time to time the Bureau has undertaken *ad hoc* investigations, sometimes to tide over a period of stringency, more often to render important public service, such as the investigation of federal statistical services recently made for the Commission on the Organization of the Executive Branch of the Government. But the broad history of the Bureau has been one of concentration on relatively few subjects, not piecemeal research. The program has developed from within the investigations themselves, one study growing out of another, reinforcing the studies in progress, making its direct contribution, and in turn raising fresh problems. Thus the deliberateness and consistency which guided Mitchell's life since boyhood became imbedded in the Bureau's work and shaped its development. By creating an atmosphere in which scientific work could flourish and in which capable investigators could work cooperatively, Mitchell laid the foundation for a research program that in time became cumulative and self-reinforcing.[52] The Bureau's past accomplishments and its present strength are largely attributable to his personality, integrity, and scientific genius.

VIII

Mitchell remained a working scientist while he served as Director of Research of the National Bureau. Although he gave up this office in 1945, he continued as an active member of the research staff until his death. Mitchell did not permit administrative work at the Bureau or professorial duties at Columbia to consume all his energy, as they easily might have. He was coauthor of the first National Bureau publication, *Income in the United States, Vol. I* (1921). In 1927 his *Business Cycles: The Problem and Its Setting* was published. He was coauthor of several other Bureau volumes: *Business Cycles and Unemployment* (1923), *Business Annals* (1926), *Recent Economic Changes* (1929), *Measuring Business Cycles* (1946), and *Economic Research and the Development of Economic Science and Public Policy* (1946). He contributed to the Bureau's *Bulletin* and *Occasional Papers*, wrote enlightening introductions to many Bureau monographs, and a long series of *Annual Reports* which stimulated economic thinking and research

[52] See "The Cumulation of Economic Knowledge," [reprinted above, pp. 46-60].

at large. But the publications that bear Mitchell's name cannot by themselves convey his part in the Bureau's work on business cycles, or his role in inspiring and bringing to fruition its other investigations.

In 1921 when the study of national income was approaching completion, the Executive Committee considered what problem to take for its next investigation. The subject of business cycles was obviously "of great importance to all classes in the community." With the aid of the Bureau's resources, it could be pushed further than in Mitchell's 1913 book—already out of print. While a considerable amount of research was being done by others on the nature and causes of business cycles, no one was engaged in a "comprehensive survey of the whole." These reasons seemed sufficient to justify a thorough investigation. The plan called for a "systematic treatise" by Mitchell, supplemented by "two or three special studies of topics that have never been adequately investigated."[53] No one could foresee how the project would grow, what contributions it would make to knowledge, how much effort and time it would require, or that its vigorous director would not live to see it completed.

In economic literature there are many concepts of business cycles, not just one. Some familiarity with Mitchell's particular concept is essential if the epic proportions of the investigation he launched in 1922 are to be understood. To Mitchell a business cycle meant more than a fluctuation in a single aggregate such as national income or employment. It meant also that the fluctuation is recurrent, and that certain repetitive features run through the recurrences. And especially it meant that the fluctuation is diffused through economic activity—appearing, as a rule, in prices as well as industrial activities, in markets for securities as well as those for commodities and labor, in processes of saving and investment, in finance as well as industry and commerce. Systematic fluctuations of this character are distinct from the irregular disturbances and seasonal rhythms to which business is commonly exposed. Not only that, they emerge at a late stage in the evolution of the money economy, when processes of production and consumption have become broadly organized on the basis of making and spending money incomes. Fluctuations of this type—that is, business cycles—can hardly occur until the different parts of an economy have been linked together by complex agencies of transport and credit. To understand how business cycles have emerged

53 *A Bold Experiment,* cited above, pp. 9, 10.

is to understand how our "business economy" has developed. And if business cycles are "not one phenomenon, but a congeries of interrelated phenomena,"[54] any distinction between the problem of how business cycles run their course and of how our economic organization works cannot be other than artificial. In an outline of an Introductory Course in Economics that Mitchell once drew up, he put a section at the end entitled "Economic Process in Motion."[55] Its content was expressed in the following note: "Business prosperity, crisis, depression, and revival, discussed so as to bring in and review all that has gone before." In other words, business cycles encompassed the entire field of economics, and a theory of business cycles was to be a theory of capitalism itself.

This sweeping notion was already contained in Mitchell's 1913 volume, but he now tried to work out its implications more fully. The statistical basis of the old book was restricted to a brief period, 1890-1911. It leaned heavily upon annual data, which often obscure essential features of business fluctuations. Its statistical techniques seemed primitive in the light of devices that time-series analysts were beginning to develop. Most serious of all, there were gaps in the evidence—especially on construction, inventories, retail trade, personal incomes, and business profits. In view of the rapid accumulation of new records and the improving knowledge about business fluctuations, Mitchell was eager to make a fresh attack upon the entire problem. At the beginning he expected that a single volume would suffice for the "systematic treatise." But as his irrepressible instinct of workmanship asserted its authority, the investigation deepened and lengthened. In reporting to the Board early in 1924 Mitchell observed: "I am eager to get the work done as rapidly as possible, but I am still more eager to do it as well as I can—and that takes time."[56] The first instalment, *Business Cycles: The Problem and Its Setting*, did not appear until 1927.

In the Preface Mitchell explained that he was conducting the inquiry on the "general plan" of the 1913 volume. He added:

My earlier impressions that business cycles consist of exceedingly complex interactions among a considerable number of economic processes, that to gain insight into these interactions one must combine historical

[54] *Business Cycles: The Problem and Its Setting*, pp. 63, 454.

[55] The outline is undated. From Mitchell's correspondence I judge that it was probably drafted May 23, 1909, in preparation for Introduction to Economics, which he was scheduled to teach in the fall. Note that he was then not yet working on his *Business Cycles*.

[56] *Annual Report of the Director of Research*, February 4, 1924 (unpublished).

studies with quantitative and qualitative analysis, that the phenomena are peculiar to a certain form of economic organization, and that understanding of this scheme of institutions is prerequisite to an understanding of cyclical fluctuations—these impressions have been confirmed. . . .

The confirmation came through extensive new research. Mitchell was now investigating business cycles on a scale that made his formidable 1913 volume look like an introductory sketch. While *The Problem and Its Setting* is a book of substantial size, its scope corresponds merely to the first three chapters of the 1913 volume—that is, to ninety of its six hundred pages. In the new volume Mitchell recorded what he had discovered in his extensive intellectual travels: what hypotheses concerning business cycles the theorists have developed, what statisticians have found out about various types of fluctuations, and how reporters have described each year's business since 1790 in the United States and Great Britain and for shorter periods in another fifteen countries. But Mitchell went beyond an encyclopedic report. His interpretation of the procedures and findings of time-series specialists illuminated a new literature for both novice and expert. His description of modern economic organization, while designed from the viewpoint of a student of business cycles, is virtually a survey of the field of economics, and I believe one of the most instructive ever written. His analysis of the duration of business cycles is still the one authoritative treatment of that complex subject. His handling of the factor of time in the equation of exchange is a theoretical contribution of lasting value. Mitchell's scholarly feat was acclaimed by professional and lay readers alike. The first printing was soon exhausted, and the book has been reprinted a dozen times. It was translated into Russian and German. No volume published by the National Bureau has approximated its sales.

Only at the end of *The Problem and Its Setting* was Mitchell prepared to define business cycles, and the definition he framed was a working definition—that is, a definition to guide research. How have wage rates behaved during recent and distant depressions? Does consumer spending characteristically lead or lag behind investment at recoveries? What are the relations in time between consumer spending and national income? between consumer spending and employment? How do inventories behave from stage to stage of the business cycle? Does the volume of the circulating medium rise and fall in harmony with industrial activity? Is the volume of investment materially affected in the short run by the rate of change in sales? How are the cyclical turning points in the profits of individual concerns distributed around the turning points of aggregate profits? Questions of this character go to the very heart of the operation of our economic system. Since reliable answers did not exist, Mitchell felt that economists and men of affairs lacked a solid foundation for dealing with business cycles. "Overtaken by a series of strange experiences our predecessors leaped to a broad conception" of economic cycles, "gave it a name, and began to invent explanations, as if they knew what their words meant."[57] This method of working yielded quick results, but they could not be depended upon. To theorize responsibly it was essential to know definitely the actual behavior for which the theory was supposed to account. Instead of undertaking a fresh explanation of business cycles, Mitchell therefore first set about determining as precisely as he could what the business cycles of actual life have been like. In so doing he no more ignored the theories of other writers than he did his own; but he took existing explanations as guides to research, rather than as objects of research.

An economist who works with only a few time series can get along without a special technique of analysis. Mitchell's plan, however, compelled work with a wide range of observations. To gain a just view of business cycles and their causes, the number of time series could hardly be smaller than the number of processes that reputable theorists have alleged to be strategic. That the number should, in fact, be much larger was plain at an early stage, partly because it seemed wise to examine the records of at least several countries, partly because the frequent imperfections of statistical data made extensive crosschecks necessary, partly because new theoretical problems were suggested in the course of work with the data. But if hundreds of time series are to be compared—some covering little more than a decade and others over a century, some representing one country and others a second or third—a systematic technique becomes necessary. In the closing chapter of *The Problem and Its Setting* Mitchell sketched a novel method of analyzing the cyclical behavior of time series. This method he amended after some experimentation. Other investigators soon joined in the task of developing the technique, and improved its power to establish what characteristics of business cycles are stable and what characteristics are variable. Preliminary versions of the technique appeared from time to time as the work progressed.[58]

[57] *Business Cycles: The Problem and Its Setting*, p. 2.
[58] See, for example, Mitchell's *The Problem and Its Setting*, pp. 469-474; "A Re-

But a full and definitive account was postponed until 1946 when *Measuring Business Cycles,* on which I collaborated with Mitchell, was published. This volume shows how business cycles may be identified, describes the range of observations needed to bring out what happens in a modern economy during a business cycle, tests the assumptions underlying the general plan of measurement, and explores the fundamental question whether business cycles have been subject to substantial secular, structural, or rhythmic variations. The basic features of the plan of measurement described in this volume are Mitchell's inventions. If anyone is to be credited with the technique of time-series analysis that has come to be known as the National Bureau method, the credit surely belongs to Mitchell.

Even before *The Problem and Its Setting* was completed, Mitchell began experimenting with the results yielded by his new apparatus. The interpretation of results thus went hand in hand with compiling time series, developing a technique of measurement, and applying the technique to the data—each operation reacting on the others. In his first use of the results, Mitchell followed a plan similar to that of Part III in his 1913 volume. But as he attempted to carry out an analytical trip around the business cycle, he found gaps in his knowledge—some of which could be filled by a more thorough mastery of the statistical materials. Hence he embarked on an intensive analysis of the cyclical behavior of leading economic processes—production of commodities, construction work, transportation and communication, commodity prices, wholesale and retail trade, inventories in different hands, foreign commerce, personal incomes, business profits and losses, security markets, savings and investment, interest rates, banking and the currency. In the 1913 volume Mitchell had written:

The present theory of business cycles deals almost wholly with the pecuniary phases of economic activity. The processes described are concerned with changes in prices, investments of funds, margins of profit, market capitalization of business enterprises, credits, the maintenance of solvency, and the like—all relating to the making of money, rather than to the making of goods or to the satisfaction of wants. Only two nonpecuniary factors command much attention—changes in the physical volume of trade and in the efficiency of labor—and even these two are treated with reference to their bearing upon present and prospective profits.[59]

---

view," *Recent Economic Changes in the United States* (National Bureau, 1929), Vol. II, pp. 890-909; "Testing Business Cycles," *Bulletin 31* of the Bureau's series; "Business Cycles," *Encyclopaedia of the Social Sciences*, Vol. III.

[59] *Business Cycles,* pp. 596-597.

In his new investigation, Mitchell put greater emphasis on the physical side of economic activity. He began his examination of the cyclical behavior of individual processes with production instead of prices, and explored the organization and technology of different industries, seeking to distinguish situations in which output could respond readily to business motives in the short run from others in which output was not subject to close business control. The physical processes of employing labor and other resources, and of ordering, producing, holding, and using commodities were still interpreted in their pecuniary bearings. But Mitchell was steadily broadening his analysis of the workings of our economic organization, and he did not shrink from going as far below the 'money surface' as seemed necessary to comprehend the impulses originating changes in output, and the agencies—technical, legal, psychological, or financial—through which adaptations to new circumstances were continually being made.

By 1932 Mitchell had drafted a sizable manuscript on the cyclical behavior of leading economic activities, taken singly and in combination. He expected to follow this volume with another devoted to theoretical analysis. But he was not satisfied with the manuscript, and after rewriting it more than once continued to feel that he had not mastered adequately the vital processes of which his time series were only the symbols. "I am not a rapid worker," he wrote a friend in 1937, "and I do not like to publish materials which I have not had the time to work into as good form as I can." Mitchell was not deterred from making a fresh start by the length of time his investigation had already taken. He no more hesitated to redo a manuscript that displeased him than to scrap laborious but defective calculations. Around 1938 he reached the conclusion that the authoritative investigation of the operations of our economic system for which he was, in fact, striving required expert knowledge of business and industrial practices beyond what he possessed or could easily acquire. The upshot was an enlargement of the staff. Several collaborators took on the task of extending and refining Mitchell's analysis of the cyclical behavior of leading processes, while he shifted his focus from specific activities to the changes in the internal organization of the economy that occur during a typical business cycle.[60]

Thus the simple conception of the original plan—that is, a "systematic treatise" by Mitchell, supplemented by "two or three

[60] The next two paragraphs are adapted from my Introduction to Hultgren's *American Transportation in Prosperity and Depression* (National Bureau, 1948).

special studies of topics that have never been adequately investigated"—was progressively modified as the investigation of business cycles unfolded. In the hands of an alert investigator, empirical research has the refreshing quality of springing ever new surprises. In working on the systematic treatise, Mitchell discovered not "two or three," but numerous, topics that had never been adequately investigated, and that nevertheless seemed indispensable to a scientific understanding of business cycles in the actual world. He had the habit of examining new evidence all the time, and this kept reminding him of what he did not know. As his task grew, he invited other investigators to join in the enterprise, who in their turn opened up new problems. Work on "special studies" therefore expanded, the "systematic treatise" burst through the limits of a single volume, and various by-products of that treatise developed into independent studies. For example, Kuznets' study of seasonal fluctuations grew directly out of Mitchell's investigation of business cycles; so did Macaulay's work on interest rates and security markets, Thorp's on business annals, Wolman's on trade unionism, Clark's on 'strategic factors,' Hultgren's on transportation, Evans' on incorporations, Abramovitz' on inventories, much of Mills' on prices, and so on. A general idea of how the program developed in the course of a quarter century's research may be derived from the National Bureau's numerous publications that take business cycles as their main theme.

Through all changes of plan and conception, a systematic treatise that would deal comprehensively with business cycles and their causes remained Mitchell's goal. Its living shape is the Bureau's series, Studies in Business Cycles. The final instalment of the series was to be a theoretical account of what business cycles are, how they typically run their course, and of their tendencies towards variation.[61] Mitchell devoted his last years to this effort, trying to fit together the pieces on which his colleagues were at work. He planned a "progress report" in two volumes that would sum up what he had been able to learn about business cycles. The subtitle of the first volume was to be "The Many in the One," and of the second "The One in the Many." As a scientist and philosopher Mitchell had searched long and patiently for "the many in the one, the one in the many." His first volume was nearly completed when he died. It is only a fragment of what he had planned.

[61] Mitchell's conception of the scope of this work underwent several changes. At the last he projected two volumes, as a "progress report." He never completely gave up hope of expanding and revising this preview.

Yet no other study in existence elucidates so fully or so authoritatively how economic activities behave, both individually and collectively, during a typical business cycle. This work was published by the National Bureau in 1951 under the title *What Happens during Business Cycles*.

IX

During the long years of specialization in business cycles, which made Mitchell the foremost world authority on the subject, he remained a general economist concerned with the whole social process—at once economist and statistician, theorist and historian, philosopher and social scientist. Although he never returned to his manuscript on "The Theory of the Money Economy," its intellectual impulse remained with him. In one paper after another, he developed his basic theme that if economic theory was to play a useful role in social reform, it had to grasp "the relations between the pecuniary institutions which civilized man is perfecting, the human nature which he inherits from savage ancestors, and the new forces which science lends him."[62] Time and again, also, he developed his implemental theme that objective, quantitative studies are essential to a scientific understanding of economic life in its current institutional setting.[63]

One of Mitchell's last essays, "The Role of Money in Economic History," sums up his reflections on "how monetary forms have infiltrated one human relation after another, and their effects upon men's practices and habits of thought." I shall quote what Mitchell has to say concerning the influence of the money economy on "man's efforts to know himself":

By giving economic activity an immediate objective aim, and by providing a common denominator in terms of which all costs and all gains can be adequately expressed for business purposes, the use of money provided a technically rational scheme for guiding economic effort. It thereby paved the way for economic theory; for technically rational

[62] *Business Cycles*, p. 599.

[63] See *The Backward Art of Spending Money and Other Essays*, cited above, a selection published in 1937. Of later essays, beside those published by the National Bureau, the following are noteworthy: "The Public Relations of Science," *Science*, December 29, 1939; "Economic Resources and Their Employment," in University of Pennsylvania Bicentennial Conference, *Studies in Economics and Industrial Relations* (University of Pennsylvania Press, 1941); "National Unity and Individual Liberties," *School and Society*, June 13, 1942; "Economics in a Unified World," *Social Research*, February 1944; "Facts and Values in Economics," *Journal of Philosophy*, April 13, 1944; "The Role of Money in Economic History," *Journal of Economic History*, Supplement IV, December 1944.

conduct can be reasoned out, and in that sense explained. But money economy does this job of rationalizing conduct only in a superficial sense, and unwary observers of human behavior fell into the trap it had set. Thoroughly disciplined citizens of the money economy readily assumed that all economic behavior is rational, and when they tried to penetrate beneath the money surface of things they found no absurdity in supposing that men do psychic bookkeeping in pains and pleasures as they do pecuniary bookkeeping in outgo and income. . . . Following the money-making pattern, economic theory became, not an account of actual behavior such as historians attempt to provide, but an analysis of what it is to the interest of men to do under a variety of imagined conditions. . . .

Not only did the money economy make it plausible to explain economic behavior as a calculating pursuit of self-interest, it also long kept a more scientific treatment very difficult. . . . The humdrum processes of producing and exchanging goods, of paying and receiving money were recorded in private account books, but students had no access to these basic sources, and virtually no summaries of them were compiled. . . . But in the course of their expansion, the money economies reached a stage where businessmen, investors, and officials needed economic information more extensive than their predecessors had. . . . One consequence was that it became possible to test a wider range of explanatory hypotheses. . . . Nowadays we can begin laying the foundation for a type of economics that will have a demonstrable relation to the actual conditions with which men have to deal, because it can be based upon an analytic study of actual behavior. This empirical science, whose birth pangs we are witnessing, will be as definitely a by-product of a later phase of money economy as mercantilism and the speculations of Ricardo were by-products of earlier phases.[64]

Mitchell found much of the traditional body of economic theory faulty, not because it was mechanical, but because, lacking institutional perspective, it was naively mechanical. He well knew that "the use of money and the pecuniary way of thinking it begets is a most important factor in the modern situation." Hence "to isolate this factor, to show what economic life would be if it dominated human nature, is to clarify our understanding of economic processes." But he regretted that the theorists who worked on this plan "have not emphasized the monographic character of their work."[65] He put his criticism as follows:

A man who realizes that he is studying an institution keeps his work in historical perspective, even when he confines himself to analyzing the form that the institution has assumed at a particular stage of its evolution. By so doing he opens vistas enticing to future exploration, instead of suggesting a closed system of knowledge. He does not delude himself into believing that anyone's personal experience is an ade-

[64] *Journal of Economic History*, Supplement IV, December 1944, pp. 61, 64-66.
[65] *The Backward Art of Spending Money*, p. 158.

quate basis for theorizing about how men behave; rather is he eager to profit by any light shed upon his problem by any branch of learning —history, statistics, ethnology, psychology.[66]

Veblen's and Commons' work, Mitchell felt, was also of a monographic character, and of course the 'institutionalists' were not the only economists concerned with institutions. Let me quote another telling passage:

Veblen's analysis of the cultural incidence of the machine process and of business traffic takes for granted knowledge of how prices are fixed and of the bearing of prices upon the distribution of income. Every scheme of institutions has an implicit logic of its own, and it is no less important to know what that logic is than to know how the institutions came into being and what they are becoming. When . . . Davenport defined economics as the science that treats phenomena from the standpoint of price, and insisted that it must be written 'from the private and acquisitive point of view,' he was elaborating the logic of pecuniary institutions. . . . Though Davenport explicitly ruled cultural evolution out of economics, he was contributing toward the understanding of one set of institutions.[67]

Thus orthodox price theory was 'institutional' but 'monographic,' since it was not concerned with the evolution of economic organization. It was 'monographic' also because it failed to differentiate sufficiently between the "work of the captains" of modern business, where its reasonings applied tolerably well, and "the work of the rank and file" and "activities of consumption," where its reasonings applied badly.[68] Hence, it was critically important to determine what men actually do, and not take on faith attempts to think out what it is in the interest of men to do.

Games and puzzles of all sorts, not least those contrived by the more subtle of the economic theorists, fascinated Mitchell; but he found the solution of puzzles turned up by actual events not less delightful and much more rewarding. He looked forward to an economics that would be immersed in "the objective validity of the account it gives of economic processes." He put his "ultimate trust in observation" and expected this approach ultimately to prevail. As economists concerned themselves increasingly with actual human behavior, rather than equilibrating adjustments under assumed conditions, the efforts of economic historians and theorists would be fused and the scope of economic theory expanded. Hypothetical schedules of utility and disutility would

---

[66] *ibid.*, p. 256. [67] *ibid.*, pp. 338-339.
[68] "The Rationality of Economic Activity," *Journal of Political Economy*, March 1910, p. 201.

give way to realistic accounts of processes by which the valuations of men are moulded.

Indeed, one of the developments to be looked for is the rapid application of statistical technique to the study of demand for commodities, to the measurement of fatigue, to saving and other aspects of behavior that have seemed particularly baffling because particularly subjective. Psychological facts that can be measured are better data for science than most of the materials the economists have utilized in the past.

But the striving of economists to fashion a science of human behavior would not render equilibrium price theory useless. "On the contrary, not only will it make clear the limitations of the older work, but it will also show how the old inquiries may be carried further, and how they may be fitted into a comprehensive study of economic behavior." The theory of value and distribution, in its traditional sense, would therefore remain a concern of economists, although it would recede from its central position.[69]

Mitchell's faith in social science sprang from his faith in mankind. He expected that as economics took on the shape of a cumulating quantitative science, it would become an increasingly potent factor in social change.

Such topics as the economic serviceability of advertising, the reactions of an unstable price level upon production, the effect of various systems of public regulation upon the services rendered by public utilities will be treated with incisive vigor as we become able to make the indispensable measurements. And investigations of this type will broaden out into a constructive criticism of that dominant complex of institutions known as the money economy—a constructive criticism which may guide the efforts of our children to make that marvelously flexible form of organization better fitted to their needs.[70]

Repeatedly Mitchell pointed to the shortcomings of our economic organization. "The frequent recurrence of economic crises and depressions," he noted, "is evidence that the automatic functioning of our business system is defective."[71] Business planning had found no effective means of checking depressions, or preventing developments that tend to increase the business cycle hazard, or providing economic security for wage earners, or restraining the formation of monster combinations, or conserving the nation's heritage of natural resources, or providing for the satisfactory training of underprivileged youth for responsibilities of industry and citizenship. To Mitchell the existence of these grave problems

---

[69] *The Backward Art of Spending Money*, pp. 36, 370, 371, 376.
[70] *ibid.*, p. 30.　　　　　　　　　[71] *ibid.*, p. 91.

demonstrated a need for greater knowledge of human behavior. The following is a characteristic utterance:

When for any reason it is not profitable to make goods we are forced to sacrifice our will as human beings to our will as money makers. . . . What we have to do is to find out just how the rules of our own making thwart our wishes and to change them in detail or change them drastically as the case may require. Not that this task is easy. On the contrary, the work of analysis is difficult intellectually and the work of devising remedies and putting them into effect is harder still. But one has slender confidence in the vitality of the race and in the power of scientific method if he thinks a task of this technical sort is beyond man's power.[72]

Mitchell realized poignantly that of itself science was neither good nor evil, and that in recent years many of its findings have been put to antisocial uses. But he felt that in a free society this danger is likely to be reduced as knowledge of man's own nature is improved.[73]

Mitchell recognized also that government must play a key role in applying the results of social investigations. He favored national planning on a broad and continuing basis—by which he meant mobilization of a democratic society's intelligence "to deal seriously with social problems before they had produced national emergencies." He followed eagerly the bold experiments in social organization being made in different parts of the world, and our own modest efforts at economic planning under the aegis of the Council of Economic Advisers. That society would evolve a form of organization that will satisfy men's emotional and material needs better than our money economy was his constant hope. Mitchell admired rebels in politics as in economic theory, feeling that deliberate experimentation is essential to the learning process. Yet he thought it necessary to recall "the historical fact . . . that, in the countries that have given wide scope to private initiative . . . , the masses of mankind attained a higher degree of material comfort and a larger measure of liberty than at any earlier time of which we have knowledge, or under any other form of organization that mankind has tried out in practice."[74] The one

[72] "The Crisis of 1920 and the Problem of Controlling Business Cycles," *American Economic Review*, Supplement, March 1922, pp. 31-32.

[73] In his Presidential Address before the American Association for the Advancement of Science he stated: "Perhaps, and perhaps is all we can say, if we can come to a clearer understanding of how we behave, we can learn how to condition men so that their energies will go less into making one another miserable." *Science*, December 29, 1939, p. 606.

[74] *The Backward Art of Spending Money*, pp. 94, 100.

element in our society that he deemed worth preserving at all costs was democracy itself.

These, in brief, are the leading thoughts that run through Mitchell's scattered papers. Their moral sincerity, simplicity, humor, and literary grace won for them a large audience beyond the ranks of professional economists.[75] They played their part, beside his more technical contributions, in shunting the car of economics onto the tracks of empirical science.

X

Although the National Bureau was Mitchell's main concern after 1920, he gave much of his time to the University and to other interests. His sense of proportion and judgment made him an ideal counselor. His life was that of a student, but his later years were complicated by many calls for help from those interested in scientific, educational, philanthropic, and related undertakings.[76] He allied himself freely with progressive and humanitarian movements, such as racial equality, aid to refugees, civil liberties, settlement work, and educational experimentation. For many years he played a leading role in the affairs of the Social Science Research Council, the Bureau of Educational Experiments, and

[75] Some of Mitchell's essays have been reprinted in different places. One, "Intelligence and the Guidance of Economic Evolution," was included by Roger S. Loomis in his *Models for Writing Prose* (rev. edn., Farrar and Rinehart, 1937). Not infrequently Mitchell wrote pieces also for the popular press.

[76] Mitchell's preeminence as an economist was widely recognized during his lifetime. He received honorary degrees from the universities of Paris, Chicago, Columbia, California, Princeton, Harvard, Pennsylvania, and the New School for Social Research. The American Association for the Advancement of Science elected him its President—a distinction accorded an economist only once before in its history. The National Institute of Social Sciences awarded him a gold medal for his contributions to economic science and public affairs. The American Philosophical Society, the American Academy of Arts and Sciences, and the Institut International de Statistique enrolled him as a member. He was elected Fellow of the American Statistical Association and of the Econometric Society, and an Honorary Fellow of the Royal Statistical Society. At different times he served as President of the American Economic Association, the American Statistical Association, the Econometric Society, and the Academy of Political Science. During the academic year 1931-1932 he was George Eastman Visiting Professor at the University of Oxford, in 1934 Hitchcock Professor at the University of California, and in 1935 Messenger Lecturer at Cornell University. On the occasion of his sixtieth birthday his former students presented him with a volume of their writings, *Economic Essays in Honor of Wesley Clair Mitchell*, and many scholars and men of affairs, including President Roosevelt and ex-President Hoover, sent congratulatory messages. In December 1947 he received the highest honor the American Economic Association can confer, becoming the first holder of the Francis A. Walker medal, which is to be awarded not more often than once every five years to an American who "in the course of his life made a contribution of the highest distinction to economics."

the New School for Social Research. During 1929-1933 he served as Chairman of President Hoover's Research Committee on Social Trends. President Roosevelt appointed him to the National Planning Board in 1933. He was a member of the National Resources Board in 1934-1935, a special adviser to Secretary Morgenthau in 1937. In 1944 he prepared a report for the President's Committee on the Cost of Living, which helped to end the dispute then raging about the accuracy of official index numbers of changes in the cost of living. Except during the summer—when he retired to his camp in Greensboro, Vermont, for a few months of uninterrupted work—he devoted a portion of practically every working day to correspondence or conferences with investigators, students, educators, businessmen, public officials, journalists, social workers, and social dreamers.

Only by careful ordering of his daily routine was Mitchell able to engage in so many activities, and at the same time carry forward his own research and maintain a working familiarity with newly published writings. Mitchell's life was serene, unhurried, well balanced. He found time for relaxation as well as work, read the classics extensively without neglecting detective stories, freely exercised his skill at golf and cabinet making, loved gay repartee at the dinner table, and always had an apt remark or verse to enliven conversation.

Mitchell's influence on his students and colleagues was profound. In 1919 he left his Columbia professorship to become Lecturer at the New School for Social Research. Three years later he returned to Columbia and taught until 1944, when he elected retirement and became Emeritus Professor. Mitchell's lectures on Types of Economic Theory and Business Cycles attracted graduate students from all parts of the world. Though he did not care for popular lecturing, his classes were so stimulating that the best students often joined the poorest in repeating them. Those who took his Types of Theory in the expectation of being drilled on fine technical points were at first bewildered by the attention he gave to social and political history. When they discovered how great was his knowledge of the theoretical literature and how deftly he handled its technical issues, they sometimes found it all the more difficult to understand why he did not follow a more conventional approach. But before the year was over even the most technically minded students worked up some enthusiasm for Mitchell's course. They too came to see that economic theory was not coterminous with the neoclassical system, that the works of the major theorists had links with social conditions, and that theory was a phase of man's continuing effort to learn about himself and to better methods of living, not a self-contained system of logic.

No small part of Mitchell's success in broadening the intellectual horizon of students was his ability to make them feel that economics was still in its infancy, and that each of them might take a hand in building a useful social science. Those who went on to his course in Business Cycles discovered that Mitchell was handling on a quantitative basis the very processes they had read about in the theoretical literature, that facts studied in relation to one another could be as exciting as abstract concepts, and that qualitative analysis and empirical inquiry could be complements instead of substitutes. A considerable number were inspired by Mitchell's distinguished example to devote their energies to quantitative research. But Mitchell's own interests were very wide and he encouraged students wishing to work on technical problems in economic theory as well as those who sought to work with observations, urging only that conclusions reached by analyzing imaginary conditions be treated with a scholar's conscience when applied to the actual world. The size of his classes prevented personal acquaintance with all his students. Yet many who never exchanged more than a few words with him felt he gave a new direction and meaning to their lives.

His colleagues at the National Bureau had the good fortune to see a great deal of Mitchell, and benefited continually from his insight and judgment. He was a remorseless critic of his own work, but a generous critic of the work of others. "What counts most of all in scientific work," he once remarked, "is that free play of ideas which we understand so little, but from which emerge at rare moments the flashes that keep reorienting our search for knowledge generation after generation."[77] Mitchell prized the freedom he had enjoyed in developing his own interests, and felt impelled to use his authority at the Bureau to enlarge the freedom of others. His mind had a constructive bent. When he went over a research project or a manuscript he searched out with deliberate care its merits and potentialities, not its defects. An excellent judge of men, he made it a practice to confine criticism to such matters as the individual seemed capable of handling. However short a manuscript might fall of his own standards, he had words of encouragement if it represented honest effort.

Mitchell's understanding of people thus enabled him to bring

[77] *The Backward Art of Spending Money*, p. 82.

out the best qualities, both personal and scientific, in his associates. He did not attempt to impose his judgment or his standards
of scholarship on his colleagues. He never drove the members of
the staff and rarely preached to them. In the main he exercised his
influence by giving daily proof of scientific integrity in his own
work and of kindness towards others. Mitchell treated every member of the staff, young or old, as his scientific equal, and made him
feel that his work was respected and important. He went about
his research quietly, shared his newest thoughts with his colleagues,
sought their criticism, advised and encouraged them in their own
tasks. His characteristic attitude is well expressed in the following
comment on Thor Hultgren's study of American transportation:

Thor virtually demolishes the notion to which I attached much importance in 1913 that unit costs encroach upon profits in late expansion, and are materially reduced in late contraction—so far as
railway transportation is concerned. He leaves mere remnants of the
idea, and makes me wonder whether it has much validity in other types
of business. I have congratulated him warmly on this success in damaging my speculative construction.[78]

Mitchell's steady striving to make his own best efforts obsolete had a
subtle and cumulative influence on the working habits of the staff. A
sense of social responsibility, precision of thought and expression,
repugnance for shoddy work, ability to profit by criticism, passion
for objective evidence, even fairness and generosity are, in some
degree, habits that will grow in one environment and wither in
another. Mitchell set the moral and scientific tone of the National
Bureau so that these habits grew naturally and unobtrusively.

If Mitchell had confined himself to scientific work, he would
have carried his own studies further, perhaps much further. But
he would not have become what he is today, the voice of conscience
itself to numerous investigators within and outside the Bureau.
His varied activities advanced powerfully the research of other
students, aided the progressive undertakings of many educators
and reformers, and helped hundreds to find an honorable and useful place in life. If Mitchell had led a more sheltered existence, he
might not have retained his intellectual youth and vigor so long,
and his thinking would perhaps have taken on the stiffness that
so often accompanies preoccupation with one's own tasks. But I
am dealing here with the imponderables of life, which can be
weighed one way or another. I shall bring this hour's remembrance

[78] Letter to me, June 16, 1946. However, see in this connection the *Twenty-ninth
Annual Report of the National Bureau of Economic Research*, pp. 78-79.

to a close by dropping speculation, and simply record the fact that under the stimulus of Mitchell's leadership quantitative research on national income, prices, investment, money markets, and business cycles developed rapidly in the United States and abroad. The reconstruction of economics now under way may be traced in large part to his influence—to his bold views on the scope and method of economics, to his pioneering studies of the money economy, and to his vigor in stimulating research by others.

I am deeply indebted to Mrs. Wesley C. Mitchell for facilitating in every possible way the preparation of this essay. Milton Lipton helped me verify certain biographical data, and Joseph Dorfman called several facts to my attention. For reading and commenting on the paper I am grateful to Martha Anderson, Milton Friedman, Millard Hastay, Ruth Mack, Geoffrey H. Moore, Frederick C. Mills, C. Reinold Noyes, George Stigler, and Leo Wolman.

New Facts on Business Cycles

I. THE NEED FOR SCIENTIFIC WORK

Despite the relatively good business conditions of recent years, the business cycle continues to haunt the thinking of the American people. The reason is not only a wish to obliterate the human miseries and material wastes of recurring depressions. The reason is also political necessity. The old Marxist dogma that capitalism is doomed to collapse on the rocks of economic crisis has become a weapon of propaganda, used adroitly and energetically to confuse the uninformed and to stir discontent the world over. Our government and other democracies have met the challenge by building a variety of defenses against depression. How well the defenses have been built, no one yet knows. The business decline which started in the fall of 1948 has fortunately been checked, and some credit for this achievement can be assigned to governmental policy. But it is easy to exaggerate the influence of government on the course of events. An outstanding feature of the business situation during 1949 was the high and rising activity in the automobile and housing industries, which continued to feel the stimulus of war-induced shortages. Had these industries faced 'normal' markets, it seems fairly certain that the contraction in business would have gone deeper. For the present, obituaries on the business cycle are romantic expressions of human impatience, not records of solid achievement. They serve neither the nation nor economics, and may prove seriously harmful if they lead to any relaxation of the scientific work on business fluctuations now going forward in universities and other research centers.

The National Bureau's research on business cycles began nearly thirty years ago. Our first publication on national income was already concerned with its fluctuations, and later studies have added materially to a growing body of knowledge about business cycles. But only a relatively small part of the results reached by the Bureau's investigation has as yet been published. Scientific work flourishes best when investigators are free to permit their researches to mature, and this inevitably means a modest and highly uneven rate of publication. The current year, however, is one of plenty. Among the works on business cycles soon to be published is Wesley Mitchell's unfinished book *What Happens during Busi-*

Reprinted from *Thirtieth Annual Report of the National Bureau of Economic Research* (May 1950), pp. 3-31.

ness Cycles, which is remarkably complete as far as it goes. The list includes also Moses Abramovitz' scholarly volume *Inventories and Business Cycles* and three substantial *Occasional Papers*: "Behavior of Wage Rates during Business Cycles" by Daniel Creamer, "Cyclical Diversities in the Fortunes of Industrial Corporations" by Thor Hultgren, and "Statistical Indicators of Cyclical Revivals and Recessions" by Geoffrey H. Moore.

I feel prompted by this upsurge of publications to give some account of the National Bureau's work on business cycles. I cannot attempt to summarize either the research in process or the completed studies. Instead, I shall describe a few facts developed by our investigation that may prove of some help to economists and men of affairs facing the hard task of appraising an uncertain future. What I shall say is based largely on American experience before World War II—a period to which all students must turn when they seek to form a considered judgment of how our business economy functions under peacetime conditions.

II. Dispersion of Specific Cycles

Economic activities generally move in cycles—that is, wavelike fluctuations lasting from about two to ten years. 'Specific cycles' of this character appear in prices as well as output, in markets for securities as well as commodities, in the spending of incomes as well as saving, in the flow of goods to consumers as well as business enterprises. Of the hundreds of time series analyzed by the National Bureau, all but about 3 per cent have continuously undergone cyclical movements. The occasional exceptions include steady series like railroad commutation traffic, extremely volatile series like net gold movements between the United States and Great Britain, and series of 'list' prices that sometimes remain unchanged for a decade or longer and then rise or fall by a vertical step.

These exceptional series are excluded from Chart 1; also all annual series, and such of the monthly or quarterly reports as cover merely a small part of the period between the two wars. Otherwise, the chart includes virtually all the American series that we have analyzed. They encompass a wide range of activities—producing commodities, merchandising, employment, disbursing incomes, commodity pricing, wages, interest rates, security transactions, inventory holdings, and the behavior of the banking system. Most series summarize some activity in the nation at large—for example, production of coal or sales by department stores—but a considerable number are of narrower geographic scope. The precise list varies somewhat from one stretch of the interwar period to another; in most years the total number runs between 600 and 700.

The chart sets forth the distribution, month by month, of the cyclical turns of this large and varied collection of time series. If anyone is so naive as to believe that most economic activities reach like turns on the same or almost the same month, this chart should

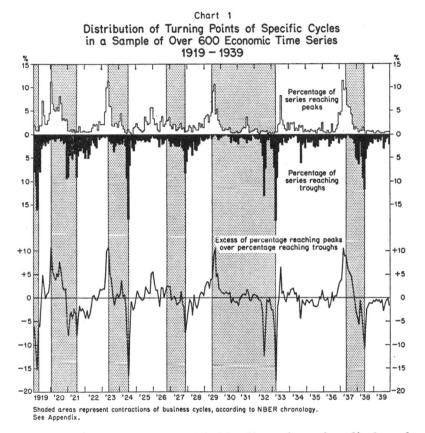

Chart 1
Distribution of Turning Points of Specific Cycles in a Sample of Over 600 Economic Time Series
1919 – 1939

Shaded areas represent contractions of business cycles, according to NBER chronology.
See Appendix.

disabuse him. What it shows is wide dispersion of cyclical peaks and troughs. Practically every month some series attain peaks while other reach troughs. The occasional gaps on the chart, it may be justly supposed, would be closed if our collection of time series were still more comprehensive.

From the wide dispersion of the specific turning points, a simple but important implication may at once be drawn. If in a given month or quarter some activities are at a peak, they must have been undergoing cyclical expansion in immediately preceding months. If in the same month or quarter other activities are at a

109

trough, they must have been undergoing cyclical contraction in immediately preceding months. Since in each month or quarter some activities attain cyclical peaks while others drop to troughs, it follows that expansions have run side by side with contractions all the time. This persistent feature of economic change is brought out vividly by Chart 2, which is simply an arithmetical transformation of the frequencies of peaks and troughs displayed on the preceding chart. Curve A shows the percentage of series undergoing expansion each month from 1919 to 1939, and curve B shows the excess of the percentage expanding over the percentage contracting. The percentages in curve A fluctuate over a wide range but never reach 100 or 0.

Chart 2

Percentage of Series Undergoing Cyclical Expansion
and Their Cumulative, 1919-1939
Based on Sample of Over 600 Economic Time Series

A Percentage of series undergoing cyclical expansion
B Excess of percentage of series undergoing cyclical expansion
   over percentage undergoing contraction
C Cumulative of B

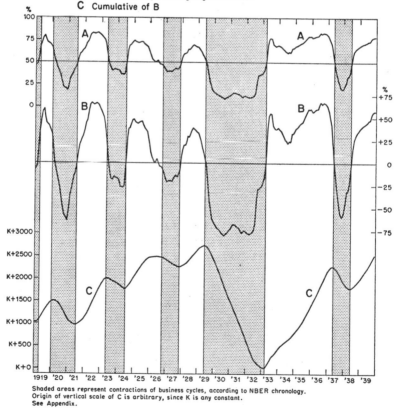

Shaded areas represent contractions of business cycles, according to NBER chronology.
Origin of vertical scale of C is arbitrary, since K is any constant.
See Appendix.

This picture of the diffusion of cyclical movements over our economic system would be very different if the cycles in individual activities followed the same temporal course. In that event curve A would be a step-line, with ordinates of 100 for a stretch of months or years, succeeded by values of 0 for another stretch, then values of 100 again, and so on. With everything rising and falling in unison, there would be little need to fuss with specific factors in business, and one might center attention exclusively on aggregate activity. But business cycles—that is, the cycles in aggregate activity encountered in historical experience—are of a very different character. They are marked by expansions and contractions that are only partially diffused through the economy, and it is therefore of the utmost importance to obtain as clear a notion as we can of how the specific cycles of different activities are tied together.[1]

III. The Business Cycle as a Consensus of Specific Cycles

We have already taken one step in this direction by registering, month by month, the frequency with which specific peaks and troughs are reached, and then combining the frequencies so as to show the percentage of series expanding each month. Let us now carry this process of combination a step further. Assume that a series rises or falls each month by one unit. If, therefore, aggregate activity encompassed 100 items, of which 80 rose in a given month and 20 fell, the total rise during the month would be 60 units. If next month 85 rose and 15 fell, the total rise would be 70 units. By starting with a base figure and cumulating the net percentage of rising series—that is, the excess of the proportion rising over the proportion falling—we should get a schematic picture of the movements in aggregate activity itself. Curve C in Chart 2 has been constructed on this principle. It traces out five remarkably clear cycles, which idealize the fluctuations in several familiar indicators of aggregate economic activity—industrial production, factory employment, and freight car loadings—plotted on the next chart. Not only that, but the chronology of turning points in curve C is nearly identical with the chronology of business cycles previously determined by the National Bureau.

[1] For further analysis along the lines of this and the next section, see the following publications by the National Bureau: Arthur Burns and Wesley Mitchell, *Measuring Business Cycles*, Chap. 4, Sec. II; *Twenty-sixth Annual Report*, pp. 22-24 [reprinted on pp. 3-25, above]; Wesley Mitchell's forthcoming volume [*What happens during Business Cycles*], Chap. 5; and especially Geoffrey Moore's "Statistical Indicators of Cyclical Revivals and Recessions," *Occasional Paper 31*.

Curve C is, of course, no better than its antecedents. It shows the net effect of the temporal distribution of the cyclical turns in our sample of series, and it shows nothing else. It is a highly artificial aggregate which abstracts from every other feature of its components. That is why its cycles are so clear and smooth, in contrast to the jagged fluctuation of most economic time series. It is significant, nevertheless, that this simple construct has enabled us to reproduce rather faithfully the familiar movements of recent business cycle history. For if 'business cycles' can be built up, so to speak, from a mere knowledge of turning points of individual activities, the path to a scientific understanding of business cycles may be considerably shortened by concentrating on the timing relations among specific cycles.

We have seen in Chart 1 that the turning points of specific cycles are so widely scattered that expansions in some activities always accompany contractions in others. But the turning points are not distributed at random through time. If they were, sustained fluctuations such as have occurred in aggregate activity would be highly unlikely. The turns of the specific cycles come in clusters which have, as a rule, definite points of concentration. When the peaks are bunched the troughs are few, and vice versa. The bunching is brought out best in Chart 1 by the excess each month of peaks over troughs, which—except for occasional stray items—is continuously of the same sign for numerous months. But the proportion of advancing series must decline when peaks exceed troughs, and rise when troughs exceed peaks. Hence the bunching of cyclical turns is reflected in protracted periods when a majority of series undergo expansion, followed by protracted periods when a majority undergo contraction.

Charts 2 and 3 add the vital fact that each period in which expansion has been dominant matches closely the upward phase of aggregate economic activity, and each period in which contraction has been dominant matches closely the downward phase; in other words, the succession in time of expanding and contracting majorities is much the same as the succession of expansions and contractions of business cycles. Hence, as Wesley Mitchell observes in his forthcoming book, "business cycles consist not only of roughly synchronous expansions in many activities, followed by roughly synchronous contractions . . .; they consist also of numerous contractions while expansion is dominant, and numerous expansions while contraction is dominant." And just as the succession of a majority of individual expansions by a majority of individual contractions, or vice versa, has been accomplished in periods lasting from about two to eight years during the interwar era, so the cycles in aggregate activity have had this order of duration.

The substitution of one of these majorities for the other takes place gradually, and indeed follows a definite cyclical course, as Chart 2 demonstrates. Rising series are only a thin majority at the

Chart 3
Simple Aggregate of Specific Cycles in Over 600 Economic Time Series, Industrial Production, Factory Employment, and Freight Car Loadings
1919 – 1939

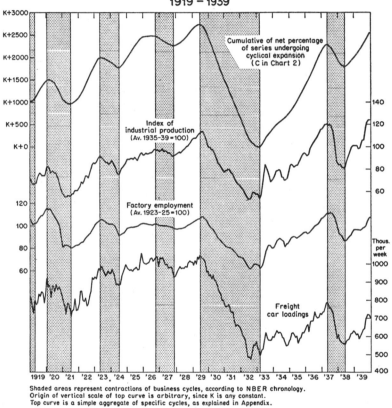

Shaded areas represent contractions of business cycles, according to NBER chronology.
Origin of vertical scale of top curve is arbitrary, since K is any constant.
Top curve is a simple aggregate of specific cycles, as explained in Appendix.

beginning of a business cycle expansion. Their number swells as aggregate activity increases, though expansion reaches it widest scope not when aggregate activity is at a peak, but perhaps six months or a year earlier. In the neighborhood of the peak, cross-currents are the outstanding feature of the business situation. Once the economy is on the downgrade, the number of expanding activities becomes smaller and smaller, though the scope of expansion does not shrink indefinitely. Perhaps six months or a year before the aggregate reaches a trough, the proportion of contracting activities is already at a maximum; thereafter the majority of contracting activities dwindles, while the minority of expanding activities becomes ever stronger and before long becomes the ruling majority.

Thus a continual transformation of the economic system occurs beneath the surface phenomena of aggregate expansion and contraction. A business cycle expansion does not mean that nearly everything within the economy is moving upward, nor does a business cycle contraction mean that nearly everything is shrinking. There are two cycles in economic activity, not one. First, there is the cycle of sustained expansions and contractions in the aggregate itself. Second, there is the cycle in the distribution of expansions and contractions within the aggregate. The first cycle is 'seen' since we are accustomed to following comprehensive records of business conditions. The second cycle is 'unseen' since few of us subject the components of comprehensive aggregates to close examination. An 'unseen' cycle in the relative distribution of expansions and contractions of specific activities corresponds to each 'seen' cycle of their aggregate. But whereas the proportion of expanding activities moves in the same direction as the aggregate in the early stages of a business cycle expansion or contraction, it moves in the opposite direction in later stages. The proportion of expanding activities is already declining months before aggregate activity reaches a peak, and is already rising months before the aggregate reaches its trough.

Further evidence on these basic propositions is supplied by Charts 4 and 5. The first of these charts compares two fairly homogeneous groups of series—production and employment—with our all-inclusive sample. The next chart comes from Geoffrey Moore's *Occasional Paper 31*. It is based on a mass of series selected on account of their rather regular conformity to business cycles. Like Chart 1, it includes widely different activities, but spans more than half a century instead of a mere two decades. It appears from these exhibits that the features of business cycles I have emphasized— the variety of cyclical movements in individual activities, their tendency towards a consensus, and an inner cycle in the distribution of expanding and contracting activities within the external cycle of aggregate activity proper—cannot be ascribed to any special characteristics of the interwar period or to the heterogeneity of our full sample of series or the fuzziness of their aggregate, but

Chart 4
Percentage of Series Undergoing Cyclical Expansion
Three Groups of Series, 1919–1939

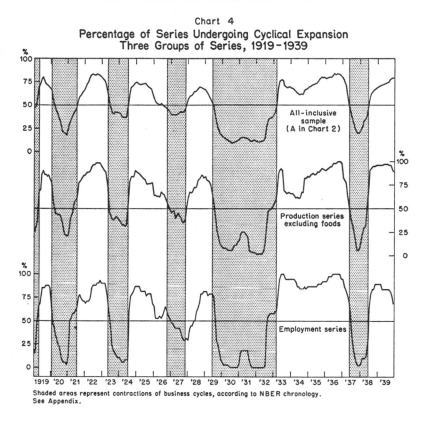

Shaded areas represent contractions of business cycles, according to NBER chronology.
See Appendix.

must be reckoned as underlying properties of over-all aggregates of economic activity however defined.

IV. Why Business Fluctuations Spread Unevenly

Before presenting more statistical results, it may be well to pause and consider the reasonableness of the picture of business cycles thus far developed. Let us suppose that economic activity, having recently moved at a depressed level, is jarred out of its routine by a moderate increase in 'spending.' The additional spending might be by business firms, governments, or consumers within the nation, or it might originate outside the domestic economy. For simplicity let it be assumed that domestic consumers, as a class, enlarge their spending, that they do so at a time when their income is unchanged, and that technological changes do not occur in the sequel. What, then, will be the likely consequences of this 'autonomous' increase in spending?

It is plain that in the very short run the direct effects will dom-

115

inate, and that they will depend upon the direction of the new outlay. If the spending is on railroad travel, theatrical performances, or the like, involving merely the use of some idle capacity, there will be an immediate increase in incomes, but both the number of men employed and their average workweek are likely to

Chart 5

Percentage of Series Undergoing Cyclical Expansion
Moore's Sample of Well-Conforming Series, 1885-1939

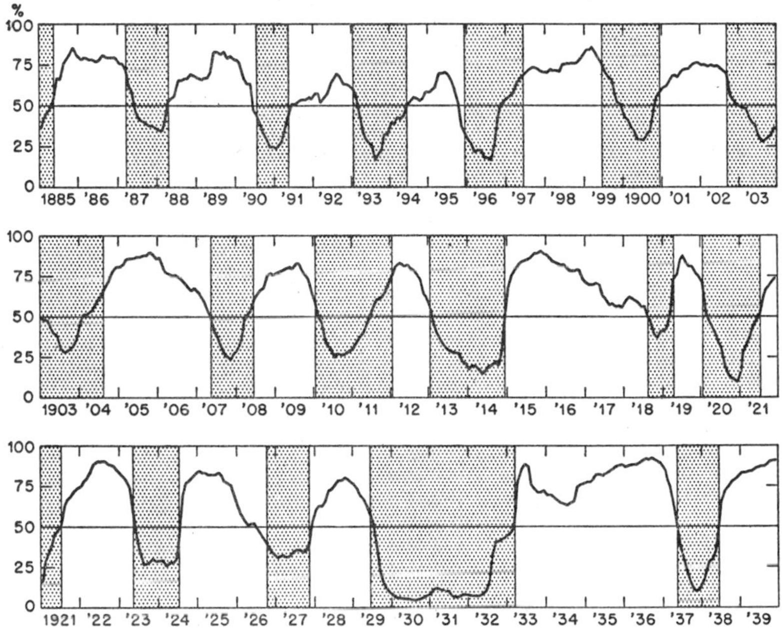

Shaded areas represent contractions of business cycles, according to NBER chronology.
See Appendix.

remain unchanged. If the spending is on personal services of barbers or lawyers, the number of man-hours worked is sure to increase at once and with it the national income, but not necessarily the number of men employed. If the spending is on imported commodities there will not be any immediate increase in domestic employment. So it may be also if the spending is on domestic commodities carried in stock; for dealers or manufacturer may not see fit or be unable to replenish their inventories. If the spending is on goods made to order, employment is likely to rise though that will not happen if the jobs generated in any short period by the new spending are insufficient to offset the decline in work on projects started in earlier periods. Even blinking this com plication, it is useful to distinguish between additional spending on custom-made articles such as furniture, which may merely lengthen the workweek in existing shops, and increased spending on new dwellings, which is practically sure to augment the numbers employed.

The preceding remarks may be generalized. Whether the consuming public or some other group is responsible for the increase in spending, as long as we look merely at what happens in the very short run we should expect spotty reactions through the economy, not over-all expansion. The impact of the new spending will be uneven, perhaps only a small minority of firms benefiting from it. Each firm has its own peculiar heritage of circumstances—size and condition of plant, goods on hand, work in process, liquid assets, outstanding contracts, customers' good will, labor relations, managerial skills. Hence different enterprises will appraise differently whatever expansion in sales they experience; those making fairly similar appraisals will still respond differently, and those who happen to respond in much the same way will not always achieve similar results. Indeed, we could not even be confident that the total number of men and women at work will increase, unless two conditions are met: first, that the new 'spending' is on goods made to specification in new 'shops' set up for the purpose; second, that purchases of this type ceased their decline some months back and are now at a stable level.

New construction meets adequately the first condition, and if we suppose that the second is also met, we can speak more definitely of the outcome. Practically all construction projects are built to fresh specifications. Each requires a new site on which a temporary factory, so to speak, is set up and a work force assembled. Hence any increase in spending on construction is reasonably certain to add promptly to the number employed. Not only will employment increase, but in view of the long period required to carry out construction projects, the increase will be sustained for months, sometimes years. The work on a construction job is unevenly distributed over time, but for every type of project there is a characteristic pattern of labor input, which often rises until the job is about half completed and then declines. Hence a jump in the rate of starting new construction will lead to a gradual increase in employment on construction sites. In the case we have supposed, employment will grow at on increasing rate for several months, the precise period depending upon the size and character of the projects initiated, then rise at a diminishing rate until a level proportionate to the higher rate of ordering is attained.

In this sketch I have tacitly assumed that the higher rate of new construction 'starts' is maintained over a period at least equaling that required to carry out a typical construction project—which nowadays is probably a little over a half year. As employment on construction sites expands over a period of this duration, there may at first be no increase in the production of building materials. Dealers or fabricators who consider their stocks excessive will permit them to go lower, and those who seek to augment their supplies may not be able to do so as readily in the case of one material as another. But if the rate of initiating construction is maintained at the new level, an increasing number of dealers will expand their purchases and more and more producers will expand their output. In the long run—which may need to be reckoned in years rather than months—orders, production, employment, shipments, inventories, and related business factors will be generally higher throughout the constructional trades.

Few industries, and none of a magnitude comparable with construction, have its power to convert a discontinuous increase in spending—whether it returns promptly or only after a few months to the old level—into a sustained expansion of employment, which for a time is even accelerative. But whatever the industry, if a higher rate of sales is maintained long enough, employment will surely rise and so will the activities associated with it. For a while the effects will be spotty, but with the passage of time adjustments will be set in motion throughout the industry as well as in those on which it closely depends for its materials and supplies. And as the higher rate of spending generates new incomes, its effects will spread out in new channels having little in common with the original direction of the new spending. People will spend part or all of their larger incomes, and their additional outlay will be swollen by that of business firms seeking to add to inventories or 'fixed' plant. In this cumulative process the banking system and the capital market will play a part; and once the movement has gathered strength, it may continue of its own momentum even if the original increase in spending, which might have been a governmental instead of a consumers' buying spurt, is no longer maintained. But it is not my purpose here to examine the actual process whereby a business cycle expansion cumulates.

My aim has been merely to suggest that there are economic reasons why crosscurrents are more prominent in some stages of the business cycle than in others. Factors peculiar to individual businesses and markets are always at work. The adoption of new technical processes, introduction of new products, opening up of new sources of supply, migration of people, shifts in demand, formation of new firms, disappearance of old ones, and the weather itself—these factors, whatever their precise role may be in generating or transmitting business changes, create crosscurrents in both good times and bad. Nevertheless, I have tried to set forth reasons for expecting the crosscurrents to be especially numerous at the beginning of a business cycle expansion. As expansion progresses, we should expect its scope to widen, as actually happens according to our statistical summary. But after some time obstacles to further expansion are likely to multiply, though aggregate activity keeps climbing. Here and there banking facilities will be inadequate to finance further expansion. Here and there in the industrial process 'bottlenecks' will emerge, and the increase in supplies slow down or vanish. Here and there prices will remain steady in the face of rising costs, and discourage programs for expansion. Here and there nearly everyone in the labor force will be at work, and the growth of some firms will be at least partly balanced by the decline of others in the neighborhood. Thus it is reasonable to expect what our charts so forcefully show, that with the passage of time the scope of a business cycle expansion will shrink though the expansion still continues.

V. TYPICAL SEQUENCES WITHIN A BUSINESS CYCLE

I need not stop to adapt these commonplaces to the phenomena of a business cycle contraction. For present purposes it is sufficient that the statistical finding on which I have dwelt is a meaningful and reasonable result; namely, that the proportion of economic activities undergoing expansion traces out a cyclical curve which precedes the movements of aggregate activity, whether it be rising or falling. In view of this finding two broad propositions may be set down. First, a business recession starts while aggregate activity is still expanding and a recovery starts while the aggregate is still contracting. Second, a recession or recovery spreads gradually over the economic system and in time reverses the tide of aggregate activity. These propositions naturally raise the question whether the transitional changes in business cycles have a stable economic character. For example, the decline in the proportion of advancing series towards the close of expansion might be produced by cyclical peaks in a random assortment of activities. On the other hand, it might be produced by substantially the same set of activities, cycle after cycle; in other words, the sequence of downturns in one cycle might be much like the sequence in any other. To grapple with this issue, the veil of anonymity clothing our time series must be lifted.

Chart 6 does this in part by segregating three highly important groups of series in our sample—those reporting orders for invest-

Chart 6
Simple Aggregates of Specific Cycles in Three Groups of Series 1919 – 1939

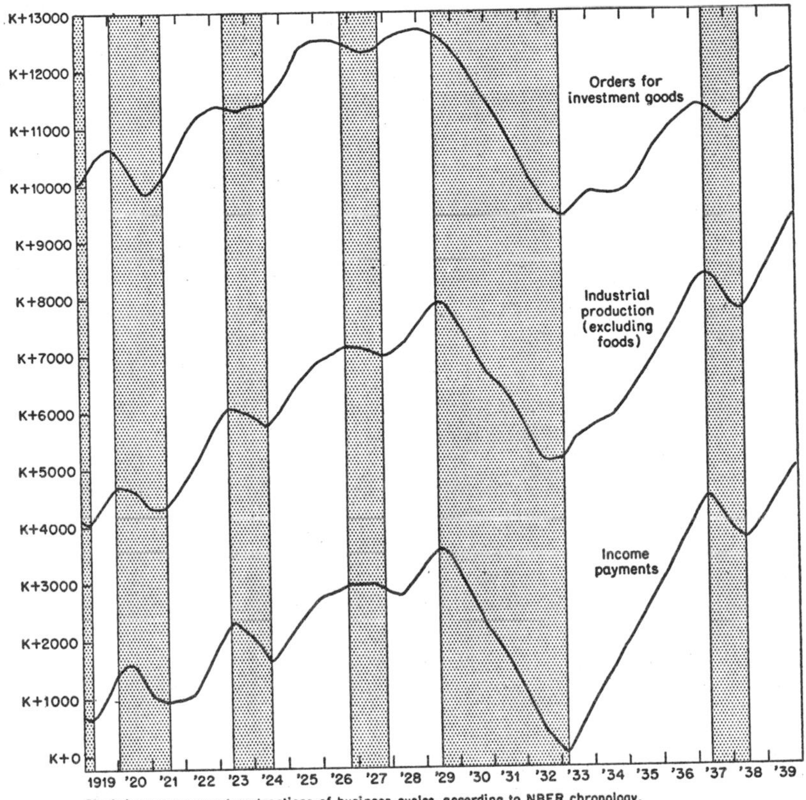

Shaded areas represent contractions of business cycles, according to NBER chronology.
Origin of vertical scale is arbitrary, since K is any constant.
See Appendix.

ment goods, industrial production, and income payments. The curves are constructed on the same principle as the cumulative in Chart 2, which, it will be recalled, is based solely on a specification of the cyclical turning points in individual series. But whereas the simple aggregate of that chart includes our full sample of series, the aggregates of Chart 6 are constructed from 'homogeneous' subgroups. The curve marked 'orders for investment goods' combines all series relating to construction contracts, building permits, equipment orders, and orders for materials such as are predominantly used in making investment goods. The curve for production includes all the production series in our full sample except foodstuffs. The curve for income payments includes all available series of this type, though it happens to be dominated by payrolls. Taken together, these three groups account for about a third of the series in the full sample.

The simple aggregates of the specific cycles in our several groups trace out movements that correspond closely to one another and to the cycles in business activity identified by the National Bureau. But the cyclical timing of the groups varies: as a rule the maxima and minima of investment orders lead the corresponding turns of production, which again lead the corresponding turns of income payments. Now, a maximum or minimum represents a point of balance between expanding and contracting series within a group. Hence the sequence of maxima means that at a downturn in aggregate activity the shift from a majority to a minority of expansions comes first in the group on investment orders, later in production, a little later still in income payments. At an upturn in aggregate activity there is a similar succession of shifts from a majority to a minority of contractions. These systematic sequences express a tendency of our several groups to occupy similar positions relative to one another within each cluster of turns surrounding a business cycle turn.

The results depicted in Chart 6 are restricted to investment decisions at the time they become effective, the physical volume of production, and the disbursement of incomes. This is only part of the evidence that a system exists in individual upturns at business revivals and in individual downturns at recessions. Speaking broadly, our studies indicate that new orders, construction contracts or permits, stock prices and transactions, security issues, business incorporations, and hours worked per week tend to lead the tide in aggregate activity; so do the liabilities of business failures on an inverted basis. On the other hand, production, employment, commodity prices, imports, and business profits tend to move with the tides in aggregate activity; while income payments, wage rates, interest rates, retail sales, and inventories are laggards.[2] These cyclical traits are not infrequently obscured or

[2] See the following publications by the National Bureau: *Bulletin 69; Measuring Business Cycles* (Chaps. 4, 9-12); *Occasional Papers 26, 31-32*; Evans' *Business In-*

deflected by special circumstances, but when numerous time series and long periods are analyzed a tendency towards repetition in cyclical sequences, such as I have described, comes clearly to the surface.

To gain more definite knowledge, it is well to concentrate on selected series of broad economic coverage. Table 1, which is adapted from Wesley Mitchell's analysis of 'comprehensive' series in *What Happens during Business Cycles*, will serve my immediate purpose. Each series in the table has some right to the claim of being a 'true' aggregate or average of its kind, in contrast to the artificial ones I have largely used hitherto. The table shows directions of movement during a typical business cycle—here divided into eight stages, four each for expansion and contraction. Of course, each stage covers several months, and the table is therefore insensitive to minor differences in timing, such as the short lag in income payments. Further, it hides many crosscurrents that would appear in less comprehensive series, and completely omits certain business factors of which we should take account—especially wage rates, inventories, banking, and governmental finance. But with all its faults, the table identifies actual time series and thus shows more concretely than have previous exhibits the typical round of developments that constitute a business cycle.

Let us then take our stand at the bottom of a depression and watch events as they unfold. Production characteristically rises in the first segment of expansion; so do employment and money income; and so do commodity prices, imports, domestic trade, security transactions. Indeed, every series moves upward except bond yields and bankruptcies. In the second stage the broad advance continues, though it is checked at one point—the bond market, where trading begins to decline. Bond prices join bond sales in the next stage; in other words, long-term interest rates—which fell during the first half of expansion—begin to rise. In the final stretch of expansion, declines become fairly general in the financial sector. Share trading and stock prices move downward; the liabilities of business failures, which hitherto have been receding, move up again; security issues and construction contracts drop; the turnover of bank deposits slackens; and bank clearings in New York City, though not as yet in the interior, become smaller.

---

corporations in the United States, 1800-1943 (Chap. 9); and the forthcoming studies by Mitchell, Abramovitz, and Creamer, previously mentioned. See also the earlier studies by W. M. Persons, especially his papers in *Review of Economic Statistics*, January and April 1919.

TABLE 1

Characteristic Direction and Amplitude of Twenty-six "Comprehensive" Series during a Business Cycle[a]

SERIES NUMBER	SERIES	TYPICAL DIRECTION OF MOVEMENT DURING A BUSINESS CYCLE[b] — EXPANSION				TYPICAL DIRECTION — CONTRACTION				NUMBER OF BUSINESS CYCLES COVERED	PERCENTAGE OF CONFORMING MOVEMENTS DURING SPAN OF STAGES IN WHICH SERIES IS SAID TO		AVERAGE AMPLITUDE[c] OF MOVEMENTS DURING SPAN OF STAGES IN WHICH SERIES IS SAID TO	
		Trough to first third	First to middle third	Middle to last third	Last third to peak	Peak to first third	First to middle third	Middle to last third	Last third to trough		Rise	Fall	Rise	Fall
1.	Bond sales, N.Y. Stock Exchange	+	−	−	−	−	−	+	+	14	86	79	35.0	14.7
2.	Railroad bond prices	+	+	−	−	−	−	+	+	19	65	74	7.4	3.8
3.	Commercial failures, liab., *inverted*	+	+	+	−	−	−	+	+	14	86	93	74.5	57.8
4.	Common stock prices	+	+	+	−	−	−	−	+	16	94	82	26.8	20.2
5.	Shares sold, N.Y. Stock Exchange	+	+	+	−	−	−	−	+	16	94	88	40.6	36.2
6.	Corporate security issues	+	+	+	−	−	−	−	+	8	100	75	46.9	46.1
7.	Construction contracts, value	+	+	+	−	−	−	−	+	7	86	75	43.2	30.4
8.	Deposits activity	+	+	+	−	−	−	−	+	16	94	88	14.3	16.7
9.	Bank clearings, N.Y.C.	+	+	+	+	−	−	−	+	18	100	89	30.8	26.6
10.	Incorporations, number	+	+	+	+	−	−	−	+	19	84	80	26.9	10.2
11.	Bank clearings, outside N.Y.C.	+	+	+	+	−	−	−	+	14	100	79	25.5	12.8
12.	Bank clearings, total	+	+	+	+	−	−	−	+	14	100	86	29.2	20.4
13.	Imports, value	+	+	+	+	−	−	−	+	16	94	75	26.1	18.9
14.	Industrial production, total	+	+	+	+	−	−	−	−	5	100	100	35.2	32.5
15.	Fuel and electricity production	+	+	+	+	−	−	−	−	5	100	100	25.5	14.6
16.	Pig iron production	+	+	+	+	−	−	−	−	16	100	100	54.2	44.9
17.	Railroad freight ton-miles	+	+	+	+	−	−	−	−	6	100	88	27.8	25.1
18.	Factory employment	+	+	+	+	−	−	−	−	6	100	100	21.8	22.8
19.	Factory payrolls	+	+	+	+	−	−	−	−	5	100	100	36.3	39.9
20.	Income payments, total	+	+	+	+	−	−	−	−	4	100	50	22.6	17.6
21.	Corporate profits	+	+	+	+	−	−	−	−	4	100	100	168.8	174.6
22.	Commercial failures, no., *inverted*	+	+	+	+	−	−	−	−	16	75	88	22.3	26.1
23.	Department store sales	+	+	+	+	−	−	−	−	4	100	75	17.6	9.1
24.	Wholesale trade sales, value	+	+	+	+	−	−	−	−	3	100	100	17.7	19.1
25.	Wholesale commodity prices	+	+	+	+	−	−	−	−	11	82	91	8.7	8.9
26.	Railroad bond yields	−	−	+	+	+	+	−	−	19	74	65	3.7	6.2

a See Appendix.

b A plus denotes rise, a minus denotes fall. Series 3 and 22 are inverted here.

c Expressed as percentage of mean value during a cycle.

These adverse developments soon engulf the economic system as a whole, and the next stage of the business cycle is the first stage of contraction. Production, employment, commodity prices, personal incomes, business profits—indeed, practically all processes represented in the table—decline. Of course, the liabilities of business failures continue to rise, which merely attests the sweep of depression. Long-term interest rates also maintain their rise. But in the next stage the downward drift of bond prices ceases; that is, the rise in long-term interest rates is arrested. By the middle of contraction, bond sales join the upward movement of bond prices. More important still, the liabilities of business failures begin declining, which signifies that the liquidation of distressed business firms has passed its worst phase. These favorable developments are reinforced in the following stage. Share trading and prices revive; business incorporations, security issues, and construction contracts move upward; money begins to turn over more rapidly; even total money payments expand. Before long the expansion spreads to production, employment, prices, money incomes, and domestic trade. But this is already the initial stage of general expansion— the point at which our hurried observation of the business cycle started.

This recital of cyclical developments is rough and inadequate. Of course, it delineates characteristic movements during business cycles, not invariant sequences. That the description fits imperfectly individual business cycles is apparent from the conformity percentages in Table 1. Yet these percentages also suggest that the deviations from type are not so numerous as to destroy the value of our generalized sketch. And if this much can be accepted, an important conclusion immediately follows, notwithstanding the omissions of the table; namely, that the check to the dominant movement of business activity, whether it be expansion or contraction, is typically felt especially early in financial processes and activities preparatory to investment expenditure.

The sequences in the table express interrelated developments; they are not disconnected facts. Even my bleak description has not escaped causal overtones. An informed reader who makes the effort will not find it hard to forge explicit causal links. Take, for example, the early recovery of the bond market from depression. The explanation can partly be found in the behavior of commercial banks. With reserves growing, short-term interest rates declining, and 'sound' loans difficult to arrange, the banks naturally seek to expand their holdings of bonds. Private investors attempt to do likewise, but at the expense of stocks since business profits are still declining rapidly. The broad result is a revaluation of security holdings: bond prices and trading move upward, while the stock market keeps going down. But high grade preferred stocks are a fairly close substitute for gilt-edged bonds, and blue-chip common stocks for preferred stocks. As the yield on bonds diminishes, stocks of strong concerns become more attractive to alert investors. In time, declining interest rates exert an upward pressure on stock prices generally, offsetting the influence of falling profits. And so one may continue to link the signs recorded in the table, and fill the blanks in our knowledge of how expansions and contractions cumulate. But if the links are to be of tolerable strength, they must be hammered out of materials beyond those in the table, and among these materials some understanding of what goes on within broad aggregates is essential.

VI. The Cyclical Behavior of Profits

Of this I shall give a large illustration. The operations of our business economy depend in a significant degree on the relation that unit costs, unit prices, and the physical volume of sales bear to one another. These three factors are summed up in profits—the driving force of business enterprise. According to Table 1 corporate profits characteristically rise throughout the expansion and decline throughout the contraction of business cycles. That this is a tolerably faithful summary of recent experience is evident from Chart 7, which sets profits against industrial production and the National Bureau's chronology of business cycles since 1920. Reliable reports on quarterly profits are not available for earlier years, and we must be content with a span of observations hardly long enough for confident generalization. However, the evidence on profits seems reasonable in view of the behavior of production, just as the latter seems reasonable in view of the behavior of security issues and construction contracts. Accepting the evidence, it appears at first blush that profits tend to favor the continuation of prosperity or depression practically until the end of the phase, and that forces capable of reversing the tides of business activity are ordinarily not to be found in profits as such. Reasoning along these lines will lead one to suppose that actual profits are an unsatisfactory gauge of prospective profits, and to seek this key to business movements elsewhere—in orders, sales, inventories, the price-wage ratio, the stock exchange, or other places.

These lines of investigation are worth pursuing. At the same time, much can be learned about changes in prospective profits from the distribution of actual profits. After all, business firms do not have a common pocketbook. As long as we reason from aggregates we assume that they behave as if they had one, and it

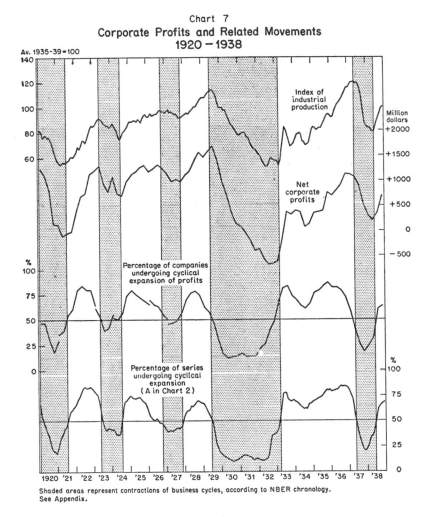

Chart 7
Corporate Profits and Related Movements
1920 − 1938

Shaded areas represent contractions of business cycles, according to NBER chronology.
See Appendix.

is only common sense to stop and inquire how much difference separate pocketbooks do make. The third curve from the top in Chart 7 supplies as good a statistical answer as now seems attainable. It is based on the cycles of profits in a sample of companies analyzed by Thor Hultgren. The curve shows that "at every stage of the business cycle the fortunes of some companies . . . ran counter to the main stream."[3] Not only that, but the proportion of firms experiencing an expansion of profits began to decline well before the peak in total profits or total economic activity, and to increase long before the trough. In other words, developments in the sphere of profits that actually foreshadow reversals in the direction of aggregate activity are obscured when we view profits in the aggregate.

Earlier in this report I noted that there are two cycles in economic activity, one 'seen' and another 'unseen,' and that the 'unseen' cycle in the distribution of individual activities throws its shadow ahead of the 'seen' cycle in the aggregate. We now find two cycles in profits, the 'unseen' cycle in the distribution of companies throwing its shadow ahead of the 'seen' cycle for all corporations. Chart 7 demonstrates, moreover, that in the period covered the 'unseen' cycles in profits and in general economic activity follow similar paths. The two curves are made from widely dissimilar and independent materials, but this fact merely corroborates our earlier conclusion that recession and recovery start well in advance of any reversal in the direction of aggregate activity. However, the causal links between the curves are as yet obscure; and while the available data will not permit exhaustive analysis, we should attempt to determine as well as may be whether the companies whose profits run counter to the dominant cyclical movement are in fact the foci of gathering recovery or recession.

Meanwhile, it may be observed that the behavior displayed on our chart accords with rational expectations. In the early stages of an expansion, unit costs often decline as industrial facilities are improved or utilized more fully. But as prosperity cumulates, unit costs tend to mount for business firms generally; and since in many instances selling prices cannot be raised, profit margins here and there will narrow, thus offsetting the influence on profits of an increase in sales or reinforcing the effects of an occasional reduction in sales. The 'squeeze' on profits becomes more widespread the longer the business expansion continues. In the first place, all firms do not have the same power to advance prices; some are prevented or limited by custom, trademarks, or governmental regulation. Secondly, errors pile up as mounting optimism warps the judgment of an increasing number of businessmen concerning the sales that can be made at profitable prices. Thus, after a business

[3] See Hultgren's "Cyclical Diversities in the Fortunes of Industrial Corporations," *Occasional Paper 32* (National Bureau, 1950). Cf. J. Tinbergen, *Statistical Testing of Business Cycle Theories: A Method and Its Application to Investment Activity*, and L. Klein's note in Part Three of *Thirtieth Annual Report of the National Bureau of Economic Research*.

expansion has run for some time, the proportion of firms experiencing rising profits begins to shrink, although the profits of business in the aggregate continue to climb. Such a development spreads doubt or financial pressure to firms whose profits are still rising, and in time moderates their investments in sympathy with that of the growing number of firms whose business fortune is waning. Of course, a check to investment from this source strengthens an emerging tendency to postpone investment projects until a time when, it is felt, construction costs and financing charges will recede from the abnormal level to which they have been pushed by prosperity.

Minor changes aside, these are some of the crucial developments generated by prosperity, as Mitchell originally analyzed the problem in his *Business Cycles*, published in 1913. A series of converse developments may be expected in depression. A great deal of evidence may now be cited in support of these expectations; though definite knowledge is not yet available of the scale on which investment projects are shelved in late expansion or resuscitated in late contraction, or of the links that tie firms with declining and rising profits into a system of cumulating responses.

One reason for emphasizing the role of profits in the business cycle is their extraordinarily wide fluctuation. Thus far I have abstracted from the cyclical amplitudes of different processes, which together with the variations in timing transform the internal composition of the economy in the course of a business cycle. Of this fundamental feature of business cycles I can say little on the present occasion; but I at least wish to call attention to the wide differences among the amplitudes of the 'comprehensive' series in Table 1, and to record the finding that in our economic system, taken as a whole, production fluctuates more widely than sales to final users. As a consequence of the latter, additions to inventories trace out cyclical movements that conform closely to the cycles in production, and account for a considerable part of the changes in it. These facts were first glimpsed by Simon Kuznets. Later, Moses Abramovitz, beside making more refined and extensive measurements, developed their rich implications in his *Inventories and Business Cycles*, now in press.[4] More recently, Ruth Mack has brought fluctuations of shorter time span than business cycles within the orbit of the original generalization, and compiled evidence suggesting that

[4] See Abramovitz' forthcoming book, especially Chaps. 1 and 21; also *Bulletin 74* by Kuznets. Cf. Alvin H. Hansen, *Fiscal Policy and Business Cycles* (Norton, 1941), Chaps. 1-2.

inventory investment plays an even more important part in the variations of production that occur every few months than in those that extend over a business cycle.

VII. FORECASTING BUSINESS CYCLES

I have stressed in this report some of the repetitive features of business cycles established by the National Bureau's studies. Yet the very charts on which I have relied as my witnesses attest also variability in the duration of business cycles, in the relative length of their phases of expansion and contraction, their amplitude, their economic scope, the speed with which a sizable majority of expanding activities is converted into a minority or vice versa, the intervals separating the upturns or downturns of different activities, and even their sequence. As everyone knows, the contraction of 1929-1933 was exceptionally long and deep, as well as very widely diffused. The contraction of 1926-1927, on the other hand, was mild though not exceptionally brief. Chart 6 gives some inkling of the dynamic impact of outlays on plant and equipment during business revivals and recessions, but this branch of expenditure was not the active factor in lifting the nation out of depression in 1914 or 1933. In recent years monetary and fiscal management has left only faint traces of the cyclical pattern of long-term interest rates which ruled before the 1930's and which I have recorded in Table 1. The same table states that stock prices move early in revivals and recessions, but is silent on the occasional lapses from this tendency. None of the exhibits in this report shows agricultural production, a major industry dominated in the short run by the weather, or singles out exports, which fluctuated in virtual independence of business cycles before World War I.

I take it as a matter of course that it is vital, both theoretically and practically, to recognize the changes in economic organization and the episodic and random factors that make each business cycle a unique configuration of events. Subtle understanding of economic change comes from a knowledge of history and large affairs, not from statistics or their processing alone—to which our disturbed age has turned so eagerly in its quest for certainty. If I have emphasized the repetitive elements in business cycles gleaned from statistical records, it is because a constructive contribution can come also from that direction. Findings such as I have reported add to the understanding of business cycles, and may even prove helpful in predicting reversals in the direction of total economic activity—or at least in identifying them as such promptly. That this hope is not entirely a pipe dream is indicated by Chart 8.

The chart shows artificially simple aggregates, struck on the plan previously described, of the specific cycles in two small groups of series. Taken together, they are the twenty-one indi-

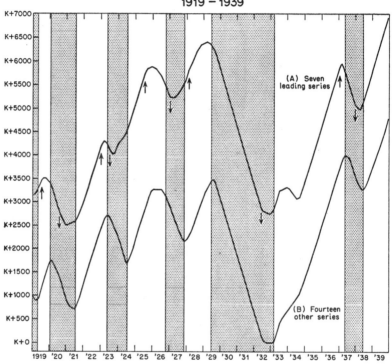

Chart 8
Simple Aggregates of Specific Cycles in Two Groups of Series
Differentiated by Their Cyclical Timing
1919 – 1939

Shaded areas represent contractions of business cycles, according to NBER chronology.
Origin of vertical scale is arbitrary, since K is any constant.
See text for explanation of arrows, and Appendix for other explanations.

cators of cyclical revivals selected by the National Bureau in 1937 on the basis of performance in past revivals.[5] After ranking these twenty-one series according to their average timing at revivals through 1933, the top third were segregated from the rest. Curve A includes this top third, which spans average leads from 7.8 to 4.2 months. Curve B covers the remaining two-thirds, the extreme series having an average lead of 3.6 months and an average lag of

[5] See "Statistical Indicators of Cyclical Revivals," *Bulletin 69*.

1.8 months. In view of the method of selecting the two groups, curve A may be expected generally to lead curve B at recoveries. There is no technical reason, however, for a lead at recessions, or for that matter at the recovery of 1938. Nevertheless, curve A turns down and up in every instance before curve B; more important still, it does so before the turning points of general business activity expressed by our chronology of business cycles. If there were no genuine tendency towards stability of cyclical sequences, the probability of attaining such regular results would be slender.

Four forecasting principles are embodied in Chart 8, and they are more significant than their particular expression. First, since the cyclical timing of single processes cannot be implicitly trusted, a measure of protection against surprises of the individual case may be won by combining the indications of numerous series. Second, since there is a tendency towards repetition in cyclical sequences, economic series may be grouped into two or more classes according to their timing. Third, while the group with the longest leads is of keenest interest, groups that tend to move later serve the important function of confirming or refuting the indications offered by the vanguard. Fourth, since the 'unseen' cycle in the distribution of cyclical expansions and contractions within an aggregate tends to throw its shadow before the movements of the aggregate, this propensity may be harnessed by the forecaster. How that practice would extend the lead of curve A over B is indicated by the upward- and downward-pointing arrows on the chart, which are placed respectively at the maxima and minima of the proportion of series in group A undergoing expansion.

These matters are being investigated further by Geoffrey Moore. Beside improving the selection of indicators made in 1937, he has devised a technique for grafting current monthly observations onto cyclical units such as I have combined in Chart 8 on empirical, and in Chart 6 on economic, considerations. His tentative results are presented in *Occasional Paper 31*, and should prove extremely helpful to the many economists who can master statistical devices without being mastered by them.

VIII. MILD AND SEVERE DEPRESSIONS

The fear of business cycles which rules economic thinking is a fear of severe depressions. The reasons for concern about the magnitude of emerging economic movements extend far beyond the sphere of private business activity or profit. Our society can readily make political as well as economic adjustments to a mild contraction such as that of 1926-1927 or 1948-1949, perhaps even to rapid but brief declines such as occurred in 1907-1908 and 1937-1938. The really serious threat to our way of life comes not from business contractions of this character, but from the long and deep depressions that devastate homes and industries—as in the 1870's, 1890's, and the early 1930's. To glimpse economic catastrophe when it is imminent may prevent its occurrence: this is the challenge facing business cycle theory and policy. A preceding generation concentrated on the causes and cures of commercial crises; later interest shifted to business cycles, and more recently to fluctuations in employment. But the crucial problem of our times is the prevention of severe depressions, not of business or employment cycles. It is in this direction that research must move in the future, and the first and fundamental task is to determine why some business contractions are brief and mild while others reach disastrous proportions.

Some insight into this problem is afforded by the experience of the 1920's. Each of the successive cyclical waves during this decade carried further the belief in a 'new era' of boundless prosperity. As speculative fever mounted, even the business declines that occurred were ignored or explained away. The boom in common stocks of that decade and its aftermath are notorious, but speculation was by no means confined to stocks. Ilse Mintz has recently added an important chapter on foreign bonds, and Raymond Saulnier has contributed another on urban mortgage lending.[6] Mrs. Mintz' study is concerned with American loans extended to or guaranteed by foreign governments from 1920 to 1930. After observing that "the 1920's were the defaultless era in foreign lending," she suggests that the quality of the loans progressively deteriorated during the decade. This was well concealed until severe depression brought a test of quality. "Only 6 per cent of the issues of 1920 defaulted in the 1930's while 63 per cent of those of 1928 suffered this fate; dividing the period into its earlier and its later half only 18 per cent of all issues from 1920 to 1924 became bad while the corresponding ratio for 1925 to 1929 is as high as 50 per cent." Saulnier's sample survey of urban mortgage loans by life insurance companies suggests a similar relaxation of credit standards during the late twenties. It shows, for example, that of the

6 See the forthcoming studies by Ilse Mintz [*Deterioration in the Quality of Foreign Bonds Issued in the United States, 1920-1930*] and Raymond Saulnier. The latter's *Urban Mortgage Lending by Life Insurance Companies* is in press. See also an earlier study by George W. Edwards, *The Evolution of Finance Capitalism*, pp. 231-232.

loans extinguished in 1935-1939 the foreclosure rate was 40 per cent on such of the loans as were made during 1925-1929, but only 32 per cent on those made in 1920-1924 and 25 per cent on those made in 1930-1934.

These new facts accord with an old hypothesis; namely, that developments during 'prosperity'—which may cumulate over one or more expansions—shape the character of a depression.[7] But the results I have cited do not explain, for example, why the revival in the first half of 1931 proved abortive. That unfortunate episode cannot be understood without study of foreign conditions, the policies pursued by the Federal Reserve System, and other matters. I make these remarks merely to suggest that a host of developments during a business decline, largely unconnected with what happened during the preceding 'prosperity,' may convert what might have been a mild contraction into a severe one. This too is an old hypothesis, and of course it supplements rather than rivals the hypothesis that the sources of deep depression are imbedded in preceding prosperity.

Our past work on business cycles has laid an excellent foundation for comparative study of mild and severe cyclical movements. *Measuring Business Cycles* demonstrates a high and positive correlation between the amplitude and economic scope of business cycle phases. Abramovitz has found an inverse correlation between the length of a business cycle phase and the proportion of the change in gross national product that is accounted for by inventory accumulation or decumulation. Geoffrey Moore has found qualitative differences in the movements of agricultural prices and production during mild and severe depressions.[8] In a forthcoming *Occasional Paper* Daniel Creamer supplies important information on the behavior of wages during business cycles of varying intensity, and Milton Friedman is now investigating monetary changes during mild and vigorous cyclical movements. But we have only begun to exploit our vast collection of records which cover expansions and contractions of widely different length and depth in several countries. Full investigation of the problem why some business declines remain mild while others reach catastrophic magnitude is a natural extension of our research program, and one for which we have long prepared. It will call for considerable new

[7] See, for example, *Measuring Business Cycles*, p. 460.

[8] See Abramovitz' forthcoming monograph [*Inventories and Business Cycles, with Special Reference to Manufacturers' Inventories*], Chap. 21. Moore's study of *Harvest Cycles* is undergoing final revision.

effort, and the merging of the skills of the historian, economic theorist, and statistician. If we can turn to it promptly and energetically, we may make a telling contribution to the economic knowledge our society so sorely needs.

I have received generous aid in preparing this report. Millard Hastay organized and recorded the statistical work, Geoffrey Moore participated in parts of this task, W. Braddock Hickman took charge of the mechanical tabulations, H. I. Forman drew the charts, and several members of the National Bureau staff read the manuscript with critical care.

Looking Forward

It is the normal business of our Annual Meeting to lay plans for the future besides taking stock of past accomplishments. We share a common faith in the power of economic research to better human life, but the specific inquiries that we pursue require constant scrutiny and reexamination. At a time when our nation is mobilizing its spiritual and economic resources to protect its way of life against the sinister force of communism, the need for critical self-appraisal is especially strong. To aid you in making this appraisal, I shall discuss the National Bureau's program in relation to some of the practical issues of our times, and suggest the general direction in which the Bureau may usefully move in the years ahead.

I

The distribution of the national income is always a vital concern of a free and progressive people seeking to raise their plane of living. The wage bargains into which we enter, the prices and taxes we pay, the subsidies we legislate, even the careers we choose, are all affected in some degree by our notions of what is a 'fair' income. These notions are naturally linked to our impressions of how incomes are actually distributed, but on this subject we have been very badly informed. Our direct knowledge of incomes is of necessity limited to a few cases. For the rest we rely on vague impressions gathered over the years, eked out by crude statistics that occasionally come to our notice. As a result few Americans and still fewer Europeans are aware of the transformation in the distribution of our national income that has occurred within the past twenty years—a transformation that has been carried out peacefully and gradually, but which may already be counted as one of the great social revolutions of history.

Let me cite several figures from Simon Kuznets' recent reworking of income statistics. In 1929 the highest 5 per cent of the income recipients obtained 34 per cent of the total disposable income of individuals—that is, the total of personal incomes, inclusive of any capital gains but after deducting federal income tax payments. By 1939 their share had dropped to 27 per cent of total income, and by 1946 to 18 per cent. Since 1946 the size structure of the income distribution does not seem to have changed materially, so

Reprinted from *Thirty-first Annual Report of the National Bureau of Economic Research* (May 1951), pp. 3-18.

that we may regard the distribution in that year as roughly representative of current conditions. If we now compare 1929 and 1946, we find that the share going to the top 5 per cent group declined 16 points. Had perfect equality of incomes been attained in 1946 the share would have dropped from 34 to 5 per cent, that is, by 29 points. In other words, the income share of the top 5 per cent stratum dropped 16 points out of a maximum possible drop of 29 points; so that, on the basis of this yardstick, we may be said to have traveled in a bare two decades over half the distance separating the 1929 distribution from a perfectly egalitarian distribution. If we turn to the top 1 instead of the top 5 per cent group, the results are still more striking. The share of the top 1 per cent group in total income was 19.1 per cent in 1929 and 7.7 per cent in 1946. Since the share of this group dropped 11.4 points out of a total possible drop of 18.1 points, we have traveled since 1929 on the basis of this yardstick almost two-thirds of the distance towards absolute income equality.[1] Regrettably, the 'iron curtain' precludes comparison of our achievement with that of the vaunted 'people's democracies,' but it is permissible to wonder whether many of them can point to so vast a democratization of the distributive process in their own countries.

Considerable income inequalities still exist in our midst, but they require careful interpretation. Imagine a static society in which differences of earnings simply reflect differences in productivity; hence youngsters earn less than middle-aged men, and men with no schooling receive less than those possessing a technical education. Imagine further that real incomes are independent of location, but that both the scale of living costs and money incomes are higher in urban than in rural areas. To an uninformed observer the income differences of such a society might seem disturbing, although age and education, each correlated with productivity, account for all real differences in income. We lack the means to

---

[1] The above figures are derived from Kuznets' report *Shares of Upper Income Groups in Income and Savings*, now being prepared for publication. For a preliminary summary of his findings, see *Occasional Paper 35* (National Bureau, 1950). Of course, the figures cited in the text refer to only two points on a Lorenz curve, and cannot be interpreted to mean that 'income inequality,' taken as a whole, has been reduced by over half. Moreover, Kuznets' figures are estimates that may be modified by later research; though it seems unlikely that the *trend* indicated by the figures would be materially changed, as long as the income concept is confined to personal incomes. If, however, the undistributed income of corporations were allocated to individuals, the change from 1929 to 1946 would be less striking. On this basis the share of the top 5 per cent group comes out 35 per cent in 1929 and 20 per cent in 1946; while the share of the top 1 per cent comes out 20.8 per cent in 1929 and 9.9 per cent in 1946.

assess precisely the influence of the various factors that shape our current income distribution, but the data assembled by Kuznets leave no doubt that a part of the income differentials in our society is attributable to urban life; that the upper income stratum is dominated by the most productive age, sex, and educational groups in the population; and that income inequality would appear smaller if incomes were reckoned by two- or three-year periods instead of by the year.

These conclusions of Kuznets' investigation have great significance for the American people. If we are to look forward constructively to a material reduction of income inequalities in the future, we must seek to attain it principally by raising the productivity of those at the bottom of the income scale rather than by transferring income from the rich to the poor. Between 1929 and 1946 the average per capita income of our population (including capital gains but after payment of federal income taxes) rose from $690 to $1,166. Meanwhile the average per capita income of the top 1 per cent of the population fell from $13,168 to $8,994.[2] Thus the upper income stratum suffered a substantial decline in money income and a still larger decline in real income. The social experimentation of our own and other countries suggests that private incentives to embark on new and venturesome investments are more firmly rooted than was generally believed to be the case a quarter of a century or even a decade ago; but there can be no doubt that as high incomes are cut, a point must come when private investors have neither the will nor the power to launch major innovations. Substantial further redistribution of incomes may therefore affect adversely the size of the national income, while it cannot improve appreciably the living conditions of the great masses. The paramount source of the rising living standards of our workers and farmers has always been an increasing volume of production, and in the years ahead it bids fair to become the only source.

II

The evening out of incomes is partly attributable to the rapid rise of wages relative to other forms of income—salaries, dividends, and interest receipts. Another significant factor has been the progressive income tax, which now dominates the federal revenue system. Lawrence Seltzer's investigation discloses that the income actually subject to tax grew three times as rapidly as total personal income

[2] See the preceding note.

between 1939 and 1948. At the same time tax rates rose sharply, so that tax payments grew twice as fast as income subject to tax. As a consequence of both developments, personal income tax payments increased six times as fast as personal incomes. The relative increase of tax revenues was still higher by 1950, and will be higher again in 1951 even if Congress accepts only partly the President's recommendations. The precise character of the additional taxes is as yet uncertain, but the raw facts on income distribution make it altogether plain that the burden will fall mainly on moderate-sized incomes. Even if the *total* income of those receiving $25,000 or more per year were paid into the Treasury, the addition to tax revenues would fall far short of the additional sums now budgeted.

The only way the government can avoid sharp increases in taxes is to finance all or a substantial part of the new military expenditures by borrowing. But experience teaches that this method of financing is nearly certain to impose greater hardships on the average citizen than would increased taxation. For, on the one hand, financial tinkering cannot of itself change the physical quantity of goods available for civilian consumption; while, on the other, debt financing will lead to a further shrinking of our shrunken dollar, and thus further obliterate the savings that ordinary folk had laid by in the form of bank deposits, government bonds, pension accounts, and life insurance holdings. It is often noted that inflation hurts the lender and benefits the borrower, but it is easy to overlook that men of small or moderate means are far more apt to be net lenders than net borrowers. The principal borrowers, of course, are governments, large business firms, and wealthy individuals.

Whether the government obtains the dollars it needs by taxing or borrowing or doing some of each, it will use the dollars to purchase a larger portion of the national output than it did previously. Hence, unless production increases or inventories are permitted to fall to dangerous levels, the quantity of goods left for purchase by civilian users must decline. In a period when industry is converting plant from peacetime to military production, an over-all increase in output per man-hour is not very likely to occur. Absorption of the unemployed into gainful occupations will tend to relieve the short supplies; but the contribution from this source will hardly be sufficient to offset the projected increase in military forces. An increase in the labor force and a lengthening of working hours are, therefore the principal means that are immediately available for attaining the military goods we need without severe curtailment of living standards.

138

Clarence Long's investigation of changes in the labor supply during recent decades in the United States and foreign countries throws considerable light on the elasticity of the labor force—a total that includes civilian workers, the armed forces, and the unemployed who are actively in the labor market. The labor force is normally one of the steadiest of economic factors, but it is nevertheless capable of increasing very sharply at a time of national emergency. During the 1930's the annual additions to our labor force were in the neighborhood of 600,000. Between 1940 and 1944, however, the total increase was close to 10,000,000, or about four times what it would have been under normal conditions. Over half of the 'extra' workers were girls and women, and most of them left industry at the end of the war. When the conflict in Korea broke out last June, the proportion of the population of working age in the labor force was not much higher than in 1940. Now the proportion is perceptibly rising again, and it seems likely that the general pattern of the recent war will be repeated in the present emergency.

Long's analysis of foreign experience during World War II is not less instructive than his analysis of the American record. The British augmented their labor force on approximately the same scale as the United States, when allowance is made for the difference in size of the two countries. Canada also added substantially to its labor force; Germany, on the other hand, fell far behind the democracies. According to Long's calculations, "for every hundred females at work before the war the United States added 35, Britain 21, and Canada 19 (compared with 1941); Germany relinquished 1. For every hundred males the United States added 9, Canada 6, Britain 2, and Germany 0.3."[3] The great contrast between the German experience and that of the democracies has many causes, but perhaps the most important is that a free and peaceful people have a resilience and energy at a time of crisis that cannot be matched by a dictatorial state. Years before launching an attack, a totalitarian government is likely to drive its citizens to fanatical effort, but the furious pace cannot be maintained physically or psychologically if the conflict turns out to be a protracted one. There is a nice balance in the energy of a people over a run of years that moral fervor may stretch but cannot override. To build up our military strength we must now act boldly and quickly, and

[3] [See Long's *Occasional Paper 36*, "The Labor Force in War and Transition, Four Countries" (1952), in the National Bureau's series.]

yet guard against the danger of draining the reserves of energy we shall need if our country is forced into full-scale war.

In view of the magnitude of our military program, a considerable expansion of the labor force during the next year or two is as desirable as it is likely. A moderate increase in working hours would also contribute to smoothing the transition to a sharply higher level of governmental spending. But over a longer run we must seek to protect living standards by looking to increases in the productivity of labor rather than to an extension of working hours or a rise in the proportion of people in the labor force. The American people will willingly work harder for the same or even a lower real income while our most urgent defense preparations are being built up, but they are not likely to continue to do that—unless, of course, the Korean war is extended. If the rightful aspirations of workers and farmers for better living standards are to be realized with a minimum of social unrest, it will be necessary to strive for even greater increases in productivity than have ruled in the past.

The extent and causes of increasing industrial productivity have long occupied the attention of the National Bureau's research staff. The investigations now being conducted by Mills, Fabricant, Stigler, and Barger will probably be completed within a year or two, and it is highly important to begin laying plans for new research in this critical area. But it is only prudent to assume that whatever gains may occur in industrial productivity during the next decade, controversy over the distribution of the national product will not be less intense than in the recent past. New research on the distribution of incomes therefore seems advisable, and it is likely to prove especially fruitful if linked with Wolman's and Long's studies of the labor market. Kuznets' work on income distribution, invaluable though it is, has covered intensively only the upper income strata. Fortunately, a great deal of information on low and moderate incomes has recently accumulated and awaits exploitation. Preliminary explorations suggest that it may be possible to work out tolerably full income distributions for every year since 1939, and to cross the size distributions with other classifications among which occupation, trade union status, and full- or part-time membership in the labor force are especially important. Statistics on income analyzed in this fashion would clarify the economic policies that have ruled in recent years, and at the same time provide a better factual basis on which current policies may be formulated. I hope that the Bureau's Board will authorize research in this direction as soon as funds and personnel can be assembled.

III

At an early stage of World War II Leonard Crum began an investigation of the outlook for the postwar federal budget, in which he was later joined by Slade Kendrick. Their successive estimates were widely discussed and had considerable influence on students of government, but they rested on so many uncertain assumptions—especially with regard to the state of international affairs—that the authors were reluctant to have them published. Recalling this experiment, it is especially noteworthy that back in 1943, when the thinking of so many was still geared to the 1930's, Crum foresaw that the postwar federal budget would run on a very much higher level than any prewar budget.

Crum reached his conclusion by examining individual items of the budget, taking such account as he could of the probable needs and political pressures after the war. Recently, in the course of an historical study of federal expenditures, Kendrick gave close attention to the influence of major wars and in the process succeeded in lifting Crum's conclusion to the plane of generalization.[4] After the War of 1812, after the Civil War, after World War I, and again after World War II, federal expenditures ran on a substantially higher level than in the years preceding hostilities. Of course, a large gap between prewar and postwar expenditures might merely mean that traditional methods of war financing have a powerful tendency to lift price levels. But Kendrick demonstrates that the gap is not a monetary illusion; it remains very substantial even after allowing for population growth and rising incomes, besides changes in the purchasing power of money. This persistent pattern arises, at least in part, from readily identifiable causes—such as heavy borrowing during a war which piles up embarrassing interest charges at the war's end, the need to care for veterans and their families, and a natural tendency to countenance what seem to be moderate increases in outlay on civilian functions at a time when military budgets are being drastically cut. Thus, although the bulge of war spending is followed by sharp contraction at the war's end, the level of expenditures remains considerably higher than before the war.

Whether and in what degree this pattern will apply to the pres-

[4] See Kendrick's forthcoming *Occasional Paper* on "Federal Expenditures for 150 Years."

ent bulge in governmental spending is a question that cannot be answered with assurance. War with Russia is by no means inevitable. Some approach to international comity within the near future cannot be ruled out. Further, the pattern depends on factors that are in considerable degree within human control even if the calamity of war cannot be averted. It is therefore premature to conclude that when full peace reigns again, the rate of governmental expenditures will be substantially higher relative to population and national income than in the past three or four years. At the same time it is well to recognize that apart from wars the broad trend of governmental expenditures has been emphatically upward. Fabricant's study, now approaching completion, reveals persistent growth in the utilization of human and material resources by government. Between 1900 and 1949 private employment in the United States approximately doubled, the combined employment of state and local governments quadrupled, while federal employment increased more than twelvefold. One out of twenty-four workers was on some governmental payroll in 1900; the proportion rose to one out of fifteen in 1920, one out of eleven in 1940, one out of eight in 1949. In 1902 one out of every thirteen or fourteen dollars of capital assets (excluding military equipment) was government property; in 1946 the proportion became one out of four. Nor do these striking figures tell the full tale, since they leave out of account the employment provided and the capital utilized through governmental purchases from private business, which in the aggregate add very materially to the government's command of real resources.[5]

It is interesting to speculate on what the trend of governmental activity might have been in the complete absence of wars. From this point of view, it is well that the figures I have cited on employment are imperceptibly affected by interest on the federal debt or by outlays on the veterans' program, both being predominantly legacies of war. The figures do include the military forces and the civilian workers employed by government in connection with the military establishment. If these were omitted, governmental employment would be notably lower but the broad trend would be unchanged. The crux of the problem, however, is the indirect influence of war on the civilian functions of government, and on this matter it is difficult to touch firm ground. It does seem clear that the domestic and international dislocations caused by war extend

[5] See Fabricant's preliminary report, "The Rising Trend of Government Employment," *Occasional Paper 29* (June 1949) in the National Bureau's series.

the need for governmental activity, and it is not unlikely that once government undertakes a new function there is a tendency to maintain it even if underlying conditions change. Not only that, but the decisive role of government in conducting a war probably fosters a tendency on the part of many to look to government for a solution of their special problems. But these and other indirect influences of war, important though they may be, can account only in part for the increasing role of government in economic life.

The broad trend of development in a progressive economy is towards sharply increasing emphasis on the service industries, and the government is merely one of the major channels through which the public's demand for services is satisfied. An economy undergoing rapid industrialization and urbanization increases the interdependence of men—their exposure to the wisdom and enterprise, also the folly and indolence, of their neighbors. Social and economic problems arise that cannot be handled adequately by private enterprise. With the spread of political democracy the demand increases for collective action to broaden educational opportunity, to improve sanitation and health, reduce slums, conserve natural resources, eliminate or regulate private monopoly, supervise banks and insurance companies, protect workers against the hazards of unemployment, and so on. Thus the line separating private enterprise and governmental responsibility is constantly redrawn, the range of governmental activities broadens, and a 'mixed economy' comes into being.

In these few sentences I have touched on one of the gravest problems of our time—namely, the proper line of division between the functions of government and private enterprise. This has always been a controversial issue in our democracy, and every significant relocation of the line has been preceded and followed by extensive public discussion. What makes the problem so acute today is that despite the notable shift towards government in recent years, Americans feel that new changes are impending—the scope and consequences of which they can but dimly foresee. Over a large part of the earth collectivism has triumphed, and even in the democracies of Western Europe the government is a more significant economic factor than in the United States. To make social changes intelligently amidst the uncertainty bred of crisis and tumult in the world is not easy. But that very fact imposes a heavy obligation on economists to clarify and set out scientifically the extent, character, and impact of governmental activities.

The National Bureau's research in this area dates formally

from 1939, when the Conference on Research in Fiscal Policy was set up. In the last two years our research on fiscal problems has been accelerated. Several investigators—Seltzer, Kendrick, Maxwell, Lent, Holland, and Dobrovolsky—now have in hand important research concerning federal finances and state-federal fiscal relations. But in our experience 'public finance' or 'fiscal policy' is a subject that cannot usefully be kept in a box by itself. The major projects on which the National Bureau has worked—that is, our investigations of national income, money flows, capital requirements, the credit system, business cycles, and employment and productivity—have attempted to cover, each in its own image, the operations of the economy as a whole. So large a factor as government inevitably obtrudes itself in such inquiries, and our research staff has been alive to the opportunity. Kuznets' papers on income originating in governmental activity, presented to the Conference on Research in Income and Wealth; Copeland's paper "Concerning a New Federal Financial Statement"; Stigler's paper "Employment and Compensation in Education"; Fabricant's monograph on trends in the government's use of resources, of which a preview was published as *Occasional Paper 29*; Wolman's *Planning and Control of Public Works* and Gayer's *Public Works in Prosperity and Depression*; Firestone's current study of cyclical fluctuations in federal revenues; Coppock's *Government Agencies of Consumer Instalment Credit*; Colean's recently published volume, *The Impact of Government on Real Estate Finance in the United States*; Harriss's *History and Policies of the Home Owners' Loan Corporation* which is ready for press; Copeland's new investigation of the capital used by government—every one of these studies has grown out of a major project concerned with the over-all operations of the economic system, and each has aided and will continue to aid the more specialized inquiries in public finance.

Thus government operations have for some time been a large factor in the Bureau's research program. It would be well, however, to give them greater prominence by making the expanding role of government one of the high themes of our research in the years immediately ahead. The National Bureau has recently taken one step in this direction by requesting Saulnier to organize a comprehensive investigation of the entire field of governmental lending, including federal loan guarantees and loan insurance. A still more important step is the authorization of a study of international trends in the governmental use of resources. Both in Europe and in the United States discussions of governmental activity,

144

especially of the socialization of industry, have hitherto been carried on without the aid of basic measurements, and great confusion and suspicion have unhappily been wrought in the process. Hence the projected study will have as its first aim the development of detailed and accurate information on governmental employment of men and other resources in each of the leading countries of Western Europe since 1900. Thus a factual foundation may be laid for comparing European trends with those set out by Fabricant in his American study. But it would be desirable to go further and search for the causes of international similarities and differences in the economic role accorded by free peoples to their governments. Such a comparative study would help everyone concerned with large affairs, whether on the theoretical or practical level, to see developments in our own and other countries in clearer perspective.

To carry out this broad and fundamental investigation properly will require larger funds than we have in hand, but we shall at least get the project launched through an exploratory survey by Abramovitz. What makes the project enticing to the economic student is the prospect that it will open up an array of problems concerning not only government, but economic development at large. To derive information on governmental employment it will be desirable, if not strictly necessary, to work out occupational tables for each country covered. Thus materials of very great significance for a study of comparative economic development will come into being, and perhaps pave the way for wide-ranging investigations of the conditions of economic progress. But it is much too early to say whether we shall be led in this way or by some other route into extending the modest international studies we are now pursuing.

IV

I have emphasized the operations of government because of the strategic role they have come to occupy in the modern economy. The government, however, is merely one agency in the complicated process by which the citizens of a democracy obtain their living. The figures on governmental employment, which I cited earlier, would have appeared less striking had I observed that 96 per cent of Americans were privately employed in 1900 and that, despite the growing complexity of economic life and our participation in two major wars, as many as 88 per cent continued to be privately employed in 1949. Even during World War II, federal income payments at no time reached a fourth of the national total, although the government's payroll was swollen by over 11 million in the armed forces. Of course, these figures convey little concerning government's regulatory functions, but these too must not be exaggerated. By and large, except in times of the gravest national emergency, the predominant mass of economic decisions concerned with choice of occupation, industrial location, production, pricing, saving, investing, financing, working, buying, and selling has remained in private hands; though, to be sure, it has become necessary for everyone to function within an expanded framework of governmental rules.

Under the impact of economic mobilization such as we are now facing, it is possible to form the impression that the size of the national income, its physical composition, and the manner in which we share it are all determined by some will of government. In fact, the end results of our economic activity depend both in times of peace and in times of war on actions taken by millions of workers and farmers, households, business firms, financial institutions of various sorts, trade unions, farmers' cooperatives, businessmen's associations, and state and local governments, beside the federal government. Our vast economy is essentially a partnership. In an emergency like the present, the federal government becomes the dominant partner. But while there are many silent as well as quarrelsome partners in the joint enterprise, none is dormant—not even in wartime.

The gains registered over the last two decades by our joint enterprise have been many and substantial. The combined output of our factories, mines, utility plants, and construction yards is now about twice what it was in 1929. The production of the service industries has increased enormously, and even agricultural production has expanded about 40 per cent. The gain in population has been 25 per cent, in the physical volume of personal consumption nearly 75 per cent. The glaring inequalities of our income structure have in large degree been eliminated. We have devised a tolerably comprehensive system of insurance against the hazards of bank failure, unemployment, and an indigent old age. And we have shared the fruits of our industry and knowledge with the peoples of less fortunate nations, including our former enemies, on a scale that is probably unique in the annals of history.

These are great moral as well as economic achievements. They deserve more attention than they have received from the American people, and they deserve vastly more attention from the peoples of other nations. But if the performance of the American economy is imperfectly understood, the reason is partly that our record is not free from blemish. Despite our great economic strength, we have failed to exercise the leadership needed to restore that measure of free international trade under which the world once prospered and enjoyed substantial peace. Nor have we as yet proved ourselves capable of conducting our economy without serious oscillations. Within the past twenty years we have lived through one of the greatest inflations of money and prices in our history, also one of the severest depressions, beside smaller movements that were sufficient to cause anxiety not only to us but to the friendly peoples of Europe.

The view has gained some currency of late, as it has in other periods of exaltation, that economic institutions and knowledge have developed to the point where the government can readily prevent sizable economic fluctuations. This view can be supported by reciting the impressive contracyclical devices that have been built into our fiscal system. Recent price history, on the other hand, casts some doubt on the expectation, and so too does the longer perspective of history. Government policy with respect to booms and depressions is not an innovation of the Employment Act of 1946 or of the Roosevelt administration.[6] It can be traced to the depression of the 1890's, and indeed much earlier. At the beginning of the century the objective of policy was to prevent financial crises, such as occurred in 1893 and 1907. After the violent monetary disturbances of 1915-1921 interest shifted to the stabilization of the price level in the hope that if price gyrations could be avoided, the economy would move forward without any serious setback. When mass unemployment developed during the 1930's, the goal of a stable dollar was abandoned, and the objective of policy became full employment. Once unemployment was wiped out, price movements and industrial productivity became a serious concern. Emphasis subtly shifted from 'full employment' to 'a high and stable level of employment' or to 'economic growth and stability.' Recently, the primary goal of government policy has been maximum production rather than employment, and so it will undoubtedly continue to be for some time. But if the price inflation of recent years extends into the next decade, the clock of policy may eventually turn back to the 1920's, when the primary emphasis was on a dollar of stable purchasing power.

[6] See Robert Warren, "Twenty-five Years of Monetary Controls," in *Economic Research and the Development of Economic Science and Public Policy* (National Bureau, 1946).

147

The shifting emphasis of our economic policies has, of course, reflected a continual effort to adjust to changing conditions and newly emerging problems. Underlying the effort there has been a growing understanding of the character and mechanism of economic fluctuations. Men seriously concerned with governmental policies have been feeling their way slowly towards a goal of balanced economic growth. The goal cannot be expressed in a simple formula because simple formulas have not conformed well to the abiding values of the American people or because they have brought new problems in the process of dealing with the old. But the goal would probably include at least the following objectives: a high and steady volume of employment relative to the size of the labor force, a high and steadily rising volume of production of goods that people wish to have, a high and steadily rising volume of imports on which the hopes of the outside world are pinned, a fairly stable level of consumer goods prices for people at every income level, and a minimal use of direct controls over prices and incomes. The conditions needed for realizing such a goal of 'balanced economic growth' are still obscure, and much experimentation may be needed before it is approximated. But the chances of success will be improved as the boundaries of objective knowledge of the interlocking processes of our economic system are extended. The National Bureau's studies of business cycles have been guided by this aim. They have already yielded results of practical value, but a vast amount of fundamental research on the pervasive problem of economic instability remains to be done.

In last year's report I presented some important facts on business cycles that have emerged from recent studies by Mitchell, Moore, Abramovitz, Hultgren, Saulnier, Ilse Mintz, and myself. I explained that our research on the typical characteristics of business cycles was sufficiently advanced to justify closer attention to the differences among the cyclical movements thrown up by history, and urged "investigation of the problem why some business declines remain mild while others reach catastrophic magnitude." Tentative plans for such an investigation have been drafted, and they are designed to handle expansions of varying degrees of intensity as well as contractions. From this matrix it would be desirable to single out two special studies for early attention. One would compare the patterns of economic change during war cycles with peacetime patterns—a comparison that might prove particularly helpful if the present phase of near-war economy stretched out, as it may, over a considerable number of years. The second study would analyze quantitatively the impact of inflation on incomes and prices, on the efficiency of production, and on the distribution of wealth. In the course of the Bureau's research on prices and business cycles, a great deal of information has been accumulated on inflationary episodes in our own and other countries. Considerable research would still be required to round out the empirical record on inflation and to analyze its ramified economic effects; but there are strong forces in our economy working towards secular inflation, and a thorough investigation of the subject might have a salutary influence on the course of events.

The problem of reestablishing confidence among the nations of the world is more important even than the problem of economic stability, but the two are not unrelated. The view is widely held by Europeans that the United States is responsible for major shifts in their economic fortunes; and for this reason, if for no other, it is important to gain better understanding of the impact of our international economic relations on us and the rest of the world. Fabricant and Ilse Mintz have begun work on important aspects of this problem, and several others of our staff are engaged in related undertakings. But we have as yet made so little progress on the international research previously projected that our immediate need is to expand the staff rather than initiate new researches.

V

The economic future of our country is now heavily clouded by political and military uncertainties. No one can tell what changes the future will bring in our daily lives or what course our economic organization will take. But in thinking of the National Bureau's research over the coming years, it is reasonable to assume that whatever happens to hearth or kin our political democracy will remain intact, that a considerable measure of economic freedom will continue to be a part of our cultural scheme, and that our national enterprise of production and distribution will continue to be a partnership in which workers, consumers, business firms, and other groups participate with the government. As long as these conditions prevail there will be a need for research on the behavior patterns of the labor market, industrial productivity, prices and incomes, capital formation, consumer spending, the machinery of credit, the finances of government—in short, for scientific study of the enduring features of economic life such as have engaged the Bureau's efforts during its entire history, and that my sketch of the future seeks to extend.

Research on basic problems makes heavy demands on an investigator's time and patience, and the usefulness of its results is not always obvious. But in the long run nothing is more practical than fundamental research. When the Bureau undertook its investigation of corporate bond experience, no one could know that results would be forthcoming to influence legislation on insurance companies, personal trusts, and savings banks. Nor did anyone know at the time our project on urban real estate finance was launched that years later the Federal Reserve authorities would need to regulate real estate credit and that our findings would be helpful in drafting the regulations. A large part of the information currently compiled by governmental agencies on the subjects of national income, money flows, capital formation, physical production, and consumer credit has grown out of or been materially influenced by the Bureau's research; but no one could know that in advance. Our studies of the national income, which were designed to promote the arts of peace, turned out to be extremely helpful also in conducting the recent war. The studies by Fabricant, Long, Kendrick, Kuznets, and others, to which I have referred in the course of this report, were started years ago and yet are capable of illuminating our most recent experiences. In planning the National Bureau's research we therefore need not be disheartened by our inability to tell what the world will be like several years hence. As long as we work on fundamental problems in the scientific spirit to which we are accustomed, we may be confident that our researches will prove of practical value to mankind.

Much of today's thinking runs of necessity along military lines. But the struggle between the Western democracies and communism is basically ideological, and we must not allow its military aspect to obscure this fact. It is a grave error to regard communism solely as a conspiracy of an unscrupulous clique to attain mastery of the world. Such a clique exists but its power derives from its ability to harness the idealistic impulses of man. To strive for peace in the world, for justice in distributing incomes, for higher living standards, for security of job and home, for protection against the ravages of disease and old age—these are natural expressions of present-day culture. Communism has made headway by promising the millennium to an anxious and partly hungry world, while exploiting our every shortcoming and diverting attention from our constructive achievements. Over a large part of the earth informed economic communication has broken down, and one of the most vital needs of our time is to find the means of reconstituting it. But fundamental economic research must also be pushed with vigor, so that our children may be better equipped with the knowledge needed to solve economic and political problems than were their fathers and teachers.

I am deeply indebted to Geoffrey H. Moore for his advice and assistance in the preparation of this report.

The Instability of Consumer Spending

I

The consumer, rarely a heroic figure in economic affairs, scored a modest but noteworthy success in the struggle against inflation during the past year. He had numerous allies—an array of price and wage controls, credit restrictions, regulations concerning the use of raw materials, and a battery of stiff taxes. Yet the consumer's role seems to have transcended all the others. He played his part without fuss or fanfare, as is his wont. A year earlier, after the outbreak of hostilities in Korea, he went on a spending spree in the expectation that shortages of civilian goods, such as had marked the recent war, would soon develop. Businessmen, acting on a similar impulse, rushed to stock up on raw materials and stepped up their production schedules. The general upsurge of spending was reflected in a rise of 17 per cent in wholesale prices and 8 per cent in consumer prices between June 1950 and February 1951. Since military orders in the meantime were only beginning their upward climb, manufacturers soon were able to add profusely to the flow of goods to consumer markets. The supply of civilian merchandise expanded along with the demand; indeed, in some lines of activity—such as textiles, television, and radio—inventories piled up and prices had to be slashed to move them. These developments led consumers to revise their outlook. Spending fell off perceptibly after the first quarter despite the steady rise in personal incomes throughout 1951; by the end of the year savings reached their highest level since the end of World War II.

Largely as a result of the lull in consumer buying, the past year was characterized by a degree of over-all stability that few economists had anticipated. The physical volume of production and employment remained substantially steady through the year. Commodity markets were also fairly stable on the average, with wholesale prices declining 2.5 per cent and consumer prices rising 2.8 per cent between the first and last quarters. Meanwhile, the nation pushed ahead towards the goal of high military preparedness. Between the first and last quarters the annual rate of expenditures on national security increased from $29 billion to $44 billion—an increase that equaled the entire increment in the gross national product and lifted security expenditures from 9.0 to 13.2 per cent

Reprinted from *Thirty-second Annual Report of the National Bureau of Economic Research* (May 1952), pp. 3-20.

of the gross national product. This fairly sharp twist of our economy from civilian to military ends was attained without serious imbalance in the federal budget as well as without any important change in the general level of commodity prices.

Whether last year's remarkable economic achievement will be repeated in the present year is problematical. The renewed increase in the money supply during the second half of 1951, the higher military spending scheduled for this year, the fresh resort to deficit financing—all suggest a revival of inflationary pressure. But there are as yet no clear indications whether consumers will extend their new taste for frugality into the months ahead or go on another spending spree. The consumer has emerged as a complex economic personality; to be sure, not quite so gifted with temperament as the investor or the entrepreneur, but perhaps not much less capable than these gentry of stirring up economic uncertainty.

II

Until very recent years the subject of consumption held a distinctly subordinate place in the main body of economic theory. Even Alfred Marshall, who felt a serious need for the study of consumption, put primary emphasis on "the science of efforts and activities" rather than "the science of wants." The problem of consumer demand seemed to him to offer few major difficulties in a search for the "common kernel" in practical problems of value. Given the "familiar and fundamental tendency of human nature" to derive diminishing increments of satisfaction from successive units of a commodity, and a few assumptions of a more technical character, Marshall was able to establish a "universal rule" of demand: namely, that the lower the price of a commodity, the larger will be the amount that the public seeks to purchase. Marshall knew, of course, that the lumpy character of many consumer expenditures, people's imperfect perception of wants and of the want-satisfying power of commodities, their shifting expectations concerning prices, and sheer impulse were factors to be reckoned with in the actual world, just as he knew that changes in the size of the national income or in the value of money or in consumer tastes could obscure the effects of the "general law of demand."[1] But Marshall did not dwell on these difficulties. A dollar of changing purchasing power fell outside the scope of his *Principles*; and while he

[1] Alfred Marshall, *Principles of Economics* (Macmillan), 1st edn., p. 383; 8th edn., pp. 90, 93, 99.

made many profound observations on the nature of economic development, he concerned himself only in passing with income fluctuations.

By and large, Marshall's theory dominated economic thinking on the subject of demand until the course of events in the early thirties forced concern with a wider range of problems. This scientific development was long overdue. It would probably have occurred even without a special stimulus from practical life, once the results of empirical research on the Marshallian demand function became familiar outside a circle of specialists. But life itself, in the shape of the Great Depression, provided a far clearer and more forceful demonstration of the need to release income and other variables from the pound of *ceteris paribus* than any calculation by technicians. As the depression deepened, it became plain to everyone that the dwindling markets for consumer goods were caused, at least proximately, by the collapse in personal incomes. Declines of output and prices were general, and even the goods whose prices declined with special rapidity did not seem exempt from the shrinkage of demand. True, the decline in the relative price of a commodity might stimulate larger purchases, but this influence was usually swamped by the opposing effect of declining income. The drop in aggregate expenditure stood out as a more important matter than shifts in demand for individual articles. An increasing number of economists began to see that however expertly neoclassical theory may have dealt with the role of prices, it had neglected the influence of income on specific demands and, worse still, it seemed to have little to contribute to the explanation of variations in aggregate consumer spending beyond a few hesitant reflections on the effects of the interest rate.

The time was ripe for a major shift in economic theory. Students of crises and depressions, who for a century or longer had practiced income analysis in an effort to make sense of the fluctuations experienced by modern nations, were at last making their influence felt. Other forces were also bending economics towards an increased emphasis on income changes and income differences. Statistical explorations of family expenditures and income, on the lines initiated by Ernst Engel during the 1850's, took on a new significance under the shadow of mass unemployment. Research on empirical demand functions, which actively got under way soon after the publication of Henry L. Moore's *Economic Cycles* in 1914, was receiving serious attention. The income investigations of the National Bureau, which in the early thirties were already beginning to branch out into studies of consumer spending and capital formation, were causing a stir in the economic and statistical world. The subtle reformulation of the Marshallian theory of demand by Hicks and Allen was widely discussed. This extensive literature offered a growing challenge to the older economics; but the most important single factor in shifting the emphasis of economic theory from prices to incomes was Keynes' *General Theory*—a highly original work that met the needs of the despondent and anxious thirties for a theory that was at once simple and reassuring, clothed with the symbols of science, and yet equipped with a political handle for economic reform.

A nation's income, Keynes reasoned in *The General Theory*, consisted of two great classes of expenditure, first on consumer goods, second on investment goods. Next he argued that aggregate consumer spending depended mainly on the amount of aggregate income, while investment expenditures were not tied down by any category of receipts and depended mainly on the state of business sentiment. Finally, he showed that if the variations in consumer spending at a *given* level of income are provisionally neglected, several conclusions of great importance immediately follow. First, consumer spending can respond to changes of income but cannot initiate them. Second, national income—or its correlative, the volume of employment—cannot increase unless investment increases nor decrease unless investment decreases. Third, since investment depends on business confidence, which is notoriously unstable, our economic system is liable to wide fluctuations. Fourth, since "far-reaching change in the psychology of investment markets" cannot be expected, "the duty of ordering the current volume of investment cannot safely be left in private hands."[2]

To fortify the argument, Keynes enunciated a psychological law and an income formula. There is a "fundamental psychological law," he declared, that "men are disposed, as a rule and on the average, to increase their consumption as their income increases, but not by as much as the increase in their income."[3] Suppose, in keeping with this 'law,' that nine-tenths of every addition to the income of a period is spent on consumer goods and the remainder saved. If the volume of investment were now to rise by one dollar, consumer spending in the current period would have to increase by nine dollars and national income by ten dollars. This was the

[2] J. M. Keynes, *The General Theory of Employment, Interest and Money* (Harcourt Brace, 1936), p. 320.
[3] *ibid.*, p. 96.

formula. Keynes realized, of course, that it could be no more than an approximation. In the first place, it takes time for consumer spending to adjust to a new level of income, and the early effects of an increased volume of investment may therefore be very different from the late or ultimate effects. In the second place, quite apart from the adjustments attendant upon the passage of time, consumer spending is not governed exclusively by the amount of income. To clarify this feature of consumer behavior, Keynes analyzed the influence of other objective factors that seemed to him capable of modifying the amount of 'real' spending at a given level of 'real' income—that is, the distribution of incomes, windfall changes in the value of assets, the rate of interest, changes in fiscal policy, and expectations concerning future incomes. Keynes did not, however, attach great importance to these factors, and he practically dismissed one of them—namely, consumer expectations. To get on with his argument, he lumped them in *ceteris paribus*. He did not stop often enough to remind the reader, or for that matter himself, of the restrictive assumptions on which his analysis proceeded.

Many of the economists who were attracted by the brilliant argument of *The General Theory* gave less attention than Keynes to the factors complicating the consumption-income relation. Not a few practically overlooked them. Whereas Keynes had merely concluded that the propensity to consume was a "fairly stable function" of income, others soon began to speak of it as a "highly stable" function or simply as a "stable" function. Even those who stopped to consider what factors, beside income, may influence the amount of aggregate spending rarely inquired about the role of changes in relative prices or in expectations concerning the value of money. A new economics arose, which devoted itself preponderantly to aggregate income analysis, neglecting variations in prices, just as the older economics had devoted itself preponderantly to individual price analysis, neglecting variations in national income. To the older generation the important problems of economics revolved around phenomena of price as they affected entrepreneurs, investors, landowners, wage earners, and consumers. To the new generation of economists the important problems revolved around the deficiency in aggregate spending such as characterized the thirties; they therefore concerned themselves chiefly with two classes—consumers and investors. To the older economists, all species of economic man were more or less efficient calculators of utility or gain. To the new economists, consumers were creatures of habit whose collective propensity to spend or save could be counted on with assurance; while investors were a dynamic group whose expenditure, no matter how well cloaked in formal calculations, was at bottom swayed by emotionally tinged estimates of a precarious future.

This psychological distinction between investors and consumers opened up a new vista before economics. For if it was approximately true that consumer spending is linked passively to income, economics was at last on the threshold of becoming an engineering science. In the years immediately following the publication of Keynes' *General Theory*, it came to be widely believed that once the desired level of income was specified, the economist would be able to estimate with tolerable reliability what amount of investment—or of some practical equivalent—would bring that income into being. But if the economist was to perform this engineering function, he needed dependable empirical estimates of the relation between aggregate consumer spending and aggregate income. For this purpose statistics had to be used. A fair number of economists therefore turned eagerly to empirical research and began mining two bodies of new information that become available during the thirties—Simon Kuznets' historical estimates of consumer spending, investment, and national income, which were later extended and developed by the Department of Commerce, and the budgetary data for thousands of families brought out by the National Resources Committee.

As these and other statistics were worked over, the results at first looked very promising. Not only did the correlation between aggregate consumer spending and income turn out to be remarkably high, but some investigators found that the correlation could be improved by adding other factors—such as the degree of income inequality, the size of population, the rate of change in total income, or time itself—to the list of independent variables. However, as the statistical experiments piled up, the disturbing fact emerged that rather minor shifts in the period covered by the correlation were capable of modifying appreciably the estimated parameters of the consumption function. The same thing happened when one reputable series on income or consumer spending was substituted for another. Further analysis suggested that what economic policy required was not so much an estimate of the consumption function as an estimate of its complement—that is, the savings function. "The most important single economic fact about the community," declared Beveridge, is "the amount which the individuals of a community will try to save under conditions of full employment, with a given distribution of income."[4] But if this was the critical fact, then the high correlation between aggregate consumer spending and income had slight significance. Clearly, since consumer spending was on the average about nine or ten times as large as saving, a small percentage error in the spending estimate could mean a large error in the saving estimate. Indeed, independent calculation showed that the correlation between saving and income was by no means so high as between spending and income, and that "the most important single economic fact about the community" was therefore a somewhat elusive magnitude. When the forecasts even of what consumer spending would be after V-J Day were found to be in error by an uncomfortable margin, faith in a stable consumption function was severely shaken.

Many believed, however, that consumer spending would emerge as a fairly stable function of income, once the shortages accumulated during the war were made good. Reflecting this view, the President's Economic Report to the Congress in January 1947 stated that "if consumer incomes should remain at current levels, we would expect savings to drop little, if any." The report also expressed doubt "whether the rate of consumer savings will or even can be reduced much further except by adversity." As it turned out, the rate of savings was reduced much further during 1947—and not by adversity, but by prosperity. More recent events, especially since June 1950, are familiar and have led to a sharp reversal in economic thinking. The President's latest Economic Report declares that "consumer spending is the most uncertain factor determining the general inflationary outlook for 1952."[5] A few years ago a statement of this character would have invited ridicule. Today it hardly causes a ripple. Few, if any, economists are any longer disposed to question the capacity of consumers to change their rates of spending and saving without prior notice. Indeed, there is some danger that the whimsical character of consumer spending will now be as roundly exaggerated as was its mathematical determinacy only a short time back.

III

The ups and downs in recent economic thinking about the consumption-income relation require appraisal. It is salutary for prac-

---

[4] William H. Beveridge, *Full Employment in a Free Society* (Norton, 1945), p. 96.
[5] *The Economic Report of the President*, January 8, 1947, p. 13; January 16, 1952, p. 20.

ticing economists to fight each year's battle; but it is not less important to try to see such activities as a historian might see them. The recent controversies and reversals of opinion about the consumption function are not likely to stir deeply a later generation. What future economists will look for are the cumulative trends, of which controversies such as this are merely a surface expression, and that is what we ourselves should try to see.

One of the trends that has been gathering force in economics, and never more rapidly than in our generation, is an interest in a widening range of problems connected with the activities of consumers. The speculations of Cournot on the elasticity of demand, which were ignored by his own generation, have been turned to practical account by businessmen and governmental agencies in ours. Budgetary studies, which several decades back were of interest chiefly to social workers, have become instruments for analyzing how the economy at large functions. Fluctuations in aggregate spending, which not so long ago many viewed as an obsession of the crank, now occupy the time and thought of reputable economists, businessmen, and even heads of governments. Perhaps no other general subject receives as much attention nowadays as the spending of different consumer groups on specific goods and in the aggregate, the shift in these patterns through time, the movement of total spending and saving, and the degree of adequacy of current living standards in our own country and other parts of the world. Vast changes in the political and economic environment, as well as many intellectual currents, have converged to produce this emphasis on mass consumption and well-being. Keynes' aggregate consumption function is a symbol of our era, just as Marshall's individual demand function symbolized an earlier time.

Another major trend which has been gaining strength is a tendency towards closer fusion between speculative theorizing and empirical testing. Already in 1838 Cournot, having expressed with theoretical precision the relation between the demand for a commodity and its price, went on to plead for the statistical calculation of demand elasticities, or at least the empirical classification of "articles of high economic importance" according as their elasticity at ruling prices was above or below unity.[6] His plea went unheeded. In 1890 Marshall went beyond Cournot, and actually sketched the basic design that would need to be followed in testing and applying his demand theory. But while Marshall's work

6 Augustin Cournot, *Mathematical Principles of the Theory of Wealth*, tr. Bacon (Macmillan), p. 54.

aroused considerable literary controversy the world over, his ideas on statistical procedure remained fruitless until Henry L. Moore took them up in the first of his books on business cycles in 1914. Thus, depending on whether we look back to Marshall or Cournot, one-quarter or three-quarters of a century elapsed between the formulation of an economic theory and its first significant statistical test.[7] There was, however, no such hiatus in the case of the Keynesian theory. The world which it entered was already accustomed in some degree to require of an economic theory that it pass the test of applicability to experience. Almost as soon as *The General Theory* was published, the question was raised whether its novel notions concerning consumer demand were valid; and while this question was more often discussed on a speculative than on a factual plane, within a year or two statistical measurements and tests of the aggregate consumption function began to appear in economic journals. The process of scientific checking and sifting is still going on. A *Technical Paper* by Robert Ferber, which I hope we may publish this year, will contribute to this essential task by examining the degree of success that has thus far attended the numerous efforts to establish the characteristics of the consumption function.

The promptness and persistence with which the Keynesian theory has been subjected to the testings of experience are not yet typical of economic inquiry generally. But the trend is definitely in the direction of an economics in which quantitative records and empirical tests play a significant part. Recognizing this need of modern times, the National Bureau has steadily sought to develop and clarify the economic facts that surround major social problems. Our very first investigation produced approximate measures of the size and distribution of the national income—a subject obviously of critical importance, yet one that at the time was still being handled on the basis of opinion and guesswork. Even while this study was in progress, Wesley Mitchell called the Board's attention to the need for investigating quantitatively the subject of savings versus current consumption. After several tentative efforts in this direction during the twenties, a fairly comprehensive investigation was started in January 1933, under Simon Kuznets' direction. Within a year or two his researches yielded annual estimates of the flow of services and commodities to consumers, beside estimates of investment, back to 1919. Later Harold Barger con-

---

[7] See Henry Schultz, *The Theory and Measurement of Demand* (University of Chicago Press, 1938), pp. 63-65.

verted the annual figures into quarterly form; Shaw and Kuznets carried the statistical record back to around 1870; Duncan Holthausen, collaborating with Rolf Nugent and Malcolm Merriam, prepared monthly estimates of consumer instalment credit; and David Wickens improved existing measures of the aggregate cost of new dwellings—a consumer good that statisticians usually prefer to treat as part of investment. More recently, in connection with a comprehensive accounting of the flow of money through the economy, Morris Copeland has developed annual estimates of money flows and year-end estimates of cash and related assets for households. Each of these statistical efforts[8] has met a widely felt need. Each has been taken over, extended, and improved by one or another agency of the federal government. Governmental agencies in turn have initiated many new statistical enterprises in this general area, one of the most interesting being the annual survey of consumer finances conducted jointly by the Federal Reserve Board and the Survey Research Center at Michigan.

I have already referred to the eagerness with which economists turned to the new statistical materials in an attempt to test, apply, or extend Keynes' theory. That some of the statistical research was done with excessive haste is a trivial matter at this distance. The vital fact, from a historical viewpoint, is that economics has reached a stage where theoretical propositions are often taken so seriously that they are not permitted to become an object of purely dialectical concern and development. The great power and promise of empirical economics lie not in its voluminous records or formal methods of handling hypotheses, but in the attitude of mind fostered by its practice—an attitude of mind that is sensitive and receptive to the teachings of experience. It is this attitude of mind, more than anything else, that has blurred the line that not so long ago separated the 'old' and 'new' economists, that has brought to light the strength and weakness of the Keynesian theory of consumer demand, and that has driven an increasing

[8] See the following: Simon Kuznets, "Gross Capital Formation, 1919-1933," *Bulletin 52* (1934); *National Income and Capital Formation, 1919-1935* (1937); *Commodity Flow and Capital Formation* (1938); *National Product since 1869* (1946). William H. Shaw, "Finished Commodities since 1879, Output and Its Composition," *Occasional Paper 3* (1941); *Value of Commodity Output since 1869* (1947). Harold Barger, *Outlay and Income in the United States, 1921-1938* (1942). David L. Wickens and Ray R. Foster, "Non-Farm Residential Construction, 1920-1936," *Bulletin 65* (1937); D. L. Wickens, *Residential Real Estate* (1941). Duncan McC. Holthausen, Malcolm L. Merriam, and Rolf Nugent, *The Volume of Consumer Instalment Credit, 1929-38* (1940). Morris Copeland, *A Study of Moneyflows in the United States* (1952). All of these titles are publications of the National Bureau.

number of investigators to probe intensively beneath the surface of economic aggregates when searching for the causes of their movements.

A generation or two ago the properties of abstract utility schedules were a favorite topic of discussion among economists interested in the subject of consumer demand. Interest later shifted to the properties of indifference curves, and later still to the properties of a supposedly stable schedule linking aggregate consumption and aggregate income. These subjects have not been outmoded by time; but nowadays economists address their theoretical questions more frequently to records of experience and less frequently to one another. The subject of primary interest concerning consumer demand has become the consumer himself—that is, his actual behavior and the kind and degree of regularity that characterize it. How, in what directions, and in what degree is the current spending of individual families influenced by the size of the family, the age of its members, their occupation, their place of residence, their income, any recent shift in their income, their highest past income, the amount of their liquid assets, their stock of durables and semidurables, recent changes in their buying, their highest past spending, their expectations concerning future incomes and prices, the amount and kind of their neighbors' buying, and by still other factors? How, in what directions, and in what degree is the consumer spending of a nation influenced by, among other things, the distribution of individual incomes, the amount of capital gains or losses, changes in the general level of prices, the dispersion of individual price movements, the terms on which consumer credit is extended, the introduction of new commodities, advertising expenditures, the rate of formation of new families, the geographic mobility of the population? These are some of the questions now being put by economists;[9] and while none have as yet been answered with precision and some have hardly been answered at all, the rough foundations of an empirical science of consumption are slowly beginning to take shape.

IV

The National Bureau has participated in this adventure by making analytical investigations, beside developing basic factual records such as I previously mentioned. In a study now approaching

[9] For a survey of recent empirical research see the paper by Ruth Mack, "The Economics of Consumption," in Volume II of *A Survey of Contemporary Economics*, ed. Bernard F. Haley (Irwin, 1952).

completion Thomas Atkinson has explored the amounts of financial assets held by individuals, with an eye to the factors that underlie the distribution of different categories of wealth among them. Another study in its closing stages, and which bears more directly on the inchoate science of consumption, is Lawrence Klein's investigation of family spending and saving,[10] based on the individual returns obtained by the Survey Research Center in recent sample surveys. These returns contain unusually extensive and varied information about each of the spending units interviewed and permit fuller empirical analysis of the forces that shape consumer saving than has hitherto been possible.

Klein has made good use of the opportunity. His basic and most suggestive finding is that family spending and saving depend upon many factors, not upon one or a few variables.[11] In contrast to the magnificent coefficients of correlation between consumer spending and national income over time, which abound in statistical literature, very humble correlations show up between the spending and income of individual families during any one year. This means, of course, that factors other than current income are much too important to be slighted. Klein finds, for example, that the greater the amount of liquid assets held, the smaller—other things equal— will savings tend to be, especially in low income groups. Again, homeowners tend to save more than occupants of rented premises; people expecting favorable economic developments tend to save less than folk expecting unfavorable conditions; and so on. By his careful comparisons of different samples, Klein also shows that the direction of the specific influences he examines is more dependable than their numerical effect. To be sure, as he points out, much of the numerical instability would tend to vanish if the samples covered a larger number of spending units. This still means that uncomfortable margins of error may attend projections based upon the present samples. Furthermore, some of the variations from one year's equation to another's cannot be attributed to sampling fluctuations; they may be due to intrinsic flaws in the equation or to 'jumps' in behavior which defy any equation. The

---

[10] For some preliminary results see two papers by Lawrence R. Klein: "Assets, Debts, and Economic Behavior," in Volume XIV of *Studies in Income and Wealth* by Conference on Research in Income and Wealth (National Bureau, 1951); and "Estimating Patterns of Savings Behavior from Sample Survey Data," *Econometrica*, October 1951.

[11] This mathematically tested finding is an extension of earlier research by the Survey Research Center. See George Katona, *Psychological Analysis of Economic Behavior* (McGraw-Hill, 1951), chap. 8.

movements of consumer spending after the outbreak of the Korean War are an outstanding example of a 'jump.' Another instance is the behavior of consumer spending and borrowing at the end of World War II. As Kisselgoff's recently published study shows, a formula that summed up effectively the forces impinging on the volume of instalment sales credit before 1941 was quite unable to cope with the conditions that prevailed after the war.[12]

To improve our ability to distinguish between the stable and capricious elements of consumer behavior, it is highly important that studies such as Klein's be repeated for future samples and that careful consideration be given to the research needs disclosed by his investigation. The noncorporate part of the business world has always been a somewhat cloudy corner of the economy to the statistician. Unincorporated firms are usually small and do not practice meticulous bookkeeping. Moreover, producing and consuming activities are much less distinct in a family whose head operates a farm or a small business than in the run of households. It is not surprising, therefore, that Klein found that his calculations of spending and saving propensities are less reliable for farmers and independent businessmen than for other groups. To remedy this defect of existing knowledge, one or more specially designed sample inquiries would be necessary. Such inquiries would probably yield a maximum of instruction if students concerned with the producing and financing activities of small business worked side by side with others interested chiefly in household operations.

Another difficulty that Klein has encountered is the absence of adequate information on the stocks of goods possessed by households. Survey techniques, which have already yielded much more than seemed likely only a few years ago, may perhaps be developed before long to a point where chairs, lamps, and shirts held in varying stages of physical decrepitude and personal incertitude can be expressed in useful numbers. An alternative approach to consumer stocks that warrants study is through the medium of time series. If consumer purchases exceed the actual consumption of a period, stocks are being built up. If consumer purchases fall short of consumption, stocks are being drawn down. Such investment or disinvestment in inventories is always taking place in the nation's households, but we have not had a systematic or continuous record of it. An interesting method for attacking this problem has re-

12 "Factors Affecting the Demand for Consumer Instalment Credit," *Technical Paper 7* (National Bureau, 1952).

cently been worked out by Raymond Goldsmith in connection with the intensive study of savings that the Life Insurance Association of America has been making under his direction.[18] Apart from price adjustments, the procedure consists in applying depreciation rates to different categories of durables, subtracting the estimated depreciation during a period from the dollar value of new purchases so as to get the net addition to consumer stocks, and then cumulating the increments to derive a series of total stocks. Goldsmith has made annual calculations of this type for consumer durables back to the beginning of the century. With further research his procedures might be extended to semidurables and the entire plan of measurement put on a quarterly basis. Estimates such as this have obvious defects, but their practical importance must be gauged in the light of experience. If tolerably dependable statistics of consumer stocks can be devised, it seems likely that they will prove helpful in judging current developments as well as in historical and analytical investigations. An incidental but not unimportant advantage of such statistics might be that their mere existence would curb the fairly common but misleading tendency to identify consumer spending with consumption proper.

I cannot dwell further on the gains to be sought by developing new statistics or by refining and testing the statistics we already have or the concepts that underlie them. Fortunately, there is no need for special emphasis on these matters; they are now well understood and will doubtless continue to receive active expression. What does require emphasis is that even existing statistics can help us go further than we have in tracing the interrelations between the activities of consumption and production. The consumer research of the last ten or fifteen years has centered primarily on the facts and causes of variation in consumer spending and saving. The intricate effects of these variations on the over-all operations of the economy—particularly, on the production of consumer as well as investment goods industries—have received much less attention. This one-sided accent was natural as long as the belief was widespread that consumer spending was merely a passive response to national income, and that private investment and governmental

[18] R. W. Goldsmith, "A Perpetual Inventory of National Wealth," in Volume xiv of *Studies in Income and Wealth*, cited above. [Dr. Goldsmith's intensive work, *A Study of Saving in the United States*, will be published by Princeton University Press in 1954.] See also Lenore A. Epstein, "Consumers' Tangible Assets," in Volume xii of *Studies in Income and Wealth* (National Bureau, 1950), and Reavis Cox and Ralph F. Breyer, *Consumer Plant and Equipment* (Retail Credit Institute of America, Washington, 1944).

spending were therefore largely, if not entirely, instrumental in driving and shaping the level of income. Now that statistical research and the course of experience itself have made it clear that this simplification is unwarranted, there are signs of a renewed theoretical interest in the dynamic interconnections of consumption, production, and income distribution. But the theorists need aid and guidance from empirical research if their models are to cope seriously with the problem of how changes in consumer spending spread their influence over the economy.

How much there is to be learned about this problem is indicated by Ruth Mack's searching investigation of the causal links between shoe buying and earlier stages of production and distribution. She finds, for example, that about a year typically elapses between the first appearance of a hide at market and its later entry, in the shape of shoes, into a consumer's closet. This long interval leaves, however, no obvious imprint on retail sales of shoes relative to shoe production or still earlier stages of the industry—all of which exhibit nearly concurrent fluctuations. Again, the retailer does not merely transmit the changes in consumer purchases to the wholesaler or manufacturer; he magnifies them. Thus the amplitude of fluctuations is larger in wholesale sales than in sales at retail, also in shoe production than in sales at wholesale, and to some degree in leather production than in shoe production. Here the intensification of the cyclical movement stops; the production of leather is preceded by the movement of hides into commercial markets but this activity undergoes narrower fluctuations than the production of leather. Of course, the varying amplitude and similar timing at successive stages of the shoe-leather industry imply that the cycle in retail sales is accompanied by a corresponding cycle of investment in shoe and leather inventories and by an inverse cycle of investment in hide inventories. These movements of sales, production, and inventories—and I have singled out only a few—raise difficult questions. How does the cyclical synchronism in the different parts of the shoe-leather industry come about? Why are the fluctuations of retail sales, when passed on to earlier stages, at first magnified and later moderated? And why does this industry, beside participating in business cycles, trace out a shorter cycle of its own? To clarify these striking phenomena Dr. Mack has put principal stress on four factors: first, the rate of change in consumer buying; second, the degree of firmness in the inventory objectives of dealers and manufacturers; third, the adjustment of orders to the varying length of delivery periods over the course of a cycle; fourth, expectations concerning price movements. But the importance of these factors differs from one branch of the shoe-leather industry to another and, of necessity, from one industry to another.

Once the full report on this investigation, which is now being revised, has been completed, it would be well to consider what additional studies may be needed to advance realistic understanding of the vertical transmission of cyclical impulses. Some useful suggestions about this problem are made by Wesley Mitchell in his posthumous volume, *What Happens during Business Cycles.* A special aspect of the problem, namely, the effects of variations in instalment credit on economic activity at large, was treated by Gottfried Haberler in *Consumer Instalment Credit and Economic Fluctuations*—a volume that has exercised a significant influence on both business and governmental policies since its publication ten years ago.[14]

V

The relation between 'wants' and 'activities' is the basic theme of economics. Numerous theoretical systems have been constructed by assigning primacy to wants, and again by assigning primacy to activities. But in actual life there is only interdependence. The principal task of economic science is to analyze this interdependence and to extract the elements of regularity that underlie or characterize the influence of wants on activities and of activities on wants, especially under conditions of change. This task is proving harder than many thought likely in the early days of enthusiasm over the new doctrines of Keynes. But some progress has been made, and knowledge concerning the interrelations of consumption, production, and income distribution is cumulating.

In addition to the general research tasks that I have already mentioned, there is one that falls peculiarly within the range of the National Bureau's experience. We have devoted over the years considerable resources to the study of trends in national income, production, employment, the labor force, and business finance; and we are now making an elaborate study of trends in capital formation and the prospective requirements for capital. Would it not be desirable, once some of our present investigations taper off, to supplement these studies by equally systematic research on

[14] Both Haberler's and Mitchell's volumes were published by the National Bureau, the former in 1942, the latter in 1951.

consumption trends? Such research would help to clarify our present and earlier investigations, and it would help the research of others as well as our own. Indeed, nothing seems more likely to contribute to perspective and informed judgment on consumer problems than a comprehensive survey of trends in consumption, analyzed so as to bring out their relation to the general development of our economy since 1900 or, better still, since 1870.

The doctrine of secular stagnation, which stirred economic circles only a short time ago, owed some of its popularity to inadequate appreciation of the historical fact that the spending of the 'average' family at a given level of family income has shown a progressive tendency to increase across the decades. One of the main explicit pillars of the stagnationist theory was, of course, the absolute decline in the year-by-year increments of our population; but this decline ceased just about the time when the theory was first articulated. The last fifteen years have witnessed a great upsurge of population and the years since the close of World War II a tremendous boom in home construction. In 1890 owner-occupied dwellings constituted 36.9 per cent of all occupied dwelling units; this proportion stood at 41.1 in 1940 and climbed to 53.3 by 1950.[15] In 1900 the value of the structures and equipment of business firms about equaled that of the dwellings, carriages, and household durables of consumers. In 1948 the consumer plant and equipment exceeded the value of business plant and equipment by about 30 per cent.[16] Spending on durables, which was 11.9 per cent of total consumer expenditure in 1929 and 10.4 per cent in 1937, rose to 13.3 per cent in 1949 and 15.1 per cent in 1950.[17] Per capita food expenditure, exclusive of alcoholic beverages and adjusted for the rise in retail food prices, increased nearly 40 per cent between 1929 and 1948.[18] These and a thousand other statistics on consumer behavior require assembly, perhaps rectification, and certainly interpretation.

Vast changes have occurred in recent decades in technology, the distribution of population between urban and rural centers, the industrial status of women, the education of children and adults, the length of human life, the range of available commodities and services, the speed of communication, the income per capita, the

---

15 Ernest M. Fisher and Leo Grebler, "A Stocktaking of Housing in the United States," *Appraisal Journal*, July 1951, Table III.

16 R. W. Goldsmith, "A Perpetual Inventory of National Wealth," *op.cit.*, p. 18.

17 Estimates by the Department of Commerce.

18 "Consumption of Food in the United States, 1909-48," *Miscellaneous Publication No. 691* of the Department of Agriculture, p. 138; see also pp. 71-103.

distribution of incomes among the people, and the activities of government. How have these and related developments affected consumer spending patterns? To what extent, in particular, has the decline in the inequality of personal incomes since 1929 helped to create mass markets for a wide range of commodities? In what ways has the recent sharp increase in the marriage rate, in home ownership, and in the number of children affected the allocation of consumer income among different kinds of expenditure and between saving and spending? How, in turn, has the modern emphasis on possession of ever larger amounts of consumer goods reacted on the pecuniary ambitions of people, their willingness to work, and their attitude towards assuming the risks of innovation and enterprise? How has the trend of employment in the service industries[19] been affected by our changing consumption standards? How has the surprisingly high rate of food expenditure in recent years affected the fortunes of farmers and the long-run prospects of agriculture? With what speed, and with what effect on saving and other types of spending, have industrial prodigies like the electric refrigerator, the radio, and the television receiver been absorbed into the consumer economy? What part has the development of consumer instalment financing played in this process? How has the extension of life insurance, social security programs, and private pension plans affected consumer spending and saving? And what does the increasing proportion of consumer outlay on goods that need not be purchased continuously, either because they have a long life of service built into them or because they are of a luxury character, signify for the problem of maintaining economic stability in the future?

These questions are of practical as well as of scientific interest. Perhaps some of them are unanswerable, and perhaps all are only partly answerable. But it will be well to keep them in mind when we come to think more concretely about a survey of consumption trends. The past studies of the National Bureau have helped to illuminate a few corners of the vast terrain of economic life. With careful planning and the help of investigators in other institutions, it should lie within our power to illuminate a few additional corners.

---

[19] This subject has already been partly elucidated by George Stigler and he is investigating it further. See his "Domestic Servants in the United States, 1900-1940," *Occasional Paper 24* (National Bureau, 1946), and "Employment and Compensation in Education," *Occasional Paper 33* (National Bureau, 1950).

I am deeply indebted to Geoffrey H. Moore for his advice and assistance in the preparation of this report.

Business Cycle Research and the Needs of Our Times

The gift of prophecy has never loomed large in the endowment of economists, whether lay or professional. A generation ago, however, the professional analyst of business conditions at least had the advantage of being able to organize his thinking around such venerable concepts as a self-generating cycle and a regularly rising secular trend. If the advantage proved ephemeral, it nevertheless kept uncertainty under decent restraint while it lasted. Looking back across the years between the Civil War and the first World War, one could see a fairly regular fluctuation in business activity emerging. Except for the lapse in 1895, each peak of an expanding wave towered above its immediate predecessor. The shortest of the nine cycles before 1914 lasted thirty-five months and the longest only forty-six months. The amplitudes of successive cycles were less uniform but severe depressions were infrequent. Through the international gold standard our economy was linked closely to the rest of the world. Every recovery and recession in Western Europe had its counterpart in American experience, although we managed to generate some special cycles of our own. The most spectacular fluctuations occurred commonly in our financial markets and activities preparatory to investment expenditure; and since these seemed to have a critical bearing on developments in the industrial sphere, the movements of stock prices, interest rates, business failures, and investment orders attracted wide attention.

The outbreak of war in 1914 brought new and difficult economic problems. It was generally expected, however, that upon the return of peace the dislocations wrought by war would quickly vanish and the world economy revert to its prewar pattern of growth and fluctuation. This expectation was scarcely fulfilled outside the United States. A wild inflation, which enabled Germany to escape the world-wide depression of 1920-1921, brought disaster in late 1923. Inflation stopped short of complete riot in France but lasted longer and likewise served to insulate its economy. England followed a path of financial orthodoxy, but could not reduce unemployment to the prewar level and faced the ordeal of a gen-

Reprinted from *Thirty-third Annual Report of the National Bureau of Economic Research* (May 1953), pp. 3-16.

eral strike in 1926. Russia, having fallen towards the close of the war under communist control, lost little time in organizing for a test of strength with the outside world. Of the great powers the United States alone enjoyed a return to "normalcy." While the depression of 1920-1921 was severe, it passed quickly and was widely accepted as a salutary check of speculative exuberance. The prosperity that followed grew marvelously except for a pause in 1923-1924 and another in 1926-1927. Business confidence ran high despite the monetary, industrial, and political disorganization in other parts of the world. No special controls beyond those residing in the Federal Reserve System seemed necessary to keep the business cycle in check. And for a brief while, as one foreign nation after another limped back to the gold standard under the umbrella of our easy money policy, the prewar world seemed restored.

As we look back to the 1920's, three facts about the business cycle stand out. The first is that it was natural to frame expectations about the business future on the assumptions of international peace and of normal business relations among nations. Second, it was natural to think of the government as playing a minor role in business fluctuations. Third, it was natural to think of business depressions as passing interruptions of progress. This concept of normal business in a peaceful and progressive world, which ruled our economic thinking in the twenties, was severely tested by stubborn depression in the thirties, and then nearly shattered by war and its sequelae in the forties. The old order did not change at once, but it changed swiftly. International disunity erupted first in currency and trade wars, later in ideological and military warfare. And prolonged depression, a second world war, and the growing menace of communism brought to the American people a vast network of controls, high taxes, still higher expenditures, but also a new conception of public responsibility for coping with booms and depressions.

II

The presidential campaign of 1952 gave clear testimony of how profoundly the economic and political storms of recent years have changed our intellectual outlook. The Republican party was not less emphatic than the Democratic party in urging the importance of governmental action to foster a stable economy. In the course of one of his addresses, Mr. Eisenhower declared that "never again shall we allow a depression in the United States." He went on to say that if signs appear "of any . . . depression that would put . . .

men and women out of work, the full power of private industry, of municipal government, of state government, of the federal government will be mobilized to see that that does not happen." This declaration of governmental responsibility goes well beyond the Employment Act of 1946. It caps a long line of social thinking that first had as its objective the cushioning of depression, next pump-priming expenditure, then compensatory fiscal policy, and, finally, comprehensive contracyclical action.

The traditional attitude of letting business depressions 'blow themselves out' had already been repudiated by the Hoover administration. Its experiments with contracyclical devices were not sufficient, however, to check the rising tide of unemployment. The Roosevelt administration moved with greater vigor and attempted both to engineer recovery and to reconstruct economic society. New measures designed to increase the money supply, raise the price level, reform the banking system and security markets, relieve the distress of farmers and unemployed workers, aid local governments, protect homeowners, strengthen trade unions, stimulate construction work, and reduce the inequality of personal incomes followed one another in quick succession. On the whole, consumer spending responded much better to the governmental measures than private investment. Unemployment was reduced but not eliminated. In 1937-1938 economic activity suffered a sharp setback and 8 million were still unemployed in 1940.

Since then the course of international events has dominated the economic scene. Military demands for men, materials, machines, and munitions started to climb after the collapse of France and became insatiable after the attack on Pearl Harbor. Taxes increased sharply, yet expenditures outran taxes and a huge federal deficit accumulated. At the same time, personal incomes mounted, unemployment disappeared, civilian consumption increased, liquid assets piled up, and curbs on inflation replaced recovery stimulants. The war experience raised the hope not only of intellectuals but of common folk everywhere that depressions could be prevented in the future by vigorous governmental policy. Before long official pronouncements of individual governments, including our own, and the Charter of the United Nations gave eloquent expression to this hope.

With the approach of victory men's minds turned again to the tasks of peace. In 1944 federal outlays on goods and services were over 40 per cent of the gross national product, and of course interest and transfer payments carried dollar expenditures far beyond the volume of purchases. Under the circumstances there was, quite naturally, considerable uncertainty whether demobilization and abrupt cuts in war production could be carried through without bringing back mass unemployment. The fears proved unfounded. The civilian economy, starved for self-expression through the war and more handsomely equipped with cash than ever before, manifested a power with which not many economists were then inclined to credit it—a power to generate activity on as lavish a scale as had the military a few years earlier. Between the first quarters of 1945 and 1946, federal purchases fell from an annual rate of $91 billion to a rate of $26 billion. But buying by the rest of the community, principally households and domestic business firms, increased sufficiently to replace two-thirds of the decline. By the first quarter of 1947 federal purchases were down to an annual rate of $16 billion, a drop of $75 billion from their peak rate. In the meantime, the gross national product had risen slightly, so that the rest of the economy fully compensated for the unprecedented reduction in governmental spending. Of course, commodity prices rose sharply after price controls were dropped and the rise continued well into 1948. At the same time the physical volume of activity also increased and all major branches of the economy— including federal purchases, which were already being lifted by Marshall Plan aid—continued to expand until the closing quarter of 1948.

The recession which began in the fall of that year was of slight consequence. Consumer expenditures continued to expand, as did housing construction, automobile production, and many other activities. In all, the gross national product declined merely 4 per cent, and this reflected principally a drop of inventory investment. By the last quarter of 1949 aggregate activity was again moving upward. Recovery was rapid and proceeded without special aid from the public purse, except for the veterans' insurance dividend, until the fateful month of June 1950, when the communists struck with guns in Korea. The noble illusion of peace in our time was now ended. Once again the government projected a heavy phase of military spending, higher taxes, and ramifying controls. Meanwhile, consumers and businessmen alike, fearing that shortages of civilian goods would soon develop, rushed to stock up on all sorts of things. For a few months prices rose at an alarming pace; but production also expanded rapidly and by early 1951 it became evident that merchandise was generally in good supply and that the anticipated shortages had failed to materialize. Presently, consumers revised their expectations and stopped adding frantically to their accumulated stocks. Manufacturers and dealers in consumer goods responded in similar fashion, and a sizable decline of output in the consumer goods industries followed. This quiescence of the civilian sector proved very timely and neutralized the inflationary pressure of military spending. Federal outlays on goods and services, which were at an annual rate of $31 billion in the first quarter of 1951, rose to $55 billion eighteen months later; but the aggregate physical volume of production increased only slightly and the level of wholesale prices declined somewhat. Of late, consumer spending has increased perceptibly, although personal savings have continued at an exceptionally high level.

Taken as a whole, the quarter century since 1929, some of whose features I have so hastily sketched, provides the sharpest contrasts of business conditions in our history—contraction running from the mildest to the most violent of which we have any knowledge, expansion ranging from hesitant recovery to a long and vigorous boom. The tendency towards regularity in cyclical fluctuations, which seemed so clear a generation earlier, became fuzzy. Social control of business cycles emerged as a political necessity, both domestically and internationally. Extensive experiments in contracyclical action were undertaken, of which a persistent tendency towards easy money and a persistent difficulty in attaining budgetary balance became the principal outward symbols. Foreign developments at times aided, at others complicated, the efforts of government to promote a stable and prosperous economy. Over a considerable part of the period the rate of governmental spending, buffeted about as it was by international developments, itself became the principal active factor in the economic situation, rather than a response to variations of private spending. In some years the civilian economy compensated for the violent shifts in public spending, in others it aggravated their consequences. At all times, even when sales and profits were eminently satisfactory, uncertainty about the course of international relations or of governmental economic policy added a note of anxiety to business planning. On the other hand, the social legislation of the period, which aimed to afford some protection against the hazards of unemployment, old age, bank failures, and declining farm prices, brought a new sense of security to millions of Americans.

III

In closing his first book on *Business Cycles* in 1913, Wesley Mitchell ventured the prediction that, since cumulative changes in economic organization are likely to occur in the future as they have in the past, the economists of each generation "will see reason to recast the theory of business cycles which they learned in their youth." The course of events in the past quarter century has borne out his historical insight. Not only have recent fluctuations in aggregate activity become less regular in duration, but many of their internal features have been modified. For example, the tendency of interest rates to rise during expansions of aggregate activity has become decidedly weaker, the ability of wage rates to resist contractions has become stronger, the conformity of the velocity of bank deposits to over-all economic movements has become irregular, the lag of dividends at cyclical turns has become shorter, the tendency of private construction contracts to lead general recovery and recession has become less dependable. But cumulative movements of expansion and contraction have continued to diversify our economic fortunes, and many features of earlier business cycles have persisted although they have been obscured by the predominantly expansive pressures since 1938. The sequence of developments in 1948-1949, as Geoffrey Moore has shown, bore a striking resemblance to earlier cyclical declines; and the shrinkage of private spending during 1951, when public spending was rapidly expanding, is another warning that the present boom will not last forever.

The only things we can be reasonably certain of in the proximate future are, first, that our economic system will continue to generate cyclical tendencies, and second, that the government will at some stage intervene to check their course. The outcome of these opposing tendencies must needs be, at this time, a matter of judgment. It is reasonable to expect that contracyclical policy will moderate the amplitude and abbreviate the duration of business contractions in the future, so that our children will be spared the sort of economic collapse that blighted lives in the early thirties. The strengthening of the banking system, the development of unemployment compensation and general assistance programs, the large and automatic reduction of taxes that now takes place when the national income contracts, and above all the assurance that the government is not likely to permit deflation to proceed unchecked support this faith. But there are no adequate grounds, as yet, for believing that business cycles will soon disappear, or that the government will resist inflation with as much tenacity as depression, or that deep but brief contractions such as occurred in 1920-1921 and 1937-1938 will never again take place. Our limited experience with contracyclical policy does not provide strong support for the belief, so often expressed by theoretical writers, that the government is capable of adjusting its spending, taxing, and regulatory policies with the fine precision and promptness needed to assure virtually full employment and a virtually stable price level at all times. Not only is the art of contracyclical action as yet imperfectly understood, but there are practical obstacles to the effective use of such knowledge as exists. In a world in which international crises keep recurring, in which the domestic population clamors for relief from burdensome taxes, and in which different groups of the community are either deserving or persuasive enough to win the special solicitude of government, considerations of economic stability neither are nor can be the sole concern of public policy.

These obstacles to effective contracyclical action are likely to continue. It may be hoped, however, that as knowledge of business cycles is extended, contracyclical policy will improve and the burden of counteracting its own mistakes will become lighter. Interest in business cycles has never been so keen, nor the social and political importance of curbing their wandering so widely recognized, as at present. Perhaps, before many years pass, an economic general staff will emerge within the government and take on some of the characteristics of military general staffs. Just as the military often find it helpful to draft plans for resisting different potential aggressors, each or a combination of whom may strike at this point or at that, so an economic staff may in the future find it prudent to work concurrently on plans for meeting a great variety of economic troubles that we loosely call booms and depressions. And just as the military staff tends to concentrate on immediate danger points, but without neglecting the lessons of past campaigns and battles, so the economic staff may come to combine historical and theoretical research on business cycles with the devising of policies to meet emerging conditions. But though much may be accomplished by a general economic staff in the future, it is unlikely that it will ever be able to pursue far enough or deeply enough all the problems that come its way. In the future, as in the past, the scientific study of business cycles will therefore continue to be a primary responsibility of our great centers of learning—the universities and private research institutes like the National Bureau.

IV

The 'new economics,' of which less is heard nowadays than a few years back, found little need for the study of business cycles as an earlier generation knew it. Equipped with a 'consumption function' that was supposed to take full account of the influence of variations in the national income on consumer outlay, looking upon investment expenditure as an 'exogenous' variable that shaped the course of the nation's income, and braced by a crisp formula of compensatory fiscal policy, the new economists had sufficient thunder without bothering much about the cumulative processes of change and adjustment in a business economy. Their bold thinking stimulated much useful analysis and research, but experience has not dealt gently with their simplification of Keynes' teaching. Under the influence of war and inflation, a strong interest has of late reemerged in the mutual adjustment of costs and prices; in the influence of consumer spending, profits, construction costs, and terms of financing on business investment; in the influence of accumulated assets, borrowing, and changing expectations of consumers on their rate of spending; in the influence of investment on industrial productivity, on business competition, and commodity prices—in short, in the numerous and lagged responses that bind economic activities together into a system. Theoretical models of business cycles are once again exciting general attention and, while they may sometimes unwittingly caricature the economic process, their emphasis on cumulative movements, lags, and self-reversing tendencies is salutary.

Except for the minor setbacks in 1945 and 1948-1949, our economy has moved steadily forward since 1938. This is undoubtedly the longest sustained expansion of recent history, yet it is not the only movement of its kind. The period from 1921 to 1929 was also one of sustained expansion broken only by minor cyclical declines; so too were the periods from 1897 to 1907, 1885 to 1893, and 1867 to 1873—if not the entire span from 1858 to 1873. Each of these major expansions culminated in a speculative boom, each was followed by deep depression, and three of the depressions lasted years. One of the important tasks awaiting students of business cycles is thorough historical study of the booms that preceded these as well as other contractions. Studies of this type are worth making, not because of any immutabilities of historical sequence, but because there is a need to clarify the work of policy makers who, while earnestly resolved to do away with depressions, sometimes seem to neglect the need of controlling booms and trust too exclusively in our ability to check any contraction that may get under way.

Of the massive materials compiled by the National Bureau, we have thus far analyzed most carefully the record of the twenties. The extravagance of its boom in common stocks is notorious, but the speculation of the time was by no means confined to stocks. It extended to urban real estate, foreign government bonds, and many types of industrial enterprise. As the decade rolled on, borrowing piled up in all directions but the quality of new loans, as measured by their later ability to meet the test of hard times, declined progressively. Thus Ilse Mintz has found that 18 per cent of the dollar amount of foreign government loans placed in the United States during 1920-1924 defaulted during the thirties. The wave of defaults caught a much larger proportion of later issues: 50 per cent of the bonds acquired from 1925 to 1929 and 63 per cent of those acquired in 1928. Saulnier's study of urban mortgage loans by life insurance companies, the study of mortgage loans of commercial banks made by Behrens, and Hickman's recent study of domestic corporate bonds likewise indicate a progressive relaxation of credit standards. Hickman finds, for example, that 17 per cent of the par amount of railroad bonds offered during 1920-1924, but fully 53 per cent of the amount offered over the next quinquennium, went into default by 1944. The defaults ran lower in the case of public utility and industrial bonds, yet each of these groups also showed a trend towards deterioration. The net result was that the bonds offered in the early twenties eventually yielded something more to investors than they had been promised, while the offerings of the late twenties—especially those issued at the very height of the boom—brought the average investor far less than the promised yield.

Hickman has also gathered some empirical evidence on the business psychology of the twenties, and this is especially interesting in view of the huge expansion in practically every category of private debt in the United States since 1945. One might perhaps expect that the investment rating agencies, if not the financial market generally, would have recognized the increasing risk that attended the new bond issues. This did not happen in the twenties: the optimism of the time was general and financial specialists did not escape infection. Judging from Hickman's compilations, the rating agencies failed to sense the declining quality of new bond issues before 1928, perhaps not even then. The judgment of the market place was poorer still, as is evident from the fact that the proportion of new offerings rated as high grade by the market rose rather consistently over the decade for each of the major bond categories —railroads, utilities, and industrials. These findings enlarge the significance of Ilse Mintz' earlier comparison of the risk premium on foreign bonds with their subsequent performance. Apparently, investors in domestic as well as foreign securities "not only were unaware of the increasing riskiness of new . . . issues but even grew more confident at the very time the quality of new bonds was lowest."

It is, of course, impossible for any people to see their own current actions, shaped as they are in large degree by expectations of an uncertain future, with the cold detachment and knowledge that a later generation can sometimes bring to the same events. Economic research will never alter this pervasive feature of life. It may, however, usefully bend the course of events, first by bringing the lessons of experience to bear on current developments, and second, by devising improved methods of diagnosing the direction in which the economy is currently moving. The latter problem, no less than the former, has long occupied the attention of the National Bureau. Our greatest contribution has been, of course, the development of national income and gross product accounts, which are perhaps the most widely used of all statistics at the present time. Morris Copeland's highly original investigation of money flows, which we published last year, provides a new set of tools that the Federal Reserve Board has already found helpful in its studies of the relation between credit and economic stability. Still another approach to economic diagnosis is the one that Mitchell, Moore, and I have used in our studies of indicators of cyclical revivals and recessions.

Recently, we have laid plans for exploring how one of the firmest and most important of the Bureau's findings about the business cycle—namely, that the cycle in aggregate activity has been invariably preceded by a remarkably regular cycle in the proportion of individual activities undergoing expansion—might be put to current use. This cycle in the structure of economic activity is a very sensitive fluctuation. Its amplitude has been large even when aggregate activity has undergone only minor fluctuations; further, its movements have led by a considerable interval the movements of aggregate activity itself. But before this knowledge, which we have wrung from observations cast in a cyclical mould, can be applied to the analysis of current conditions, it will first be necessary to carry out extensive experiments and see if it is possible to construct from raw data a tolerably stable monthly or quarterly measure of the degree of preponderance of expansions over contractions or vice versa in individual lines of economic activity. In contrast to our earlier efforts, such an index of diffusion would not involve any assumptions about regularity of leads or lags of particular series, and this should enhance its usefulness in times of stormy change such as ours.

But even if its predictive value turned out to be small, a soundly conceived index of diffusion—preferably, a set of such indexes covering output, employment, prices, and profits—should at least help students in their efforts to arrive at informed judgments about the current state of the economy. For if it is well to know whether aggregate activity has recently risen, it is surely desirable to know also whether the scope of expansion in our complex economy has broadened or narrowed. A few figures based on a cyclical index of diffusion that we built up several years ago from a sample of over 600 time series for the interwar period may perhaps be suggestive. At each peak of aggregate activity, the expansions and contractions of individual activities were approximately in balance; that is to say, the proportion of expanding series then stood at or close to 50 per cent. This proportion declined to 47 per cent three months later, in the downturn of 1926; to 41 per cent in the downturn of 1923, 38 per cent in the downturn of 1920, 31 per cent in the downturn of 1937, and 29 per cent in the downturn of 1929—the specific date for the figure last cited being September or one month before the stock market crash. This ranking, based on the *scope* of the contraction almost at its beginning, turns out to be precisely the same as that of the *depth* which the several contractions eventually reached. Whether this correspondence has any predictive significance is uncertain. It does seem, however, that if compact and up-to-date information on the scope of the several contractions had been available at the time, whether through a diffusion index or some other statistical device, men charged with responsibility for formulating economic policy could have gone about their tasks with a somewhat keener awareness of the economic state of the nation.

V

The figures I have cited on the contractions of the interwar period reinforce the judgment, long entertained by observers of economic conditions, that the causes of varying degrees of severity of business contractions are to be sought primarily in the developments that precede them, rather than in the fresh complications that crop up while the contractions are in progress. However, although it is justifiable in the current setting to emphasize study of booms, it would be shortsighted to neglect the study of depressions. The high goal of business cycle research is to disclose and, as far as possible, clarify the multitude of problems with which contracyclical programs must grapple. The business cycle of a speculative thinker may be one phenomenon; the business cycles of experience are many. Governmental measures that are well suited to one decline of aggregate output may be poorly suited to another, even if its magnitude and momentum are no different. An age which takes contracyclical policy seriously must seek to improve knowledge of how an economic organization based on substantial freedom of individual enterprise typically generates cumulative movements of expansion and contraction. Not less important, however, especially in times like ours, when international factors and governmental policy loom so large, is the need to push on from knowledge of the typical course of business cycles to their special circumstances and to the direct examination of the effectiveness of alternative contracyclical devices.

A significant part of the National Bureau's research is gradually moving in these directions. The development of factual knowledge about governmental economic activities has become one of our major themes. Kendrick is investigating federal expenditures over the past century and a half, giving special attention to the influence of wars on later spending. Seltzer, Holland, and Dobrovolsky are making historical and statistical studies of the impact of the federal income tax on individuals and corporations. Copeland is investigating the behavior of federal and local finances over the past sixty years, concentrating on the factors that have given rise to changes in the public debt. Robinson is studying how the federal government has managed its debt, especially during the great wars of our history. Earl Rolph, who is also concerning himself with debt management, is analyzing the effects of different policies on economic conditions in the United States and several other countries in the turbulent years since 1920. The federal government is now, of course, an important lender and guarantor of loans as well as borrower. The recent growth in these lending operations and their ramifying economic effects are being explored by Saulnier, Jacoby, Halcrow, and their associates. Further, Stigler and Abramovitz have begun an inquiry into the trends of governmental employment in several foreign countries, with the aim of broadening the factual basis for interpreting the economic growth of government in the United States over recent decades, which Fabricant has recorded in our recently published volume.

In addition to these basic studies, Firestone has compiled new monthly series on federal receipts and expenditures since the 1870's, which lay the groundwork for more thorough analysis of the role of fiscal policy in past business cycles than has hitherto been possible. Even a rough inspection of these records suggests how instructive they are likely to prove. For they show that even before World War I federal revenues tended to move in close harmony with the business cycle, while expenditures ordinarily rose during contractions as well as expansions. In other words, 'built-in' fiscal stabilizers are not an invention of recent years, although their importance has gained immensely with the growth of the federal budget. Nor can unbalanced budgets qualify as a new development of peacetime finance. It is only proper to add, however, that although annually balanced budgets have been elusive in experience, earlier generations had far better success than our own both in restraining the size of public deficits and in alternating them with surpluses.

International economic relations, which have been a constant source of anxiety in our times, are also assuming some importance in the Bureau's research program. To facilitate informed judgments about the prospects for enlarging our foreign trade and investment, Fabricant is now devoting himself to a close study of their trends. Penelope Hartland is investigating the influence of international capital movements on Canadian development. Ilse Mintz is analyzing the cyclical fluctuations of our foreign trade. Morgenstern is completing a study of the cyclical behavior of international financial transactions, and Woolley is drawing plans for extensive statistical research on the structure of world trade and payments.

While only some of our studies of governmental activities and international economic relations are directly concerned with cyclical behavior, they all are likely to enrich, and to a considerable extent have already enriched, those of our investigations that are more narrowly devoted to cyclical issues. The like is true of the studies of secular changes in domestic capital formation under Kuznets' direction, of production and productivity under Mills, of wages and the labor force under Wolman, and of the workings of financial institutions under Saulnier. All these investigations are developing new information on the changing institutional setting within which business cycles have run their course, or are adding to the statistical knowledge needed to construct realistic models of the business cycle, or are contributing directly to the understanding of economic fluctuations. Partly under their influence, partly as a result of progress internal to our specialized work on business cycles, our current research on economic fluctuations—even when it seems immersed in distant periods or issues—is sensitive to newly emerging conditions. We continue to investigate the typical features of business cycles, seeking in the spirit of science well-founded generalizations having a wide range of application. But our research has reached a stage where we can usefully give increasing attention to variations among business cycles and to the workings of contracyclical policies. Several members of our business cycle group are now engaged in significant research in these directions.

Thirty years have passed since *Business Cycles and Unemployment*, our first study of business cycles, was published. This volume was devoted to an objective analysis of the contribution that the government, the banking system, and individual business firms could make to economic stability. Since then we have returned from time to time to explicit research on contracyclical policies—as in the studies of public works by Wolman and by Gayer in the early 1930's; Maxwell's recent study, *Federal Grants and the Business Cycle*; and the Conference papers on *Regularization of Business Investment*, which are now in press. Might it not be well, however, to pursue research on contracyclical policies more deliberately? For some time we have been considering the feasibility of undertaking a full-scale empirical study of the contracyclical efficacy of our unemployment insurance system, another of the experience gained since 1930 in the use of public works as a contracyclical weapon, still another of the probable changes in disposable income that would result under a given set of conditions from specified changes in personal income tax rates or deductions. But the time seems ripe, if we could manage it without injury to the basic research now in hand, for a comprehensive investigation of business cycle policies—an investigation that would have the same general aim as our first book on business cycles, but which would deal with the new as well as old instruments of policy that have figured in the economic thinking and practice of our generation.

A broad inquiry of this sort, carried out by a corps of outstanding scholars, could make a contribution of the first importance to public welfare as well as economic knowledge. It would be well for us to keep this project before our minds, even if we cannot find the way to it promptly. And we should not be deterred by the prospect that the new investigation, like its predecessor of thirty years back, will leave many questions unanswered. For not the least of our current needs, as Cournot so well expressed it for his time, is to make "clear how far we are from being able to solve, with full knowledge of the case, a multitude of questions which are boldly decided every day."

I owe a heavy debt to my colleagues, especially Geoffrey H. Moore, for advice and assistance in the preparation of this report.

PART TWO

Related Essays

Mitchell on What Happens during Business Cycles

Shortly before his death Wesley Mitchell put in my care the completed parts of the "progress report" he was preparing on his long and elaborate investigation of "what happens during business cycles." This book is substantially the document he left behind. I have felt free to make numerous changes of detail, but I have not interfered with the design, nor attempted to complete the narrative. The work of a major scientist, even if not half done, deserves a life of its own, unencumbered by the hand or voice of another. So it is especially when, as in the present case, the fragment has well-defined contours, balance, and direction. But for the guidance of students who may take up the book for the first time, I shall put down a few remarks about Mitchell's objectives and what he accomplished.

I

Business cycles are not merely fluctuations in aggregate economic activity. The critical feature that distinguishes them from the commercial convulsions of earlier centuries or from the seasonal and other short-term variations of our own age is that the fluctuations are widely diffused over the economy—its industry, its commercial dealings, and its tangles of finance. The economy of the Western world is a system of closely interrelated parts. He who would understand business cycles must master the workings of an economic system organized largely in a network of free enterprises searching for profit. The problem of how business cycles come about is therefore inseparable from the problem of how a capitalist economy functions.

This conception governs Mitchell's posthumous book, as it does his earlier writings. Mitchell was not content to focus analysis on the fluctuations of one or two great variables, such as production or employment. His concern was with *business* cycles and he therefore sought to interpret the system of business as a whole—the formation of firms and their disappearance, prices as well as output, the employment of labor and other resources, the flow of incomes to and from the public, costs and profits, savings and in-

Reprint of the introduction to Wesley C. Mitchell's *What Happens during Business Cycles: A Progress Report*, National Bureau of Economic Research, Studies in Business Cycles 5 (1951), pp. vii-xxi.

vestments, the merchandising of securities as well as commodities, the money supply, its turnover, and the fiscal operations of government. Not only that, but he sought to penetrate the façade of business aggregates and trace the detailed processes—psychological, institutional, and technological—by which they are fashioned and linked together.

Thus Mitchell took as his scientific province a terrain as far-flung and intricate as Walras's and Marshall's. But he explored more fully than his predecessors the obstacles to the mutual adjustment of economic quantities in a disturbed environment. "Time . . . is the centre of the chief difficulty of almost every economic problem."[1] Pursuing this Marshallian theme through uncharted jungles of statistics, Mitchell detected systematic differences in the rates of movement of economic variables, and arrived at an early stage of his scientific work at the conception that our economic system of interdependent parts generates a cyclical path instead of moving towards an equilibrium position. This fateful twist aside, Mitchell's economic outlook was thoroughly Marshallian. Had he lived to finish this book, he would have inscribed on its title page Marshall's motto: "The many in the one, the one in the many."

The hypothesis that each stage of the business situation tends to develop out of the preceding stage and to grow into the next in a cyclical pattern poses two major questions: Does economic life actually proceed in recurrent fluctuations having similar characteristics? If so, by what processes are continuous and repetitive movements of this character brought about? In a search for definite and dependable answers, Mitchell examined "facts on a wholesale scale," as had Darwin before him in a related field, and Lyell before Darwin. "My success as a man of science," wrote Darwin, "has been determined . . . by complex and diversified mental qualities and conditions. Of these, the most important have been—the love of science—unbounded patience in long reflecting over any subject—industry in observing and collecting facts—and a fair share of invention as well as of common sense."[2] These, too, were the sources of Mitchell's scientific strength. In his quarto on *Business Cycles*, published in 1913, he anchored a theory of fluctuations to an array of empirical observations unprecedentedly full

[1] Alfred Marshall, Preface to the first edition of his *Principles of Economics* (Macmillan).
[2] Charles Darwin, "Autobiography," in *Life and Letters*, ed. Francis Darwin (Appleton, 1888), Vol. I, pp. 68, 85-86.

for its time. But Mitchell was not content with this achievement. World War I had ushered in a new era of economic statistics, able theorists were elaborating new hypotheses, and statistical analysts were rapidly fashioning new devices for disentangling economic movements. Eager to exploit the new materials for research, Mitchell launched in 1922 a fresh investigation of business cycles.

II

The science of economic fluctuations is only beginning to pass into an inductive stage. Even today the descriptions of business cycles by economists often resemble the descriptions of plant life by writers of antiquity, who commonly relied on "casual observations, no experiments and much speculative thinking."[3] If later botanists often "could not identify the plants by the descriptions," so it has also been in economics. As long as investigators worked by themselves, they could not very well "collect the masses of raw data pertinent to the study of cyclical behavior, segregate the cyclical components from movements of other sorts, and assemble the findings to form a realistic model of business cycles by which explanations could be judged."[4] In recent decades the organization of scientific institutes has greatly enlarged the possibilities of empirical research in economics. Mitchell made the most of the opportunity afforded by the resources of the National Bureau. Taking his own and others' explanations of business cycles as "guides to research, not objects of research" (p. 5), he delved deeply into the facts of cyclical behavior and the relationships among them. The wish to contribute to economic policy was strong in Mitchell. Stronger still was his conviction that intelligent control of business cycles depends upon sound theoretical understanding, which requires tolerably full and accurate knowledge of what the business cycles of experience have been like.

Business Cycles: The Problem and Its Setting, the first major instalment of Mitchell's investigation, was published in 1927. The second appeared in 1946 under the title *Measuring Business Cycles*. In the meantime numerous studies of special aspects of cyclical fluctuations were prepared by the Bureau's staff, and a small group was steadily engaged in analyzing the cyclical behavior of economic processes.[5] It was Mitchell's hope to integrate

---

[3] William Crocker, "Botany of the Future," *Science*, October 28, 1938, pp. 387, 388.
[4] Mitchell, *What Happens during Business Cycles: A Progress Report*, p. 4. All other page references, unless otherwise indicated, are to the text of Mitchell's report.
[5] See the list of publications on business cycles at the end of Mitchell's report.

the findings of his collaborators with his own and other investigators' results; that is, to develop a model of business cycles from carefully screened observations, to use it in explaining how the cycles of experience are typically propagated, and then press on to account for the outstanding differences among them.[6] But he would have fallen short of the goal even if he had lived to complete the present book. Many of the needed materials—especially for foreign countries—were not in shape for use, and the subject of business cycle differences required systematic investigations yet to be undertaken. As it stands, Mitchell's report barely covers the first three of the seven parts he had planned. Part I sets out his aims, methods, and materials. Part II deals with the great variety of cyclical movements characteristic of individual economic activities. Part III, not fully completed, shows how the cyclical movements of different parts of the American economy fit together into business cycles, and paves the way for analyzing the processes of expansion, recession, contraction, and revival, to which the last four parts were to be devoted.

Thus the book is a 'progress report,' both in the sense in which Mitchell intended the phrase and in the poignant sense forced by his death. Yet no existing publication elucidates so fully or so authoritatively what happens during business cycles as Mitchell's fragment. The accent of the book is on characteristic behavior, formalized in the concept of a 'typical cycle.' "The only normal condition" of business, as Mitchell once expressed it, "is a state of change";[7] but some states of change are 'normal' and others 'abnormal,' and Mitchell's 'typical cycle' is designed to take account of such differences. Hence, this concept is similar in some respects to the classicists' 'normal.' The role of each is to segregate the effects of complex causes: both are devices of abstraction: both are tools for analyzing new, concrete situations. Mitchell was keenly concerned about the wide variations among the business cycles of experience and eager to press investigations of them. But he deemed it essential, as a first step, to lay bare the typical characteristics of the alternating waves of prosperity and depression that have swept the economic world in modern times. In this emphasis he conformed to the usual practice of business cycle theorists. He broke with tradition, however, by extracting what is 'typical' or 'aberrant' from mass observations, and thus substitut-

[6] For a fuller account, see "Wesley Mitchell and the National Bureau," in the Bureau's *Twenty-ninth Annual Report* [reprinted above, pp. 61-106].
[7] *Business Cycles: The Problem and Its Setting*, p. 376.

ing fact and measure, as well as may be, for the impressionistic judgments that have ruled business cycle literature.

III

Mitchell begins his survey of what happens during business cycles by illustrating the varieties of behavior characteristic of economic activities in the United States. Some of the figures in his introductory chart merely confirm common knowledge. For example, commodity prices generally rise and fall with the tides in production; business failures increase during contractions of aggregate economic activity and diminish during expansions; the output of durables fluctuates more widely than the output of perishables; and prices are more stable at retail than at wholesale. It is less generally known, however, that crop production moves rather independently of business cycles, or that production typically fluctuates over a much wider range than prices, that the liabilities of business failures usually turn down months before economic recovery becomes general and turn up months before recession, that both durables and perishables experience their most vigorous decline well before the end of contraction, and that retail prices characteristically move later as well as less than wholesale prices.

Students who will take the trouble to ponder these facts are not likely to leave Mitchell's chart quickly. They will notice that orders for investment goods tend to lead the tides in aggregate activity; that private construction is more closely related to business cycles than public construction; that call money rates or even commercial paper rates greatly overstate the fluctuations in the rates of interest at which bank customers ordinarily borrow; that interest rates in New York tend to move before, and more widely than, those in the interior; that the number of business failures lags behind the liabilities; that bond prices tend to lead stock prices, which themselves lead the turns in aggregate activity; that bank deposits appear to be comparatively steady during depressions; that imports conform closely to business cycles while exports do not; that grocery sales fail to show the regular response to business cycles characteristic of retail trade at large; etc. And if the reader looks beyond the large processes that have dominated theoretical literature, he will see how peculiar the cyclical behavior of smaller sectors of activity can be. For example, cattle slaughter tends to move with the tides in aggregate activity while hog slaughter moves inversely; the dollar volume of residential construction contracts fluctuates less, not more, than the physical volume; cotton stocks held at mills run parallel with mill production, while stocks in public storage move inversely.

Thus business cycles are complex phenomena—far more so than has been commonly supposed. The sales of a large firm may be dominated by the tides in aggregate activity; the fortunes of a small firm are rather at the mercy of personal factors and conditions peculiar to the trade or locality. Some activities, like local transit or net gold movements between the United States and Great Britain, are apparently free from cyclical fluctuations. Others, notably farming, undergo cyclical movements, but they have little or no relation in time to business cycles. And these irregular responses, passed over lightly by theoretical writers, accord with reason: "We cannot expect any activity to respond regularly to business cycles unless it is subject to man's control within the periods occupied by cyclical phases, and unless this control is swayed, consciously or not, by short-period economic considerations. The domination of harvests by weather, the 'migratory property' of petroleum underground, the mixed motives of governments in undertaking construction work, the long-range planning that weighs with many men in a position to set 'administered prices,' the time-consuming negotiations that prevent prompt adjustments of certain other prices and many wage rates, the existence of long-term contracts, the years required to complete some large undertakings—these are concrete examples of the multifarious obstacles that interfere with prompt and regular response to the cyclical tides" (p. 95).

The processes that fail to bear the imprint of business cycles are nevertheless a minority. Almost nine-tenths of Mitchell's basic sample of approximately 800 time series fluctuate in sympathy with the tides in aggregate activity, but the movements of this imposing majority are far from uniform. Between the cyclical recalcitrants, like farming, and the cyclical regulars, like factory employment, there is a continuous gradation. Coal and iron production conform more closely to the tides in aggregate activity than the production of textiles or gasoline. The prices of industrial commodities do not conform as well as their production, while the opposite relation rules in farming. Employment conforms better than wage rates, bank loans than investments, open-market interest rates than customer rates, stock prices than bond prices, etc. Some conforming processes move early in the cyclical procession; for example, orders for investment goods. Others, like interest rates, are laggards.

Of course, most processes respond to the tides in aggregate activity by rising during expansions and declining during contractions, though they may do so with a lead or lag. But business cycles also generate countercyclical movements: "Brisk business increases the domestic demand for textile goods and so diminishes the exports of raw cotton; it increases the sale of fresh milk and so restricts the production of butter; it increases the volume of coin and paper money held by the public and stimulates borrowing from the banks, thereby enlarging demand liabilities and tending to impair reserve ratios; it leads department stores to carry larger stocks of merchandise and lowers the piles of iron ore at blast furnaces; it activates share transactions on stock exchanges and discourages transactions in bonds. The declines in this list, and many others, are as characteristic a feature of business cycles as the advances" (p. 66). However, the processes that run counter to business cycles do so, by and large, with less regularity than those that respond positively. An expansion of money incomes stimulates a general increase in buying, and this influence may obscure the concomitant impulse to shift demand away from inferior articles to goods of higher quality. As it turns out, purchases of staples such as pork, flour, coffee, and potatoes frequently decline during expansion, but their inverted response is less regular than the positive response of more costly articles. "In general, influences that tend to repress an activity in expansion encounter more opposition than influences favoring an increase, and when repressing influences win out, their victories are less regular from cycle to cycle than the victories won by influences that push forward. *Mutatis mutandis*, the like holds true in contraction" (p. 96).

Large as are the variations in the cyclical timing of economic processes, the differences in amplitude of fluctuation are more impressive still. In high grade bond yields, for example, the cyclical wanderings are confined to a narrow range; the total rise and fall is typically only about 10 per cent of their average value during a business cycle. The amplitude of the over-all index of wholesale prices, excluding war episodes, is nearly twice as large; the amplitude of factory employment four or five times as large, of private construction contracts over ten times and of machine tool orders over twenty times as large. On the other hand, stocks of industrial equipment are remarkably steady, expanding usually during contractions as well as expansions of business cycles. The proportions among economic quantities keep changing so systematically over a business cycle that the "very essence of the phenomenon is omitted unless the chart of business cycles contains numerous lines that indicate the wide differences among the rates at which, and also some of the differences in the times at which, various elements in the economy expand and contract. For, unless these divergencies in cyclical behavior are pictured by fit symbols, we have no suggestion of the basic business-cycle problem: how an economic system of interrelated parts develops internal stresses during expansions, stresses that bring on recessions, and how the uneven contractions of its varied parts pave the way for revivals" (p. 295).

IV

So much for the varieties of cyclical behavior that come to the surface once the lid is lifted from aggregate activity. What sort of whole do the parts make up? When the individual pieces are put together it appears that every month some activities reach cyclical peaks and others decline to their troughs; so that expansion and contraction run side by side all the time. But the peaks tend to come in bunches and likewise the troughs. Hence, when troughs gain on the peaks, expansions grow more numerous and in time dominate the economy. Their supremacy is short-lived, however, and gradually gives way to the encroachments of contraction. The business cycle of experience is the alternating succession of these sustained majorities: first, individual expansions; next, contractions; then expansions once again; and so on. "Business cycles consist not only of roughly synchronous expansions in many activities, followed by roughly synchronous contractions in a slightly smaller number; they consist also of numerous contractions while expansion is dominant, and numerous expansions while contraction is dominant" (p. 79). According as the expansions or contractions of individual activities dominate, the aggregate activity of the economy surges forward or recedes. And when economic crosscurrents are at or near their maximum, the direction of aggregate activity is reversed: it begins to rise if it has been falling, or to fall if it has been rising.

The turmoil that goes on within the cycles in aggregate activity has a systematic core. A highly simplified picture of the system is afforded by the accompanying table,[8] which condenses Mitchell's analysis of "comprehensive series" in Chapter 10. The table shows directions of movement during a typical business cycle—here divided into eight segments, four each for expansion and contrac-

[8] [Omitted here. The table appears on page 123, above.]

tion. Of course, each segment includes several months, and the table is therefore insensitive to minor differences in timing, such as the short lag in income payments. Further, it hides many cross currents that would appear in less comprehensive series, and omits certain business factors of which we should take account—especially wage rates, inventories, banking, and governmental finance. But with all its faults, the table gives an effective glimpse of the typical round of developments that constitute a business cycle.[9]

Let us then take our stand at the bottom of a depression and watch events as they unfold. Production characteristically rises in the first segment of expansion; so do employment and money income; and so do commodity prices, imports, domestic trade, security transactions. Indeed, every series moves upward except bond yields and bankruptcies. In the second stage the broad advance continues, though it is checked at one point—the bond market, where trading begins to decline. Bond prices join bond sales in the next stage; in other words, long-term interest rates—which fell during the first half of expansion—begin to rise. In the final stretch of expansion, declines become fairly general in the financial sector. Share trading and stock prices move downward; the liabilities of business failures, which hitherto have been receding, move up again; security issues and construction contracts drop; the turnover of bank deposits slackens; and bank debits in New York City, though not as yet in the interior, become smaller.

These adverse developments soon engulf the economic system as a whole, and the next stage of the business cycle is the first stage of contraction. Production, employment, commodity prices, personal incomes, business profits—indeed, practically all processes represented in the table—decline. Of course, the liabilities of business failures continue to rise, which merely attests the sweep of depression. Long-term interest rates also maintain their rise. But in the next stage the downward drift of bond prices ceases; that is, the rise in long-term interest rates is arrested. By the middle of contraction, bond sales join the upward movement of bond prices. More important still, the liabilities of business failures begin declining, which signifies that the liquidation of distressed business firms has passed its worst phase. These favorable developments are reinforced in the following stage. Share trading and prices revive; business incorporations, security issues, and construction contracts move upward; money begins to turn over more rapidly;

[9] This and the three following paragraphs are adapted from the National Bureau's *Thirtieth Annual Report* [reprinted on pp. 107-134, above].

even total money payments expand. Before long the expansion spreads to production, employment, prices, money incomes, and domestic trade. But this is already the initial stage of general expansion—the point at which our hurried observation of the business cycle started.

Of course, this recital delineates characteristic movements during business cycles, not invariant sequences. That the description fits individual business cycles imperfectly is apparent from the conformity percentages in the table. Yet these percentages also suggest that the deviations from type are not so numerous as to destroy the value of a generalized sketch. And if this much is accepted, an important conclusion immediately follows, notwithstanding the omissions of the table; namely, that the check to the dominant movement of business activity, whether it be expansion or contraction, is typically felt especially early in financial processes and activities preparatory to investment expenditure.

The contraction phase of business cycles is not, however, the precise counterpart of expansion. This is clear from the table and becomes clearer still when numerical values are attached to its signs and intervals. The arrays of individual turning points at business cycle troughs "are more dispersed and skewed toward leads" than are the arrays at peaks. Expansions of aggregate activity average longer than contractions. They are also more vigorous, so that the trough from which a given expansion starts is ordinarily above the level from which the preceding expansion started. In the first segment of expansion the rate of improvement "is more rapid than at any other stage of the cycle." A "sharp and general retardation" of the advance occurs in the next segment. In the third, while "reacceleration is the rule," the advance "does not regain the speed" it had at the beginning of expansion. In the final stage of expansion "the business tide . . . becomes fuller of eddies." Contractions follow a different pattern. "The fall accelerates somewhat in the second segment of contraction, whereas the rise is much retarded in the second segment of expansion." The next stage "brings a moderate retardation" of the decline, whereas it "brought a moderate reacceleration" of the advance. The closing stages of expansion and contraction are similar "in that the rate of change becomes slower; but this retardation is much more marked at the end of contraction than at the end of expansion. . . ." "Thus the notions often suggested by the picturesque phrasing beloved of writers upon 'booms and busts'—that prosperity grows at a dizzier pace the longer it lasts, and that

196

slumps gather momentum as they proceed—are wrong if our measures are right. Scarcely less misleading are the implications of the mathematical constructions often used to represent business cycles. A set of straight lines sloping upward to represent expansion, connected at a sharp peak with downward sloping straight lines to represent contraction, misrepresents the facts. . . . Sine curves are not less objectionable. . . . What our observations suggest is that the shapes of business cycles are phenomena *sui generis*."

V

These, then, are some of the broad results that emerge from Mitchell's examination of the cyclical process of the American economy. The full range of the book, its suggestions for further research, and its exemplary scientific care await the reader. Economists anxious to wield a simple formula of the causes of business cycles or the means of controlling them will not find Mitchell's fragment to their liking. Those willing to take conclusions on faith may chafe at its patient elaboration of evidence. But men who seek so earnestly to understand how our economic organization works that they insist on judging evidence for themselves are more likely to lament that too much detail has been suppressed. Scholars will respect Mitchell's pronouncement that his report on findings, after many years of research, is "ill proportioned, tentative, and subject to change as the investigation proceeds" (p. 5).

This book is not easy and everyone will save time by a careful reading of Part I, which, beside outlining aims and methods, provides the modicum of technical vocabulary required for comprehending what follows. Economic theorists are likely to find especially suggestive Chapter 7, which sets out the facts and inquires into the causes of the changing proportions among economic quantities in the course of a business cycle; also Part III, which centers on the consensus of fluctuations in leading sectors of the economy. Chapter 8 is a useful reminder to all that, despite their persistent traits, business cycles are changing phenomena; and that just as each new member of a group has traits of his own, which cannot be inferred from knowledge of the 'average man,' so each business situation must be judged in the light of its own circumstances as well as according to historical patterns. The bulk of this chapter is devoted to technical problems in the decomposition of time series, and only specialists will want to study it fully. Readers pressed for time might move lightly through Chapters 5 and 6 also

—except for the closing sections, which will repay careful reading.

The modern theory of employment, which for a time pushed aside both value theory and business cycle theory, is now slowly being fitted into older economic knowledge. The younger economists are rediscovering that cost-price relations play a significant role in shaping the national income and its movements, that the 'consumption function' itself moves cyclically, that investment is not an autonomous variable, that price inflation does not wait for full employment, and that both investment and consumption are heterogeneous aggregates that cannot be understood without separate analysis of their parts. If our harassed generation can win the opportunity to pursue the arts of peace, the fruit and example of Mitchell's work will have their quiet but decisive part over the years in bringing the theory of fluctuations into ever closer contact with the ebb and flow of experience.

Railroads and the Business Cycle

The first modern railroad built was the 12-mile line from Stockton to Darlington in England, opened to traffic in 1825. Several years later railroad construction got under way in the United States, France, and Germany. From its modest beginnings in the 1830's the construction of new railroad lines increased rapidly, but the period of expanding construction was comparatively brief. The peak of new railroad mileage was apparently reached in 1848 in Great Britain, 1875 in Germany, 1884 in France, and 1887 in the United States. The general trend thereafter was downward.

Secular expansion of new investment in railroads nevertheless continued. The wave of new line construction was followed by progressive improvement of existing railroads, especially in the United States where many of the original roads were lightly built. A tremendous effort was put into extensions and betterments, sometimes to accommodate the growing traffic, sometimes to reap the benefits of advancing technology. Over widening stretches of the railroad system single track roads were converted to double track, sidings added, grades reduced, curves eliminated, automatic signals installed, iron rails replaced by steel rails, light rails by heavy rails, wooden bridges by bridges of steel or concrete, and a hundred other improvements in road and equipment made. Whereas additions to road mileage in the United States reached a peak in 1887, additions to auxiliary track reached a peak in 1904; additions to total track mileage were about as large in 1904 as in 1887; the peak in rail consumption came in 1906, in additions to leading types of equipment between 1907 and 1911, in additions to book value of investment around 1910. Thus the peak in railroad investment expenditures apparently came after the turn of the century, or some twenty years after the building of new mileage had passed its maximum.

Meanwhile the total capital invested in the railroads of the country continued to grow. Traffic grew faster still. It increased partly in response to the economic growth and the territorial expansion of the country; partly at the expense of coaches, canals, and other waterways which the railroads gradually superseded. It is difficult to fix the precise date when railroads ceased gaining

Introduction to Thor Hultgren's *American Transportation in Prosperity and Depression*, National Bureau of Economic Research, Studies in Business Cycles 3 (1948), pp. vii-xiv.

on competing means of transport, but it could not have been much before 1910. By 1920, at any rate, the competitive trend was already definitely reversed. New agencies of transportation had arisen—trolley lines, trucks, motor buses, passenger automobiles, pipelines, the airplane, and revived waterways—and they battled the railroads for traffic as vigorously as railroads in their youth had fought their rivals. Passenger traffic reached a maximum in that year, dropped a full third by 1929, and declined further during the thirties. Freight traffic continued to grow during the twenties, but at a lower rate than production. In 1937 the number of ton-miles of railroad freight was only about four-fifths the 1929 figure, despite an unchanged volume of mineral production, an increase of 6 per cent in the output of agriculture, and of 3 per cent in manufacturing.

The adverse turn in the fortunes of railroads did not arrest technical progress in the industry. On the contrary, more powerful locomotives were installed; trains became longer and faster; maintenance work was largely mechanized; and economies of labor, fuel, and equipment were generally extended. Between 1929 and 1939, while the combined freight and passenger traffic of railroads fell off a fourth, traffic per man-hour increased a third. But physical progress did not leave a visible imprint on the annual statements of profit or loss. By the end of 1939 nearly a third of the railroad mileage of the country was in receivership.

The secular shifts in investment and operations were accompanied by changes in the organization of the industry and in its place in society. Once the continent was crisscrossed with railroads, the addition of new mileage not infrequently resulted in a duplication of existing facilities. A period of rate wars, maneuvers for control, and outright consolidations set in. Government, at first the eager patron of the industry, later became its vigilant overseer. Competitive pricing gave way to restrictive practices and sticky prices. Labor was unionized, and collective bargaining evolved into nation-wide negotiations and contracts. The federal government added its taxes to those long levied by local authorities, and a progressively larger part of the traffic dollar was diverted to tax collectors. In the meantime, the character of entrepreneurship was itself subtly modified. Financing by stock issues gave way increasingly to bond flotations, and in more recent years internal financing supplanted both forms of external financing. Posts of authority, once so largely occupied by financiers, passed to managerial experts and technicians.

II

These momentous changes in the life of the railroad industry raise exciting questions for the student of business cycles. How closely was the current investment geared to the volume of traffic or its rate of change? What of the accumulated supply of facilities and equipment? Did traffic respond the same way to business cycles in the early stages of the industry as in the later stages? How did employment react to fluctuations in traffic? While the trend of traffic moved upward, did cyclical expansion create more jobs than were lost in the preceding contraction? By what process did railroads first encroach on other transport agencies, then lose out to new competitors? Did business depression accelerate or retard the competitive pressure of the innovator? Did the amplitude of fluctuations in traffic widen as the industry matured? What of the fluctuations in costs and revenues? Did government regulation modify the behavior of railroad rates during business cycles? If so, what were the repercussions on profits?

Thor Hultgren's scholarly study clarifies most of these vital issues, and some of his findings have a significance that extends well beyond the boundaries of the railroad industry. For example, the market for freight service can be estimated for the years 1920 to 1925, and measured with some precision since 1926. The record discloses that the share of the business going to railroads fell almost uninterruptedly, year after year, from 1920 through 1938. However, the new transport agencies penetrated the market faster during contractions of business cycles than during expansions. I have noticed a similar cyclical regularity over much longer periods in the encroachment of open-hearth steel on Bessemer steel and of by-product coke on beehive coke, and suspect that it is characteristic of the onrush of new products or processes at large.

But if cyclical shifts do occur in the rate at which markets are diverted from old to new industries, are the shifts not induced by changes in price relations between the cyclical phases of expansion and contraction? In the railroad case there seems to be little need to speculate on this issue. General rate changes "became a conspicuous feature of the industry's price-making around the end of World War I and again in the great depression."[1] Every one of the general changes ordered by the Interstate Commerce Commission "promoted inverse conformity to freight traffic" (p. 248); in other

---

[1] Hultgren, *American Transportation in Prosperity and Depression*, p. 248. All other page references, unless otherwise indicated, are to the text of Hultgren's report.

words, the increases in rates came during contractions and the decreases during expansions of traffic. "During 1929-32 and 1937-38 rail freight rates, on the whole, declined little or rose" (p. 12). On the other hand, the rates charged by operators of trucks—which made the most serious inroads on the railroads' freight business— not only declined, but probably declined sharply.

Another finding of broad significance concerns equipment. The era of secular growth in railroad traffic "was one of rather steadily increasing supplies of cars and locomotives." The succeeding period "was one of persistently diminishing stocks" (pp. 150-152). But the positive relation between equipment and traffic over these long periods eluded the much briefer periods of traffic cycles. Up to the First World War railroads added to their stocks of equipment in cyclical expansions and contractions alike. From the middle of the 1920's or earlier, depending on the type of equipment, stocks diminished whatever the cyclical phase. The rate of growth or decline in equipment stocks of course varied, but not in any regular relation to traffic cycles. Judging by the orders placed for equipment, Hultgren finds that railroad managers did make an effort to build up stocks faster during expansions. But they were not highly successful: partly because fairly long intervals elapsed between the placing of orders for cars or locomotives and their installation, and partly because retirements moved in quasi-independent fashion.

It is notable, however, that orders for railroad equipment conformed with substantial regularity to traffic cycles, and that cyclical downturns in orders usually preceded downturns in traffic. A familiar explanation of the early timing of orders is the 'acceleration principle'—which asserts that equipment stocks tend to maintain a rather constant ratio to output, and that requirements of additional equipment therefore tend to vary with the rate of change in output. If this investment formula applied to railroads, the early decline in equipment orders would imply (except for possible complications arising from retirements) that the rate of increase in traffic tapers off towards the close of expansions. According to Hultgren's tests this has not often happened; and when it has, the cyclical peak in equipment orders has sometimes preceded, instead of accompanied or followed, the maximum rate of growth in traffic. After a minute examination of movements during successive traffic expansions, Hultgren concludes that orders have not, in general, been geared to the rate of growth in traffic. He carefully notes that his statistical tests may have put excessive strain on the rough statistics of equipment orders; yet he accents the negative verdict on the acceleration principle by observing that good economic arguments are lacking for any firm belief in the principle.

Details aside, it is my impression that Hultgren's conclusions on the cyclical behavior of railway equipment have a wide range of application. Other studies of the National Bureau suggest that during periods of business cycle length a rather inflexible supply of plant and equipment is characteristic not only of railroads, but of industry at large. Contracts for industrial plant and orders for equipment—not to be confused with the volume of work currently done or the facilities currently installed—commonly turn down while national income is still rising, and turn up while national income is still falling. But the early timing cannot be satisfactorily explained by the acceleration principle. In tests over a range of industries, I have found that the contracts for new plant or orders for equipment placed by an industry are fairly closely geared to its output, but not to the rate of change in output as the acceleration principle would require. The acceleration principle seems to misrepresent the play of forces on investment in the short run; nevertheless, it is sometimes the key to movements over long periods.

III

As Hultgren takes the reader through the round of railroad operations, one fact emerges above all others and in a degree sums them up. That fact is the pervasive influence of business cycles on railroading. Secular changes in traffic, technology, and organization have sometimes modified the response to business cycles and frequently obscured it; they have rarely erased it. So also with wars, blizzards, strikes, and other major disturbances that diversify railroad history. The influence of business cycles can be detected in almost every feature of railroad operations: in the volume of traffic, its composition, the length of hauls, the load of cars and locomotives, their active time, the speed of trains, their length, the size of the labor force, its age composition, the length of the work month, the fuel consumed, prices received, prices paid, etc. But the direction, amplitude, and timing of the multitudinous adjustments to business cycles are highly variable. To find one's way through the maze of cyclical reactions, a plan is needed. Hultgren's plan is to focus attention on the behavior of costs and profits.

The relation of costs to prices during business cycles is of great theoretical and practical interest. If unit costs rise during expansion and prices are pushed up, sales may be inhibited. If the rise in unit costs outstrips the rise in prices, unit profits will decline; which may darken the prospect for profits and discourage investment. Both influences are widely thought to play a key role in bringing cyclical expansions to a close. Are the facts of the railroad industry consistent with thinking along these lines? What, in general, do they teach concerning cost-price relations during expansions and contractions? At this juncture Hultgren makes his most striking contribution to knowledge. As far as I know, no work since Mitchell's California classic of 1913[2] has dealt with cost-price relations during business cycles with equal thoroughness.

The behavior of costs depends partly on physical input-output relations, partly on rates of payment for the factors of production —labor, fuel, materials, and so on. In a strictly physical sense, unit costs appear to move inversely to cycles in railroad traffic. Labor requirements per unit of traffic tend to decline when traffic is expanding, and to rise when traffic is declining. Unit fuel requirements likewise tend to move inversely to traffic cycles, and so too does the ratio of equipment to traffic. But factor rates of payment normally increase during traffic expansions, while prices of fuel and materials—if nothing else—tend to decline during contractions. These movements of factor prices oppose the movements of unit physical costs, but do not dominate except during violent inflation such as accompanied World War I. Unit operating expenses therefore usually move inversely to traffic cycles, as do unit physical costs. Taxes per unit of traffic behave similarly, since this category of expense fluctuates over a narrower range than traffic. Rent and interest do likewise. Railroad rates, on the other hand, are sluggish. As a net result, unit 'profits' are normally higher at the end than at the beginning of cyclical expansions in traffic, and are normally lower at the end than at the beginning of contractions.

I have put Hultgren's conclusions baldly, without stopping to allow for leads or lags. When they are taken into account, it appears that unit costs have often started to rise before expansion ceased, or started to decline before contraction ended. However, the tendency has not been especially strong; in a fair number of instances the decline in unit costs continued to the end of expansion, or the rise to the end of contraction. There has also been some tendency for unit profits to reverse their movement before a

[2] Wesley C. Mitchell, *Business Cycles*, University of California Press (1913).

phase closed. But "an ominous narrowing of the profit margin while the physical volume of business is still growing, and an auspicious widening while volume is still diminishing, were not highly characteristic of the cyclical course of events. Yet . . . the maximum level was reached before the end in more than half the expansions . . . , and . . . the minimum level was reached before the end in more than half of the contractions. . . . The maximum and minimum were sometimes early, never late" (p. 315).

To what extent does Hultgren's demonstration of the power exercised by expanding output on unit costs apply to other major industries? What of the rest of his conclusions concerning costs and profits? What, in particular, of the highly regular tendency of railroads to defer maintenance during depression, or the tendency of their unit profits to rise fastest early in expansion and to fall fastest early in contraction—conclusions of great theoretical promise that I can no more than mention? And how seriously is the celebrated account of cyclical changes in efficiency, presented by Wesley Mitchell thirty-five years ago,[3] now in need of amendment? Reliable answers to these questions will not be forthcoming until studies similar to Hultgren's are carried out for other important industries. The statistical records of railroads are unique in their excellence, abundance, and time span. Useful statistics nevertheless exist also for other industries. They merit intensive study, not only for their vital bearing on the cumulative and self-reversing processes that constitute the business cycle, but also because so much of the economic controversy that rages in the practical world centers about the relation of unit costs, prices, and profits to the volume of production and hence to employment and national income.

IV

Transportation events after 1938 are not traced in Hultgren's volume, except in passing. The war years were marked by an amazing burst of activity. By 1942 the number of passenger-miles was larger than in 1920, and by 1944 it was twice as large. Freight ton-miles likewise expanded at a furious pace, doubling between 1937 and 1944. But the tremendous traffic was due partly to the peculiar circumstances of war, and would not have accompanied a peacetime economic expansion of equivalent size. Between 1944 and 1947 the number of ton-miles fell off 11 per cent, and the number of passenger-miles 52 per cent.

[3] *ibid.*

In 1944 the National Bureau published *Occasional Paper 15*, which examined the experience of railroads during the war. Hultgren reached a conclusion of basic importance in this paper; viz., despite the vastly increased traffic, the behavior characteristic of costs and profits during earlier peacetime expansions reappeared. The duration and amplitude of future cycles in railroad traffic are, of course, no more predictable than is the course of business cycles itself. Who could have foreseen ten years ago that railroad passenger movement would ever again reach the 1920 level? But the concomitants that business cycles will have in railroad operations can probably be anticipated with considerable assurance. Hultgren rounds out his expert contribution to the economics of railroading in a chapter on "Future Cycles" that merits the most careful attention of economists.

Keynesian Economics Once Again

Professor Hansen's paper in this number of the *Review* deals with important issues of economic theory. It expresses the judgment of a leading Keynesian thinker, who has had full opportunity to weigh and refine his reasons for repudiating my interpretation of Keynes.[1] Every mature economist knows how barren controversy can be and, in fact, usually is. But Keynes' theory is now at the center of much of our economic thinking, and Hansen is its outstanding exponent. Under the circumstances, it may serve the interests of economic science to examine Hansen's strictures with some care. I am grateful to the Editors of the *Review* for according me the opportunity.

In the following pages I shall consider the major issues raised by Hansen. Section I is devoted to the essentials of Keynes' theory of income and employment, Section II to its determinacy, Section III to the consumption function, and Section IV to the Keynesian apparatus as distinguished from the Keynesian theory. An appendix on Keynes' business cycle theory brings the paper to a close.

I. KEYNES' THEORY OF INCOME AND EMPLOYMENT

In the essay on *Economic Research and the Keynesian Thinking of Our Times*,[2] I boldly attempted to set forth the essence of Keynes' *General Theory* in a few paragraphs. To enable the reader to follow closely the questions raised by Hansen, I shall reproduce the main part of the original sketch before taking up the criticisms:

Reprinted by permission from *The Review of Economic Statistics* (published by Harvard University Press), November 1947, pp. 252-267.

[1] In the November 1946 issue of this *Review* Alvin H. Hansen comments on the great difficulty that economists have experienced in grasping Keynes' *General Theory*. In this connection he makes the following pronouncement: "A recent example disclosing a number of elementary misconceptions is the pamphlet by Arthur F. Burns, on *Economic Research and the Keynesian Thinking of Our Times* (National Bureau of Economic Research, 1946). However, the pamphlet does strikingly reveal (perhaps inadvertently) how economic theory—whether Ricardian or Keynesian—serves the highly useful purpose of pointing up what factual data are relevant to a useful investigation" (p. 187). Since this statement was not accompanied by any evidence, I was of course interested and eager to know what my misconceptions may be. In the course of the ensuing correspondence, Hansen eventually set forth his views in some detail. I replied as fully. Hansen's paper in this *Review* presents the critical remarks that he developed in correspondence, with such elaborations and modifications as he has deemed necessary to present his case properly before the scientific public.

[2] Hereafter referred to as *Keynesian Thinking*. [Reprinted on pages 3-25, above; page references that follow are to the present volume.]

". . . Keynes' theory of underemployment equilibrium . . . attempts to show that a free enterprise economy, unless stimulated by governmental policies, may sink into a condition of permanent mass unemployment. The crux of this theory is that the volume of investment and the 'propensity to consume' determine between them a unique level of income and employment. The theory can be put simply without misrepresenting its essence. Assume that business firms in the aggregate decide to add during a given period $2 billion worth of goods to their stockpiles, using this convenient term to include new plant and equipment as well as inventories. This then is the planned investment. Assume, next, that business firms do not plan to retain any part of their income;[3] so that if they pay out, say, $18 billion to the public, they expect to recover $16 billion through the sale of consumer goods, the difference being paid out on account of the expected addition to their stockpiles. Assume, finally, that the 'consumption function' has a certain definite shape; that if income payments are, say, $18 billion, the public will spend $17 billion on consumer goods and save $1 billion, and that one-half of every additional billion dollars of income will be devoted to consumption and one-half to savings. Under these conditions, the national income per 'period' should settle at a level of $20 billion.

"The reason is as follows. If income payments were $18 billion, the public would spend $17 billion on consumer goods. But the firms that made these payments expected to sell $16 billion worth to the public and to add $2 billion worth to their stockpiles; the actual expenditure of $17 billion on consumer goods would therefore exceed sellers' expectations by $1 billion, and stimulate expansion in the consumer goods trades. On the other hand, if income payments were $22 billion, the public would spend $19 billion on consumer goods; this would fall short of sellers' expectations by $1 billion, and set off a contraction in the output of consumer goods. In general, if income payments fell below $20 billion, the sales expectations of business firms would be exceeded; while if income payments rose above $20 billion, the expectations of business firms would be disappointed. In either case, forces would be released that would push the system in the direction of the $20

[3] This assumption is not essential to the Keynesian system; I make it here in order to simplify the exposition. The figures used throughout are merely illustrative. Further, the exposition is restricted to the proximate determinants of employment in Keynes' system; this simplification does not affect the argument that follows. (This note appeared in the original essay.)

billion mark. Hence, in the given circumstances, $20 billion is the equilibrium income, and it may be concluded that the basic data— that is, the volume of investment and the consumption function— determine a national income of unique size. If we assume, now, a unique correlation between income and employment, it follows that the basic data determine also a unique volume of employ- ment—which may turn out to be well below 'full' employment."[4]

This theoretical sketch can be readily translated into the lan- guage of diagrams, and it may perhaps prove helpful to some read- ers if I do that. In Figure 1 line CC' represents the consumption

Figure 1

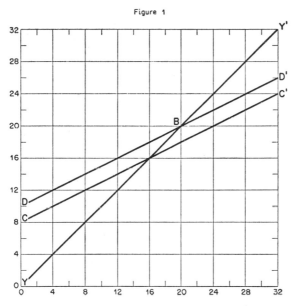

function, or the propensity to consume at levels of income speci- fied along the horizontal axis. DD' represents the aggregate de- mand—that is, consumer outlay plus intended investment—at the specified levels of income.[5] YY' represents the aggregate supply function—that is, the sum that is just sufficient to induce business firms to pay out to the factors of production each sum along the horizontal axis. At B income payments are 20 and DD' equals YY'. At lower levels of income DD' exceeds YY'; at higher levels DD' is less than YY'. Hence, as said above, "if income payments

4 *Keynesian Thinking*, pp. 5-6. In later paragraphs, I distinguished between this general theory of income and employment, and its characteristic special variant—the theory of secular stagnation.

5 Of course, DD' and CC' need not be linear; see note 3.

fell below $20 billion, the sales expectations of business firms would be exceeded; while if income payments rose above $20 billion, the expectations of business firms would be disappointed. In either case, forces would be released that would push the system in the direction of the $20 billion mark." Figure 2 illustrates

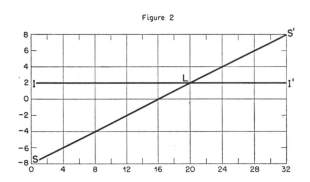

Figure 2

the same relations in another way. Here *II'* represents the volume of intended investment, and *SS'* the propensity to save at specified incomes. At *L* income payments are 20 and the intended investment equals the propensity to save. At other levels of income, the two are unequal. Since, in the given circumstances, any discrepancy between *II'* and *SS'* merely expresses in a roundabout way the excess of *DD'* over *YY'*, any deviation of income from *L* will set forces in motion that will tend to restore this level of income. Hence *L*, or the point of intersection of *II'* and *SS'*, defines the equilibrium income. And since employment and income are assumed to be uniquely correlated, it defines also a unique volume of employment.

Turning now to Hansen's paper, I am forced to point out that Hansen has not made a single explicit criticism of the substance of my summary of Keynes' theory. Hansen begins by saying that I depart seriously from Keynes' terminology [in using the term 'planned' or 'intended' investment]. He then makes miscellaneous remarks, some of them critical of certain portions of my essay, but says nothing in explicit criticism of pages 5-7, where I summarize Keynes' theory of income determination. If my terminology were all that troubled Hansen, there would be no cause for concern. For when I speak of 'planned' or 'intended' investment, I imply merely that 'actual' investment *may* be something different; I do not imply that it *will* be different. If the reader will substitute 'actual' for 'intended' whenever I refer to 'intended investment,'[6] he will discover that the only consequence is that business firms can no longer experience surprises with regard to their inventories. My sketch of Keynes' theory is perfectly general on this point—that is, I deliberately do not specify whether surprises are absorbed in price changes or in inventory movements. Hence anyone who wishes to rule out unintended changes in inventories, regardless of the fact that Keynes himself did not,[7] is entirely free to do so. This restriction will make the Keynesian theory less general; it will have no other effect.[8]

Can it be, then, that Hansen's trouble is not merely my terminology: that despite his failure to specify error, Hansen feels that my summary sketch misses something vital in Keynes' theory of income? There can be no serious doubt on this matter. Hansen says more than once that I have failed to present Keynes' theory accurately, and actually makes an effort—I wish it had been more systematic—to put down his own understanding of the theory. The drift of Hansen's thinking on Keynes' theory of income is indicated by statements such as these: "With an initial income of $16 billion, with new investment of $2 billion, and with a marginal propensity to consume of ½, income would rise to $20 billion." "Investment actually made in fixed capital was presumably 'intended,' while part of the net investment in inventories may at times be 'unintended.' In any event, the actual investment in any given period is the relevant factor" for income determination. "As time unfolds from day to day, the rate of investment at any moment is a given amount; and whatever that given amount is, the flow of income is affected by the magnitude of the actual rate of investment. . . . Thus, as the flow of investment unfolds, income rises or falls by a magnified amount according to *the actually prevailing marginal propensity to consume*" (my italics).

[6] At one point I speak of 'planned investment' in an equivalent sense.

[7] See *General Theory*, for example, pp. 123-124, 288.

[8] To illustrate in terms of the preceding example: Assume that income payments are $24 billion. This would imply that business firms expect to recover $22 billion through the sale of consumer goods and to add $2 billion worth to their stockpiles. The consumption function being what it is, they can recover only $20 billion from the public. Under the present restrictive hypothesis they cannot absorb the difference by leaving an extra $2 billion worth on the shelf; hence (barring destruction of unwanted goods), they must slash prices. The outcome for the given period is as follows: consumption, 20; investment, 2; income, 22; income payments, 24; consumer saving, 4; business dissaving, 2; aggregate saving, 2. In the next period, investment being a datum, business firms will presumably curtail the output of consumer goods. And so they would also under the less restrictive hypothesis; that is, if inventories in the given period piled up, or if the failure of expectations to be realized led partly to price cuts and partly to a piling up of inventories.

Now the remarkable thing about this representation of Keynes is that Hansen does not feel impelled to say anything about an economic process whereby one level of income supplants another, that he eschews all analysis of expectations or motivation, that he omits any reference to incentives that may induce business firms to maintain employment at one level or to shift from that level to some other; in short, that he sees no need for inquiring whether the balance of forces is such as to produce an equilibrium. He says blandly that if investment rises by $2 billion, and the marginal propensity to consume is ½, income will rise by $4 billion. Given equality between saving and investment, this statement is, of course, arithmetically incontrovertible. But so also is the proposition that if income rises by 4 and the marginal propensity to consume is ½, then investment must have risen by 2. If the first statement expresses Keynes' theory of income determination, as Hansen seems to suggest, then by parity of reasoning the second expresses a theory of investment. And indeed, if it were as simple as all this, we would have at hand a veritable machine for grinding out theories on significant economic problems. Thus if we craved a theory of the propensity to consume, we could find it in the suppressed syllogism that if investment rises by 2 and income by 4, the marginal propensity to consume must be ½.

There is something—one might say a good deal—in Keynes to support such tautological propositions, but it is a little strange to find a devoted follower of Keynes giving them prominence. Obviously, Hansen is echoing *one* of Keynes' theories of the multiplier —specifically, "the logical theory of the multiplier, which holds good continuously, without time-lag, at all moments of time."[9] Need I say that Hansen is not honoring Keynes by identifying this unfortunate appendage of the *General Theory* with Keynes' theory of income? While Keynes at time lapses into tautologies, there can be no doubt that he sought to explain the level of income and employment in terms of underlying human motives and expectations. In seeking to establish "what determines the volume of employment at any time,"[10] Keynes recognized that a solution requires proof. He therefore attempted to show that the factors isolated by his theory were sufficient to establish a "unique equilibrium value" of income and employment; that is, a value "at which there is no inducement to employers as a whole either to expand or to contract employment."[11] When the task was done, Keynes

9 *General Theory*, p. 122.   10 *ibid.*, p. 313.
11 *ibid.*, pp. 26, 27.

felt justified in remarking that the *General Theory* offered, "properly speaking, a Theory of Employment because it explains *why*, in any given circumstances, employment is what it is."[12]

In condensed and nontechnical prose, Keynes' proof is simply the sketch that I gave in my essay on *Keynesian Thinking*. In this proof two propositions are crucial, and both relate to the consumption function. The first is that consumption is a fairly stable function of income in experience; hence, what is actually a fuzzy band may be treated, for analytic purposes, as narrowing to a line. This proposition fixes the consumption function as such, and sets the stage—so to speak—on which investment can play. The second proposition is that as income expands, consumption also increases but by less than the increment of income. This proposition limits the shape of the consumption function. It is necessary if an equilibrium solution is to emerge, just as the first proposition is needed if the equilibrium is to have some relevance to the actual world.

Let Keynes now speak for himself: "The amount of labor . . . which the entrepreneurs decide to employ depends on . . . the amount which the community is *expected* to spend on consumption, and . . . the amount which it is *expected* to devote to new investment. . . . When our income increases our consumption increases also, but not by so much. *The key to our practical problem* [i.e., what determines the level of income and employment] is to be found in this psychological law."[13] But why is this the key to the problem? Let Keynes continue: "What the theory shows is that if the psychological law is *not* fulfilled, then we have a condition of complete instability. If, when incomes increase, expenditure increases by more than the whole of the increase in income, there is no point of equilibrium. Or, in the limiting case, where expenditure increases by exactly 100 per cent of any increase in income, then we have neutral equilibrium, with no particular preference for one position over another. Neither of these conditions seems to be characteristic of the actual state of affairs. . . ."[14] Keynes' meaning is conveyed simply by Figure 1. Given the "psychological law," *DD'* must be (as drawn) above *YY'* to the left of *B* and below *YY'* to the right of *B*. It follows that profits of entrepreneurs as a class will be maximized at the point of intersection of *DD'* and *YY'*; that is, when income is the abscissa of *B*. Given

[12] J. M. Keynes, "The General Theory of Employment," *Quarterly Journal of Economics*, February 1937, p. 221. The italics are Keynes'.

[13] *General Theory*, pp. 29-30. My italics.

[14] See Keynes' letter to Elizabeth Gilboy, *Quarterly Journal of Economics*, August 1939, p. 634. The italics are Keynes'. Cf. *General Theory*, pp. 117, 118, 251-252.

213

the propensity to consume and the intended investment, any erratic displacement of B is self-restorative; that is, B defines a position of maximum profit, or of stable equilibrium. But if the marginal propensity to consume exceeded unity, the slope of DD' would exceed that of YY'; hence DD' would cut YY' to the left of B from below. Any displacement of B, whether erratic or systematic, would now be cumulative; in other words, profit-seeking entrepreneurs would drive the system to full employment or to extinction, depending on whether the displacement was to the right of B or to the left.

It should now be clear that Hansen's purely arithmetic reasoning[15] fails to convey Keynes' fundamental meaning. It is possible, however, to bring the one into harmony with the other. First, the "actually prevailing marginal propensity to consume," if it is to be taken as a historical datum at all, must be treated as a property of a stable consumption function; for, otherwise, it cannot have causal significance. Second, the marginal propensity to consume must be less than unity. Hansen reasons that if the initial income were 16, new investment 2, and the marginal propensity to consume $\frac{1}{2}$, income would rise to 20. If the Keynesian theory of income were reducible to a formula of this type, we should have to say that if the marginal propensity to consume were $\frac{3}{2}$, other circumstances of the case remaining unchanged, income would fall to 12.[16] This statement, arithmetically, is on a par with the preceding one. But whereas the first statement makes economic sense in Keynes' basic scheme, the second does not; for, as we have just shown, new investment in the second case will set off a cumulative movement that in real terms has no stopping point short of full employment, and in monetary terms no stopping point whatever.[17]

15 I am referring to Hansen's explicit argument. He may well have taken some things for granted.

16 To explain: Since new investment is 2, a reduction of income by 4 and of consumption by 6 is necessary to satisfy the assumption that the marginal propensity to consume is 3/2. In a more technical jargon, if the marginal propensity to consumer is 3/2, the marginal propensity to save is –1/2, and the investment multiplier –2; hence, if investment goes up by 2, income must come down by 4.

17 Keynes was an extraordinarily effective teacher, but a poor pedagogue. A good one would have defined the stability conditions of his system with some care. It is not necessary to assume (though there is a gain in realism in doing so) that the marginal propensity to consume is greater than zero and less than unity (*General Theory*, p. 96); it is sufficient to assume that it is less than unity. If the marginal propensity exceeded unity, the system would be completely unstable, as Keynes states. If the marginal propensity equals unity, three cases are possible: neutral equilibrium as defined in the quotation in the text (i.e., when $II' = SS'$ for all values of income

I have only one additional comment at this juncture. Hansen advises the reader to "compare the highly rigid picture which he gets from the discussion of the Keynesian determinants of income as stated in Burns' pamphlet, with the flexible treatment found" in different portions of the *General Theory*. If by this warning Hansen means merely that my summary fails to convey much that is contained in Keynes' book, I of course agree. My summary was designed to convey the "theoretical skeleton that underlies the Keynesian system,"[18] not as an abstract of the *General Theory*.[19] There are, to be sure, numerous and enlightening asides and qualifications throughout the *General Theory*. But Keynes was much inclined to operate with the bare bones of his system, and the Keynesians have done so preponderantly. My summary represents rather faithfully, I think, the analytic foundation on which the Keynesian school has built its theories, prognoses, and programs.

II. THE DETERMINACY OF KEYNES' THEORY

My essay on *Keynesian Thinking* carried a warning against what I consider to be the oversimplified doctrines of Keynes, especially as they are being used by his more zealous followers. I asserted

---

in Fig. 2), progressive inflation (when II' exceeds SS' by a constant), and progressive deflation (when SS' exceeds II' by a constant). Keynes doubtless was aware of these possibilities. Thus he writes: If the public seeks "to consume the whole of any increment of income, there will be no point of stability and prices will rise without limit" (*ibid.*, p. 117). This statement does not contradict the quotation in the text; the two treat of different cases in the event of a marginal propensity of unity. But both statements also illustrate Keynes' carelessness about proper qualifying clauses (cf. *ibid.*, p. 261). This, indeed, is the main reason why the *General Theory* is difficult and so frequently misunderstood.

[18] *Keynesian Thinking*, p. 6.

[19] The proper comparison is with the summaries of fundamentals sketched by Keynes himself, not with the parts of the *General Theory* selected by Hansen (though I hope that these parts as well as the rest of the treatise will receive the reader's attention). I refer to pages 25-30 of the *General Theory*, and to pages 219-221 of Keynes' paper in the February 1937 number of the *Quarterly Journal of Economics*. See also pages 247-249 of the *General Theory* (contained in one of Hansen's recommendations), though this summary is less successful in exposing the skeleton of the system than the summaries just cited. Cf. the following: A. P. Lerner, "Mr. Keynes' General Theory of Employment," *International Labor Review*, October 1936, especially pp. 446-447; P. A. Samuelson, "The Stability of Equilibrium: Comparative Statics and Dynamics," *Econometrica*, April 1941, pp. 113-120, and "Lord Keynes and the General Theory," *ibid.*, July 1946, especially pp. 192, 199; O. Lange, "On the Theory of the Multiplier," *ibid.*, July-October 1943, pp. 227-228; L. Klein, "Theories of Effective Demand and Employment," *Journal of Political Economy*, April 1947, pp. 109-117, and the review in the same, pp. 168-170; L. Tarshis, *The Elements of Economics* (Houghton Mifflin, 1947), Part IV, especially pp. 346, 360-365. (As far as I know, the sympathy of these authors for Keynes is not suspect.)

that the widespread opinion "that Keynes has explained what determines the volume of employment at any given time . . . reflects a pleasant but dangerous illusion."[20] After pointing out the essentials of the Keynesian theory and its structural similarity to the Ricardian model, I made the following comment:

". . . Let us go back to the theoretical skeleton of the Keynesian system and examine it more carefully. Suppose that the volume of intended investment is $2 billion, income payments $20 billion, and consumers' outlay at this level of income $18 billion. On the basis of these data, the economic system is alleged to be in equilibrium. But the equilibrium is aggregative, and this is a mere arithmetic fiction. Business firms do not have a common pocketbook. True, they receive in the aggregate precisely the sum they had expected, but that need not mean that even a single firm receives precisely what it had expected. Since windfall profits and losses are virtually bound to be dispersed through the system, each firm will adjust to its own sales experience, and within a firm the adjustment will vary from one product to another. Under the circumstances the intended investment cannot—quite apart from 'autonomous' changes—very well remain at $2 billion, and the propensity to consume is also likely to change. Our data therefore do not determine a unique size of national income; what they rather determine is a movement away from a unique figure. Of course, we cannot tell the direction or magnitude of the movement, but that is because the basic data on which the Keynesian analysis rests are not sufficiently detailed for the purpose.

"I have imagined that Keynes' aggregative equilibrium is realized from the start. But suppose that this does not happen; suppose that, in the initial period, the intended investment is $2 billion, income payments $16 billion, and that savings at this level of income are zero. Will income now gravitate towards the $20 billion mark, as the theory claims it should? There is little reason to expect this will happen. In the first place, windfall profits will be unevenly distributed, and the adjustment of individual firms to their widely varying sales experiences will induce a change in the aggregate of their intended investment. In the second place, unemployed resources will exercise some pressure on the prices of the factors of production, and here and there tend to stimulate investment. In the third place, if an expansion in the output of consumer goods does get under way, it will induce additions to inventories for purely technical reasons; further, the change in the business outlook is apt to stimulate the formation of new firms, and to induce existing firms to embark on investment undertakings of a type that have no close relation to recent sales experience. In the fourth place, as income expands, its distribution is practically certain to be modified; this will affect the propensity to consume, as will also the emergence of capital gains, the willingness of consumers to increase purchases on credit, and the difficulty faced by consumers in adjusting many of their expenditures to increasing incomes in the short run. These reactions, and I have listed only the more obvious ones, are essential parts of the adjustment mechanism of a free enterprise economy. Under their impact the data with which we started—namely, the amount of intended investment and the consumption function—are bound to change, perhaps slightly, perhaps enormously. It is wrong, therefore, to conclude that these data imply or determine, even in the sense of a rough approximation, a unique level at which the income and employment of a nation will tend to settle. In strict logic, the data determine, if anything, some complex cumulative movement, not a movement towards some fixed position.

"If this analysis is sound, the imposing schemes for governmental action that are being bottomed on Keynes' equilibrium theory must be viewed with skepticism. It does not follow, of course, that these schemes could not be convincingly defended on other grounds. But it does follow that the Keynesians lack a clear analytic foundation for judging how a given fiscal policy will affect the size of the national income or the volume of employment."[21]

This criticism can be summed up in a sentence: viz., the consumption function and the volume of intended investment, which are impounded in *ceteris paribus* by the Keynesian theory, *cannot* (except by accident) remain constant, since the very process of adjusting to the data (the consumption function and the volume of intended investment) will, quite apart from independent influences that may operate on these data, induce changes in them. Nevertheless I have thought it well, for reasons that will become apparent, to reproduce the original criticism in full.

Hansen observes that if my criticism simply means "that there are dynamic effects of the approach to equilibrium," that much had already been "admirably stated" by Keynes. I do not think it worth while to dwell on this comment.[22] The important thing is

21 *ibid.*, pp. 8-9.
22 However, I wish to note, first, that Hansen gives no reference to Keynes' statement; second, the faint suggestion on page 249 of the *General Theory* (if this is the

Hansen's attempt to dismiss the criticism on the ground that it is not basic. Hansen does not argue the case directly, but proceeds by analogy. He invites attention to Taussig's "temperate remarks concerning the 'penumbra' area of price determination," and informs the reader that Taussig's "highly interesting comments, elaborating dynamic aspects of the problem, were, however, not believed by Taussig himself to be damaging to the Marshallian theory of supply and demand." The reader is left to infer that my criticism, which elaborates dynamic aspects of the income problem, is likewise not damaging to Keynes' theory of income. And has not the reader been gracefully prepared for this inference by Hansen's earlier remark that the substance of my criticism had been "admirably stated"—and presumably properly handled—by Keynes himself?

I can explain Hansen's dialectical feat only on the ground that he has not fully understood my argument.[23] I shall therefore try again, and this time guard against deceptive analogies. Let us consider the output of a firm operating under conditions of pure competition. With minor modifications, Figure 2 will serve as an illustration of the case. Assume that the horizontal line II' represents the demand curve facing the firm, and that the rising line SS' (the vertical scale being adjusted to eliminate negative values)

---

statement Hansen has in mind) hardly covers the case; third, it would be impossible to show, on the basis of citations from Keynes, that he submitted his work to the criticism I make; fourth, while Hansen's phrasing of my criticism (in view of the surrounding text) suggests that, in a general way, he has grasped my meaning at this point, it is not the phrasing I would use. (I should not speak of "dynamic effects of the approach to equilibrium," since the very point of the argument is that there are no good theoretical reasons for believing there will be such an approach.)

23 Of that there is some evidence, apart from what I say in the text and in the preceding note. (1) When I assert that "our data . . . do not determine a unique size of national income," Hansen inquires "what data?" The answer is the consumption function and the intended investment assumed in my example. (2) In commenting on my illustrative figures Hansen fails to notice that, when I suppose that "in the initial period, the intended investment is $2 billion, income payments $16 billion," etc., I explicitly proceed from a position of disequilibrium. (3) Hansen asserts that he is "forced to disagree both on the basis of theoretical and statistical studies" if, in questioning the determinacy of the Keynesian theory of income, I believe "that the consumption schedule and levels of actual investment must be moved *capriciously* by the dynamic process of adjustment" (my italics). I am puzzled how Hansen could have imagined I meant any such thing, since I at no time referred to capricious movements but did suggest that the "data" determine a cumulative movement.

A parenthetic item remains: what theoretical and statistical studies does Hansen have in mind? I do not know of any statistical studies that indicate absence of capricious shifts in the consumption function. It seems to me that it is exceptionally difficult to determine short-run shifts (other than seasonal) of the consumption function empirically, and that this seriously limits the effective use of the Keynesian analytical apparatus for many problems of short-run economic change.

represents the marginal cost of different possible quantities of its output (indicated on the horizontal axis). According to the standard theory, these data suffice to determine the output of the firm in "the short run." The solution is indicated by the abscissa of the point of intersection of II' and SS', which in our diagram is 20. The proof is simple. If output were smaller, an extra unit of output would add more to revenue than it would to costs; while if output were greater, a reduction of output by one unit would cut costs more than revenue. Since profit is at a maximum when output is 20, any deviation from that figure will stimulate a movement towards it. In this sense output is uniquely determined.

Within its own framework, this theory of the firm is strictly valid. There is nothing in the situation surrounding the indicated equilibrium output that could of itself induce changes in the demand curve facing the firm (the market price) or in its schedule of marginal costs. Hence the theory cannot be challenged on the ground that if output happened to be at the indicated equilibrium value, it could not be maintained. Nor can the theory be challenged on the ground that if output happened to be out of equilibrium, the process of adjusting to the data—that is, to the demand and supply schedules of the firm—would of itself modify these data. Any criticism along these lines would overlook the condition of pure competition—which reduces the firm to an atom. To be sure, as output varies, there will be changes in the resources employed and in income payments. But since the firm can have only a negligible influence on the demand for resources or on the industry's output, it cannot perceptibly influence any price; in other words, the demand curve facing the firm and its schedule of marginal costs can remain virtually intact as its output undergoes variation.

Let us now return to Keynes' theory of income. In essence, it is an extension of demand and supply analysis to output as a whole. The vital factors in this analysis are the consumption function and the intended investment. These are the data to which business firms, in the aggregate, are supposed to adjust. These are also the data that the theory impounds. But processes of reasoning that are valid for the output of a single firm or small industry cannot be carried over mechanically to output as a whole. Indirect effects can be ignored or slighted in the case of an economic atom, but not for the economy taken as a whole. Infinitesimal adjustments, which might still save the situation formally, are of no practical relevance. By failing to analyze the far-flung repercussions of adjustment processes, Keynes' theory of aggregate income moves on a superficial level, and misrepresents the forces at work. This is the upshot of the criticism of the determinacy of this theory, quoted at the beginning of this section. To dispose of the criticism it would be necessary to show that the induced changes in the consumption function and intended investment are inappreciable, or that they are self-correcting even if large. I suggest that the reader, whether or not he thinks the criticism justified, now turn back and see whether Hansen has come to grips with the issue.[24]

While I concluded in my essay that Keynes has failed to justify his claim of explaining what determines the volume of employment at any given time, I did not claim that my criticism was decisive. Let the reader note carefully the following sentences, which express the essence of what I tried to convey in the essay: "The problem of unemployment facing our generation calls for realistic, thorough, and unceasing investigation. The great and obvious virtue of the remedies proposed by the Keynesians is that they seek to relieve mass unemployment; their weakness is that they lean heavily on a speculative analysis of uncertain value. This weakness attaches also to my critical remarks on the theory of underemployment equilibrium. Granted that the simple determinism of Keynesian doctrine is an illusion, it does not follow that secular stagnation is another, or that the consumption function may not be sufficiently stable in experience to enable public officials to forecast reliably some consequences of their policies. These questions raise factual issues of the highest importance. . . ."[25]

III. THE KEYNESIAN CONSUMPTION FUNCTION

I have already suggested how important the consumption function is in Keynes' scheme. This was emphasized in *Keynesian Thinking*, where I argued that the consumption function occupies much

[24] The Taussig analogy, as used by Hansen, skirts essentials: (1) Taussig assumed that the *underlying* conditions of demand and supply in a given industry were independent of adjustment processes. Can a similar assumption be reasonably made for the economy as a whole? (2) Taussig did not assume independence in the short run; on the contrary, he emphasized changes in the "data" induced by adjustment processes. If this much be granted for the Keynesian theory, can it be claimed that it explains what determines income and employment at any given time? (3) Taussig considered the indeterminacy of the Marshallian price theory in the short run (days or weeks or months) a matter of real importance. Can it be argued that the indeterminacy of the Keynesian income theory in *its* short run (surely a longer span) is of slight consequence? (See F. W. Taussig, "Is Market Price Determinate?" *Quarterly Journal of Economics*, May 1921, especially pp. 401, 402, 405, 411. Compare the passages quoted by Hansen with Taussig's conclusion in full.)

[25] *Keynesian Thinking*, pp. 10-11.

the same place in Keynesian economics as the agricultural production function in Ricardian economics. Since the Ricardian parallel is not immediately relevant, I shall confine quotation to the passages on Keynesianism: "The most important proposition in Keynesian economics is that the consumption function has a *certain shape*, that is, consumer outlay increases with national income but by less than the increment of income. . . . The Keynesians treat the consumption function as *fixed*, and deduce the effects on the size of the national income of an increase or decrease in private investment, or of an increase or decrease in governmental loan expenditure. . . . To be sure, the . . . Keynesians . . . recognize that the consumption function is not absolutely rigid, and they frequently insert qualifications to their main conclusions. But I have formed the definite impression that the Keynesians—except when they discuss changes in personal taxation—attach even less importance to their qualifications than did the Ricardians. . . ."[26]

I have put in italics the words singled out by Hansen as evidence of my "misconceptions" with respect to the consumption function. That these words do not suffice to convey my meaning is evident from the context in which they appear. I charged the Keynesians with minimizing the importance of shifts in the consumption function; I did not claim that Keynes or his followers believe that the consumption function is "fixed." Once more, I do not say merely that Keynesian economics postulates a "certain shape" of the consumption function. The rest of the sentence, which identifies the meaning of "certain shape" reads: "that is, consumer outlay increases with national income but by less than the increment of income." Since this is nothing other than Keynes' 'psychological law,' which in Keynes' own words[27] is the "key" to the problem of income determination and "absolutely fundamental" to his theory, is it not strange that Hansen sees a misconception in my statement?

The best interpretation I have been able to put on Hansen's strictures is that he is concerned less with what I actually say about the Keynesian treatment of the consumption function[28] than with

---

[26] *ibid.*, p. 7 (italics added).

[27] *General Theory*, p. 29, and "The General Theory of Employment," *op.cit.*, p. 220.

[28] Thus Hansen alleges other misconceptions of Keynes' views (or is it the views of Keynesians?) "about these matters," and quotes four statements from pages 9-10 of my essay as evidence. By "these matters" Hansen is apparently referring to the consumption function, since that is the subject he is discussing. But three of the quoted statements do not even relate to the consumption function (for example, the statement that "monopolistic practices of business firms can safely be neglected"). Hansen also

the general drift of my remarks. I suspect that Hansen is troubled because my essay conveys the impression that the Keynesians are excessively mechanical in their thinking, that they gloss over the turbulent life that goes on within aggregates, that they give little heed to adjustment processes in our society, that they subject *ceteris paribus* to excessive strain, that they slight in particular the instability of the consumption function; and that while Keynes is guilty on all these counts, the Keynesians—among whom Hansen is outstanding—are guiltier still. If that is what is troubling Hansen, I do not think the fault is mine.

---

claims there is a misconception—or is it misconceptions?—on page 19, but fails to specify what it or they are.

The four statements on pages 9-10 which Hansen construes as misconceptions "about these matters" are lifted (a bit inaccurately) from my analysis of the types of assumption needed to reach a conclusion—of which much has been made lately by Keynesian writers—concerning different fiscal paths to 'full employment'; namely, that the loan-expenditure method "avoids . . . the excessively large expenditures" of the tax-financing method "and the excessive deficits" of the tax-reduction method (*Keynesian Thinking*, p. 9). This conclusion is advanced, among others, by Hansen in "Three Methods of Expansion through Fiscal Policy," *American Economic Review*, June 1945. Since Hansen did not indicate how he reached this "highly suggestive conclusion" (*Keynesian Thinking*, p. 9), I tried in my essay to pin down the theoretical steps that would lead rigorously to his assertions, and that apparently underlie them. My analysis may be right or it may be wrong; instead of dealing with it, Hansen amasses phrases without regard to the context, and declares they are misconceptions "about these matters"—by which he seems to mean the consumption function, though what he actually means is uncertain.

However, Hansen makes one comment (later and quite incidentally) that possibly relates to this fiscal analysis. The comment begins as follows: "The last paragraph on page 7 relating to recent developments in income theory discloses a mistaken view with respect to the nature of these contributions." (In the paragraph cited, which runs over a page in length, just two sentences bear on recent developments in income theory: "Of late this theory [of the Keynesians on employment policy] has been refined and elaborated, so that 'deficit financing' need no longer be the key instrument for coping with unemployment, and I shall refer to one of these refinements at a later point [this comes on pages 9-10 of the essay]. But the *practical significance* of the modifications of the theory is problematical, and in any event the theory as I have sketched it still *dominates* the thinking of the Keynesians when they look beyond the transition from war to peace" [italics added].) Hansen then refers to Haavelmo's paper on "Multiplier Effects of a Balanced Budget" (*Econometrica*, October 1945), which takes for granted "that expenditures financed by progressive taxation (effecting a redistribution of income) may raise income," and goes on to discuss (as do the papers it stimulated) "the question whether tax-financed expenditures may be expansionist even though there is no redistributional effect upon the propensity to save." Hansen stops abruptly at this point. The best I can make of this incomplete argument is that Hansen sees an inconsistency between my method of handling the effects of taxation on the propensity to consume on page 10 of the essay and Haavelmo's method. But there is no inconsistency, since my schedule of the propensity to consume is tied to income before taxes (as is Hansen's in "Three Methods of Expansion through Fiscal Policy," *op.cit.*), while Haavelmo's is tied to disposable income.

Keynes says quite definitely: ". . . we are left with the conclusion that short-period changes in consumption largely depend on changes in the rate at which income (measured in wage-units) is being earned and not on changes in the propensity to consume out of a given income."[29] Keynes did not stop with this generalization. He proceeded to build a system from which "changes in the propensity to consume" were excluded. To be sure, the "changes" are brought in, now and then, by way of qualification. They are also brought in, now and then, in comments on policy. But they do not enter the grand theorems. The 'blade' of investment carves out economic fortune; the 'blade' of the propensity to consume remains stationary while the carving is done. Or to change the metaphor, investment is the actor in the drama of employment, and the consumption function is the stage on which this actor—a rather temperamental one—performs his antics. Why is national income a function of investment? Why is Keynes equipped with an investment multiplier, which accomplishes wonders, but does not even mention a consumption multiplier? Why should an extra Ford car fructify income if acquired for business use, but not if acquired for pleasure? To these questions there is only one logical answer: In Keynes' scheme investment is a free variable, while consumption is rigidly and passively tied to income.[30]

But what of Hansen's views on the consumption function? Taking his extensive writing of recent years as a whole,[31] I feel that he is more prone to identify the formal Keynesian model with the operations of the actual world than was Keynes himself. To Keynes a stable consumption function is an analytic convenience, as I mentioned earlier. True, he sometimes loses sight of the restriction. But when he is explicitly engaged in empirical generalization, his characteristic phrase is a "fairly stable" function. To Hansen a stable consumption function seems to be a tight description

[29] *General Theory*, p. 110. Cf. *ibid.*, pp. 95-97, 248. I do not believe that in expressing the consumption function in wage units, Keynes meant more than that consumption "is obviously much more a function of (in some sense) *real* income than of money-income" (*ibid.*, p. 91, Keynes' italics). I do not know of any evidence that will support Hansen's tentative suggestion that Keynes meant to allow by this device for secular shifts in the consumption function. See Hansen's "Keynes and the General Theory," this *Review*, Vol. xxviii (1946), p. 184.

[30] Samuelson has put the matter accurately: "The crucial assumption upon which it [the doctrine of the investment multiplier] stands or falls is that consumption expenditures and savings are rigidly related to the level of national income. The passive character of consumption cannot be sufficiently stressed." See his "Theory of Pump-Priming Reexamined," *American Economic Review*, September 1940, p. 498.

[31] I have not, however, as yet examined with any care Hansen's recent book on *Economic Policy and Full Employment* (McGraw-Hill, 1947).

of reality, at least in the short run. His characteristic phrase is "highly stable." The following is a typical specimen of his thinking on the subject: "There is no evidence that the cyclical consumption-income pattern *has shifted, or is likely to shift in the near future, so* as to increase consumption and reduce savings. . . . The fact is that, at moderately high income levels, persistent institutional factors determine within *rather rigid limits* the ratio of consumption to income. . . . The superficial view that the persistence of vast unsatisfied consumer wants is an answer to the problem of limited investment outlets—outlets inadequate to fill the gap fixed by the consumption-savings pattern—overlooks the *stubborn fact* that this pattern is, according to all the available evidence, a *highly stable* one. It is not likely to be radically changed from one decade to another except by important modifications in fundamental institutional arrangements. . . . But whatever the net trend . . . there can be little doubt that *no important shift* in the consumption-income pattern can be expected within a short period. We have to recognize that we are dealing here with a function that is *highly stable and is not easily changed.*"[32]

In his present paper Hansen protests that he does not hold that the consumption function is "fixed." The above quotation would definitely support him in that statement. Hansen also protests that he does not hold that the consumption function is "practically invariant." Whether the quotation also supports *that* statement, I must leave to the readers' own sense of adjectival subtlety. Hansen protests that he has himself called attention to the upward secular shift in the consumption function, and indeed he has. He even grants that seasonal movements in the function "might conceivably . . . be found to exist."[33] All this is to the good. I prefer, however, to stick to the issue, which is not that the Keynesians regard the consumption function as fixed, but that they attach slight importance to its wanderings.[34]

I know of only three ways of testing the position of an author. The first is to determine whether his writing as a whole has a definite pattern. The second is to examine with special care what

[32] *Fiscal Policy and Business Cycles* (Norton, 1941), pp. 247-249 (my italics). See also *ibid.*, pp. 62-63, 237, 238, 250.

[33] Hansen's caution here is admirable, even if a little excessive. Of all the positive propositions that have been laid down in the literature on the consumption function, its seasonality is almost certainly the one that can be most firmly buttressed by statistical evidence on the American economy.

[34] Except, perhaps, "when they discuss changes in personal taxation" (*Keynesian Thinking*, p. 7).

he says when he attempts to sum up his own thinking.[35] The third is to observe how he handles major economic problems. The last test is the most important of all. I judge that if shifts in the consumption function over the course of a business cycle seemed at all significant to Hansen, he would not assert unequivocally that "it is just because of the *high stability* of the consumption function that fluctuations in the rate of investment *produce* the business cycle."[36] Nor would he say, without further ado, that the "essence" of the depression of 1929-1932, "as indeed of *all* depressions, can quite simply and plainly be stated"; this essence being the decline in private capital outlays, which "*caused* unemployment in all the heavy goods industries, and in turn *induced* a decline in consumption expenditures."[37] Again, I judge that if Hansen took the upward secular drift in the consumption function seriously, he would not have ignored it in his Presidential Address (American Economic Association, 1938), which dealt with the forces that shaped national income in the "nineteenth century" and how these forces have lost strength in "our times." In this important paper—still the fountainhead of stagnationist thinking—Hansen freezes the consumption function almost at the start,[38] then (quite logically) maintains silence on its part in economic evolution.

[35] See the above quotation, identified in note 32, which comes from the concluding section of Hansen's fullest discussion of the consumption function, Chapter xi of *Fiscal Policy and Business Cycles*. I may add that much of that chapter seems to me to be in conflict with the conclusions quoted above.

[36] *ibid.*, p. 249 (my italics).

[37] See Hansen's essay on "Stability and Expansion," in *Financing American Prosperity*, ed. P. T. Homan and F. Machlup (Twentieth Century Fund, 1945), p. 210 (my italics). On the stability of the consumption function, see also *ibid.*, pp. 219, 225.

[38] This is accomplished in a single sentence (which purports to sum up both the thinking of economists and the economic past): "Thus we may postulate a consensus on the thesis that in the absence of a positive program designed to stimulate consumption, full employment of the productive resources is essentially a function of the vigor of investment activity." This, of course, is the kernel of Keynes' short-run theory, and Hansen makes it serve a theory of long-run economic development. See page 372 of the Blakiston volume on *Readings in Business Cycle Theory*, where Hansen's paper on "Economic Progress and Declining Population Growth" is reprinted from the *American Economic Review*, March 1939.

Can it be that Hansen was not aware of the upward secular drift of the consumption function at the time he wrote this paper? His first mention of it, as far as I know, comes in Chapter xi of *Fiscal Policy and Business Cycles* (1941), p. 233. Chapter xvii of that book reprints the Presidential Address, with various modifications. The sentence quoted at the beginning of this note does not appear in Chapter xvii. Was Hansen led to make the omission by what he says on page 233? If so, he must have felt that, as far as the consumption function was concerned, no further change was necessary; for he did not add one word on the role of the upward drift in the consumption function in economic development. (The new paragraph inserted on pages 357-358 is of some interest in this connection.)

There is much more that might be said of the manner in which the consumption function is handled by the Keynesian school, but I think I have gone far enough to indicate that the "rigid picture" of Keynesianism in my essay—while displeasing to Hansen—is painted from life. I wish merely to add a few methodological remarks on the consumption function per se, which is a schedule or curve relating aggregate consumption to aggregate income. If the curve is to mean more than a line on a piece of paper, time must somehow enter. It does so in three ways, as in a demand curve of the Marshallian type. First, the curve relates to a definite period— day, year, or something else. Second, both consumption and income are rates per unit of time, which of course need not be the same as the specified period. Third, the curve shows the response of consumption to income after a certain period of adjustment, which may be 'short' or 'long.' These simple observations have several significant implications: (a) The curve shows a relationship between hypothetical—not existential—magnitudes. (b) For any given period there is not one curve relating consumption to income, but a family of curves, each corresponding to a different period of adjustment. (c) Since there is no fast line[39] between consumer and investment expenditure, another family of curves—one for each reasonable pair of definitions of income and consumption—corresponds to every member of the first family. (d) Finally, since tastes, technology, and resources keep changing in the world we know, the ensemble of curves may be expected to shift from one period to the next.

This, I think, expresses the essentials of the theoretical framework that faces the economist who seeks to determine the empirical properties of the Keynesian consumption function. Quite obviously, vigorous short cuts must be taken, if anything useful is to be accomplished on the problem. I take it as a reassuring sign of our times that the *General Theory* was promptly followed by efforts to measure the consumption function; that there was no gap of a quarter century, such as separated Moore from Marshall. But I feel that it is regrettable that some of the work has been

[39] Keynes says that "any reasonable definition of the line between consumer-purchasers and investor-purchasers will serve us equally well, provided that it is consistently applied" (*General Theory*, p. 61). This is entirely proper for a formal system. But Keynes' "fairly stable" consumption function is not a property of his formal system; it is an empirical generalization, as is Hansen's "highly stable" function. Can the empirical properties of the aggregate consumption function be determined reliably without an analysis being made of the parts that make up the whole—especially the parts that shade into the volatile category of investment?

done in haste, and that much of it has been used uncritically. Man is a slave not only to his theories, but to the very words in which theories are expressed. I venture the guess that if Keynes' theory had been worded in terms of a 'propensity to save' instead of a 'propensity to consume' (which would not of itself change the theory one iota), some of his doctrines would have fewer adherents today. My reason is simply that the evidence which *seems* to support a "stable" consumption function would less readily support a "stable" savings function.

IV. KEYNESIAN APPARATUS VS. KEYNESIAN THEORY

A considerable part of Hansen's paper is devoted to methodological questions. Here I see no great issues raised. When all is said and done, there is no methodological problem in economics other than straight thinking and the competent use of evidence. The important question always is whether this or that theory is sound, not what role this or that investigator assigns to economic theory. I have, perhaps, more faith in the possibility of a science of economics than Hansen.[40] I surely think that economists should work unceasingly towards that end, and that they fail to do so when they grow impatient with their intractable material. I look forward to the day when economists will not rest content until they have at least specified the observable conditions that would contradict their theories, when the conformity of a theory to facts is respected no less than its logical consistency, and when carefully formulated theories are tested promptly and thoroughly in a score of research centers. But my views on economic methodology, such as they may be, are quite apart from the issues of Keynesian economics raised in my essay and so roundly challenged by Hansen.[41]

I do not see that Hansen's methodological comments have anything to do with the validity of Keynes' basic theory of underemployment equilibrium. Nevertheless, it may be worth while to clarify the distinction between "theory" and "theoretical apparatus" which seems to underlie Hansen's methodological remarks.

[40] That does not mean I believe that massive statistical studies will provide us with "a definitive understanding of economic developments which is no longer subject to doubt by competent economists." See, for example, page 17 of *Keynesian Thinking* ("The data necessary to develop adequately the secular aspects of consumption and saving will not be easy to find or to interpret when found, but the importance of the question may justify our taking the risk") or page 24 ("True, the most painstaking studies of experience will not always lead to conclusive answers; but they should at least narrow the margins of uncertainty, and thus furnish a better basis than now exists for dealing with grave issues of business cycle theory and policy").
[41] See above, note 1.

This distinction is blurred in Hansen's account, with the result that my views, if not also his own, are not represented accurately.

I have no quarrel with the Keynesian theoretical apparatus as such, any more than with the Ricardian or Marshallian. The Keynesian theoretical apparatus is merely an analytical filing case for handling problems of aggregate income and employment, and is logically akin to Marshall's filing case for handling problems of price. Marshall's files are labeled 'demand' and 'supply,' and there are subdivisions in each on the 'length of the run.'[42] Keynes' files are labeled 'propensity to consume,' 'marginal efficiency of capital,' 'liquidity preference,' and 'supply of money.' The usefulness of Marshall's files in facilitating orderly analysis of price problems is, I think, universally recognized. Keynes' filing case is a more brilliant construction; it is also more novel, and is still fighting its way.[43] On its effectiveness in handling some problems, especially those of short-run change in income and employment, I happen to have serious doubts.[44] But I should readily grant its promise for analyzing certain broad problems of economic organization and evolution, and I think that much more experimenting needs to be done before its range of usefulness can be justly appraised.[45]

But the Keynesian *theoretical apparatus* is one thing, the Keynesian *general theory of income and employment* is another, and the Keynesian *theory of income and employment in the current institutional setting* is still another. My essay was concerned with the second and third, not the first. I questioned the determinacy of Keynes' general theory on the ground that it proceeds on a *tacit* assumption that is open to grave doubt—namely, independence of the consumption function and intended investment from the

[42] The sublabels on time are indistinct for demand, but I think they are there; in any case, they can be put there (as they can and should be throughout the Keynesian file).

[43] No one questions Keynes' enormous influence, but there are better sources than gossip for ascertaining its extent. The files of the *Economic Journal* and other English periodicals do not support Hansen's report (based on what he heard from an unnamed English economist) that "every economist in Britain is now a Keynesian . . . in the sense that all use the Keynesian terminology and the Keynesian theoretical apparatus."

[44] I have in mind here the apparatus as a whole. Chapters 19 and 22 of the *General Theory* deserve very careful study from the viewpoint of the effectiveness of the Keynesian theoretical apparatus, as do also some later contributions—among them the treatment of business cycles in Tarshis, *op.cit.*

[45] I have the impression that the Keynesian file itself is being recast: that the files on 'liquidity preference' and 'supply of money' are fairly inactive, and that the file on 'marginal efficiency of capital' now usually carries the label 'investment.'

adjustment processes of a free enterprise system. If the criticism is valid, it bears also on the doctrine of secular stagnation, which I consider the characteristic expression of the Keynesian theory of income and employment in "our times." But two *explicit* assumptions of the stagnationist doctrine have a more vital bearing on its validity. The first is that "consumer outlay is linked fairly rigidly to national income and is unlikely to expand unless income expands," the second that "investment opportunities are limited in a 'mature' economy such as our own."[46] Since these assumptions raise factual issues of the highest importance, it surely is desirable to put them to a thorough test.[47] "A scientific theory cannot require the facts to conform to its own assumptions," and to urge this homely truth—I have now put it in Keynes' words[48]—is not to raise, as Hansen seems to believe, "important issues concerning the value and validity of theoretical analysis."[49]

An economic theorist is justified on many occasions in oversimplifying facts to clarify in his own mind what he believes to be significant relationships.[50] He is likewise justified in bringing the results of his speculative inquiries before his colleagues, whether to seek their critical appraisal before going further or to stimulate them by his work. As long as the economist moves within these boundaries, he may be excused even for not making a strenuous effort to discover how seriously he has distorted the facts by his simplifying assumptions. But when he attempts to give practical advice, he loses his license to suppose anything he likes and to

[46] *Keynesian Thinking*, p. 6.   [47] See *ibid.*, pp. 10-17.
[48] *General Theory*, p. 276.
[49] When I assert that "Keynes and his followers . . . by and large . . . still seek to arrive at economic truth in the manner of Ricardo and his followers" (*Keynesian Thinking*, p. 4), I mean that the Keynesians manifest a strong tendency to take logical consistency with *explicit* assumptions as their criterion of economic truth and that this is insufficient, first, because the *explicit* assumptions may collide with facts of experience; second, because the *tacit* assumptions (they are always present) may do likewise. Hansen is not concerning himself with my views when he first interprets the above quotation to mean "searching for fruitful general hypotheses whose deductive implications are carefully assessed," then adds, "fortunately, this charge is indeed true as far as it goes."
Noting my statement on page 8 of the essay that "there is, of course, nothing unscientific about Ricardianism [i.e., the deductive method] as such," Hansen inquires why I wrote "the section dealing with 'the fate of the Ricardian system.'" The answer is contained in the beginning words of the next sentence on that page: "But *ceteris paribus* is a slippery tool. . . ." Hansen has apparently been misled by the phrase "the fate of the Ricardian system," which occurs at one point in the section on "The Lesson of Ricardianism." The context makes it plain (I think) that in that section I was concerned exclusively with Ricardo's *dynamic* theory (in Mill's sense), not with his *static* theory.
[50] See *Keynesian Thinking*, pp. 9-10.

consider merely the logical implications of untested assumptions. It then becomes his duty to examine with scrupulous care the degree in which his assumptions are factually valid. If he finds reason to question the close correspondence between the assumptions and actual conditions, he should either not undertake to give any practical advice, or frankly and fully disclose the penumbra that surrounds his analysis and the conclusions drawn from it. Better still, he should rework his assumptions in the light of the facts and see whether he is justified on this new basis in telling men in positions of power how they should act. Economics is a very serious subject when the economist assumes the role of counselor to nations.

I cannot agree with Professor Hansen that "the only realistic question is whether or not Keynes has given a fruitful direction to the study of income determination and employment." To this question a hearty affirmative is the only answer, but it is not the only realistic question. In view of the part that Keynes and his school have played in the theoretical and practical worlds, it is not unrealistic to inquire whether their theories bear out the claim that they explain what determines the volume of employment at any given time.[51] I do not think this claim could be readily accepted, even if my doubts concerning Keynes' general theory of underemployment equilibrium—or its special variant, the theory of secular stagnation—turned out to be baseless. Somehow the business cycle, and the various technical and institutional lags on which it so largely rests, would have to be brought into the theoretical system. But as Professor Hansen himself suggests, Keynes' theory of business cycles is a mere sketch, quite incidental to the theory of underemployment equilibrium. In my essay I had something to say about the loose relation between Keynes' thinking on business cycles and the facts of experience, and Professor Hansen has challenged my interpretation. While our differences on Keynes' business cycle theory must not be overlooked, they have practically no bearing on the Keynesian doctrines that have stirred the world, and I therefore relegate this theme to an Appendix.

[51] Hansen asks whether I meant to imply that various governments, "misled by Keynes, have embarked upon a mistaken policy" in announcing their assumption of responsibility for the maintenance of a high and stable level of employment (the quoted words are from Hansen's paper). I meant to convey merely that in view of the existing state of knowledge governments are assuming a responsibility they may be unable to discharge adequately; hence "the need for authentic knowledge of the causes of unemployment in modern commercial nations is now greater than ever" (*Keynesian Thinking*, p. 10).

APPENDIX ON KEYNES' THEORY OF BUSINESS CYCLES

After considering Keynes' theory of underemployment equilibrium and the issues of fact raised by the Keynesian doctrine, I went on to stress "the need for tested knowledge of business cycles."[1] I tried to develop the simple but fundamental proposition that unless "precise and tested knowledge of what the business cycles of actual life have been like . . . is attained, any explanation is bound to bear an uncertain relation to the experiences we seek to understand or to guard against." Keynes' theory was brought in only incidentally, to illustrate "the consequences that may flow from a disregard of this elementary precaution." In a single paragraph I informed the reader of my purpose (just quoted), informed him also—on the chance that he did not already know it—that Keynes' theory is a "sketch" put "at the end of his long treatise on underemployment equilibrium," summarized the essentials of the sketch, and commented on its failure to square with experience. I then noted that "Keynes' adventure in business cycle theory is by no means exceptional. My reason for singling it out is merely that the *General Theory* has become for many, contrary to Keynes' own wishes, a sourcebook of established knowledge."[2]

It will help to clarify the substantive issues if I reproduce my account of Keynes' point of departure: "Keynes starts by saying that a theory of business cycles should account for a certain regularity in the duration and sequence of cyclical phases—that the duration of contractions, for example, is *about three to five years.* Second, the theory *should account for the sharp and sudden transition* from expansion to contraction, in contrast to the gradual and hesitant shift from contraction to expansion."[3] I have placed in italics the phrases singled out by Hansen for criticism. They seem brittle to Hansen and inspire this conclusion: "The version of Keynes which Burns criticizes is a straw man; it cannot be found in Keynes."

But is not Hansen's verdict too sweeping? In reviewing the *General Theory,* Hansen had this to say about Keynes' view on the duration of cyclical contractions: "The carrying costs of surplus stocks is the second important factor, *in Keynes' view,* which determines the *duration of depression.* The carrying charges tend to force the absorption of surplus stocks within a certain period,

---

[1] See *Keynesian Thinking*, pp. 17-24.

[2] *ibid.*, p. 19. In reading Hansen's critique, the reader may find it useful to take cognizance of this background.

[3] *Keynesian Thinking*, p. 18 (italics added).

usually within three to five years. While the process of stock absorption is going on there is . . . deflation and unemployment."[4] Hansen not only found in Keynes a contraction of about three to five years, but also that his theory was designed to explain *the* sharp and sudden transition from expansion to contraction. Hansen put Keynes' view as follows: "A complete explanation of the cycle must, moreover, involve an analysis of the crisis—*the sudden and violent turning point* from boom to depression."[5] In a later paper, Hansen found once again the sudden transition, not in any straw man, but in Keynes. Hansen even nodded in approval: "The reason why *the spurt comes to a sudden halt* is well stated by Keynes in his chapter on the Trade Cycle when he says that the essential character of the Trade Cycle is mainly the result of the way in which the marginal efficiency of capital fluctuates."[6]

I do not know Hansen's reasons for shifting his position, but I am reasonably confident that he was right the first time. When Hansen was trying to summarize Keynes' business cycle theory, he adopted the same interpretation that I did. The passages he now cites from Keynes are isolated remarks, which do justice mainly to Keynes' mischievous style; they do not convey his meaning faithfully. Take the following sentence by Keynes: "There is, however, another characteristic of what we call the Trade Cycle which our explanation must cover if it is to be adequate; namely, the phenomenon of the crisis—the *fact that the substitution of a downward for an upward tendency often takes place suddenly* and violently, whereas there is, as a rule, no such sharp turning-point when an upward is substituted for a downward tendency."[7] Hansen lifts one clause (the words in italics) from this sentence. To be sure, this clause suggests that downturns are merely *often* abrupt; but the sentence as a whole, I think, suggests that downturns are *as a rule* abrupt. This is the interpretation Hansen put on Keynes originally, and it is also the interpretation against which the critical remarks in my essay were directed.[8] And can there really

---

[4] See, for convenience, A. H. Hansen, *Full Recovery or Stagnation?* p. 33 (my italics).
[5] *ibid.*, p. 32 (my italics).   [6] *ibid.*, p. 51 (my italics).
[7] *General Theory*, p. 314. (Italics mine. In Keynes' text, crisis is italicized.)
[8] My statement that in Keynes' view "the theory should account for the sharp and sudden transition from expansion to contraction" can of course be read (as can the citations from Hansen just given) as implying that Keynes meant that downturns are *invariably* abrupt. Had I wished to convey this meaning, I need not have cited more than a single exception. Instead, I referred to Keynes' "rule," and cited several exceptions (four out of a possible seven during the period covered) to show that there was no such systematic difference between the upper and lower turning points as Keynes had supposed (*Keynesian Thinking*, p. 18).

be much doubt on this matter, in view of Keynes' theory that the (typically) sudden break in prosperity is caused (typically) by a "sudden collapse in the marginal efficiency of capital"?[9]

And what shall we say of Hansen's contention that when Keynes spoke of the duration of contractions as being "between, let us say, three and five years," he did not mean "about three to five years"? Hansen bases his argument on a part of this sentence from page 317 of the *General Theory*: "There are reasons, given firstly by the length of life of durable assets in relation to the normal rate of growth in a given epoch, and secondly by the carrying-costs of surplus stocks, *why the duration of the downward movement should have an order of magnitude which is not fortuitous, which does not fluctuate between, say, one year this time and ten years next time, but which shows some regularity of habit between, let us say, three and five years.*" Now it is possible, to be sure, to interpret Hansen's quotation (I have italicized it) as meaning merely that the longest contraction is less than twice the duration of the shortest.[10] But does this interpretation seem plausible? Did Keynes mean nothing by the "length of life of durable assets" or by the "carrying-costs of surplus stocks"? Hansen overlooks the fact that the sentence from which he quotes is part of a discussion of the factors that render "the slump so intractable." The discussion starts on page 316. Keynes first expresses the view that a "considerable interval of time" must elapse before a recovery can get under way. The passage quoted by Hansen comes a little later, and should be read against the background of Keynes' obvious concern with the *absolute* duration of contractions. This, I think, narrows the uncertainty. If doubt remains concerning the meaning of the phrase "between, let us say, three and five years," it is whittled away by a similar phrase on page 318, which definitely refers to the absolute period required for the absorption of stocks during a slump.[11] And there is additional evidence of Keynes' meaning. He makes a recovery wait not only on the absorption of stocks, but also on the "shortage of capital through use, decay and obsolescence" causing "a sufficiently obvious scarcity to increase

[9] *General Theory*, p. 315. Cf. *Keynesian Thinking*, pp. 18-19.

[10] On this interpretation (which seems to be Hansen's now) Keynes happens to be as wrong on the facts as in my interpretation (and Hansen's of earlier date). One can escape the discomfort once for all: if the passage quoted by Hansen is taken literally, I doubt if any facts could ever contradict it. There is, unhappily, a great abundance of ambiguous remarks throughout Keynes' chapter on business cycles. Under the circumstances, it is essential to work patiently, back and forth, over the text as a whole.

[11] See also *General Theory*, pp. 331-332, where stocks are further discussed.

the marginal efficiency" (p. 318). In view of the great durability of 'fixed' capital and the sharply reduced demands upon it during depression, can it be seriously argued that Keynes meant that this process could work itself out in a period much shorter than "say, three to five years"?

So much for the issue of the "straw man," which Hansen raised in connection with my account of the starting point of Keynes' theory. The theory itself I summarized as follows in the essay: "His [Keynes'] theory is that a collapse of investment brings prosperity to a close; that this in turn is caused by a collapse of confidence regarding the profitability of durable assets; and that the contraction which follows is bound to last, say, three to five years, since recovery is possible only after stocks have been worked off, and more important still, after the 'fixed' capital of business firms has been reduced sufficiently to restore its profitability."[12] Hansen passes over this summary, but attempts to refute what I say of the collision between Keynes' theory and the facts of experience. I cited three such facts. Hansen asserts that "not one of them collides with Keynes' cycle theory," but he stops to examine only one—namely, that "the stock of durable goods in a growing country is virtually free from any trace of business cycles, increasing as a rule during contractions of business activity as well as during expansions."[13] Hansen's argument, as best I can make out, is that

[12] *Keynesian Thinking*, p. 18.

[13] *ibid.*, p. 19. Hansen disputes a portion of the statement just quoted. He states that the latter half is "quite all right," but "the first half is definitely in error." Here the difficulty rests on a purely verbal misunderstanding. The latter half of the statement, modifying as it does the first half, merely serves to explain the first half. If, therefore, the latter half is "quite all right," there is no real difficulty.

Although I meant to convey no more than what I have just stated (nothing else was required by the question under examination), it may be well to note that statistics (expressed in a physical unit, for individual industries) suggest that the stock of industrial facilities not only increases, as a rule, during contractions as well as expansions of business cycles, but that the rate of increase itself is not systematically higher during a business cycle expansion than during adjacent contractions. How can this happen in view of the large fluctuations in the output of investment goods and of their close relation to business cycles? The reasons, put briefly, are as follows: (1) If the output of investment goods ascended linearly from the trough of a business cycle to a peak, then descended linearly to the date of the next business cycle trough; if, further, the output at successive troughs were identical, and likewise at successive peaks; if, finally, retirements were zero; then (barring qualitative distinctions) the stock of industrial facilities in place would increase at a consistently higher rate from midexpansion to midcontraction of business cycles than from midcontraction to midexpansion. (2) None of these assumptions is fulfilled in fact; and a little experimenting will indicate to what extent plausible departures from the model will introduce a haphazard element in the cyclical interval during which the rate of increase in the stock of industrial facilities is especially high or low. The most important randomizing factor in practice (I think) is the unevenness of the successive troughs and of

this fact does not collide with Keynes' theory, since everyone—including Keynes—knows that net investment in fixed capital is usually positive even in depressions.[14]

If this is Hansen's argument, it is needlessly indirect. The question at issue is simply whether I am right or wrong in reporting Keynes' theory to be that "recovery is possible only . . . after the 'fixed' capital of business firms has been reduced sufficiently to restore its profitability." If I am right, Keynes' theory requires that net investment be, typically, negative in depressions. I maintained that this did not happen. Since Hansen agrees, the way to redeem Keynes is to demonstrate that I misrepresented his theory of recovery. Hansen has not tried to do this, and I do not believe that he would find the task especially easy.[15]

---

successive peaks in output; for this means, roughly speaking, that the *level* of output of investment goods is greater in some business cycles during expansions and in others during contractions. (3) The preceding statements are based on the tacit assumption that the output (in the sense of value added, in constant prices) of investment goods and the installation of completed facilities are coincident. Of course, there is apt to be here a substantial and highly variable lag, which serves powerfully to distort and diversify the timing of the accelerations and retardations in the stock of industrial facilities.

The whole subject of the cyclical behavior of the stock of industrial capital requires extensive statistical and theoretical analysis. What I have said merely scratches the surface. But I have thought it advisable to indicate that Hansen's remarks concerning what is possible and what is not possible are very hasty.

[14] An earlier statement of Hansen's may be of interest: "The depression is a period of cessation of growth. There need be no actual relapse in capital formation—the existing stock being fully maintained" (*Full Recovery or Stagnation?* p. 51). See also *General Theory*, p. 329.

[15] On this question, see *ibid.*, especially pp. 105, 253, 317-318, and the Keynesian primer by Joan Robinson, *Introduction to the Theory of Employment*, p. 116. Cf. Tarshis, *op.cit.*, pp. 384, 444, 448.

Hicks and the Real Cycle

The theory of business cycles has been in a peculiarly unsettled position since Keynes' *General Theory* first appeared. The older students of the subject were, as a rule, concerned with the fluctuations in business activity at large—not with the movements of a particular economic factor such as production, employment, prices, or incomes. Keynes shifted the emphasis violently in two directions. First, he made the level of employment his major interest. Second, he concentrated on the factors that tend to make this level at one time higher or lower than at another. Thus the fundamental unit of analysis became the 'volume of employment at any time' rather than 'the business cycle.' This shift of emphasis was well suited to the thirties, when unemployment overshadowed every other economic and political problem. Before long Keynes' theory was eagerly embraced and ingeniously simplified. Not only business cycle theory but the theory of value itself fell for a time by the wayside. For if Keynes was able to explain what determines the volume of employment without troubling much about the cost-price structure, some of his followers could do so without troubling about it at all.

But economic life does not stand still, and every change in its underlying conditions sooner or later stimulates fresh economic thinking. Under the impact of war and inflation during the forties, theoretical interest in the behavior of prices, production, efficiency, and the business cycle has slowly reemerged. Hicks' recent book on the 'trade cycle' is a significant expression of renewed concern with the cycle, in contrast to the level of employment.[1] A fundamental task of modern economics, as Hicks sees it, is to pass from the Keynesian theory of employment to a theory of business cycles. And that is what he has set out to do. "It is . . . a mistake," he tells us, "to begin one's investigation with a definition of the kind of fluctuation which one is going to regard as basic—deciding whether one is going to regard the cycle as being fundamentally a fluctuation in employment, or output, or prices, or interest rates, or money supplies. It is better to allow the definition to emerge as the theory develops" (p. 2). This suggests that the interdependence of the money supply, costs, prices, profits, income disburse-

Reprinted by permission from *The Journal of Political Economy* (published by the University of Chicago Press), February 1952, pp. 1-24.
[1] J. R. Hicks, *A Contribution to the Theory of the Trade Cycle* (Oxford: Clarendon Press, 1950).

ments, consumer spending, investment, employment, and other economic factors will be fully displayed in unfolding the drama of the cycle. And if this suggestion carries a promise of useful achievement, so too does Hicks' awareness of the hard road that must be traveled in building knowledge. For while he believes he has found the "main part of the answer" to the puzzle of business cycles, he candidly describes his work as "little more than an untested hypothesis" which will need to be tested "against the facts" before it can be accepted as a basis for prescriptions of policy (p. v).

I

The literature on business cycles is rich in formal models. That is hardly surprising in view of the widespread tendency to theorize about the cycle with little regard for the facts of experience. Any competent logician, especially if he has the command of mathematics, can select a set of simplified conditions and deduce a cyclical path from what he has assumed. Hicks recognizes that such a theory cannot be a "true theory" unless one can show that the causes it isolates "are actually those which are the most important in practice" (p. 83). His objective is not a formal model of the cycle but one that will enable us to make sense of our concrete experiences. Hence, as he puts it, "it is . . . wise to begin by attempting to explain what has been experienced; anything else must be a matter of prophecy, or at any rate, extrapolation" (p. 8).

But what precisely *are* the business cycles of experience in which Hicks' interest centers? And to what features or aspects of that experience is his explanation directed? Early in his book (p. 2) he notes that "the economic history of the last 150 years organizes itself . . . easily into a series of 7- to 10-year cycles." On page 57 he states that a 3 per cent annual "trend rate of growth . . . seems to have been characteristic of the nineteenth century." On page 89 he suggests that a perfectly uniform cycle superimposed on an exponential trend "is extraordinarily like the cyclical oscillation for which we are looking"—that is, like the cycle "we find in reality" during the past "two centuries." On page 2 he records that business cycles "differ among themselves quite considerably; but there can surely be no doubt of their family likeness." On pages 108-109, on the other hand, he remarks that "certainly the cycles of reality do not repeat each other; they have, at the most, a family likeness." On page 3 he speaks of the "underlying repetitiveness" of the business cycle; and on page 123 he suggests that the cycle is marked by a "fundamental regularity" on which "superficial irregularities" are "superimposed."

These remarks, and others like them, fail to convey a clear idea of the economic nature or the historical range or the geographic scope of the actual phenomenon or phenomena that Hicks is trying to explain. Nor is it possible to infer with complete confidence the temporal or spatial boundaries of the alleged cycles from the institutions analyzed by Hicks, since his theory moves on an extremely abstract level. Hicks treats the real output of any period as uniquely determined, except for a portion constituting "autonomous investment," by the outputs of past periods. This, in a sentence, is the essence of his theory of output; and his theory of the business cycle is simply a theory of the cycle in output, despite the wider scope suggested by the passage I have previously quoted. Now a fixed link between past and current outputs, if it exists at all, is no more a property of the economy of modern England than of the economy of the modern Ukraine (or, for that matter, the economy of Adam and Eve after they had strayed from virtue), and it is not entirely clear that Hicks would be averse to lumping them. To justify his assumption of a closed economy, he observes that "after all, the world as a whole is a closed economy; and the processes which the real theory studies are not made different in character by the fact that they extend across national frontiers" (p. 155). But if Hicks' theoretical arm really aims to stretch across the world, I am not at all sure, judging from some long-range production indexes I have seen, whether it could reach any actual cycle in world output. One need not go back very far to find agriculture dominant in the world economy and its fluctuations in different areas offsetting one another in the earthly aggregate. Such offsetting is considerable even in industrial output and down to the current day; though I have no doubt that an occasional catastrophe, like that of the 1930's, leaves its imprint on world output.

My main purpose in making these realistic observations is to bring out the abstract character and limited objective of Hicks' inquiry. Unless that is understood, a fair appraisal of his work is impossible. It is no part of Hicks' problem whether business cycles are five or ten or twenty years long, whether the amplitude of the cycles is large or small, whether the cycles are of national or international scope, whether they extend over all or only a few of the economic activities of a nation. We should not expect him to explain why business cycles in the United States have been shorter than in England or more violent than in Germany, or why the

United States and England experienced a cyclical downswing in 1920-1921 and 1937-1938 while Germany did not, or why the amplitude of a cyclical expansion in aggregate activity is rather closely correlated with the amplitude of the preceding but not of the following contraction, or why stock financing usually moves with the cycle in aggregate activity while bond financing moves contracyclically, or why the ratio of the change in inventory investment to the change in gross investment during a cyclical phase tends to vary inversely with the length of the phase—or to explain any of a hundred other features of the business cycles of experience. The essential object of Hicks' inquiry is the cycle in output rather than the cycle in business activity as a whole; and this object is sufficiently defined for his purpose by the generally familiar facts that the aggregate production of industrialized nations has fluctuated along a rising trend and that these fluctuations do not look at all like random movements.

To explain the fluctuations in real output (or income), Hicks makes effective use of the principles of the 'multiplier' and the 'accelerator,' as these terms have come to be used in recent literature. The 'multiplier mechanism' shapes the movements of consumption in his model, while the 'accelerator' shapes the movements of investment—except for a certain autonomous part. Hence "the theory of the multiplier and the theory of the accelerator are the two sides of the theory of fluctuations, just as the theory of demand and the theory of supply are the two sides of the theory of value" (p. 38). As these remarks may suggest, Hicks' theory has severe modern lines, runs in terms of very broad aggregates, stresses technical connections between them, and reaches its goal with only incidental reference to costs, prices, profits, or human motivation. To evaluate Hicks' ingenious theoretical construction, it is necessary to examine with some care its two main pillars—the theory of the multiplier and the acceleration principle.

II

The theory of the multiplier goes back to Kahn and Keynes. In earlier economic literature, we do not find any explicit 'consumption function,' or a 'marginal propensity to consume' of less than unity, or an 'investment multiplier' in the guise of a reciprocal of 'the marginal propensity to save.' All these are innovations of modern theory, principally associated with the name of Keynes. The older economists were, of course, more or less aware of the processes which the theory of the multiplier condenses into a formula. They realized that an increase in investment would tend to increase the flow of incomes, that the spending of all or a part of the newly received income by the public would tend to generate new income, and that investment therefore has a multiplier effect on consumption and national income. They did not, however, attach mechanically the dollars spent on 'consumption' to the prior receipt of income any more than they attached the dollars spent on 'investment' to any category of prior receipts. They did not think of the multiplier as a determinate number which summed up the effects of successive respendings of income, or which defined a new equilibrium via a change in investment. Confronted with the modern theory, they would have acknowledged the processes telescoped in the multiplier, though they would have expressed skepticism concerning the stability of the consumption function and concerning a marginal propensity to consume that is always less than unity. This, in any case—and here I can be definite—was the position of Mitchell and Schumpeter. Nor do I suppose that Keynes would have seriously disagreed with them in the precise context of the theory of the cycle rather than of the general level of employment. It is well to recall that in his famous letter to Elizabeth Gilboy he explained that the assumption of a marginal propensity to consume of less than unity was not a necessary premise of his theory of employment; for, if the assumption were not valid, it would merely follow that the economic system is inherently unstable.[2] And, of course, Keynes explained in *The General Theory* that consumption was a function of several variables beside income (Chap. VIII), and actually developed some reasons (Chap. XXII, "Notes on the Trade Cycle") why the propensity to consume out of a given income would shift in the course of a business cycle.

But the most striking and novel part of Keynes' work was the formal theory of underemployment equilibrium, and here he permitted himself to treat consumption as a numerically unique and invariant implicate of income. It was, of course, this feature of Keynes' work that caught the fancy of economists. For, if the step was legitimate, economics was on the threshold of becoming an engineering science. In the years immediately following publication of *The General Theory* the belief was widely held that, once the desired level of income or employment was specified, the economist could tell to a good approximation what amount of invest-

[2] *Quarterly Journal of Economics*, Vol. LIII (August 1939), p. 634.

ment—or of some practical equivalent—would bring that income or employment into being. But, if the economist was to function as an engineer, he needed good empirical estimates of the consumption function. Thus under Keynes' influence extensive research on the relation between consumer spending and national income got under way. At first the results looked very promising, for the correlation between consumption and income turned out to be remarkably high. As the research moved forward, it appeared however that the computed value of the marginal propensity to consume was sensitive to comparatively slight shifts in the character of the underlying data, to slight shifts in the period covered by the statistics, and to shifts from annual data to quarterly or vice versa. Not only that, but it became increasingly plain that the critical matter for purposes of control on Keynesian lines was the savings function rather than the consumption function, and that the correlation between savings and income was decidedly lower than between consumption and income. Under the pressure of empirical studies, faith in an early engineering science of economics perceptibly weakened. Numerous investigators left Keynes' precise formulations behind them, and immersed themselves in exploring the facts of consumption and disentangling the numerous forces that influence the spending of consumers and the saving of individuals and business firms.

But, while many took the path of empirical inquiry, others devoted themselves to refining Keynes' consumption function and elaborating its theoretical implications. Hicks' contribution clearly belongs in this compartment. His consumption function links consumption exclusively to aggregate income as does Keynes', but the relation is not the same. Keynes' consumption and income are expressed in a wage unit, while Hicks' are expressed in an output unit. Keynes' income is gross of depreciation allowances, while Hicks' is net. Keynes' income is current income, while Hicks' is a set of past and current incomes. The first of Hicks' modifications is capable of leading to analysis of productivity as well as employment changes, and Hicks rightly attaches importance to this. The second modification seems less fortunate from the viewpoint of realistic analysis; for in the Keynesian version a change in gross investment will tend to generate a change in consumption and net income even if net investment is constant, while this cannot happen in Hicks' version. However, both the one modification and the other have merely formal consequences within the range of Hicks' inquiry. What does make a substantial difference is the consumption lag. At this point Hicks' work links up with the empirical branch of post-Keynesian investigation—as represented, for example, by the researches of Ezekiel, Duesenberry, Modigliani, and Ruth Mack, who have stressed the influence of past income on current consumption.[3] It appears, therefore, that there is good empirical justification for Hicks' twist to the consumption function; and it also opens the road to process analysis—a road that every student of business cycles must sooner or later follow.

To show how the 'multiplier mechanism' shapes the movements of consumption, it is necessary to have in mind some rule about investment. Hicks explores whole families of such rules. Thus he allows investment to shift from one steady level to another, and shows how—under various assumptions about the consumption lag—consumption and income will adjust to the investment path. Consider the following elementary case. Consumption in any 'period' is, say, nine-tenths of the income (or output) of the preceding period; in period 0 current output is in 'equilibrium' with investment at 5 and consumption at 45; then, for some reason, investment in period 1 shifts to 10, and this level of investment is maintained in later periods. It follows, as a matter of arithmetic, that consumption in periods 1, 2, 3, etc., will be 45, 49.5, 53.55, etc., converging to a value of 90; that the corresponding series for output will be 55, 59.5, 63.55, etc., converging to a value of 100; that the increase in consumption ultimately becomes 45, or nine times as much as the increase of investment, while the increase in output ultimately becomes 50, or ten times as much as the increase of investment. This, or course, is the Kahn theory of the multiplier; but Hicks generalizes it to cover consumption lags of any degree of complexity. Besides, he shows with exemplary skill how consumption and income will respond when investment follows a more complicated path—as when it expands progressively, contracts progressively, or undergoes periodic fluctuations. The result is a very elegant generalization of the multiplier theory.

Hicks' lucid prose enables even the nonmathematical reader to see that, as he moves from one situation to the next, the multiplier

[3] M. Ezekiel, "Statistical Investigations of Saving, Consumption, and Investment," *American Economic Review*, Vol. xxxii (March 1942); F. Modigliani, "Fluctuations in the Savings-Income Ratio," in Vol. xi of *Studies in Income and Wealth* by the Conference on Research in Income and Wealth (National Bureau of Economic Research, 1949); Ruth Mack, "The Direction of Change in Income and the Consumption Function," *Review of Economics and Statistics*, Vol. xxx (November 1948); J. S. Duesenberry, *Income, Saving and the Theory of Consumer Behavior* (Harvard University Press, 1949).

mechanism keeps ticking away without pause or misadventure. It always includes two 'parts'—a rigid consumption function, some rule about investment, and nothing else. It is well to stop and examine each part because in Hicks' theory the multiplier mechanism is not a mere tool of analysis but the whole—or at least the preponderant part—of what needs to be understood about the economics of consumption in the cycle of experience. With respect to the first part of the mechanism, it may be asked what basis Hicks has for treating consumer spending as if it were a purely passive response to past and current income. Is it proper, to be more specific, to ignore the influence of changes in income distribution on consumer spending? Hicks disposes of this question by remarking (p. 36) that his consumption lag already allows for a changing income distribution, but he does not supply any reasons to bolster the naked assertion. Again, is it proper to ignore the vicissitudes of corporate and other nonpersonal saving in formulating the relation of consumer spending to total national income? Hicks apparently feels that the consumption lag also disposes in principle of this complication, the reason being that "undistributed profits are in principle temporary" (p. 22). Surely, when he writes in this vein, Hicks cannot be thinking of the financial processes whereby small firms in this country or England have grown large. And what of the other factors that have been troubling empirical investigators of the consumption function? How and in what degree is consumption influenced by movements of the price level? by changes in relative prices? by capital gains or losses? by the stock of liquid assets or other accumulation from past effort? by the terms on which consumer credit is extended? by expectations concerning income or price changes in the near future? by the rate at which new families are being formed and other demographic variables? If national output equals the sum of consumption and investment, are government expenditures on currently produced commodities and services to be split in some fashion between consumption and investment? If so, is consumption still to be expressed as a simple function of past and current income? Hicks does not comment on these issues. I assume his position is that, while they may need to be considered in examining long periods, they can be safely ignored over the period of a business cycle. But, if that were the case, one should be able to make a good short-run forecast of savings from a consumption function of Hicks' type. To my knowledge the statistical literature on the consumption function, which already includes some experiments on Hicks' lines, does not justify a strong faith in that possibility.[4] I find it difficult to suppress the feeling that Hicks' theory of consumption is quite inadequate and that this part of his multiplier mechanism limps as a consequence.

But what of the second part of the mechanism? This, it will be recalled, is the rule about investment; and here the basic question is what economic forces can be relied on to maintain any particular rule and how they do so. Surely, some theory of production is implicit in the multiplier mechanism, but Hicks does not tell what it might be. To go back to our preceding illustration, what are the economic incentives or pressures that will keep real investment at the assumed figure of 10? Or, to put the same question another way, how is it possible for real output to exceed real consumption, period after period, by the exact figure of 10? It seems clear that the multiplier theory requires that an increase or decrease in demand during any period be precisely matched by an adjustment of supply; but how is this adjustment achieved? Are we to assume that every firm has a perfectly elastic supply schedule until the 'ceiling' to output is reached? That monopoly is absent or that its presence can make no difference to the process of adjusting supply to demand? That no businessman ever makes a mistake or that errors and other obstacles to proper adjustment cancel out? Until the theory of production secreted in the multiplier mechanism is made explicit, there is bound to be a lingering suspicion that the mechanism is merely a stimulating suggestion of how the arithmetic of certain economic quantities may work out. Unless I have missed something vital in Hicks' theory of the multiplier, that is the point at which he leaves it. To be sure, in his model of the cycle the rule about investment flows from a theory of investment process; but, as we shall see, this theory is confined to the demand side of investment and takes for granted conditions of supply except for the recognition of a 'ceiling' to output and a 'floor' to investment.

III

The theory of the multiplier is "only a half-theory" (p. 38) in Hicks' system. The other and accented half is the acceleration

---

[4] A careful statistical analysis of how well various consumption and savings functions have fared as forecasting devices has been made by Robert E. Ferber, "A Study in Aggregate Consumption Functions" (unpublished University of Chicago dissertation, 1951). [A revised version was published by the National Bureau as *Technical Paper 8*, 1953.]

principle. So strong is this emphasis that at times the multiplier seems to fade out. For example, we read that "the multiplier theory does in itself offer no shadow of an explanation why fluctuations occur" (p. 31)—which is true only if we treat consumption as a rigid function of income and interpret fluctuations to mean reversals in direction. Again, we read that, when "the multiplier mechanism . . . is analyzed completely," it "proves . . . to be a stabilizing influence; its general tendency is to diminish the propensity to fluctuate" (p. 37). This suggests that, if consumption were entirely independent of income, the economy would undergo larger absolute fluctuations than it does in fact; but Hicks cannot mean that. Probably all that he wishes to convey is, first, that the rise or fall in consumption resulting from the multiplier mechanism is not so large in the presence of a consumption lag as it would be in its absence; second, that "the fluctuations in consumption . . . can at the most only reflect *initiating* fluctuations in investment" (p. 37; my italics). But how do the fluctuations in investment arise? Hicks' answer is that they are in part autonomous but primarily a response to the rate of change in total output. Hence the big half of the theory of the cycle is the acceleration principle.

It is necessary to pin down the meaning of the acceleration principle, for shades of difference in its interpretation can make a good deal of difference in one's judgment of what the principle contributes to the explanation of business cycles. Everyone appreciates that, if the output of a firm grows substantially, it may find that its 'fixed plant' is cramped and that beyond a certain point production cannot increase at all unless the plant is expanded. It is equally clear that, if production is sharply reduced on account of a drop in sales, the firm will have 'surplus capacity' on its hands and there will be no immediate technical reason for adding to its plant. If the acceleration principle meant no more than this, there would be no reason to doubt its validity. Everyone could agree that it has some bearing on investment and that no explanation of the cycle which ignored it could possibly be complete.

Doubt enters the moment the acceleration principle becomes more imperial than this, and there has been a certain tendency on the part of economic theorists to make it both imperial and mechanical by postulating a fixed ratio between the stock of real capital and current real output. On this interpretation the curve of net investment[5] becomes, except for a multiplicative factor ('the investment coefficient') and a possible lag, a replica of the curve

---

[5] I assume here, for simplicity, that replacement equals depreciation.

of the rate of change in output. Thus put, the acceleration principle is still capable of interpreting broad secular changes in real investment, especially when industrial techniques change slightly and gradually. For while the durability of capital goods—such as factories, office buildings, machinery, and other equipment— may make their stock inelastic on the side of decrease, and the heavy cost of additions may make the stock inelastic on the side of increase, these are limitations of the short run. Let enough time pass and a plant that is poorly adapted to the average run of output will shrink or grow; so that, in the absence of a great change in technology, the stock of capital will tend to correspond, more or less, to the *trend* of output.

The question from the viewpoint of the business cycle is whether the adjustment of capital to output can be at all effective in the short run. Here we bump on two critical facts. First, the rate of utilization of industrial capacity, and therefore the extent of surplus capacity, is itself a cyclical phenomenon. Second, cyclical expansions or contractions in over-all economic activity rarely last longer than two or three years. Over periods of this brief duration an improvement in the ratio of output to 'capacity' cannot well come from a diminution of capital; it must come principally from an increase of output. New additions to effective capacity do not cease when a cyclical expansion of output stops. On the contrary, they are apt to continue increasing, since some time must elapse before investment expenditures materialize in installations. To be sure, the existing stock of capital deteriorates through use and obsolescence, but this is a slow process and not one to be counted on to offset the new installations. As an empirical matter, we know that the stock of capital in the United States, if not also in other countries, has as a rule continued to grow even in periods of depression. It would seem, therefore, that a theory which presupposes a fixed ratio of net investment in fixed capital to the rate of change in output—whether as an approximation to industrial fact or to entrepreneurial design—may well miss the forces that, over the short run, dominate such investment.

Hicks is aware of this difficulty, and he attempts to meet it by immobilizing the acceleration principle over a part of the cycle. He not only recognizes, but formally incorporates into the structure of his model "the fact that falls in output cannot induce disinvestment in the same way as rises in output induce investment" (p. 83); that is, if output shrinks, gross investment in fixed capital can at the most fall to zero, and while net investment may become negative, it can do so only to the extent of the depreciation charges. Hence, except for inventories, Hicks restricts the acceleration principle to a stretch of the cycle—the latter stages of expansion and the beginning of contraction. Over this part of the cycle the accelerator is assumed to work on the plan made familiar by the mathematical theorists; but even here Hicks attends explicitly to the factor of time. His position is that, if output increases, "investment will not take place all at once—it will be spread over a certain length of time, partly because businessmen will not react at once to the need for new capital goods, partly because the process of making the new capital goods itself takes time" (p. 40). Suppose that output moves from 100 in period 0 to 110 in period 1 and that this development occurs at a time when the capital of the economy is not "in excess of requirements" (p. 105). The increase in output will then induce new investment of $10x$, where x is the investment coefficient. This investment will not be made in period 1; it will come in period 2, or perhaps in 3, or perhaps partly in 2 and partly in 3, or in some other period or set of periods; in other words, the investment lag may be simple or complex.[6] But, whatever the lag, Hicks assumes it to remain unchanged over intervals relevant to the cycle, just as he assumes the investment coefficient to be constant.

The economic system that emerges from Hicks' theory is therefore governed by a fixed investment function as well as by a fixed consumption function. The consumption function—and hence the multiplier—is operative throughout the cycle. The investment function—and hence the accelerator—is dormant during part of the cycle. Nevertheless, the accelerator is the chief cycle-maker in Hicks' theory. The business cycle, "regarded as a periodical fluctuation in output, can be explained," he holds, "in terms of simple reactions, by entrepreneurs and by consumers, which are not in any mysterious sense psychological, but are based upon the technical necessities of a capital-using economy" (p. 117). The general meaning of this central proposition seems unmistakable. "The technical necessities of a capital-using economy" are its need to enlarge or diminish the stock of real capital as output changes; net investment is the actual change in the stock of capital; the

[6] In Hicks' mathematical appendix current consumption depends on past outputs, not on current output; his literary exposition stresses current output as much as past outputs. In his appendix current investment depends on the change in past outputs, not on the change in current output; and (except at one point, p. 61) this is also true of his literary exposition. I therefore follow Hicks' appendix on the theory of investment and his text on the theory of consumption.

rate of change in output induces the investment or disinvestment; variations in consumption reflect the variations in investment; the "technical necessities" of the economy thus propel its movements; and the acceleration principle rationalizes the "technical necessities." In Hicks' language: "The main cause of fluctuations is to be found in the effect of changes in output (or income) on investment. There is nothing new in this contention; it is . . . nothing else but the familiar 'Acceleration Principle' which already has a long history. But it does not seem . . . that the consequences of this principle have hitherto been developed in a completely convincing manner" (p. 37).

Hicks has surely made the acceleration principle more convincing by allowing for the phenomenon of surplus capacity. This bold step in the direction of realistic cycle analysis is blunted, however, by the aggregative character of his adjustment. The change in output that counts in his theory is the change in aggregate output, regardless of the mixture of pluses and minuses in individual sectors of the economy. But since, as he has properly argued, "falls in output cannot induce disinvestment in the same way as rises in output induce investment" (p. 83), it is wrong to allow a plus to be annihilated by a minus. Imagine two industries of about the same size whose respective outputs trace out an identical cyclical path. Let A be a single-firm industry all of whose plants are geographically bunched, while B numbers a thousand scattered firms operating on competitive lines. Assume, further, that every firm adjusts its investment in plant and equipment according to the rate of change in its output as long as its stock of capital is not in "excess of requirements." If A happens to be operating at 50 per cent of capacity, no new investment need or will be undertaken. But the same figure for B is merely a statistical average derived from the percentages for a thousand firms, some of which may be as low as zero and others as high as 100. The firms that have forged ahead in the competitive struggle may be operating at or close to "full capacity," and the low industry average will be no bar to launching extensions of their individual producing capacities. Suppose that six months later the ratio of output to capacity rises from 50 to 75 per cent in both A and B. Then the number of B firms operating at or close to full capacity may well be higher and the investment undertaken in the industry larger, while investment in A continues at a standstill. It is clear, therefore, that both the timing and the volume of investment may be very different in two industries, although their aggregate outputs move similarly and everyone's investment is in line with Hicks' version of the acceleration principle. It follows that the curve of "induced investment," which Hicks derives from the aggregate output of the economy, bears no determinate relation to the desired curve, which can be gotten only by going to the outputs of individual sectors.

Hicks' handling of the acceleration principle would be free from this defect if the individual outputs all moved in the same direction, or if there were full mobility of capital from one sector to another. In the latter case there would even be no need for concern over the size of the capital-output ratio. Of course, the real world is nothing like that. The ratio of capital to output is somewhat higher in agriculture than in manufacturing, is very much larger for public utilities than for manufacturing, and varies extensively over the field of manufactures. Since the distribution of investment among industries varies considerably both within a cycle and from one cycle to another, there is no empirical justification for Hicks' constant investment coefficient. Nor is there any empirical warrant for treating aggregate output as if it summarized a set of individual outputs always keeping the same direction. Even during the catastrophe of the early 1930's the outputs of a not inconsiderable number of American products increased in volume.[7] In general, the milder the cyclical phase, the more extensive is the crisscrossing of individual sectors; but, whatever the amplitude of the cycle, the crisscrossing of individual outputs is itself a cyclical phenomenon. "Whereas the proportion of expanding activities moves in the same direction as the aggregate in the early stages of a business cycle expansion or contraction, it moves in the opposite direction in later stages. The proportion of expanding activities is already declining months before aggregate activity reaches a peak, and is already rising months before the aggregate reaches its trough."[8] To reckon with these facts, Hicks would need to activate the accelerator, though in shifting degree, over the entire cycle—instead of releasing it fully over one stretch of the cycle and immobilizing it over another.

A revision of Hicks' accelerator along these lines, while it would deepen his theory of the cycle, would not necessarily change the

---

[7] There is an interesting tabulation of the rates of change in output of 407 commodities from 1929 to 1933 and 1933 to 1937 in Appendix E of the Temporary National Economic Committee's *The Structure of Industry*, Monograph No. 27.

[8] A. F. Burns, "New Facts on Business Cycles," *Thirtieth Annual Report of the National Bureau of Economic Research* (1950), p. 11. [The essay is reprinted above, pp. 107-134.]

broad conclusions. Under certain simple assumptions concerning the distribution of a change in aggregate output among individual sectors, it can be shown that my reformulation of Hicks' accelerator actually strengthens its cyclical power at downturns and gives it an active role even at recoveries—a stage where his accelerator is found hibernating. It might be interesting, and perhaps instructive, to develop these theoretical implications. For present purposes, however, it is more important to see that Hicks' acceleration principle, even after adjusting it to allow for declines in individual outputs, remains a rigidly technological theory of investment; and that, unless good evidence is brought in its support, it may misdirect our thinking about the short-term changes that are the essence of the business cycle. Hicks' principal justification of the acceleration principle seems to be that, unless the capital stock is expanded to accommodate an increase in output, it will be necessary to use the existing "capital equipment at more than its optimum intensity" (p. 39). Reasoning along these lines may justify faith in the acceleration principle as an explanation of long-run tendency. But the accelerator of Hicks' model is supposed to do its work in successive short periods, and I do not think it can be trusted for this purpose.

The capital goods that count in modern business—factories, power plants, shipyards, dwellings, locomotives, large machinery, and the like—ordinarily take months or years to produce. They are costly and, once acquired, may last a decade, a generation, or still longer. A decision to invest in goods of this character is much too important to be left to routine or some mechanical rule, like the rate of change in output. If an increase in output occurs, no one can be sure whether it represents a transitory or a permanent change in business conditions. No one can therefore be sure whether an addition to the capital stock is justifiable. A decision to make or not to make a new investment in capital is reached through the exercise of business judgment—that subtle and as yet little understood process whereby a businessman combines his knowledge of what seems to be the relevant past with his estimates of the present and his hopes, fears, and dreams of the future. One firm may respond to the increase in output by ordering promptly an expansion of capital facilities; another may decide to wait and see. For the time being both will have to get on with the existing plant and put up with marginal costs that may have become uncomfortably high. If the increase in output proves 'transitory,' the first firm will be saddled with the cost of maintaining an excessive plant. If the increase proves 'permanent,' the second firm will miss the opportunity of participating adequately in the advance of prosperity and will perhaps do a year or two later what, in the absence of uncertainty, it would have done sooner. But no firm is likely to deem it worth while to reappraise its capital stock in the light of every change in output. For, in the first place, the rate of change in output—whether taken by the month, or quarter, or year—moves rather erratically in practice. And, in the second place, instruments of production are divisible only to a limited degree. A ship, turbine, or locomotive, a new factory, or a wing added to an old factory can vary in size considerably; but unless each conforms to some rough standard of efficiency, it becomes a toy, not an instrument of production.

In view of the imperfect divisibility of industrial facilities and their long period of gestation, the additions to fixed capital made by the individual firm come in substantial lumps.[9] May it not be, however, that the discontinuities, deflections, and irregular lags of the individual case tend to iron out when aggregates are struck, so that aggregate investment corresponds fairly closely to the rate of change in aggregate output? In other words, may not the acceleration principle fit badly the investment behavior of individuals and yet fit neatly investment in the aggregate? This result is conceivable. But the theorists who emphasize the acceleration principle—Hicks among them—have not addressed themselves to the question of how such a result may be brought about. In any event, it seems doubtful if a question of this sort can be handled with much assurance on a speculative plane alone. The problem must be settled, if it can be settled at all, by seeing what the facts show.

This matter has received some attention from empirical investigators—notably Kuznets, Tinbergen, and Hultgren.[10] I think it is fair to say that they have not found any substantial statistical support for the acceleration principle, taken as a general theory of investment in fixed capital over the business cycle. My own statistical searchings, which have covered a fair time span and

[9] See below, Sec. v, for a further analysis of the investment process and of the limitations of the acceleration principle.

[10] Simon Kuznets, "Relation between Capital Goods and Finished Products in the Business Cycle," in *Economic Essays in Honor of Wesley Clair Mitchell* (Columbia University Press, 1935); J. Tinbergen, *Statistical Testing of Business-Cycle Theories: A Method and Its Application to Investment Activity* (Geneva: League of Nations, 1939); Thor Hultgren, *American Transportation in Prosperity and Depression* (National Bureau of Economic Research, 1948), Chap. vi.

range of industries, have led me to the conclusion that the cyclical movements of this type of investment are rather closely geared to the output of an industry but not to the rate of change in its output. None of these statistical results, however, is decisive from the viewpoint of Hicks' version of the acceleration principle. To test that version faithfully it would be necessary to convert his "period" into a unit (perhaps a changing unit) of calendrical time, to translate the unspecified structure of his investment lag into some concrete equivalent, and to delimit the historical intervals within which the acceleration principle is supposed to be active and those within which it is supposed to be dormant. These are formidable difficulties; but they are minor compared with still another hurdle that the statistician would need to overcome—namely, to separate out the "induced" part of investment from the "autonomous" part.

It will be recalled that Hicks does not attribute all investment to the rate of change in output. This distinction belongs solely to induced investment, to which autonomous investment must be added to get the whole of investment. But how is induced investment to be identified in the course of an empirical test of the acceleration principle? It would obviously not do to estimate it from the rate of change in output and to call the rest of investment "autonomous." This would be traveling in a circle. But if we start at the other end and seek to estimate autonomous investment directly, we are handicapped by the lack of a definition. Hicks' "autonomous investment is only autonomous with respect to the multiplier and accelerator mechanism" (p. 120), but this merely tells us what autonomous investment is not. His only positive identification is through the medium of illustrations: "Public investment, investment which occurs in direct response to inventions, and much of the 'long-range' investment . . . which is only expected to pay for itself over a long period, all of these can be regarded as *Autonomous Investment* for our purposes" (p. 59). This leaves us uncertain what kind or how much of the long-range investment is autonomous; whether the installation of *improved* machinery, if it happens to follow an expansion of output, belongs to the induced or autonomous category; and whether investment associated with railroading, mining coal, distributing mail, etc. is to be counted as autonomous when conducted by a public enterprise but as induced when conducted by a private enterprise. And while Hicks is to be commended for returning to realism at the close of his book, he seems to whittle his own distinction away when he declares that "by the exercise of foresight, investment which would naturally have been of the induced type . . . can be transferred to a time at which it is more convenient" and that "by this means induced investment is, in effect, converted into autonomous investment" (p. 168).

It is precisely the element of foresight that to me seems decisive in the short-run variations of investment,[11] in contrast to Hicks' "technical rigidities" (p. 49). A new invention, a change in relative prices, an expansion in output, or some other factor or combination of factors may stimulate a decision to invest, but there is always some technical as well as business leeway in the timing of the investment. Investment in plant and equipment is governed, in the short run, by foresight, not by technical rigidities; practically all of it is "autonomous," practically none of it is "induced"—if we are to use Hicks' terminology. The "technical necessities" that Hicks sees in the acceleration principle are undoubtedly significant to the economist in analyzing secular trends of investment; also in connection with the long swings lasting from about fifteen to twenty-five years—such as have characterized residential construction in our own and other countries. Even over the short periods of the business cycles these technical necessities help to explain the behavior of certain categories of inventory investment—particularly, of goods in process.[12] Thus a mechanical acceleration principle has its place in economic analysis; but its role in the business cycle of experience is much more modest than in Hicks' model.[13]

IV

"The crucial question which a theory of the cycle has to ask," as Hicks sees it, "is whether fluctuations are possible, and if so, how they are possible, in the absence of exogenous disturbances" (p. 63). From the viewpoint of this question it need not much matter how long the cycles in output may actually be, or how far back they go in history, or in what parts of the world they may be found, or what shape they characteristically assume, or in what degree different industries participate in the successive stages of the over-all cycle, or how the cycle in output may be related to

[11] Cf. J. S. Duesenberry, "Hicks on the Trade Cycle," *Quarterly Journal of Economics*, Vol. LXIV (August 1950), pp. 473-475.

[12] See M. Abramovitz, *Inventories and Business Cycles, with Special Reference to Manufacturers' Inventories* (National Bureau of Economic Research, 1950), Chaps. VIII and XVI.

[13] See Sec. V, below.

prices, profits, employment, or other economic factors. But Hicks appreciates that what he regards as the "crucial question" is by no means the only question which a theory of the cycle has to ask. Necessary though it be to develop "some reasons why the economic system may be liable to cyclical fluctuations," the fact of fluctuations must yet be traced to the causes "which are the most important in practice" (p. 83); in other words, it must be dependably linked to other facts.

In his quest for an explanation Hicks passes from the general behavior of output to the special case of a cycle in output, first through a model that allows output to move freely, then through a model that constrains the movements of output. I shall not attempt to sketch the details of the theory, or to show how much and how ingeniously Hicks has added to the work of other theorists who have concerned themselves with the interaction of the multiplier and acceleration principles—notably, Harrod and Samuelson.[14] For present purposes it will suffice to convey the general character of Hicks' theory and to show why he concludes that "in the real theory it is the accelerator which is ultimately responsible for producing the cycle" (pp. 136-137).

Let us suppose that the economic system is in stationary equilibrium, with consumption at 100 and net investment at zero. Assume also that the consumption of any period depends on the income (or output) of the preceding period; that the investment of any period depends on the change in output during the preceding period; that the marginal propensity to consume from the income of the previous period is 0.9; and that the investment coefficient is 0.2. Let the equilibrium now be disrupted through an autonomous investment of 5, which comes in period 1 and never turns up again. What will be the consequences of this solitary disturbance? In period 1 consumption remains at its equilibrium value of 100; and, since autonomous investment is 5, total output is 105. In period 2 consumption becomes 104.5; autonomous investment is zero; but, since output has increased by 5 from period 0 to period 1, there is now an induced investment of 5×0.2; hence total output is 105.5. In period 3 consumption rises to 104.95; induced investment falls to 0.1 and total output to 105.05. In period 4 consumption falls to 104.545; induced investment becomes a negative quantity, -0.09, and total output

[14] R. F. Harrod, *The Trade Cycle* (Oxford: Clarendon Press, 1936); Paul A. Samuelson, "Interactions between the Multiplier Analysis and the Principle of Acceleration," *Review of Economic Statistics*, Vol. XXI (May 1939).

104.455. In later periods output continues to decline but approaches more and more closely its equilibrium value of 100. Thus, after an initial kickup, the system converges to equilibrium. But if we had allowed the investment coefficient to be 0.6 instead of 0.2, other things remaining the same, the result would be quite different. Output would first rise for a time, then decline below the equilibrium value of 100, later rise again but to a lower peak, fall again but a to higher trough, and so on; thus equilibrium would be approached only after a series of oscillations. If the investment coefficient were as high as 1, the system would convert the initial disturbance into a cycle of constant amplitude around the initial equilibrium value. If the coefficient were somewhat higher, cycles of progressively increasing amplitude would emerge; and if the coefficient became sufficiently high (i.e., if it exceeded 1.73), the system would move "relentlessly away from equilibrium" (p. 71)—upward if the solitary disturbance were positive, as in our illustration; downward if the disturbance were negative. It seems clear therefore that, "even if there are no exogenous causes making for fluctuations" (p. 84), a cycle may be generated by the multiplier-accelerator mechanism.

But Hicks wishes to portray cycles against a rising trend of output, since "the cycles which have been experienced have all of them taken place against a background of secular expansion" (p. 8). With this in mind, he proceeds to show that "the deviations of actual output from equilibrium output have exactly the same properties" (p. 86) if a progressive equilibrium is disrupted as when a stationary equilibrium is disrupted. That is, the character of the response of a "regularly progressive economy" (in which autonomous investment and equilibrium income are both rising at the same, constant percentage rate) to a solitary deviation of autonomous investment from its normal path depends on the marginal propensity to consume and the investment coefficient—just as in the case of stationary equilibrium which we just examined. It therefore seems natural to inquire which of the various possibilities turned up by theory "is most likely to correspond with actual experience, and which of them could be an element in the explanation of a cycle such as we find in reality" (p. 89).

It appears that, once the rate of growth of the system is given, an investment coefficient of a particular size will yield a perfectly regular cycle. Hicks rejects this possibility because it seems rather unlikely that the "world . . . had got stuck for two centuries with an investment coefficient" (p. 89) of this precise value. Another hypothesis is that, given the marginal propensity to consume, the investment coefficient has been such as to yield damped oscillations. In this case, of course, "a single disturbance cannot produce the fairly regular cycle which has been experienced" (p. 89); but may not a stream of disturbances following thickly on one another keep the cycle from vanishing? Hicks feels that this "theory of damped fluctuations and erratic shocks" (p. 91) is also unconvincing. The hypothesis he embraces is that the marginal propensity to consume and the investment coefficient are of such size as to generate "explosive cycles" or even outright "explosions." At first blush this seems utterly implausible, and so it would be if Hicks stopped here. But Hicks goes on to impose limits on output—something I failed to do in tracing the consequences of a disturbance of stationary equilibrium. The upper limit is fixed by the "scarcity of employable resources" (p. 95), so that there is a "full employment ceiling" (p. 96). Although there is no direct lower limit on output, one is indirectly provided by the fact that "disinvestment in fixed capital can only take place by a cessation of gross investment" (p. 101). This hypothesis of "constrained explosion," Hicks feels, "is the one which really fits the facts" (p. 92).

To see how the model works, it is simpler to take his stationary than his progressive equilibrium as a point of departure. Let us therefore revert to our preceding illustration with its solitary burst of autonomous investment. The consumption function we can leave unchanged; but we must now raise the investment coefficient to suit its "explosive" mission, and we must also put limits on output. Let us say that the investment coefficient is 2, that the ceiling to output in any period is 130, and that disinvestment in any period cannot exceed 6. In period 1 total output and its components are now the same as in the previous illustration. In period 2 consumption is again 104.5; but the induced investment is 10 and total output 114.5. In period 3 consumption is 113.05; the required investment is 19; but, since output cannot exceed 130, investment is only 16.95. In period 4 consumption is 127, and the output ceiling keeps investment down to 3. In period 5 consumption remains at 127, since output in period 4 is the same as in period 3; for the same reason induced investment is zero, and the expansion in output is not only halted but converted into a decline. In period 6 consumption, reflecting the lower output in period 5, falls to 124.3; induced investment becomes —6 and total output 118.3. In the next period the required disinvestment is 17.4; but, since disinvestment cannot be more than 6, surplus capacity emerges, which will have to be worked off in later periods. The accelerator mechanism is now suspended, and the multiplier carries on by itself. Total output keeps declining, period after period, but the decreases in output become progressively smaller. If the disinvestment continued at 6, a new equilibrium output of 40 would be gradually approached. However, as the change in output becomes smaller, so too does the required disinvestment. When the change in output is numerically smaller than —3, the disinvestment required in any period can already be carried out in that period. For a time, however, the disinvestment must remain at 6 to allow the unfulfilled disinvestments of earlier periods to be consummated. Once this process is completed, the accelerator goes into action again; the disinvestment now becomes smaller than 6, and before long the decline in disinvestment more than offsets the decline in consumption; in other words, total output again rises. From this point consumption as well as investment must increase; both advance energetically until the ceiling is hit, which chokes off the accelerator and sets off a fresh decline.

In this model the expansion of output is carried forward by the combined action of the multiplier and accelerator mechanisms. The expansion cannot taper off into a plateau, with output remaining at the ceiling level, because the decline in the rate of increase in output generates an absolute decline of investment. When output bumps along the ceiling, the induced investment must soon be zero; and the decline of investment cannot be offset by a rise of consumption, since consumption is determined by earlier outputs and the output along the ceiling is not rising. Thus the cyclical downturn of output is fundamentally due to a retardation in the growth of output itself, and the ceiling is sufficient to produce the retardation. So it is also in Hicks' regularly progressive economy, where the ceiling keeps rising but only at the moderate rate at which autonomous investment is rising. In both the stationary and the regularly progressive models the multiplier mechanism is responsible for the protracted contraction of output. But, whereas in the former model there cannot be a resumption of the expansion until excess capital has been worked off, in the latter model the continued growth of autonomous investment will check the decline of output and enable it to rise again before the surplus capacity has been eliminated; the resumption of a rise in output hastens the adjustment of the stock of ordinary capital to output; and, when this adjustment is completed, induced investment adds its strength to that of autonomous investment in driving the economy forward. Thus, in the regularly progressive economy the accelerator is suspended, not only during practically the whole of contraction as in the stationary economy, but also during the early part of the expansion. But the intermittent activity of the accelerator should not mislead us concerning its role as a cycle maker. If the accelerator failed to function at all, there would be no cycle in the model; on the other hand, a multiplier of unity would not alone suffice to obliterate the fluctuations. Thus it is permissible to say, in the interest of brevity, that induced investment or the accelerator is principally responsible for the cycle.

This, as I read Hicks, is the essence of his theory. To be sure, the theory has more flexibility than my sketch conveys. Hicks recognizes that there is no technical limit on disinvestment in inventories, such as characterizes fixed capital. However, in line with the general drift of his argument, which rather minimizes the part of inventories,[15] he feels that "the accelerator, in the form in which it persists into the slump, is a mere ghost of what it was in the Boom" (p. 104). He recognizes that autonomous investment cannot be expected to follow a regularly rising path in actual life and that "it must experience autonomous fluctuations on its own account" (p. 120); but he regards these fluctuations as "superimposed upon the cycle" (p. 121) of a regularly progressive economy. He does not insist that the boom is always killed off by hitting the ceiling; on the contrary he shows that the investment coefficient may be "explosive" and yet generate a decline before the ceiling is struck—though here, too, the retarded growth of output is responsible for the decline in investment and the eventual downturn of output. Again, Hicks' theory requires uniformity in the consumption and investment functions over any one cycle, but not from one cycle to the next. Nor does the theory necessarily depend on the simple lags of my exposition.[16] These various elements of flexibility leave, as Hicks sees it, "plenty of room for those divergences from a standard model which are needed in order to cover the historical facts" (p. 3).

As a result of his inquiry Hicks deems it possible to point to "a short list of fundamental facts which are sufficient to account for the cycle" (p. 3). Let us assemble this list of "facts" or "assump-

[15] See the authoritative study of Abramovitz (op.cit.), which goes a considerable distance towards establishing the highly significant role of inventories in the business cycle.

[16] However, certain types of lag may cause serious embarrassment, as Hicks recognizes, though perhaps insufficiently.

tions" (pp. 2, 83, 92, 95): (1) Consumption is a lagged function of income; induced investment is a lagged function of the change in income; and these functions are such that "an upward displacement from the equilibrium path will tend to cause a movement away from equilibrium." (2) The system has an upward trend of output geared to autonomous investment. (3) "Output is not indefinitely extensible against an increase in effective demand." (4) "Falls in output cannot induce disinvestment in the same way as rises in output induce investment." From such a list of "assumptions," Hicks concludes, it is possible to show that "a cyclical sequence, which is (to say the least) remarkably similar to that which is experienced in practice, is *inevitable*" (p. 2; Hicks' italics).

This conclusion suggests more than Hicks has proved. By what is "experienced in practice" Hicks cannot mean more than the abstraction I previously delineated (Sec. I); which still leaves, even if his theory turned out to be right, work for other times and other hands. His argument concerning consumption, induced investment, even autonomous investment, runs in terms of effective demand. On the processes whereby supply is adjusted to demand his list of assumptions is distressingly inarticulate. It seems impossible to me to make a useful pronouncement about what is or is not *inevitable* in Hicks' world until the tacit assumptions concerning conditions of supply, apart from the ceiling to output and floor of investment, have been spelled out. Aside from this, the cycle in Hicks' expanding economy is, strictly speaking, a cycle in *deviations* from an "equilibrium rate of growth," as he himself elsewhere recognizes (p. 101). Hence his assumptions do not necessarily lead to an expansion of output followed by an *absolute* decline of output; nor—therefore—necessarily to the sort of cycle which has bothered the practical world.

But I do not wish to multiply doubts along these lines. From the viewpoint of a theory which aims to be something more than an exercise in logic, the important issues, as I see them, lie elsewhere. The foundation stones of Hicks' theory are the multiplier and accelerator. These are the matters on which I have dwelt in earlier parts of this paper. And if what I have said on these subjects is at all valid, it will not do to treat consumption as a technical echo of output; it will not do to treat investment as a technical echo of the changes in past output; it will not do to treat the business cycle as a reflex of any "technical necessities of a capital-using economy." To come to grips with the economic realities of a capitalistic system, which is a capital-using economy of a very particular sort, it is necessary to give far greater scope to market phenomena—the movements of costs, prices, profits, credit, and business sentiment itself—than one finds in Hicks.

V

The process of investing in fixed capital, which plays the key role in Hicks' theory of the cycle, cannot be understood outside its business setting. I have already commented on the imperfect divisibility of industrial facilities and their long period of gestation. In view of these characteristics of investments goods, a business firm will normally seek to have a margin of plant capacity to take care of contingencies, both such as may be foreseen and such as cannot, just as it normally carries a reserve of raw materials and finished wares in its inventories. Seasonal maxima—which sometimes exceed the average for a year by more than cyclical maxima exceed the average for a cycle—will be realized by working the plant more intensively, not by varying its scale. So also will the responses to sudden and irregular flutterings of demand, which are an ever present feature of business life and sometimes strong enough to leave their impress on fairly comprehensive economic aggregates. And the firm will look to the future, not only to the past—as in Hicks' model. There the increase in output comes first; the "investment in new capital to support that increased output" (p. 43) comes later. But in a growing economy a firm relies on "increased output" to support "investment in new capital" just as it relies on "investment in new capital" to support "increased output."

A new business commonly begins operations with a modest plant. As sales expand, all sorts of inconvenience and waste are suffered for a time. A year or two later better equipment may be added and perhaps a site acquired to accommodate a larger plant in case that proves necessary. As sales keep mounting, a new factory is built or a substantial addition made to the old. This may come soon or years later, but in either event the plant is expanded with an eye to what output may be several years hence as well as to its current level. In time the business becomes cramped for space once again, and the cycle of development is repeated. This, or something like it, is typically the investment path of a small business as it grows up. In a stationary firm or one that grows very slowly, the intervals between capital expenditures will of course be longer than in a rapidly growing business. And what is true of a manufacturing concern is equally true of farming, mining, commercial, or financial enterprises. Thus, investment in plant and equipment on the part of a small or medium-sized business comes in substantial lumps, discontinuously. And while the investment of large firms seems continuous by comparison, this merely reflects the overlapping of many processes of the same kind, going on in various sections of the firm, combined with the fact that the projects undertaken are apt to be much larger and therefore remain longer in the stage separating the investment decision and the final installation.

In the actual world, therefore, the stock of capital in the individual firm cannot well move in any close adjustment to its output in the short run. If we broaden our view over the whole of an industry, we encounter a fresh impediment to the acceleration principle in the formation of new firms, which undertake new investment although they are still innocent of any past output. And if the economic process as a whole comes into view, the linkage between current investment and the rate of change in output seems to vanish in a cloud. One railroad is built by a dreamer who sees bustling centers of industry and commerce when he looks at pasture and forest. Another is built by a wily promoter who sees an opportunity to embarrass a rival railroad or to appease the public's hunger for securities. One firm builds a factory to incorporate a new technical process, another to make a new product, a third because it is cramped for space, or because it has new business in prospect, or because it wishes to acquire a 'new look,' or because a new location promises lower taxes or a cheaper labor supply. One independent builder 'sees' a housing shortage and lays down a score of new dwellings. At the same time a colleague 'sees' that the residential market is overbuilt but nevertheless puts up a house or two to keep his organization intact; while a third, who shares the somber vision of the second, adds liberally to the supply of houses because he can borrow from his banker as much or more than what it costs him to build.

There is no need to enlarge on these remarks. It is clear that numerous influences play on investment and that one or another special influence is sometimes decisive in the individual case. This suffices to show why hardly a day passes in a large country without bringing forth a new crop of investment projects and why their volume must vary over time. But the special influences do not explain the heavy bunching of investment projects at certain times, their sparse numbers at other times, the fairly regular ascent from small numbers to large and the fairly regular descent from large numbers to small—in short, why there is a *cyclical* movement in investment. To explain this feature of investment, it is necessary to abstract from the multitude of special influences and to analyze the forces that govern fairly homogeneous sections of the investment market—such as free versus controlled industries, large- versus small-scale industries, new versus old enterprises, housing versus business enterprises, private versus governmental agencies, and so on. Once separate generalizations have been framed for the leading parts of the investment market, it becomes possible to determine with assurance how the broad forces of the market—principally, the movement of the national income and its distribution, the movement of building and equipment costs, and the movements of 'finance'—impinge on investment at large. All these matters still require empirical investigation; but enough is already known to make it fairly clear that it is the pervasive forces of the market, rather than Hicks' mechanical accelerator, that give rise to fluctuations in a community's outlays on fixed capital.

Suppose, for example, that an expansion in aggregate output and employment has for some reason gotten under way. Then the income of individuals and business firms will expand also. Since the community as a whole is better off, spending on consumption goods rises; and so too does spending on investment goods—many of which seemed "necessary" months or years earlier but which were not acquired earlier because of financial stringency or business uncertainty. As spending expands, new 'shortages' appear, and men's minds turn to ways of meeting them. The spread of expansion gradually generates in people a feeling of security, later a mood of optimism. Many who have been eager to carry out new investments, and yet have postponed action because uncertain whether the time is 'right,' decide to go ahead now, while construction and equipment costs are still close to the level reached during the preceding slump. The new spirit of enterprise fosters all sorts of projects that are related very loosely, if at all, to the shortages of facilities which keep arising here and there or to the improved ability of investors to pay for new facilities. Individual dishoarding is now easier to rationalize, credit is easier to get, and equity capital easier to attract. Many families that in the past have dreamed about building a home 'decide' to build one, in some cases because their income is larger, in others because they feel more secure about their income or because lenders feel this way about them, in still others because they look forward confidently to still better times. Business firms brush up their long-range plans for expansion, promoters push projects that will exploit new products or techniques, new firms are organized to share in the growing markets for standard commodities, and legislatures authorize improvements worthy of an 'era of prosperity.' Thus, as everyone knows, a rising national income and the state of exaltation that accompanies it pile up decisions to invest; and investment expenditures follow suit—though with an irregular lag and diminished amplitude.

But why does not the expansion of investment continue more or less indefinitely? By what processes is the upward movement of investment brought to a halt and its direction reversed? Here two facts are vital. First, the rise in construction and financing costs generated by the expansion itself. In thinking of the investment process, it is essential to keep in mind that a 'decision to invest' is one thing and a 'decision to invest *now*' is quite another. Investors generally realize that building a new house, factory, or power plant is not the same thing as purchasing a hat or even an automobile. They know that when investment judgment proves bad, the penalty is severe. In reaching a 'decision to invest,' they may have given little or no conscious attention to the protracted increase that has already occurred in construction and financing costs. But this decision must be followed by another, whether to carry out the project now or later. At this stage investors are likely to consider very carefully the economic outlook in the months immediately ahead. They know that they may have the new plant or equipment on their hands for a generation and that the annual carrying charges with which they saddle themselves depend a good deal on the cost of construction, if not also on the rate of interest. They have gotten along thus far without the desired investment and in any event will have to manage without it for months or years—for as yet the investment good is only an amorphous wish or a sketch on a piece of paper. In some cases a postponement will clearly bring hardship or a business loss, and the interval between the 'decision to invest' and the start of investment expenditure will be governed entirely by technical factors—such as surveying, acquiring a site, designing plans, securing loans, contracting out the job, etc. In many other cases investors, who judge that they can let the construction job and finance it on appreciably better terms six months or a year later, will bide their time. And not a few of those who are eager to move promptly will have a chance to reconsider their 'decision to invest' in the light of market prospects, for the arrangements preparatory to investment expenditure are often very time-consuming.

The rise in construction and financing costs during an expansion impinges broadly on the investing class and would check the investment boom sooner or later even if prosperity diffused itself uniformly over the economic community. But this does not happen, and the uneven spread of expansion is our second vital fact. True, business conditions are generally good and improving; yet some firms and even entire industries are unable to expand their sales, and others find it hard to advance their selling prices. At the same time unit costs of production are already rising over the range of business enterprise—first here and there, then on a broad front, despite improvements of technique and fuller utilization of facilities. At every stage of the business cycle there are bound to be some firms whose profits are declining or whose losses are increasing. But these firms are not a steady fraction of the business population; and after a business expansion has continued for some time there are various reasons for expecting their numbers to multiply. As a mounting optimism infects a widening circle of businessmen, errors concerning the sales that can be made at profitable prices tend to pile up. Supply 'bottlenecks' keep developing, now in one locality or industry, then in others; in consequence the output of numerous enterprises—particularly those suffering from a shift in demand or an outworn technology—is restricted. Business custom, long-term contracts, or governmental regulation make it difficult or inexpedient for many firms to raise their prices; and, as the rise in unit costs continues, more and more of them are apt to find their profits diminishing. We therefore find in experience, as we may reasonably expect, that "after a business expansion has run for some time, the proportion of firms experiencing rising profits begins to shrink, although the profits of business in the aggregate continue to climb."[17] This development adds to the mood of hesitation that is already emerging among investors generally, on account of the protracted rise in construction and financing costs. The firms whose fortunes are waning are likely to be among the first to reduce investment expenditure, and their curtailments will spread doubt among others whose profits are still rising, but many of which have come to feel that investment

17 [See New Facts on Business Cycles, above, pp. 107-134]; and Thor Hultgren, Cyclical Diversities in the Fortunes of Industrial Corporations, National Bureau Occasional Paper 32 (1950).

costs will be reduced before long from the abnormal level to which they have been pushed by prosperity.

It is along lines such as these, I believe, that the cyclical downturns of investment in fixed capital are to be explained, if we hold in view an economy organized predominantly on the basis of free private enterprise. In Hicks' system the expansion of investment is brought to a halt and reversed by a mere retardation in the growth of physical output. But I do not know of any evidence that a declining rate of growth has generally characterized the closing stages of actual expansions in aggregate output[18] or that investment expenditure has been at all closely geared to the actual rate of growth of output. Even if empirical evidence fitted in more congenially with Hicks' theory of the downturn, it would still be wise for the economist, when in search for the causes of the breakdown of an investment boom, to look in the direction of business life, including the government once it has become a major factor in the economy, rather than in the direction of Hicks' hypothetical technology. And it is to the processes of business life that Hicks himself seems to turn when he comes to the case of an upturn in investment. That depends in his system on the continued advance or spurt of autonomous investment; and while his autonomous investment merits another name and more analysis than it receives, it at least opens the route along which business processes might be seen.

VI

Hicks' slight of psychological and pecuniary factors is deliberate. At the opening of his penultimate chapter he states plainly: "It has been one of the main objects of this work to show that the main features of the cycle can be adequately explained in real terms" (p. 136). In line with this resolution there is hardly a mention of the price or monetary systems in the first eight of his twelve chapters. In Chapter IX Hicks concedes that "it is very possible that some important aspects of the actual cycle can only be explained" by the aid of "the price-mechanism and the monetary mechanism" (p. 117). In Chapter X he examines the consequences of a supposed cyclical movement in the ratio of investment goods prices to consumption goods prices; but the only result derived is a blurring "at the edges" of the previous argument

[18] See the study of this subject by Abramovitz, *op.cit.*, Chap. xv. On the technical difficulties in ascertaining rates of change over a cycle, see A. F. Burns and W. C. Mitchell, *Measuring Business Cycles* (National Bureau of Economic Research, 1946), Chap. viii.

(p. 133). The last two chapters are devoted to the "monetary factor," which he regards as a "secondary force" whose effects are "superimposed" on the "*main* cycle" (p. 3; Hicks' italics). I shall say nothing of this interesting monetary supplement. To examine it at all adequately would require not much less space than I have already taken; and it is perhaps just as well to leave the emphasis where Hicks himself has put it.

This emphasis on the 'technical' or 'real' aspects of economic life is not peculiar to Hicks' new book. It has been characteristic of a good part of recent economic theory, just as it was characteristic of a good part of classical political economy in its formative phase. The emphasis is an understandable and, to a considerable degree, a justifiable reaction against the price and monetary theorizing which flourished before the 1930's and which was found so seriously wanting when the Great Depression struck. In the midst of the confusion and despondency of the day, Keynes articulated a new theoretical system, couched in a wonderful language, from which governmental policies seemed to peel off as simply and naturally as skin from an onion. He saw in a business depression, not any maladjustment of costs and prices, but a deficiency in spending, which he attributed principally to a deficiency in investment. The latter he analyzed in terms of the supply of money, liquidity preference, the supply price of investment goods, and the expectations of the business community concerning the future earnings stream from new investment. He put the emphasis on the expected earnings stream in his theory of investment, just as he put the emphasis on actual income in his theory of consumption. He saw in investment the great driving force of employment, but one that a modern society could not safely leave to the unrestrained impulses of private enterprise. These teachings of Keynes paved the way for drastic simplifications by later economists. Before long a literature arose in which costs, prices, and profits were pushed aside, sometimes completely ignored. Consumption emerged as a passive response to income, without any link to the system of prices or the range of economic choice. Investment became an exogenous variable—a mere technical datum for the economist, like the consumption function. Investment opportunity itself became a sort of physical fact; and not a few economists formed the habit of speaking of investment outlets as if they were some objective quantity, independent of the dreams of men, their hopes and fears about governmental policy, or their expectations about costs, prices, and profits.

It is against this background that I see Hicks' book on the business cycle. It is based on a profound appreciation of the work of Keynes, yet consciously departs from Keynes' doctrines at numerous points. It is written in a scholarly spirit and is devoted to scientific issues, not to questions of immediate policy. It is a sophisticated work, not to be confused with vulgar Keynesianism. It shares, however, the aggregative, mechanical, 'real' slant of much of the recent literature on economic theory. It stresses the role of effective demand but has practically nothing to say about the organization and conditions of effective supply. It sees investment as an addition to output but overlooks its part in modifying the state and intensity of competition in the business world. It restores investment to an endogenous role, which it had long played in earlier economic theory, including that of Keynes; but the restoration is carried out through a theorem of impersonal technology, not of human conduct in a business environment. The sophistication of Hicks' work derives from the pressures of a subtle and inquiring mind, not from a large knowledge of practical affairs or the teachings of history and statistics. The result is a closely reasoned[19] and attractively written essay about a possible cycle, but—as far as I can see—a dubious aid to students seriously concerned with the actual alternations of good and bad trade to which the Western world has been subject in modern times.

[19] Although the book sets a very high standard in this respect, a professional logician might yet have something to say about Hicks' method of arriving at what is or is not "probable" both in his explicitly supposititious world and in the alleged real one.

Current Research in Business Cycles

All students of business cycles owe a debt of gratitude to Professor Koopmans and to Professor Gordon for laying bare their approaches to the study of business cycles. Koopmans has sketched what he calls the econometric approach; Gordon has outlined what he calls the quantitative-historical approach. Both routes have been pictured attractively and persuasively by their authors, and I suspect that many members of this audience may now be struggling to decide whether it is best to follow the Muse of History or the Queen of Mathematics. An alert participant in the discussion might take advantage of this delicate uncertainty by staking out a claim for still another approach to the understanding of business cycles. I shall not succumb to this temptation. For I think that the paths being followed in business cycle research—whether by Koopmans, Gordon, or others—are not so far apart as may appear.

It is clear that both Gordon's and Koopmans' approaches are statistical, in the sense of involving extensive use of quantitative data. But this is not the only point of agreement. I notice that in listing the essential characteristics of the historical approach, Gordon notes that it may involve "a variety of statistical techniques—including econometric studies." In turn Koopmans observes that the econometric approach is not "a competitor of the historical approach, but . . . an important instrument of it." I notice, too, that both Koopmans and Gordon assign a strategic place to economic theory in their respective approaches. Gordon states that the historical method "entails initial theorizing—setting up working hypotheses," and that one of its essential characteristics is "full use . . . of qualitative as well as quantitative information." Koopmans likewise observes that the econometric technique is conditioned upon initial theorizing; that it is "not a substitute for theory, but one of the servants of theory." If, therefore, I have understood our two authors correctly, the approach of each can be described as theoretical, statistical, historical, and mathematical. I might even add 'psychological' to the list, for both Gordon and Koopmans confess to an "unseen hand" in their operations. Gordon notes that in the historical approach "causal inference depends

Discussion of two papers presented at the Christmas 1948 meetings of the American Economic Association, "Business Cycles in the Interwar Period: The 'Quantitative-Historical' Approach," by Robert A. Gordon, and "The Econometric Approach to Business Fluctuations," by Tjalling C. Koopmans. Reprinted by permission from *Papers and Proceedings, American Economic Review*, May 1949, pp. 77-83.

upon personal interpretations and judgment"—to be sure, "after detailed examination of the available evidence." Koopmans is no less explicit. He tells us that "intuitive considerations" play a large role in setting up econometric models; and that while there is "an optimum degree of detail" in excursions of this type, "we are far from knowing at which point . . . this optimum . . . is reached"—which means, I take it, that matters of this sort must be resolved by personal interpretation and judgment.

As I see it, then, the methodological approaches of Gordon and Koopmans have much in common. Not only that, but both seem to be concerned primarily with business cycles in a brief segment of history—the period since World War I. They further agree in suggesting that their approaches—whether to the business cycles of this period or some other—will not necessarily yield a complete and final solution to the puzzle of business cycles. Koopmans asserts that the "true calling" of the econometric approach "is not to answer all questions," and "that in certain circumstances it may leave important questions unanswered." Gordon in his turn notes that in the historical approach it is frequently "impossible to arrive at convincing judgments regarding the actual magnitude of various forces which we may be able to isolate as probable causes of particular fluctuations"—which means, I take it, that in certain circumstances the historical approach may leave important questions unanswered.

Shall we conclude, then, that the approaches of the two authors may turn out in the long run to be very similar? I think that as far as the present evidence goes, this is an entirely permissible conclusion. Koopmans might begin, for example, by constructing a simple model with very few linear equations, estimating the parameters by using annual data. If the model yields unsatisfactory results, he might add additional equations by breaking down the endogenous variables of the system, or by shifting exogenous variables to the endogenous category, or by dipping into the random catchall for variables hitherto neglected. If the results are still unsatisfactory, he may substitute quarterly or monthly data for annual, or devise methods for handling nonlinear parameters, or modify the distributional hypothesis underlying the treatment of the random variance. If it should turn out in the meantime that the estimating techniques recently devised by the staff of the Cowles Commission are in practice no better than the techniques used by a Schultz or a Tinbergen, Koopmans may abandon his criteria of simultaneous fitting and thereby win the freedom to work with a larger number of equations. If none of these devices helps sufficiently, he might put historical boundary dates to the model, devise different models for different periods or cyclical phases, perhaps even experiment with a different model for each phase of each business cycle. If Koopmans should undergo this evolution, he would come very close indeed to Gordon's position— if the latter in the meantime stood still. But I have no more reason for supposing that Gordon will remain still than that Koopmans would, and it is therefore equally possible that Gordon will come out at Koopmans' mathematical pole. If any here should think that what I am saying is fanciful, I can only plead that they may be relying on information outside the two papers before us— something I am scrupulously trying not to do.

The cold fact is that discussions of business cycle methodology, carried on in the abstract, are merely intellectual exercises in which experience, philosophical insight, and temperament mix in varying proportions. To appraise different methodological approaches responsibly, it is essential to scrutinize the actual findings or results to which the different approaches lead. The critical question is never whether a method is quantitative or qualitative, mathematical or historical, elegant or pedestrian, theoretical or statistical. In 1913 Wesley Mitchell's *Business Cycles* appeared; one year later Henry L. Moore's *Economic Cycles* was published. Mitchell used no special apparatus apart from ordinary charts and tables, but that did not prevent his reaching generalizations about the cyclical process of economic life that stood up well in the next generation. At the same time, Moore's elaborate mathematical techniques did not prevent his results from being discredited by later research. It is possible to cite illustrations of an opposite tenor, but they would only reinforce my point, which is simply that the merits of a technique cannot be judged in the abstract. The purely personal element in the scientific process is sometimes more important than anything else. A method that yields reliable results in the hands of one investigator may produce nightmares when tried by another investigator of comparable intellectual stature.

The important question about business cycle methodology, or for that matter any other body of techniques in economics, is simply whether it does or does not lead to dependable answers to significant questions. Unhappily, this pragmatic test can hardly be applied to the papers presented at this meeting, since both Gordon and Koopmans are still in the early stages of their research.

It would be manifestly improper to use the tiny samples of results that the two investigators have put before us as a basis for appraising the merits of their approaches to the vast problem of how business cycles are generated. If a pragmatic criterion is to be applied at all, we must restrict ourselves to the issues underlying the particular results illustrated by Gordon and Koopmans. What I have to say on this subject must be brief.

Koopmans has cited two illustrations of results yielded by the econometric technique. One relates to the influence of liquid assets on consumer outlay, and here he tells us that the econometric approach has failed to yield a definite conclusion. Gordon has not taken up this complicated subject, but I do not think I am being reckless in asserting that the historical approach is capable of yielding a similar result. Koopmans' second illustration is Tinbergen's negative verdict on the acceleration principle as an explanation of fluctuations in investment. Since Gordon has not discussed this subject, a direct comparison is again impossible. But I can testify that the National Bureau of Economic Research has reached results similar to Tinbergen's, indeed of larger scope, by using an approach that is similar to Gordon's. Furthermore, if the validity of the acceleration principle really hinged, as Koopmans states it does, "on the implied assumption that productive capacity is at all times in substantially full use," then anyone who had doubts on this issue could bring the acceleration principle to a critical test merely by examining some statistics on the degree of utilization of productive capacity—a procedure so simple and straightforward that there is no need to dignify it by any special name. Finally, while I can readily agree that the acceleration principle misrepresents the play of forces on investment in the short run, it seems to me that Koopmans overlooks an important point; namely, that the acceleration principle is sometimes the key to movements of investment over long periods.

Let us turn next to the illustrations cited by Gordon of the results yielded by his approach. To me the most interesting finding is that a severe depression seems to have been followed as a rule by a "submerged" cycle, but I doubt if this suggestion will stand up under critical examination. Gordon's sketch of the cyclical contours of the interwar period I can confirm in large part, though I cannot accept some of the detailed findings. I find it difficult, for example, to square the conclusion that the depression of 1920-1921 "led to only the most temporary impairment of the business community's 'propensity to invest' " with a drop of 67 per cent between October 1919 and December 1920 in the floor space represented by construction contracts, or with a drop of 91 per cent in machine tool orders between January 1920 and September 1921. At this point, as at some others, I think that Gordon has been misled by using annual data on investment expenditures instead of monthly data on investment undertakings. But I do not wish to press criticism along these lines or even to note Gordon's omissions. He has put his results tentatively and with great candor, and I have confidence that his historical sketch will vastly improve as the investigation progresses. I find it pertinent, however, to observe that Gordon's illustrative results deal largely with the magnitude of certain ups and downs, in contrast to Koopmans' illustrations, which deal with questions of causation. As things stand, the number of variables handled by Gordon is small and well within the econometrician's range even if the latter worked mechanically, which of course he need not do. I fail to see why the kind of economic history Gordon has sketched could not also be written, if someone thought it worth while to take the trouble, in mathematical curves with explicit equations; though it is only proper to add that some of the questions raised by Gordon have no obvious mathematical equivalent.

This is about as far, I think, as a pragmatic test applied to the papers by Gordon and Koopmans can take us. If we are to go further in appraising their methodological approaches, we must revert to speculations. It seems reasonable to suppose that if Gordon and Koopmans persist in their present emphases, their results will be cast in different forms—one mathematical, the other literary. That may impede understanding for a time, but economists have become inured to this sort of inconvenience. Even the nonmathematical literature of economics does not lack identical theories expressed in different idioms, to say nothing of different theories expressed in identical words. Thus economist A may assert that, *ceteris paribus*, demand is a monotonically decreasing function of price, while B states that under stable conditions demand increases as price diminishes. Or economist A may claim that in a competitive market the rate of interest equilibrates the amount of money that households and firms seek to hold with the amount of money in existence—i.e., the amount they do hold—while B asserts that the rate of interest equates the demand for money loans with the supply. Again, economist A may asseverate that if intended investment exceeds the propensity to save, the national income expressed in a wage unit is to the left of its equilibrium position and will therefore rise to its equilibrium value, while B may assert that if the aggregate profits of business firms exceed expectations, they will tend to increase their working forces. Thus the extraordinary richness of the English language has brought its joys and embarrassments. I think that Koopmans and Gordon may at least take comfort in the thought that, if it should turn out that they impose a linguistic ordeal upon one another and upon the rest of us, they may do so in no greater degree than have economists conversing in different varieties of English.

Of course, it is possible—perhaps even likely—that Koopmans will present us with a single, comprehensive generalization, while Gordon will end up with as many generalizations as, or more than, the number of business cycles he covers. But this outcome need not mean that their results will be contradictory. To the extent that Gordon tracks down variables treated as exogenous in the econometric model or secreted in its random variances, his work might prove complementary to Koopmans'. To the extent that Gordon neglects the common features of business cycles, Koopmans' work might prove complementary to Gordon's. Furthermore, I take it as a matter of course that, although Gordon is now chiefly concerned with the features that differentiate business cycles rather than with the features they have in common, he is intensely interested in the latter and will go as far as he can to account for them. I therefore see a basis for hope that Koopmans' and Gordon's results may prove not merely complementary, but actually confirm one another.

In any event, we may look forward eagerly to what they turn up. I anticipate a stimulating account of the interwar period from Gordon's pen. While there is a greater continuity in business cycle experience before and after World War I than many students realize, there can be little doubt that certain structural changes in the world economy did occur around that time. The period surely deserves intensive study, especially if the background of earlier business cycles is not neglected. Between the 1870's and 1914 the fluctuations of economic activity in the leading commercial nations of the world—Great Britain, Germany, France, and the United States—moved in unison, except for the fact that American experience was occasionally diversified by extra cycles. After 1919 the business cycles of different countries tended to drift apart, though practically all shared in the catastrophic contraction of 1929-1932. There can be little doubt that the international gold standard tied together the business fortunes of different nations before World War I, and that monetary individualism is imprinted on the divergent business fluctuations of different countries in later years. The United States emerged as an international creditor after the war, and both foreign lending and foreign trade assumed a new significance in our economy. Exports, which conformed poorly to business cycles before 1914, later fell into step with business cycles. Perhaps the most dramatic evidence of the economic unity of the period 1921-1933, which Gordon has described as a major cycle, is to be found in our record of foreign lending. Up to about 1925 the volume of foreign loans placed in this country was substantial. Yet the loans were on the whole of sound quality, as attested by later experience. The rest of the decade witnessed a further expansion in the volume of foreign loans, and a very sharp deterioration of their quality.[1] The speculative craze was not confined to foreign bonds, but expressed itself also in the real estate and stock markets. Consumer credit shared mightily in the upsurge, the largest part being devoted to the purchase of durable consumer goods. For decades before the outbreak of World War I the share of consumer durables in the total value of finished commodities had fluctuated around an average of about 10 per cent. In the twenties the percentage doubled, and this swift and momentous change in the nation's consumption habits brought a new element of potential instability to our system.

These and a thousand related facts will emerge from Gordon's study. I expect that he will make the business cycles of the interwar period stand out as individuals, without pushing the interpretation of particular events further than the intrinsic complexity of individual experience or the quality of available records will allow. I look forward to an integrated interpretation that will test current understanding of the twenties and thirties—a period that is decisive in any attempt to form a reasoned judgment of the economic outlook over the next decade. But I think that if Gordon is to accomplish what fully lies within his power, he needs a more definite framework of analysis than he has presented. His marshalling of evidence on the major cycle of 1921-1933 may, perhaps, be facilitated by putting financial accounts side by side with national income accounts, and watching the shifts from one form of speculation to another, as well as the changing proportions between the speculative and industrial activities.

[1] See a forthcoming study by Ilse Mintz [*Deterioration in the Quality of Foreign Bonds Issued in the United States, 1920-1930*, published by the National Bureau in 1951].

It is more difficult for me to appraise the prospects of Koopmans' investigation than of Gordon's. The attempt to describe the essential workings of the economic system in a comparatively small number of equations is a new and magnificent conception. Whether the attempt will prove successful, I have no way of knowing. I think, however, that the chances of success will be improved if econometricians note carefully the results of systematic factual studies of cyclical behavior such as Abramovitz' on inventories and Hultgren's on cost-price relations. I think, too, that the econometricians' work would be improved if they made an explicit effort to wrestle with the historical problem of marking off the boundary dates to which their models are supposed to apply. I think that further theoretical and statistical work on short-run versus long-run economic functions is seriously needed, and that the econometricians should experiment with timing relations that shift systematically over the course of a business cycle—a matter I believe I can demonstrate is of some importance. I think, finally, that econometricians might benefit from better record-keeping. General econometric models are barely a decade old, but simpler models go back to Moore and embrace a generation of research in agricultural economics. As far as I have been able to discover, no one is now keeping a reasonably full record of how well or how badly the many different models constructed by econometricians have worked or are working. Such a record would serve as a measure of progress, and at the same time provide an instrument that might effectively hasten progress. Imagine a file kept for each model, excluding of course those that seem too absurd to follow or those that have turned out badly, for, let us say, a dozen consecutive years. Once a year a trained analyst would go through the files and see how well the prediction for an additional year compares with the observed figure. Each year he would prepare an analysis for publication, classifying the errors of the various models according to the type of equation used, the method of estimating its parameters, the period covered by the model, the economic terms it includes, and so on. Such an analysis would aim to segregate the factors in econometric model-building that seem to promote success from those that promote failure, and thus pave the way for improvements in the technique. I devoutly hope that someone will undertake this arduous but necessary task of scientific verification and accounting.

If what I have said is not too wide of the mark, both Gordon and Koopmans are engaged in empirical investigations of high importance. True, neither author has as yet specified the economic theory that guides him, or listed the variables on which he deems it desirable to concentrate, or commented on the quality of the available statistics or other information bearing on his study, or discussed the influence that any of these matters has had or may have on his methodological approach. But I infer from these silences, as I do from the soul-searching in which each has engaged and from the points of agreement between them that I noted in my opening remarks, that the approaches of our two investigators are still fluid. This fact promises well for their inquiries. Experimentation is essential in the present state of our knowledge of business cycles, and I see in the experimental cast of mind of our two investigators the best of reasons for expecting that their researches will prosper.

Frickey on the Decomposition of Time Series

I. The Conventional Technique

The Review of Economic Statistics came to life with the publication of two remarkable papers by Professor Warren M. Persons on the nature and measurement of time-series fluctuations. Persons conceived of an economic time series as a composite of four types of movements—secular, seasonal, cyclical, and irregular. His main interest was in the problem of analyzing business conditions, and his hope was to develop, on the basis of historical records, a system of forecasting cyclical sequences in business life. Hence he eliminated secular trends and seasonal variations from time series, expressed the adjusted data in units of their standard deviation, and used coefficients of correlation to sort series according to their time sequence. This novel technique of handling economic data instantly attracted wide attention. Before long it was adopted by numerous investigators in this country and abroad; within a few years of its inception, it became the 'customary' or 'conventional' method of handling time series.

But as its use spread, there came criticism and dissent. Some questioned the propriety of some of the detailed methods employed by Persons and his associates. Others questioned the classification of economic movements, and proceeded to develop hypotheses of structural changes, of secondary versus primary trends, of special cycles in different branches of trade, of the intermittence of cyclical waves, and of the coexistence of several sets of cycles—each perhaps periodic but combining with others to produce the irregular waves of the familiar business indexes. Still others directed criticism at the 'empiricism' of Persons' methods. Will not the conventional technique decompose a series of random numbers as elegantly as an historical series? If movements of a given type are 'eliminated' from a time series, are the effects of a corresponding cause or group of causes likewise eliminated? Do not the forces of development within a capitalistic economy move in waves, cyclical depressions being the incidental wreckage of economic progress? If so, will the conventional technique bury real problems and create false ones? To the charge of empiricism, that of 'narrowness' was added. Is it wise to measure secular trends, seasonal variations, and cyclical amplitudes, only to discard them

Reprinted by permission from *The Review of Economic Statistics* (published by Harvard University Press), August 1944, pp. 136-147.

without further ado? Is not even the timing of cyclical fluctuations being handled with excessive simplicity? Is it proper to treat the problem of sequences without regard to the stage of the business cycle?

Criticism along these and similar lines was inevitable as the study of business cycles deepened. But it is worth noting that critics have all too frequently laid at Persons' door and that of his collaborators abuses committed by a host of ill-trained imitators. Today, few economists seem to remember that Persons' technique was originally developed for handling the problem of constructing a set of forecasting indexes of business conditions, or appreciate that, taken as a whole and in the light of the statistical data available at the time, it was well suited to the purpose for which it was designed. But it is also fair to add that while the 'conventional technique' gave a strong stimulus to economic research in general and to business cycle research in particular, it has proved of little aid in advancing the frontiers of our theoretical knowledge. There can be no regret that it is losing its preeminence. If economists are to gain authentic knowledge about business fluctuations, they must steadily test their tools of observation and seek to improve upon them.

Professor Edwin Frickey has worked by this creed. His book on *Economic Fluctuations*[1] makes an outstanding contribution to the methodology of time series. It is an original, painstaking, and scholarly work by an economist who for some years was closely associated with Persons. Frickey's book is directed mainly to the problem of trend-cycle separation. From some points of view, the methods that he presents for decomposing time series may be considered a rehabilitation of the customary technique; but if Frickey is the rehabilitator of Persons, his relation to Persons is much like Marshall's to Ricardo. Frickey sees the problem of time-series decomposition as essentially a problem in economic theory; it can never be solved by statistical procedure alone. Mathematical curve-fitting "enters not as the first step, but as the last in a long analytical process. It has its modest function, but it is in no way fundamental" (p. 335). Quasi-mechanical methods for separating secular and cyclical movements are to be shunned. Indeed, "the author's great misgiving in presenting this study is that there may somehow be supposed to be such a thing as the 'Frickey method' for

[1] Edwin Frickey, *Economic Fluctuations in the United States*, Harvard Economic Studies, No. 73 (Harvard University Press, 1942).

278

analyzing time series, capable of being applied automatically and universally" (p. 342).

II. THE GENERAL PLAN OF FRICKEY'S WORK

The conventional method of adjusting data for secular trend involves a series of more or less arbitrary decisions. The statistician must decide upon the form of the mathematical equation that will represent the trend, on the period to which the trend is to be fitted, on the method of fitting the trend, on the time unit in which the data are to be expressed for this purpose, and on the manner in which the trend is to be removed. A similar range of decisions is necessary if moving averages are used instead of mathematical curves. There is thus ample opportunity for whim and judgment. Readers of this *Review* may recall Frickey's 'pig iron production case,' published in the October 1934 issue. Frickey assembled twenty-three mathematical trends fitted by other investigators, counted the number of full swings about each trend line, and ascertained the average duration of the 'cycles.' The results ranged, more or less gradually, from 3 or 4 years to 40 or 45 years.

This dramatic illustration sets the problem of the book. How are 'cycles' that are merely technical creatures of mathematical processes to be distinguished from economically significant cycles? Is it possible to anchor trend lines to firmly established knowledge, and thus narrow, if not eliminate, the range for discretionary judgment? These questions cannot be handled satisfactorily by analyzing series one at a time. A far more promising method is to "attack the problem as a *unified whole*" (p. 52). Ideally, this will involve a search for "consistencies and uniformities of behavior" (p. 53) over a wide range of economic data; some proximate solution of the puzzle of time-series decomposition; an interpretation of the results as a whole in the light of economic theory and history; finally, a reconsideration of the statistical work done earlier, "with a view to obtaining . . . a systematic and connected composite array of statistical results, accompanied . . . by a systematic . . . theoretical and historical interpretation" (p. 57).

The volume is concerned with the earlier sections of this far-reaching program. Part One poses the problem and the method of attack. Part Two is devoted to a "search for patterns of fluctuation" (p. 63) in economic time series for the United States over the half century between the close of the Civil War and the outbreak of World War I. From this search three major conclusions

279

emerge. First, in the period covered, "there is a clearly-defined pattern of short-run fluctuation which permeates the whole structure of the nation's industrial and commercial life" (p. 230). Second, the evidence suggests "the presence of one, and only one, definite pattern of fluctuation" (p. 231). Third, in the array of series analyzed, "certain long-run tendencies" are present, "which were gradually . . . overcoming the cohesiveness of these series and driving them away from one another" (p. 233). These conclusions serve as "foundation stones" (p. 20) for the decomposition of time series undertaken in Part Three. They also have considerable significance in their own right, and it is well to ponder them before passing to Frickey's decomposition.

III. A Standard Pattern of Short-Run Fluctuations

For many years Wesley C. Mitchell has worked with the concept that business cycles are not merely fluctuations of a certain order of duration in aggregate economic activity; they are also units of roughly concurrent fluctuations in many economic activities, and it is this feature, more than any other, that distinguishes them from the fluctuations in aggregate activity that occurred prior to the emergence of a business economy, and from other types of fluctuations in modern times. This concept finds striking confirmation in Frickey's entirely independent study.

The conclusion that a "smooth, wave-like fluctuation of particular form" (p. 230) has pervaded the nation's commercial and industrial life is reached by Frickey at the close of an extensive investigation, conducted with meticulous care, and therefore deserves the most serious attention. The investigation starts with an analysis of thirteen important series[2] in quarterly form: bank clearings in New York City, clearings in seven cities outside New York, loans of New York banks, railroad earnings, immigration, imports, exports, sensitive commodity prices, wholesale commodity prices, railroad stock prices, industrial stock prices, bond prices, commercial paper rates. After adjustment for seasonal varations, where needed, the series are converted into link relatives, which are then adjusted for differences in their average level (by taking deviations from geometric means of the relatives, series by series), for differences in amplitude (by expressing the deviations in units of their quartile deviation), and for differences in timing (by shifting the adjusted relatives forward or backward, also by in-

2 The substance of this part of the study was published in the December 1934 issue of this *Review*.

verting them for two series). These adjusted series, Frickey finds, "exhibit a remarkable degree of correspondence" (p. 95). There is a "close approach to parallelism" among the curves showing quartiles of the adjusted link relatives; this fact "taken in conjunction with the presence of most clearly distinct 'zones of distribution'" of the relatives at successive quarters "affords decisive evidence as to the presence of a common pattern of movement among the series" (p. 96). By taking averages of the seven middle items, quarter by quarter, a "link-relative standard pattern" is obtained. As a final step, this pattern is converted from quartile-deviation units to percentages (by using the mean of the middle seven of an array of the thirteen quartile deviations), and then chained. The result is a "standard pattern" of *original items*, which delineates by quarters the common, pervasive, short-run fluctuation of the entire group of series; its oscillations "may be clearly traced—sometimes, to be sure, exaggerated or minimized; occasionally distorted by irregularities—in the movements of the original series" (p. 99).

I have described the derivation of this pattern in some detail, because it is the general method—modified slightly in some instances, considerably in others—pursued throughout the pattern studies. I must now summarize more boldly, even at the cost of conveying to the reader no more than an inkling of the methodical tests that Frickey employs to guard his results against unconscious bias. On the basis of a sample of about 100 annual production series, he derives patterns for major groups of industries— agriculture, mining, manufactures eventuating in capital equipment, manufactures eventuating in consumption, and transportation and trade. Agriculture aside, a "high degree of intrinsic correspondence" is found among the several groups in "the fundamental form of short-time fluctuation" (p. 167). This suggests the derivation of a pattern for industrial and commercial production as a whole. When the new pattern is compared with the standard pattern for thirteen series earlier described, "the correlation is truly remarkable" (p. 170). The patterns of commodity prices and of a group of miscellaneous series likewise confirm the standard pattern. So too does the form of the short-run fluctuation of various index numbers of production (excluding agriculture), employment, and wholesale commodity prices. Thus, whether a given group of series is examined collectively or combined in an index number, the same basic pattern emerges.

In view of the consilience of the evidence, Frickey is fully justi-

fied in drawing the conclusion that the standard pattern for thirteen series represents the form of a fluctuation that has pervaded
the nonagricultural sphere of the economy.[3] This does not mean,
however, that there are no flaws in the analysis. (1) In designing
the sample of thirteen series, Frickey included "only important
basic series" (p. 65); "highly inflexible" and "extremely erratic
series" (p. 66) were rejected. The sample contains just one series
expressed in a physical unit. The rest are price or value series, one
of which—the index of sensitive commodity prices—is not only a
subdivision of another price index included, but a subdivision deliberately made on account of sensitivity to business cycles. May
not such a sample bias the results in the direction of 'consistencies
and uniformities'? (2) The method of partition values, in the presence of distinct 'zones of distribution,' is said to yield a decisive
test of a common or general pattern of movement. But in order
that the test be decisive, the zones of distribution must not merely
be distinct; they *must not overlap*—and this condition is obviously not fulfilled by Frickey's data. Under the circumstances
either no test is decisive or this distinction belongs to a method
not employed by Frickey; namely, a count, simple or weighted, of
the rises and declines (allowing, of course, for leads or lags),
period by period.[4] (3) Frickey relies on visual readings of charts
to describe the degree of correspondence among his numerous
curves. I think that he occasionally exaggerates the 'uniformities'
and never the 'discrepancies' among the curves. I may, of course,
be mistaken. If objective measures of correlation, with all their
defects, had been presented, there would be less room for uncertainty on this score.

There are also several questions that Frickey's demonstration of

[3] I may add that this pattern agrees closely with the chronology of business cycles
of the National Bureau of Economic Research. Allowing for leads or lags, every movement keeping the same direction for three quarters or longer in Frickey's standard
pattern is matched by a corresponding movement in the Bureau's chronology of
business cycles. Again, every phase of expansion and contraction in the Bureau's
chronology (restricted, of course, to the period covered by Frickey) is reflected in a
movement of corresponding direction, lasting three quarters or longer in the standard pattern; so that the two sets of cyclical waves are throughout in one-to-one correspondence. For a fuller comparison, see Chap. 4, Sec. vi of the forthcoming publication on *Measuring Business Cycles*, by Wesley C. Mitchell and the present writer.

[4] Curves of partition values are an extremely powerful device for bringing to the
surface any tendencies towards a common rhythm in a mass of time series, but the
device is a little too powerful—it can extract false rhythms as well as true ones. If
the actual items of a group of series move chaotically between two dates, the partition
values may still move uniformly in the same direction. Indeed, it is possible for all
partition values to rise, while every series but one falls; or for all partition values to
fall, while every series but one rises.

a pervasive, common, wave-like fluctuation leaves unanswered. What is the precise statistical meaning of the standard pattern? Does every wrinkle in this curve depict a movement that is diffused through the economy? That cannot be Frickey's meaning. But what, then, *are* the main movements, in historical time, that are supposed to be diffused? In what degree has each of these unit movements been in fact pervasive? What are the activities whose fluctuations correspond to the standard pattern? And what is the degree of correspondence or noncorrespondence in each instance? There are no answers to these questions in Frickey's book. They either are not considered at all, or are treated in an incidental fashion.

Nor has sufficient attention been given to the fact that the 'pervasiveness' of business cycles is relative to the units of observation. Assume a group of monthly series that cover rather comprehensively the nonagricultural sphere of the economy—say, aggregates or indexes of production, income payments, employment, freight traffic, bank clearings, wholesale prices. The cyclical fluctuations of these series will harmonize closely, though clearings and prices will occasionally fall out of step with the others. Now let each composite be broken down into 'major groups,' and numerous discrepancies of cyclical behavior will begin to appear. Carry the breakdown another step, and the divergencies will again multiply. Imagine this process of breakdown to continue until the 'ultimate' economic units are reached. What will the constellation of time series now look like? The smooth, wave-like fluctuations, keeping in close step with one another, will be gone. Their place will be taken by a confused network of millions or billions of curves, some inflexible, others erratic, perhaps some wave-like, crossing one another in crazy fashion. Hence if one economist 'sees' different branches of the economy moving in harmonious cyclical waves, and another 'sees' divergent fluctuations as dominant, the first is not necessarily right and the second wrong. Each may be essentially right in terms of the 'units' on which his mind's eye is centered; that is, with reference to the 'stage' at which economic behavior is being considered.

The crucial task that faces business cycle theory comes precisely at this point. No student of business fluctuations is, or can be, concerned with the ultimate units into which time series may, in principle, be broken. On the other hand, there are some—their number and influence seem to be growing—who believe, or write as if they believed, that the mechanism whereby business cycles are generated can be adequately disclosed by analysis of a few broad aggregates. No one can be sure at present how far it is wise to go in breaking down comprehensive aggregates; the issue will be resolved, if at all, by experiment and performance, not by debate. I think, however, that Frickey is on the right track when, in outlining his program of research, he remarks that the search for 'consistencies and uniformities' must be followed by "investigation of inconsistencies and departures from uniformity" (p. 53). In other words, if we are to explain business cycles, we must know in some detail what activities participate in the general rhythm, what activities do not, what activities participate by rising and falling in harmony with the general tide, and what activities participate by rising throughout but more moderately during general contractions than during general expansions, what activities move early and what late in the general progression, what activities swing over a wide range and what have narrow amplitudes, and the changing relations of different activities in these respects from one business cycle to the next.

IV. The Problem of Long and Short Cycles

When economists discuss the dating of business cycles, they are apt to differ endlessly from one another. But when they get down to the task of measurement, their results are surprisingly similar. There is some disagreement over whether there was a contraction in 1918-1919 or 1926-1927; but practically everyone who has worked extensively with American data will agree that a contraction occurred in 1903-1904, 1907-1908, 1910-1911, 1913-1914, 1920-1921, 1923-1924, 1929-1933, and 1937-1938—to mention only the declines in business since the turn of the century. At this point agreement stops. Some believe that there is a single cyclical wave only; others believe that the 'short cycles' are subdivisions of 'long cycles,' and this group is divided into numerous sects, each devoted to its own brand of 'long cycles.'

The analyst who seeks to 'decompose' a time series must take a position on this question. If a time series is affected by just a single cyclical wave, one kind of statistical operation will be in order; if several sets of cyclical waves are simultaneously running their course, a more complex technique will be necessary. It is natural, therefore, that Frickey should seek to determine whether, in addition to the pattern of short-run fluctuation that stands out so clearly in his materials, patterns of long-run fluctuation are also present. His conclusion, already given, does not imply that long cycles do not exist. What Frickey means is, simply, that cogent evidence in favor of the hypothesis of long cycles has failed to turn up in the course of his work; consequently, for the time being, he deems it best to take an agnostic position.

This judgment is based on an analysis of the thirteen quarterly series from which the standard pattern was originally derived. Frickey begins the search for new patterns by transforming the series into annual averages, and applying to them the technique used with such striking success on quarterly data. The results are negative: "we have merely in effect derived the old pattern over again" (p. 107). Next, this technique is applied to biennial averages, with the same results; to triennial averages, and again the same results; to sextennial averages—and once again "we see that the basic pattern of fluctuation first discerned in the quarterly analysis persists in practically unmodified form" (p. 123). Finally, the technique is tried on nine-year averages; the intercorrelation of the series is now weaker and the amplitude of the pattern narrower, but "so far as a pattern of movement does still remain in the nine-year results, it is altogether consistent with the patterns previously derived from quarterly data" (p. 127). Since the methodology has now "reached almost the point of technical breakdown" (p. 130) and the results remain negative, Frickey brings this phase of the investigation to a close.

Is Frickey's interpretation of the results correct? Imagine the standard pattern—I shall call it a quarterly index of business conditions for the present purpose—converted into annual form, then biennial form, triennial, etc. Since each wave of the index lasts several years, and since the successive waves vary considerably in duration and still more in intensity, it will not be surprising if the annual curve bears a good resemblance to the quarterly curve, and if the same is true, up to a point, of curves based on progressively coarser time units. Given such results, we may say that the wave-like form of the quarterly index is merely being reproduced by the curves based on broader time units. But will it not seem a little strange if wave-like fluctuations appear in six-year averages, even in nine-year averages, and analysis discloses that these fluctuations (though less pronounced than was the case when a finer time unit was used) are diffused among the constituents of the index? Can these fluctuations be dismissed on the mere ground that they trace out a curve that has a resemblance to the original curve of the quarterly index?

That, in essence, is what Frickey does. But the evidence may be read differently. Insofar as full waves can be marked off in his patterns of six- and nine-year averages, their duration is eighteen years. If six- or nine-year *moving* averages had been used instead of straight averages, the waves would probably stand out more clearly than they do. These waves may be a genuine and distinct species of fluctuations, that is, 'long cycles.' On the other hand, they may be merely an illusion, resulting from the failure of the short waves, which vary in duration and intensity, to cancel out even in the six- or nine-year averages. That possibility could be tested by recognizing the long waves provisionally as higher units of fluctuation, and then seeing whether the short waves that occur during the upswing of the long waves differ from the short waves during the downswing of the long waves in a manner consistent with the long-cycle hypothesis.[5] If this test should be met, the provisional long cycles might still be suspect; for example, because they are not uniform multiples of short cycles, or because they are so few in number, or because they are not confirmed by evidence—statistical or historical—outside the thirteen-series sample, or on all these grounds. Frickey has not tracked down any of these possibilities. He does note that the results of the pattern studies are "at least consistent" (p. 132, n.) with the Kondratieff hypothesis, but it would seem that they are more nearly consistent with certain other long-cycle hypotheses than that of Kondratieff.

At the close of the book Frickey reasserts his agnosticism on the perplexing subject of long cycles. He notes, however, one interesting relationship suggested by a group of twelve series subjected to intensive trend analysis. "While our time period of analysis is . . . too short to afford any decisive test of the Kondratieff long-wave hypothesis, we may nevertheless note in passing that the showing of the trend-indication lines . . . , and especially the behavior of these lines around the turn of the century, is at least consistent with this hypothesis . . . ; and the array of evidence . . . can be made to fit into his statistical scheme" (p. 340). This comment seems to overlook the fact that the Kondratieff hypothesis posits *general* long waves—that is, long waves in both the production and price spheres—and that its significance for business cycle theory turns on this point. If Frickey's representations of the trends of the employment and production indexes (the former is an exponential, the latter a logarithmic parabola, showing retardation) are valid, they seem to argue against Kondratieff. Nine other series relate to prices or values; their behavior is consistent

[5] See *Measuring Business Cycles*, cited above, Chap. XI.

with Kondratieff's hypothesis, but also with the simpler and older hypothesis of long waves in prices. The behavior of immigration, the one remaining series, is again consistent with Kondratieff's hypothesis; but the most striking feature of this series is its tendency to move in waves that are about a third of the Kondratieff period—waves found also in railroad construction and, among Frickey's series, in railroad stock prices. I do not think, therefore, that the Kondratieff hypothesis gains much support from Frickey's trend analysis.[6]

These doubts arise solely in regard to some of the methods used by Frickey and the interpretation that he has placed on the results. They are not directed at his conclusion concerning "the presence of one, and only one, definite pattern of fluctuation." On the contrary, agnosticism on the subject of general long cycles seems, at the present time, definitely the better half of wisdom.

V. The Nature of Time-Series Variations

It is only after the extensive search for patterns and certain supplementary investigations have been completed that Frickey feels prepared to define the nature of time-series variations, and even then does it merely to a first approximation. This procedure is in decided contrast to that followed by Persons in his basic memoir on time series. Why does not Frickey follow Persons' example —make common sense his ally at the start, define forthwith the movements in time series, and get down to the business of segregating them? Why are so many elaborate preparations necessary? The answer is simple. Frickey is concerned with fundamentals. His aim is to "build from the bottom," to carry through the analysis of time series in such a manner "that in the end the results shall portray only relationships inherent in the original data" (p. 50). This explains the avoidance of the conventional technique, even of moving averages and other smoothing devices, in the pattern studies.[7] If the task of time-series decomposition is to isolate variations that are "inherent in the material" (p. 254), these varia-

[6] See George Garvy, "Kondratieff's Theory of Long Cycles," this *Review*, Vol. xxv (1943), pp. 203-220.

[7] Of course, it is impossible to avoid elements of these techniques completely. In deriving the standard pattern, Frickey in effect eliminates exponential trends, passed through the first and last data points of the individual series. Again, annual figures, on which he is forced to rely heavily, may be considered a degenerate form of a twelve-month moving average, one term being used and eleven dropped, in repetitive sequence.

tions must disclose something of their true economic nature before refined methods can be justified.

And that is precisely what the pattern studies have accomplished. If a smooth, wave-like, short-run fluctuation pervades the industrial and commercial life of the nation, if there is definite evidence of only one such pattern, and if the mutual attachment of the series tends to weaken as successively longer periods are analyzed, then it is plain "that elements of short-run and of long-run movement are present" (p. 241) in the statistical material. But what is the precise nature of these two elements and the relationship between them? To throw light on this question, Frickey subjects twelve important series to further analysis—an index of production, an index of employment, and ten of the original thirteen-series sample.[8] The series are broken into subperiods according to several different plans, and differences in amplitude and timing in each subperiod are eliminated, in order to see how the "form of short-run fluctuation . . . is affected by the long-run tendencies" (p. 244). Within each subperiod "distinct differences" emerge "with respect to general direction of movement" (p. 245). There is a "strong and ubiquitous tendency for the various curves . . . to drift apart from one another in a comparatively smooth and gradual way. . . ." On the other hand, "setting aside . . . relatively minor and incidental features" of the curves, "the general impression is one of striking congruence in the contours of short-run movement" (p. 247).

In view of these findings Frickey concludes that "it is a good first approximation to the truth to say that the time-series variations (setting aside seasonal and irregular fluctuations) are resolvable into smooth, continuous, gradually-changing long-time movements which may appropriately be designated 'secular trends,' and wave-like short-time oscillations which may appropriately be designated 'cyclical variations.'" Further, since investigation had disclosed a tendency towards a simple proportionate relationship between the short-run absolute fluctuations of time series and the size of original items, it is also "a good first approximation to assert that the relationship" between secular trends and cyclical variations "is that of being logarithmetically additive" (p. 253). These are, of course, familiar propositions; the novelty lies in their demonstration.

Frickey is careful to explain that this demonstration has been

[8] Loans of New York banks, exports, and bond prices are dropped because of their irregular conformity to the standard pattern.

carried through for only a small group—though a highly important group—of time series. He also recognizes that since the demonstration is limited to a fifty-year period, the movements designated as secular trends may, in fact, be segments of long-wave movements, and that the movements designated as cyclical variations may, in fact, be a composite of major and minor cycles. Nor can we assume that secular trends and cyclical variations are due to independent causes; "we should think here, not in terms of distinct sets of causal forces, but in terms of *lines of causal influence*" (p. 256). By this Frickey means, apparently, that 'economic forces' produce divergent trends in different activities, while they simultaneously produce cyclical movements which, apart from variations in timing and amplitude, have substantially the same contours in one activity and the next over a considerable part of the economic system.

This interesting interpretation of the nature of time series is bound to excite the reader to raise some questions. For example, what happens to the postulate that secular trends and cyclical variations are logarithmetically additive, in the case of series that conform well to the short-term general rhythm but that consist of plus or minus values—series like net incomes of business firms or net additions to inventories? Is it proper to assert, even as a first approximation, that certain causal impulses impinge with substantial uniformity on the short-run fluctuations of different parts of the economic system? Do not the very developments that produce variations in timing and amplitude among different activities also produce variations in the contours of their fluctuations? For example, pig iron production, as a rule, has registered its maximum rate of advance early in cyclical expansions, and its maximum rate of decline late in cyclical contractions. Commercial paper rates, on the other hand, have tended to register their maximum advance late in expansions and their maximum decline early in contractions. Such differences have been essential parts of the business cycle mechanism. They cannot be disregarded by economic theorists or statisticians. It is only proper to add, however, that Frickey's neglect of this feature of time series is not of serious moment in connection with his method of decomposing time series.

VI. THE DECOMPOSITION OF TIME SERIES

The method devised by Frickey to separate secular trends and cyclical variations is highly ingenious. Putting qualifications aside, he removes the cyclical variations from a series and gets its secular trend as a residual—which is the very opposite of the conventional technique. The method is a logical sequel to the findings reached earlier in the book. For if a time series is resolvable into a secular trend and cyclical variations,[9] and the standard pattern delineates the cyclical variations that permeate economic life, then it should be possible to derive the trend of a series by dividing its successive values by corresponding values of the standard pattern. The actual statistical operations, however, must be more elaborate, partly because the standard pattern is an imperfect gauge of the cyclical variations, partly because the observable fluctuations of individual series—even after allowing for differences in cyclical timing and amplitude—are not precisely congruent with the standard pattern.

The first task is to refine the standard pattern. In deriving this pattern, link relatives were used in the form of deviations from their geometric mean—an operation that implies exponential trends. In fact, there is very great diversity in the relationships of the secular trends over successive decades; but this very fact makes it probable that the diverse trends have largely offset one another in the standard pattern. Frickey therefore proceeds to eliminate from the twelve series selected for experimentation the particular form of variation traced out by the standard pattern. Once modified, the series are broken into several subperiods and a logarithmic straight line fitted to each. With these 'trend indications' as a guide, tentative trend lines are drawn. The standard pattern[10] is now recomputed, the adjustments for trend being made on the basis of the tentative trend lines instead of the crude corrections originally applied. But the revised pattern makes it possible to derive secular trend lines more accurately than before; hence the whole round of operations is repeated. The new tentative trend lines, in their turn, make it possible to revise the standard pattern once again. Since this revision turns out to be almost an exact replica of the first revision, "the logical stopping place in the present line of procedure" has manifestly been reached. "The process of gradual attenuation of the secular elements in the standard pattern" has been practically completed; in other words, the second revision constitutes "a rather faithful picture of *the cyclical element in isolation*" (p. 329).

With this objective realized, the remaining operations are straightforward. In general, they follow the model just sketched.

---

[9] Setting aside, of course, seasonal and irregular fluctuations.
[10] Based on ten series. See note 8.

The full period is broken into seven subperiods, each corresponding approximately to a full fluctuation of the standard pattern
about its base line. The logarithms of the standard pattern are
then adjusted for differences between their amplitude and that
of the series during each subperiod. Next, the figures thus derived
are subtracted from the logarithms of the original items—which
are first shifted a little, here and there, to allow for leads or lags.
The resulting modified series are "primarily and essentially representative of secular variations" (p. 290). To remove minor errors
and irregularities from the modified series, straight lines are fitted
for each subperiod, and these 'trend indications' serve as a guide—
followed closely but not slavishly—for drawing up a final schedule
of trend lines.

Two series—the production index and the employment index—
are fitted by simple mathematical curves, the first by a logarithmic
parabola, the second by an exponential curve. Of the remaining
ten series there are "few, if any, for which the secular variations
are capable of satisfactory representation by a single simple mathematical curve" (p. 292). Hence the series are split into subperiods,
and a trend line fitted separately to the logarithms of the data in
each subperiod. For example, the secular trend of industrial stock
prices is represented by a straight line during 1866-1904 and a
parabola during 1904-1914. Other series are broken into three or
even four subperiods, the interval varying from four to thirty-nine
years.[11] The trend lines involve, of course, a certain degree of

[11] Frickey believes that "wide diversity and decided individuality as regards the
form of secular variation" (p. 315) are by no means peculiar to his sample. Although
simple mathematical curves fit a few broad aggregates admirably for half a century,
they cannot be generally trusted to represent secular trends. True, individual industries predominantly grow at a declining rate, but their "long-time tendencies . . .
are much less simple than has commonly been supposed" (p. 151). The logarithmic
parabola is satisfactory for pig iron production in the period studied, but few individual production series "can be suitably represented" (p. 340, n.) by this function.
A broad range of evidence "strongly suggests that the secular movements of economic
series over long periods do not in general tend to proceed in accordance with 'laws'
embodied in simple mathematical functions" (p. 292). I think all these broad observations are well founded, though here and there a special interpretation clause
may be desirable.

A few of Frickey's detailed observations concerning secular trends seem a little
careless. I shall restrict comment to one point, which is of some significance. Frickey
compares (a) the median of average rates of retardation for individual production
series ending in 1929 with (b) the average rate of retardation of a chained median of
link relatives for the same series ending in 1914. Such comparisons are made for
several groups of series. The results show that (a) is consistently and appreciably
higher than (b), which leads Frickey to state that the evidence strongly suggests that
the "predominant general tendency *is not simply for the pre-war retardation rate to
continue into the post-war years 1915-29, but rather is for the retardation to become*

discretionary judgment; but the difference in this respect between the new method and the conventional technique is "great enough to constitute a difference in kind" (p. 340). The trend lines and curves of cyclical variations[12] are presented as "first approximations to the truth" (p. 339).

Frickey's method of decomposing time series is the product of careful reasoning, searching, and testing. The most attractive feature of the technique is that both secular trends and cyclical variations are determined in a series of successive approximations, the entire group of series being handled as a unit to facilitate consistent judgments. In contrast to the conventional technique, which can be applied to any series whatever, Frickey's method can be properly used only in the case of series whose fluctuations bear a close correspondence to the standard pattern. "The application of our present procedure to a series not possessing this property of correspondence . . . would be unjustified, and the results would in all probability be absurd and meaningless. We must . . . enter an emphatic caveat against any such perversion of the methodology" (p. 288). But what series and how many series will meet the criterion of close correspondence? That depends, of course, on how strictly the criterion is applied. Between series like sugar meltings, which move in virtual independence of business cycles, and series like pig iron production, which move in almost perfect harmony, there is a continuous gradation. The criterion of close correspondence could be applied so strictly as to disqualify one of Frickey's mainstays—the index of wholesale prices, which suffers some notable lapses from conformity. On the other hand, it could be applied so liberally as to admit bond prices, which Frickey excludes. If the standard pattern were extended into the thirties, commercial paper rates would become a somewhat doubtful case, while exports might beckon for reinclusion. These difficulties must not, however, be exaggerated. Frickey's method is likely to prove satisfactory even if a series shows serious lapses from conformity during some periods. If that is true, the method can be applied rather extensively.

---

more severe in these later years" (p. 166). No degree of qualification can make this anything but a very dubious statement. The question of fact involved here is difficult to handle even by explicit calculation for the shorter period on plan (a). It surely cannot be handled by a mere process of inference from (a) and (b), for there is no fixed or simple relationship between (a) and (b). For example, it is mathematically possible for (b) to show a zero rate of retardation or even acceleration, although every series but one shows definite retardation.

12 The latter, as in the conventional technique, are considered as percentages of corresponding trend ordinates.

But is not the method far more expensive than the conventional technique? It is difficult to answer this question, because in practice the 'conventional technique' means different things to different investigators. Some statisticians fit and remove trend lines with speed and authority; others need to make many experimental calculations before they 'hit upon' a curve they are willing to accept even tentatively. In any case, the elaborateness of Frickey's technique is not likely to prove a deterrent for long. Practical statisticians who may wish to use the method are sure to discover, sooner or later, how to 'cut corners' and yet get results that do not differ seriously from those obtained by a literal application. For example, satisfactory approximations of Frickey's results might possibly be obtained by (1) passing a moving average through a series so as to remove approximately the cyclical variations, (2) fitting freehand straight lines to the moving averages for subperiods such as Frickey's, and (3) using these trend indications as a guide to the final trend line—which may again be a freehand curve.

Frickey's method clearly has a scientific foundation; its superiority over the conventional procedure of treating series one at a time, with only vague ideas tying the operations together, is beyond question. This does not mean, however, that the actual statistical results will necessarily be very different from those yielded by the conventional technique. If a statistician fits a line of secular trend to pig iron production in a mechanical manner, without specifying in advance his conception of the secular trend or of cyclical fluctuations, he may get 'cycles' averaging four years in duration, or ten times as long. But a judicious and informed investigator who is seriously studying cycles of a given order of duration will examine the series closely before choosing the trend line; he will seek to mark off the cycles observable in the original data or their first differences, and then fit a trend line that cuts through and exposes the cycles in which his interest centers. Discretionary judgment will enter into the operation, but the scope for its wanderings will be comparatively narrow—though perhaps not so narrow as in Frickey's method. What chiefly distinguishes Frickey's method is its explicit and thorough foundation, not the shapes of the curves finally derived by its use.

These shapes, as Frickey carefully notes, still involve *some* discretionary judgment. Let the reader examine Frickey's results closely. Is he not tempted to draw the trend line a little differently here, and a little differently there? But how tell whether the one drawing is better than the other? "We are confronted here with a problem in probabilities" (p. 333); but there is no mathematical technique for rendering the probabilities. Granting that the trend lines are 'approximations to the truth,' how can we test the goodness of the approximations? If some indeterminacy persists, should we recognize that fact explicitly, by giving up trend *lines* and drawing trend *zones* instead? One way, perhaps the only way, of making any headway with these difficult questions is to check 'decomposed' time series against historical information. Thus, if we accept Frickey's trend lines provisionally, we must also accept each full swing about the trend lines as a cycle, and we can then inquire how well these cycles check against historical evidence of business fluctuations. To cite an example, it seems rather clear that a general contraction in American business activity occurred in 1869-1870, 1890-1891, 1895-1897, and 1899-1900. Each of these contractions is reflected in Frickey's production index, but the first two appear in their entirety above the trend line and the last two are sunk below the trend line. If the historical validity of these cyclical movements is accepted, the trend line of the production index requires some adjustment. On the basis of the criterion just suggested, I should be inclined to modify most of Frickey's trend lines, but the modifications would in most instances be slight. I am, of course, anticipating here the next stage of Frickey's program of research—which, it should be recalled, requires an interpretation and reconsideration of the statistical results in the light of economic theory and history.

VII. THE PROBLEM AHEAD

It will be interesting to see what use Frickey makes of the segregated trends and cycles in the next stage of his research. The secular trend lines that he has developed are 'real' in the sense that they delineate, to a first approximation, certain tendencies in time series conforming to business cycles; that is, the direction and rate of change of the series, when cyclical variations and still shorter movements are put out of sight. The cyclical variations are 'real' in the sense of being diffused over a considerable part of the economic system. An array of trend lines and curves of cyclical variations—especially when the latter are left without adjustment for differences in amplitude—yields a highly useful description of the paths of change followed by different business factors. But how will activities that conform irregularly or badly to the general cyclical rhythm—for example, agricultural production, most food manufactures, some branches of textile output, public construction—be brought into the statistical picture? Frickey is fully aware of this problem, and undoubtedly will find some solution.

But too much must not be expected from trend-cycle separations, no matter how that problem may be solved. By eliminating cyclical variations (and still shorter movements) it is possible to isolate for scrutiny relationships among basic economic factors that persist over periods longer than business cycles. By eliminating secular trends, it is possible to isolate approximately the cyclical path of economic change, and demonstrate the imprint of business cycles on the economy. That much is clear. But what else can the separation of secular trends and cyclical variations accomplish? Specifically, is it likely to contribute materially to knowledge of causal relationships? Will time series adjusted for secular trend by Frickey's technique add more to an understanding of the mechanism of business cycles than have time series adjusted for secular trend by the conventional technique?

There is room for skepticism on these matters. Let us recall the history of electric power production during recent decades—its amazing growth, its resistance to moderate business depressions. Does it seem at all likely that this activity, and others correlated with it, have played a role in business recoveries similar to that of, say, the beehive coke industry? Yet when the secular trends are removed, whether by Frickey's method or the conventional method, electric power production becomes merely another 'index of business conditions'; there is little to distinguish it, except for a difference in amplitude, from the output of beehive coke or a dozen other industries. That which is most characteristic of the industry, most suggestive of its part in economic development, has been put out of sight. Or take another example, railroad investment. If the secular trend is left in the data, it soon becomes apparent that during the seventies and eighties this process tended to lead American recoveries by a substantial interval; but as the decades rolled on, the leads became shorter, and now have disappeared. This fact suggests that the industry shifted from an 'active' to a 'passive' role in business cycles, and raises the question whether the same may not be true generally of industries as they pass through successive stages of development. All this is lost or blurred when the secular trend is removed from the data; for the characteristic effect of this statistical operation is to standardize cyclical movements.

295

These observations are not directed against the decomposition of time series in general, or even against trend-cycle separations. No one who has seen seasonal variations fairly step out of charts, or watched important series climb rapidly during business cycle expansions and hesitantly during contractions, can question the value of even crude attempts to decompose some time series. The separation of secular trends and cyclical variations—especially by Frickey's technique—is sure to prove highly useful in tracing the imprint of business cycles on economic life. It seems unlikely, however, that trend-cycle separations will prove of equal advantage when effort shifts from statistical description to the explanation of business cycles. If these comments are valid in their general drift, the student of business cycles will want to remove secular trends at one stage of his work and leave them in at another stage.[13]

Frickey has kept his own counsel on the specific methods he intends to pursue in carrying his investigation to the next stage. But he remarks that "it is precisely in the course of the investigation of inconsistencies and departures from uniformity that we may hope to find those clues which, traced back, will enable us to surprise basic economic forces in the course of their operation" (p. 53). This attitude, combined with the fact that Frickey has lavished considerable attention on secular trends as matters of curiosity in their own right, indicates that he has broken with the tradition built up by the conventional technique and promises well for his future studies.

VIII. Concluding Comments

To give emphasis to some of the points covered in this review as well as make partial amends for its omissions, I conclude by listing what seem to me to be the leading contributions of Frickey's book. These include:

1. Elaboration of a technique for searching for 'consistencies and uniformities' in time series, capable of wide application.

2. Demonstration, on the basis of an extensive sample, of a rhythmic fluctuation pervading the economic life of the United States during the period from 1866 to 1914.

3. Delineation of the cyclical pattern of economic change by a quarterly index covering this period.

---

[13] Cf. *Measuring Business Cycles*, cited above, especially Chap. 3, and Joseph A. Schumpeter, *Business Cycles* (McGraw-Hill, 1939), Vol. I, Chaps. 3-5.

4. Careful formulation, and partial test, of a hypothesis concerning the nature of time-series variations.

5. A new and improved technique for separating secular trends and cyclical variations.

6. An improved technique for fitting secular trend lines.

7. Development of some new statistical series, the most important being an index of manufacturing employment, of manufacturing production, of the output of the transportation and communications industry, and a composite of the two preceding indexes.[14]

8. Presentation of a large body of significant economic measurements.

A good craftsman knows how to make a chain that will be stronger than its weakest link. He does it by doubling and tripling the links, especially when he suspects a link may be weak, and also when he believes it to be strong, so that the chain may stay firm even if some of the links break. This basic methodological principle has been observed by Frickey on a scale rarely equaled in economic research. The result is a book that, beside making substantial contributions to knowledge, bids fair to become a significant educational instrument.

[14] Only a brief description and graphs of the indexes are now given. The full record will be presented by Frickey in a later publication.

America's Capacity to Produce

In a notable volume on *America's Capacity to Produce*, Dr. E. G. Nourse and his associates take their problem to be "America's capacity to produce during the period from 1900 to 1930 with the capital goods and labor force which she then possessed and with the technology and the general pattern of operative and commercial organization then prevailing" (p. 415). The measurements of capacity are made, it is said, on the basis of "technological considerations" alone (p. 21). Considerations of ability to pay and of costs are ruled out, and "excess capacity" is interpreted as technically unnecessary idleness. The general plan is to make estimates of "practical," not "theoretical," capacity. This end is attained by striking estimates for each industry on the basis of (a) prevailing techniques in the industry, (b) prevailing customs as to number of shifts, length of working day, and so on; and by scaling down the estimates thus reached to allow for (c) whatever seasonal variations in output exist in fact, (d) "unavoidable" interruptions resulting from breakdowns of machinery, fires, strikes and so on, (e) the capacity of idle plants. For the sample of industries covered in the study, the final estimates are expressed as ratios of actual output to "practical capacity" output. The trends in these ratios of utilization are examined, and on the whole no tendency towards a secular rise is found. Further, a weighted average of the ratios of utilization is struck for the period 1925-1929 and the single year 1929. The average ratio is 80 per cent for 1929, which means that output might have been larger by 25 per cent. To allow for "failures of coordination," the estimate of potential increase in output is reduced to 19 per cent. This estimate is checked against data on labor power in 1929, and it is found that with some redistribution the labor force would have proved adequate for full utilization of the industrial plant.

The study results, then, in two outstanding conclusions: (1) there has been no cumulative piling up of "excess capacity" over the last three decades; (2) our production even in boom times falls considerably short of possibilities. These statistical findings are significant as such and also have a critical bearing on the thesis of the broader inquiry. In examining how firmly these find-

The first section of a lengthy review, originally published under the title "The Brookings Inquiry into Income Distribution and Progress." Reprinted by permission from *The Quarterly Journal of Economics* (published by Harvard University Press), May 1936, pp. 477-492. *America's Capacity to Produce* was published by the Brookings Institution in 1934.

ings have been established, nothing is more important than the adequacy of the concept of "capacity to produce" which underlies the statistical work.

I. THE CONCEPT OF CAPACITY TO PRODUCE

No concept of "capacity to produce" can be satisfactory unless five elementary propositions are clearly recognized. The first is that the central notion of "capacity to produce" is one of a maximum—that is, the maximum attainable production. The second proposition is that "capacity to produce" is an economic and not a technological problem, the thing to be maximized being human satisfactions. Since productive resources can be assigned to ends of varying urgency, the real problem is what allocation of resources will maximize production in the sense of a sum of satisfactions, not in some technological sense—say, in terms of weight or bulk. The third proposition is that an indefinite number of answers may be given to the question of what is the maximum attainable production. The answer will depend upon what assumptions are made concerning economic practices—that is to say, the rules of the economic game. A relatively minor change in economic organization might be assumed, for example, that protective tariffs are eliminated or that the run of technical practices is brought closer to the best. Or else a revolutionary change might be assumed, for example, that our farms, forests, mines, factories, railroads, highways, and so on, are made to turn out all that the available laborers working the optimum hours per week are capable of producing when directed by the most skilful engineers aiming only at maximum production of goods. The fourth proposition is that, while an investigator of a nation's "capacity to produce" may choose whatever assumptions he pleases, this raises rather than settles the matter of their 'significance.' The final proposition is that an estimate of potential increase in output, whether high or low, has little meaning unless it is accompanied by a theoretical analysis which indicates how the increase may be realized.

The Brookings inquiry faces squarely the problem of a maximum. However, it gets off to a bad start because the second proposition is not observed with sufficient care. The authors do not really rely, as they state, merely on technological considerations, but their technological bias causes difficulty all the same. Before turning to this difficulty, a few observations may be set down to indicate that in the plan of measurement described above considerations of price are, in fact, inextricably mixed with considerations of technology. (a) To make estimates of capacity on the basis of "prevailing techniques" is to assume the whole network of prevailing price relationships. As prices change the least cost combination of productive agents also changes and technical practices follow suit. (b) If an enterpriser is on the margin of doubt as to whether or not it is worth his while to introduce a night shift, a rise or fall in the price of labor will probably resolve the doubt. (c) Production of ice cream is highly seasonal, but it might not be if an ice cream soda sold for $2 in the summer and 2 cents in the winter. (d) Let enough money be expended on a repair force, and the loss of time due to breakdowns will be less than any assignable quantity. (e) If selling prices rise sufficiently, all or nearly all idle plants will resume operations.

Clearly, the 'price' factor enters into the Brookings estimates of capacity. But the difficulty is that its role is blurred by the technological factor. The technological bias results in treating ratios of plant utilization as so many observations on the inability of our economic system to obtain the fullest production of which it is capable. In effect the Brookings investigators multiply actual output by the reciprocal of a weighted average of ratios of utilization for a sample of industries and consider this quantity an estimate of our "capacity to produce." But this quantity has an indefinite relation to maximum attainable production, since maximum utilization of the "practical capacity" of our industrial plant is not the same as our maximum ability to produce. What is required by our second proposition is that output be maximized in an economic sense, not that existing plant be worked to the full on whatever products it is now making. Ratios of utilization are, and must always be, ambiguous 'observations' on a nation's efficiency in production. Even in a business economy a low ratio for beehive coke ovens may indicate that too much coke is produced by a notoriously wasteful process rather than too little. If we had simultaneously a sharp increase in birth rates and decline in death rates, the emergence of excess capacity in old casket factories and in newly erected baby carriage factories might mean that the goal of maximum national production is being approached more closely than if the unchanged plant of casket and carriage makers operated at full capacity. Putting the cyclical problem aside, in a dynamic society low ratios of utilization, no less than high ratios, may mean that productive resources are currently being used efficiently.

To estimate the maximum attainable production, productive resources must be considered as mobile. What degree of mobility is proper will depend on the system of economic practices postulated. If we assume a reorganization of economic life along collectivist lines, a considerably greater degree of mobility of industrial plant and labor may be envisaged than if we assume that protective tariffs are eliminated. For our present purpose, we need merely note that the Brookings investigators assume considerable technical and geographic mobility of the labor force; that the assumptions governing their estimates of plant capacity—such as acceptance of prevailing techniques, customs of operation, and seasonality—do not preclude some mobility of industrial plant; and that mobility of labor is more important to estimates of capacity than mobility of plant. There is nothing about the underlying assumptions of the Brookings inquiry, other than the technological bias, that seems to require an identification of maximum use of plant with maximum ability to produce. It is, of course, more difficult to estimate the output that would obtain under a rearranged industrial pattern than to estimate the output that would be realized with full use of the existing plant; though there is an offsetting gain in escaping the need to consider the capacity of each industry as a fixed quantity when we know, in fact, that the output of any given industry is usually indefinitely expansible, even in the short run, under adequate stimuli.

It may, of course, be argued that an estimate of "capacity to produce" made on the assumption of full use of the existing plant gives *one* answer to the question of what is the maximum attainable production. However, it is obvious that full use of every part of the industrial plant will lead not only to returns that are in many cases disproportionate to cost, but also to an unusable accumulation of considerable quantities of all sorts of intermediate products. This is recognized by the authors of *America's Capacity to Produce* at the end of the volume, where they attempt a correction for "failures of co-ordination."[1] Apart from the arbitrariness of the correction, the important point to note is that it serves to reduce the estimate of "capacity to produce," while the preliminary figure of capacity might actually need to be raised to make it approximate an estimate of capacity carried through on the assumption of optimum allocation of productive factors within a postulated framework of economic practices.

Let us now consider the 'significance' of the explicit assumptions concerning economic practices made in the Brookings survey. Following the Brookings investigators, we may say that our

[1] See below, p. 307.

"capacity to produce" is equal to actual output plus the additional output that could be got through use of the idle plant. The former quantity can be ascertained more or less definitely. The latter quantity, as already stated, is estimated by assuming prevailing techniques, customs of operation, and seasonality, by making further allowance for more or less unavoidable interruptions, and by excluding the potential output of plants that are shut down. These assumptions seem excessively restrictive. They appear to doom in advance estimates of capacity, for all but declining industries, to the neighborhood of actual output; they therefore rule out what is most needed for a significant appraisal of America's capacity to produce. An instructive though somewhat extreme example is the treatment of the Southern branch of the cotton textile industry. The problem here is how to take account of the custom of multiple shift operation followed by some of the mills. The authors decide to take as their estimate the capacity "as it would be if spindles were always operated on as full a schedule as they have occasionally attained, and if the spindles idle even in these times of maximum activity were also operated on at least a single-shift basis" (pp. 199-200). This formula yields a ratio of utilization of 89.8 per cent for 1925-1929. Actually, the "times of maximum activity" are seasonal peaks and the spindles idle "in these times" are relatively few. Thus the seasonal factor accounts for the greater portion of the gap between 89.8 and 100. The circularity of the estimate of capacity is not obvious from the ratio put down for this industry, mainly because this happens to be an instance where the rule requiring adjustment for seasonality is not applied.

Another serious shortcoming of the assumptions that underlie the Brookings estimates is their lack of theoretical unity. These assumptions, as we have already shown, presuppose the price system as it now functions. On the other hand, the additional output that could be attained by putting the 'idle' capacity to work is, of necessity, estimated on the assumption that the present price system is suspended or materially modified. Once either assumption is made, it would seem that such price-conditioned factors as a large portion of seasonal variations, customs of operation, and so on should be reexamined in the same stroke. What is equally if not more important, the assumptions of the Brookings estimates are not fitted into an analytic framework of a functioning economic system, and therefore fail to indicate *how* the calculated slack of productive capacity could be taken up. In the absence of a plan for realizing what is set down as a potential increase of output of 19 per cent in 1929, this figure has little meaning even if all other doubts are set aside. The final volume of the Brookings series supplies a corrective to *America's Capacity to Produce* by presenting a program for economic reconstruction; but as will presently be indicated this plan is incapable of closing the gap between actual output and "practical capacity" output.

II. THE ESTIMATES OF PLANT CAPACITY

The doubts aroused by the Brookings concept of productive capacity extend also to the multitude of decisions made in applying the concept statistically. At times these decisions violate the basic assumptions of the inquiry; at times they seem slipshod. All too frequently they are unexplained and even unstated.

We may illustrate by examining the manner in which the rule of scaling down estimates of theoretical capacity to take account of seasonality has been employed. (1) The adjustment factor applied to theoretical capacities is the crude ratio of the average monthly output to peak output. This method may result in serious error when the secular trend is steep. (2) Except for a few industries (high explosives and electric power production, and to a minor extent the meat packing, dairy, and automobile industries) no account is taken of intraindustrial differences. This makes the seasonal allowances too low whenever the seasonal patterns of different regions, of leading producers, or of leading products fail to synchronize perfectly. (3) Inadequate attention is given to the fact that seasonal variations are rarely constant for more than a few years.[2] For the bituminous coal and the meat-packing industries the seasonal factors are based on periods covering a quarter of a century. (4) Changes in seasonality are recognized in a few instances, but not in a manner consistent with the governing assumptions of the estimating procedure. The intensified seasonality of automobile production in recent years is classed as unnecessary and the seasonal correction is therefore worked out on the basis of 1923-1926. For a similar reason the seasonal allowance for anthracite coal is based on the period 1905-1914. The notion of "necessary seasonality" enters also into the analysis of the iron industry. All this is accomplished in the face of repeated stress that existing seasonality will be treated as a fact. (5) Little information is given on the seasonal allowances. The period on which the seasonal factor is based and its size can be made out for

[2] See Simon Kuznets, *Seasonal Variations in Industry and Trade* (National Bureau, 1933), Chap. XI.

only five of the twenty-nine manufacturing industries covered in the survey (meat packing, dairy, automobiles, black powder, and high explosives). In another four or five cases it is clear that a seasonal allowance has been made, but its magnitude is undiscoverable. In the remaining manufactures there are varying degrees of uncertainty whether any seasonal allowance has been made.

A similar list of criticisms might be drawn up with respect to each of the major rules of the Brookings procedure; but it would serve no good purpose. We may, however, take Table 1 as a rough measure of the workmanship that has gone into the study. This table relates to manufactures, which have "special importance for the hypothesis" of the study and for which, along with mining, "the most definite and satisfactory measurements" are claimed (pp. 162, 415). It will be noticed that in almost half of the cases the ratios of utilization set forth in the conclusions have no exact counterpart in the basic narrative or tables. The discrepancies may mean mainly that an incomplete account is given of the methods used; but they at least suggest the lighthearted manner in which many of the estimates are presented. Of course, disagreement does not necessarily mean that the method of estimating is poor. Neither does agreement prove that it is good; for example, the capacity of the machine tool industry is treated as constant during 1925-1930, without citing any evidence or authority in support of the estimate, and the ratio of utilization of 110 for 1929 raises further doubts.[3] Judging from the first column of the table, capacity data apparently are lacking for many industries for 1925-1929. Again, the fact that an estimate is somehow produced for each industry for this period is more conclusive with respect to the workmanship in general than the quality of any estimate in particular.

The entries in the first column of the table throw light also on what the Brookings investigators consider one of their outstanding results. Of the twenty-nine industries in the list only eight have data covering three decades and four of these fall in the iron and steel group. Clearly, this is a slender sample on which to base any definite conclusions concerning secular changes in the ratio of utilization of the manufacturing plant since 1900.[4] The sample

[3] A ratio in excess of 100 for a month or two may be easily explained, but not an average ratio of 110 for a year—particularly since the ratio is above 100 for ten consecutive months. See p. 586.

[4] This is recognized on page 297, but the note of caution is removed in the final conclusions on page 421. In later volumes, the absence of a secular trend in the degree of utilization of plant capacity in general is treated as an established fact.

TABLE 1

Data Bearing on Brookings Estimates of Capacity of American Manufactures[a]

| | | Percentage of "practical capacity" utilized in manufacturing industries during | | | |
| | | 1925-1929 | | 1929 | |
Industry[b]	Year when continuous data on capacity utilized begin	According to basic chapters or appendix	According to chapter on "Conclusions on Manufacturing"	According to basic chapters or appendix	According to chapter on "Conclusions on Manufacturing"
Meat packing	..	86	86	..	89
Dairy products	..	90–95	95	..	98
Fruit and vegetable canning	..	83–87[c]	80	83–87[c]	87
Beet sugar	1900	70	70	..	67
Flour milling	1900	44–46[d]	50	46–49[d]	53
Cotton manufactures	1900	80	80	83[e]	82
Wool manufactures	1921	..	70	..	69
Silk and rayon manufactures	1925	..	85	..	88
Full-fashioned hosiery	..	..	97	..	92
Men's clothing	..	..	78	..	76
Boot and shoe	..	80	80	..	80
Automobile	1910	83	83	85	85
Automobile tire	1921	85	85	76	76
Paper[f]	1899	92	92	92	92
Printing and publishing	..	90	90	..	92
Pig iron	1900	85	85	93	93
Steel	1900	93	93	..	100
Rolled (steel) products	1898	..	73	..	81
Tin plate	1899	68	68	74	74
Wire	1919	74	74	..	74
Locomotive	..	30	40	..	45
Textile machinery	..	55	55	..	58
Machine tool	1925	71	71	110	110
Lumber	..	..	72	72	72
Window glass	..	62	62	52	52
Plate glass	..	85	85	93	93
Black powder	1917	53	53	51	51
High explosives	1917	80	80	81	81
Chlorine and allied products	..	..	75	90	90

a The dots in the second and fourth columns mean that no figure is specified. In the few cases where no figure was given but one could be derived from data presented, an entry has been made. The dots in the first column mean absence of continuous data. The term "continuous data" is interpreted liberally. For example, there is an entry for rolled steel products, though there are only six unevenly spaced figures in a period of thirty-two years.

b The industrial designations are as given in the chapter on "Conclusions on Manufacturing." The only important conflict between these headings and the basic narrative is in men's clothing. The text discussion covers both men's and women's clothing.

c Derived from the statement that "the canning industry as a whole was equipped at the close of the 1920's to handle some 15 or 20 per cent of additional output" (p. 185).

d Derived from statements that rated capacity utilized was 41.4 per cent in 1925-1929 and 44.1 per cent in 1929, and that rated capacities should be reduced by "some 5 to 10 per cent . . . to keep the estimates in line with our criterion of practical operating conditions" (pp. 187, 193, 572).

e Derived by reducing the computed ratio of utilization of spindle capacity by 2.3 per cent, this being the reduction factor applied to the ratio for 1925-1929 (pp. 200, 204, 575).

f Judging from page 239, it seems that the figures should be 94 instead of 92.

for industrial divisions other than manufactures is better in some cases but worse in others, so that the table is fairly representative of the industrial field as a whole. It thus appears that the conclusion that there has been no secular change in "excess capacity," one of the most important in the book, is inadequately grounded in actual statistics. We shall find that this conclusion plays a major role in the later analysis.

The examples we have presented show that the statistical work of *America's Capacity to Produce* falls short of expectations, and that the conclusions both for all industry and for individual industries must be used with the greatest caution even by those who are ready to accept the conceptual framework of the study. However, it is only fair to bear in mind that the measurement of capacity is an undeveloped statistical field. Bold estimating at critical points is often necessary and this naturally breeds carelessness on matters of detail. Also, divided authorship, while probably unavoidable in a large undertaking carried through in short time, does not promote consistency. It is a pleasure to add that the statistical work of Dr. F. G. Tryon on mineral industries and electric power production is on the whole an excellent piece of craftsmanship.

III. THE ESTIMATES OF LABOR CAPACITY

The estimates of labor capacity are restricted to 1929 and play a subsidiary role in the Brookings calculations. But some account of them is essential, since they constitute a vital check on the estimate of the additional output that could be gotten in that year by putting idle plant capacity to work.

The conclusion is that with some redistribution of the labor force the available labor power would have proved just sufficient to man fully the available plant in 1929. This conclusion is based on the following statistical argument. By increasing the labor force of mines 6 per cent and of manufactures 12 per cent,[5] the output of each could be increased by about 20 per cent. Mines would need to draw upon other industries for 20,000 laborers and manufactures would require 1,000,000 additional laborers. They would come mainly from agriculture and trade. Agriculture could relinquish 500,000 workers and at the same time increase output

[5] We get this figure by (a) increasing the estimated number of laborers attached to manufactures by 1 million, the figure suggested; (b) multiplying (a) by 0.965, as the authors do, to allow for illness and job changing; (c) expressing (b) as a percentage of the average number of workers employed in 1929. See pp. 512-518.

by 10 per cent. The merchandising trades could release 200,000 workers and still accommodate the increased output of industry. Other industrial divisions, after stepping up operations and re-employing labor attached to them, would have a surplus of 305,000 workers, which is only 15,000 short of the remaining requirement of 320,000.

This balance is as fragile as it is neat. The estimates are not built up by individual trades or types of skill, but are made in broad strokes for major industrial divisions. Little or no evidence is cited in support of the estimated number of laborers that the various industries could release. The arithmetic assumes both technical and geographic mobility for over a million men, but no indication is given either in *America's Capacity to Produce*[6] or in later volumes of how this mobility would be effected. Nor is provision made in the labor accounts of the construction industry for the new demand for housing that would accompany a redistribution of the population. In estimating the labor requirements of mining and construction, allowance is made for seasonal variations, but not so in the case of manufactures. No explanation is given of the different rates of increase of labor which it is said would be required to effect an equal increase in the output of mines and manufactures. Further, with due recognition of the relative fixity of the salaried force, the output per worker would be more likely to diminish than to increase as output approached "practical capacity" in these industries, because of the use of poorer grades of equipment and labor, increased militancy and mobility of labor, and relaxed supervision. It seems that agriculture and merchandising are invidiously singled out with respect to ineffectiveness of labor—inadequate application in the former, both that and unfruitful application in the latter. Finally, the change in industrial practices called for in agriculture and merchandising seems to contradict the basic assumption of prevailing techniques. These several factors suffice to indicate that the data on labor power provide no real confirmation of the estimate of the extra output to be gotten by eliminating plant idleness.

IV. THE POTENTIAL INCREASE OF OUTPUT IN 1929

Putting aside the statistical defects of the estimates of plant and labor capacity, we must still face the fundamental question of how the potential increase of output of 19 per cent in 1929 could have

---

[6] At one point (p. 395) it is stated that this problem "must be dealt with in the fourth volume"; but it is not considered in the fourth volume.

been harnessed. There is nothing definite on this point in *America's Capacity to Produce*. We are offered just two clues to the business of reform. The first is in the Foreword, where the promise is more or less clearly given that "only evolutionary modifications and readjustments" (p. 2) will be considered. The second comes in the final chapter and is somewhat bolder. Here the authors rightly note that it is not "realistic" to assume a rise of ratios of utilization in all industries to 100 per cent, since this would lead to "piling up huge stocks of certain types of goods" (p. 417). They claim that this factor calls for a reduction of the preliminary estimate of the potential increase of output, as does the obsoleteness of much unused equipment and also the inevitability of interindustrial dislocations. But the correction required is slight—from 25 to 19 per cent. For, while the "present unutilized capacities are not coordinated in such a way as to make possible anything like full utilization of the existing slack, the most serious limiting factors could promptly be removed" through "the direction of new productive effort towards coordinating the various industries and leveling up those which threatened to become limiting factors" (pp. 417-418).[7]

The notion of centralized control so vigorously suggested by these observations is abandoned in later volumes. The promise of the Foreword, on the other hand, is fulfilled in the final volume. The principal idea there advanced is that "the broad highway along which continued economic progress must be sought is the avenue of price reductions."[8] By passing on to consumers the benefits of technical progress, the buying power of the masses will be stimulated, profits will be maintained if not enhanced, and the motive force to fuller utilization of our productive resources and to accelerated growth of these resources will be supplied. The appropriateness of this proposal to our basic economic difficulty, as the Brookings Institution has diagnosed it, is a question best deferred to a later point. Our present problem is simply whether the proposal supports the estimate of potential increase of output in 1929; that is to say, whether intensified competition could have closed the gap in the late twenties between actual output and "practical capacity" output.

Perhaps the simplest way to approach this question is to set

[7] As already stated, these interesting dicta are at variance with the basic assumptions of the estimate which they purport to correct; also, the correction is entirely arbitrary. See above, p. 300.

[8] H. G. Moulton, *Income and Economic Progress*, p. 126.

down some of the ways in which our economy with intensified competition would *not* have differed from the actual system we had (and have). Two considerations are here of chief importance. In the first place, an appreciable portion of the slack in productive capacity in 1929, as measured in the Brookings study, is properly attributable to the cyclical factor. While a cyclical peak was reached in 1929, business was not uniform through the year. The average level of the Federal Reserve Board's seasonally adjusted index of industrial production in 1929 is only 95 per cent of the level reached in June. Since a boom culminates at different times in different industries, it is conservative to say that cyclical forces alone kept output for the year at least 5 per cent below capacity. Presumably, business cycles would exist under the new scheme no less than under the old.

In the second place, slow adjustment in the supply of productive capacity to the demand for its use would continue, quite apart from the cyclical factor, to make for idleness of industrial plant. Oil refineries would still find at times that cracking equipment is insufficient to permit continuous operation of stills, natural gasoline plants that their supply of natural gas has disappeared, and beet sugar mills that crops are short. New coal mines would still be opened in the face of "excess capacity," electric power plants built in anticipation of growth, cotton mills built in new areas because of the recalcitrance of labor, and flour mills because of changes in freight and custom tariffs. The beehive coke industry would continue on its career of decadence with large excess capacity, and factories everywhere would still find that some obsolete equipment does not repay use.[9] Partial idleness of industrial plant is inevitable in a dynamic economy and is to some extent a condition of industrial growth.

In the short run an increase in the purchasing capacity of the masses would probably increase the rate of use of plant capacity. But there is little reason to believe that a program of price reductions, whatever its effect on the relative income of the masses, would of itself lead over a period of years to a substantially closer adjustment of plant capacity to the purchases by households and industry than what we had during the twenties.

[9] The factor of "frictions" is summarily dismissed in *Income and Economic Progress* (p. 35), but at the cost of misrepresenting the nature of the calculations in *America's Capacity to Produce*. It may also be noted that practically all the illustrations given above are based upon the latter book and that any number of additional instances are there given. These data merited some attention in the final volume.

Long Cycles in Residential Construction

I. THE PROBLEM

When we examine monthly figures we find that construction activity has cyclical fluctuations that correspond fairly closely to the cycles in general business, but when we examine annual figures these fluctuations tend to vanish before the eye, while cycles lasting from fifteen to twenty years obtrude themselves. These longer cycles consist of actual rises and declines, not merely of variations in the rate of growth such as are found in the secular trends of all industries. Long cycles of large amplitude characterize railroad construction as well as building construction, and appear to be a feature of investment in fixed capital wherever economic life is organized on a business basis.

The long cycles in building construction have recently received considerable attention in this country. Numerous historical studies for individual localities have been published. The results are remarkably uniform: they show that in one locality and the next there are long cycles of large amplitude in the construction of buildings, and that similar cycles are found in subdivision activity and real-estate trading—so that the cycles in construction are but one phase of the long cycles that characterize real-estate 'activity.' The most painstaking and scholarly of the local studies is Homer Hoyt's *One Hundred Years of Land Values in Chicago*, recently published by the University of Chicago Press.

While the local cycles diverge considerably, they also show a fair degree of similarity in their timing. Hence, it is to be expected that clearly defined long cycles will be found in national construction. This problem has been investigated by Dr. John R. Riggleman, and in June 1933 he published in the *Journal of the American Statistical Association* a preliminary index of building construction in the United States, based on building-permits data, for the period 1875 to 1932. The index has lately been revised and extended. In its present form it begins in 1830 with three cities, includes twenty cities by 1875, and sixty-five cities by 1900, this number being retained through 1933. Dr. Riggleman's index

Reprinted by permission from *Economic Essays in Honor of Wesley Clair Mitchell* (Columbia University Press, 1935), pp. 63-104.

shows long cycles of large amplitude across a century of American experience. The following quotation from an unpublished manuscript by Dr. Riggleman on "Building Cycles in the United States" indicates their duration and amplitude: "The curve moved up from 49 per cent below normal in 1830 to 81 per cent above normal in 1836, down to 57 below in 1843, up to 74 above in 1853, down to 58 below in 1864, up to 19 above in 1869, down to 45 below in 1878, up to 58 above in 1890, down to 30 below in 1900, up to 33 above in 1909, down to 75 below in 1918, up to 66 above in 1925, and down to 87 below in 1933." Dr. Riggleman has tested his national index by constructing separate indexes for seven geographic regions for the period since 1875. The regional indexes show a fair degree of synchronism.[1]

Dr. Riggleman's index does not segregate residential buildings from other types of buildings. The same is true of most of the long-range studies for localities. But it is to be expected that if there are long cycles in the total construction of buildings there will also be long cycles in the construction of residential buildings, first, because residential construction is a substantial part of the total,[2] and second, because much other building is closely correlated with it. Such figures as we have confirm this expectation. Data for St. Louis since 1880, for New York City since 1902, and for Chicago since 1912 show that the long cycles in the total construction of buildings represent fairly well, except for a dampening of the amplitude, the long cycles in the construction of residential buildings. The short series of broad coverage—the Dodge figures since 1919 and the Bureau of Labor Statistics figures since 1921—reveal the same tendency.

The indications are, then, that there are long cycles in residential construction, that these cycles attain enormous amplitudes, and that they synchronize roughly in the various regions of the country. We attempt in this paper to explore the rational basis of the long cycles in residential construction. Other types of building and alterations are left out of account. But the major forces that impinge on residential construction are not peculiar to it

[1] The writer is sincerely indebted to Dr. Riggleman for permission to quote from his manuscript.

[2] The Bureau of Labor Statistics figures on estimated expenditures for new buildings, covering from 257 to 364 cities, indicate that residential construction accounted for 61 per cent of the total during 1921-1933. The F. W. Dodge Corporation figures on contracts awarded, covering from twenty-seven to thirty-seven states, indicate that residential construction during 1919-1933 accounted for 55 per cent of the floor space and for 49 per cent of the dollar value represented by all contracts exclusive of public works and utilities.

alone. Much of our analysis, though with qualifications that we do not make, applies also to other types of construction.

II. The Governing Hypothesis and Method of Approach

The long cycles in residential construction are a result of certain characteristics of dwellings and of men. Normally, our dwellings have a long life; they provide accommodations for their occupants that admit of some shrinkage; they are not subject to transportation; and they are standardized only to a moderate extent. Normally, the inhabitants of this country move more freely from one district of a town to another than from one town to another; they move more freely from dwellings of one class to dwellings of the same general class than to dwellings of another class; they grow in numbers at a rate that varies considerably from year to year whether we consider a hamlet or the country as a whole; and the wisest among them are unable accurately to forecast the future state of the residential market. These characteristics of dwellings and of men are the 'basic' factors in the long cycles of residential construction. We can say more simply that they consist of variability in the rate of population increase, durability of dwellings, immobility of dwellings and men, inconstancy of the housing standard, and the uncertainty of men.

These basic factors provide a peculiarly apt setting, even when not worked upon by pecuniary institutions, for the formation of long cycles in residential construction. Their cyclical power will be clearly exposed if we analyze an imaginary economy that aims to provide residential facilities on some standard of need. We shall assume, therefore, that the Planning Council of a collectivist state sets a standard of one residential unit per person, that the Council ordinarily fixes building programs in the light of this standard, and that the construction scheduled for a year is fully executed in that year. It is perhaps necessary to stress that we shall use collectivism merely as a vehicle for expressing the basic factors in the residential cycles of our business economy, which is the sole object of our inquiry and to which we return explicitly in the last section of the paper.

Let us first dispose of some matters of definition. We shall understand by a residential district the area over which the physical distribution of dwellings exercises an important influence on the shifts of persons from one residence to another. If a surplus of residential units in A affects the movements of the population of

B and a surplus in B affects the population of A, but neither the one nor the other exercises any appreciable influence on the population of C, then A and B belong to one residential district and C belongs to another. We shall assume that the country consists of a large number of residential districts whose boundaries remain unchanged over the period which concerns us. We do not exclude migration across the boundary lines; all that we assume is that such migration is not influenced perceptibly by housing conditions.

We shall consider the population of a residential district to be composed of several communities, each community to consist of members of a residential class who normally dwell in a distinct type of residential unit. The Council might classify persons for residential purposes according to their industrial grade, marital status, age, or all these and others; so that persons may or may not be permanently attached to the same residential class. But whatever the principle of classification, the members of a residential class will shift freely, as occasion requires, among the residential units corresponding to their class, but reluctantly—if at all—among other residential units. In view of our definitions of a residential district and a community, any surplus of residential units in one community will be of no more use to any other community in the same district than to any of the communities in any other district. The community, therefore, will be the fundamental unit for the accounts of construction.

Residential units we shall consider as durable over time and immobile over space. The residential units intended for the various communities will differ in design, but the units intended for a particular residential class will always be of the same construction. We shall assume that residential units of various types call for an equal expenditure of productive effort. It will therefore be permissible to add the various types of residential units to obtain totals of construction. However, comparisons of the demand for the use of residential units with the supply will still be ambiguous if the totals embrace more than a single community.

The Council cannot hope that the number of residential units in each community will invariably equal the size of its population, but under normal conditions it will use one means or another of approximating this end. The Council might set annual quotas for communities on the basis of estimates of population change and of replacement needs, taking due account of any surplus or shortage that is known to exist. Or else the Council might follow

313

the convenient mechanical rule of basing the building quota for a year on the change in population during the preceding year, plus the number of residential units retired by nature or the state during the preceding year. The first method proceeds partly on known demand and partly on estimated demand. The second method proceeds entirely on an artificial conception of known demand. Let us suppose that the Council uses this method.

III. CONSTRUCTION IN A SINGLE COMMUNITY UNDER COLLECTIVISM

We begin with a single community. If the community is new, but established upon a sound basis, it will tend to grow in numbers year in and year out. There will be no need to replace residential units except when fire or tornado cause destruction. We assume that we have a new community which escapes destructive visitations by nature. The volume of construction will then vary to the extent that increases in population vary. Suppose that the community numbers successively, as of the first of the year, 10,000, 10,140, 10,230, 10,290, and 10,400 persons. The annual increases are, then, 140, 90, 60, and 110. The number of residential units constructed annually will correspond exactly to these increases of population, but it will lag by one year. While the percentage changes in the population are small and positive (+1.4, +0.9, +0.6, and+1.1), the percentage changes in the increases of the population and in the volume of building are large and oscillatory (-36, -33, and +83). To be sure, the violent fluctuations in building reproduce the increases of what are merely hypothetical figures of population. But the fluctuations in the increases of our imaginary community are as nothing compared to what will frequently happen in small areas.[3] Should the increases in population have a rising tendency for a half dozen years or so, and then a declining tendency, the construction industry would trace out long cycles; and, since the relative fluctuations of the increases in population tend to be large, the cycles in construction would also tend to show large amplitudes.

While the variability of population increases will introduce a violent rhythm in building activity, it will have no such effect on

[3] It may be of interest to note that the relative fluctuations of the increases in the entire population of the United States have at times been greater; though this is of dubious relevance in the present connection, since pecuniary forces have played an important role in these fluctuations.

the output of a relatively perishable commodity such as shoes.[4] Suppose that the Council sets a standard of one pair of shoes per person per year and that the production quota for a year is set at the level of the population at the beginning of the year. The annual output of shoes intended for the community will then rise successively by 1.4, 0.9, 0.6, and 1.1 per cent. There will be no cyclical fluctuations in production; there will be fluctuations only in the rate of increase in production. Our buildings and shoes can therefore be viewed as rough instances of a general principle: If real income is to bear a fixed ratio to population, the output of a commodity admitting of only a single use will vary with the size of population, while the output of a commodity admitting of perpetual use will vary with the increases in population. The fluctuations of an empirical population series are virtually always much smaller than the fluctuations of the increases in the series. Hence the fluctuations in the production of residential units will be much greater than in shoes. The reader may, if he so chooses, consider the fluctuations in shoes as the standard of comparison when reference is made in this paper to 'large' fluctuations in construction. In this sense the fluctuations in construction will be 'large' even if the fluctuations of the increases in population are regarded as 'small.'

Our preceding example assumes an uninterrupted rise in population. Let us next consider a decline in population. The community has, let us say, entered the phase when decreases in population take place occasionally, but it has not yet reached the age when residential units must be retired because of physical depreciation. Continuing with the last figure in the example, the population numbers may run 10,400, 10,360, 10,350, 10,350, 10,360, 10,400, 10,450. The volume of construction required on account of population change will then be −40, −10, 0, +10, +40, +50. Since the volume of construction cannot drop below zero, it will remain at zero until the earlier peak in total population has been passed. This means that when an upward trend in population is intermittently marked by declines, the amplitude of construction will be smaller both absolutely and relatively than that of changes in population[5]; that if the level and amplitude of changes in population are on the average the same in the present

[4] Cf. J. M. Clark, *Strategic Factors in Business Cycles* (National Bureau of Economic Research, 1934), pp. 27-44.

[5] In this paper we consider the standard deviation (σ) as the measure of absolute amplitude and the ratio of the standard deviation to the mean as the measure of relative amplitude.

'stage' as in the 'stage' of steady growth, the amplitude of construction in this 'stage' will be smaller both absolutely and relatively than in the preceding 'stage'; that the volume of construction may lag by more than one year after changes in population; that a minor cycle following upon a negative population change may not appear at all in the construction curve; and, finally, that whenever the population remains below a peak figure for some years and then rises above that figure a temporal skeleton of a long cycle in construction may be formed.

Let us now take account of replacements. They will become an appreciable factor in construction when the age of the community has outgrown the useful life of residential units. But first we must indicate more exactly the procedure of the Council in arriving at building quotas. The quota for each year measures the actual construction during the year. The quota is set at the beginning of the year according to the difference which then exists between the size of population and the number of residential units available for residential use. If the former is larger than the latter— that is, if the difference is positive—the quota for the coming year will equal the size of the difference. If the difference is negative or zero, the quota will be zero. Thus the difference always measures the 'required construction' in a year, but it is a theoretical quantity when negative. Were the difference invariably positive the Council could reach the same quota by taking the algebraic sum of the following preceding-year quantities: change in population, number of residential units destroyed by natural elements, and number retired from use as living quarters by state order. The sum of the last two items gives the 'required replacements.' The sum of all three items gives what may be called the 'presumptive construction.' If the required construction is negative or zero the actual construction will be zero; if the presumptive construction is negative or zero the actual construction will also be zero; if the presumptive construction is positive the actual construction may still be zero, for the required construction may be negative or zero. The actual construction would be the same as the presumptive construction only if the negative construction required in any year could actually be realized in that year. We shall therefore need to pay as much attention to presumptive construction as to actual construction when we come to consider the influence of immobility on the amplitude of construction cycles.

We can gain some idea of the role of replacements in total construction by making simple assumptions. Suppose that residential units are retired by order of the Council when they reach a fixed age but are not retired in any other way. Let R stand for the ratio of replacements to total construction in a year, the subscript n for the year, k for the age at retirement, and a for the largest whole number obtained by dividing k into $(n-1)$. Then, if population increases annually by a constant amount,

$$R_n = \frac{a}{a+1}$$

Assume that $k = 50$; R will then be zero from the first through the fiftieth year of the community, 0.5 from the fifty-first through the one hundredth year, 0.67 from the one hundred-first through the one hundred-fiftieth year, and so on. But if the population increases annually by a constant percentage,[6]

$$R_n = \frac{r^{ak}-1}{r^{ak+k}-1}$$

where r is the ratio of the population of any year to that of the preceding year, and where n is not equal to $(ak+1)$. The replacement ratio will now approach $1/r^k$ as a limit, instead of 1. Suppose that $r=1.02$ and $k=50$; then, $R_{52}=0.27$, $R_{102}=0.34$, $R_{152}=0.36$, and $R_{n\to\infty}=0.37+$. In general, R increases as a increases, decreases as r increases, and decreases as k increases.

The fluctuations in the number of residential units destroyed by the elements are likely to be uncorrelated with the fluctuations of population changes. The same remark applies to voluntary retirements—at least if we assume that the retirements are based on a standard of fitness, that there is no periodic cycle in changes of population, and that replacements on account of natural destruction are not a negligible portion of total replacements. Hence, if the required construction is at no time negative the absolute amplitude of construction will on the average tend to be larger than that of population changes.[7] This means, of course, that if population conditions are similar, the construction of a community advanced in age will tend to be of larger amplitude than the construction of a community requiring no replacements. However, population decreases may counteract this tendency. If the

[6] The writer is indebted to Mr. Arthur Stein and to Mr. Milton Friedman for this expression.

[7] See G. U. Yule, *An Introduction to the Theory of Statistics* (8th edn., Charles Griffin and Company, 1927), Chap. XI, paragraph 2.

decline in population is numerically larger than the volume of required replacements, construction will drop to zero and remain at zero until after equality between the number of residential units in existence and the number of persons has been restored by the movement of either or both variables. Under such conditions the amplitude of construction may be smaller than that of changes in population. Irrespective of the sign of population changes, the timing of building fluctuations in the replacement stage will no longer be regularly related to the timing of population changes; there will now be leads and lags of varying duration and occasional coincidences.

Population changes and required replacements will form all sorts of combinations. This is of great importance, for out of these combinations long cycles may be formed in construction even when there are no such cycles in population changes. While required replacements and population changes will tend to be uncorrelated over long periods, they will nevertheless be correlated over short periods—now positively, then inversely. Although the fluctuations of required replacements will ordinarily be smaller than those of population changes, for a time they may be larger. The peaks or troughs of the two variables may at some turns be approximately coincident. At others the peak of one variable may be coincident with the trough of the other. In the neighborhood of such turning points both variables may undergo especially violent movements, those in required replacements perhaps being the more violent. Chance alternations in the character of the short-time correlation between the two variables are thus likely to promote to some extent the formation of long cycles in construction. This tendency will gain in strength if such declines as occur in population occasionally exceed the volume of required replacements, so that the presumptive construction is negative. The actual construction curve will now be apt to skip completely some minor cycles in the curve of presumptive construction. And if this curve remains below the zero line for several years the curve of actual construction will form a zero trough over a longer period; a temporal base for a long cycle will thus be fashioned, which the construction contributed by other communities may transform into an actual long cycle for the residential district.

IV. NATIONAL CONSTRUCTION UNDER COLLECTIVISM

Let us now abandon the community for a larger area. If the population of each of the communities that compose a residential district increases every year and replacements are not needed, the construction of the district will reproduce with a one-year lag the annual fluctuations of the increases in the population of the district. Under similar conditions the residential construction of the country will reproduce with a one-year lag the increases in the national population. The relative fluctuations of increases in population will be smaller in the country taken as a whole than in the generality of communities. Hence the relative fluctuations of construction will be smaller; but they are still apt to be large, since the fluctuations of the increases in national population are likely to be large. The volume of national construction will trace out long cycles only if there are such cycles in the increases of national population; but long cycles may characterize the increases of national population even if there are no such cycles in the generality of residential districts or communities. Under the simple assumptions we have made, the fluctuations in the construction of a residential district or of the country as a whole, no less than of a single community, reflect the force of only two factors: variability of population increases and durability of residential units.

But variability of population increases would have little cyclical power if the longevity of buildings were no greater than of shoes. Suppose that there are long waves in the increases of national population. They will not suffice to generate long cycles in the production of shoes. With a footwear standard of one pair of shoes per person per year and quotas based on the population at the beginning of the year, the output of shoes will simply reproduce the curve of national population. There will be no cycles of any sort in this curve. Hence there will be no cycles of any sort in the output of shoes, though there will be long cycles in the rate of increase in output. Only the immobility of shoes in use could disturb the rigid relation between their production and total population; but for this to happen a net decline would have to take place in the national population of some 'footwear class.' Given a constant standard of housing and footwear, there will need to be long cycles in the population of the country if there are to be long cycles in the production of a perishable good such as shoes, while long cycles in the increases of the population will suffice to generate long cycles in the production of a lasting good such as dwellings.

Residential units, however, do not have everlasting life and in growing communities will sooner or later need to be replaced. If the presumptive construction is at no time negative in any of the communities—that is, if there are no declines in population, or if declines in population are smaller than required replacements—the actual volume of national construction, no less than that of a single community, will be the same as the presumptive construction. We have previously argued that the fluctuations of required replacements will tend to be uncorrelated with the fluctuations of population changes. Under present assumptions, therefore, the absolute amplitude of construction, whatever the area, will tend to be larger than the amplitude of changes in population. The timing relationship between construction and changes in population will tend to be irregular. And, just as the combination of required replacements and population changes may produce long cycles in the construction of a community even when there are no such cycles in its population changes, so the combination of required replacements and population changes may produce long cycles in the total construction of the country even when there are no long cycles in changes of population in either the component areas or the country as a whole.

Let us next consider the possibility that the presumptive construction is at times negative in some of the communities. This will be the case if there are occasional declines in population but no replacements, or if in certain communities at certain dates the volume of required replacements is smaller than the decline of population. If residential units or men were perfectly mobile, the theoretical requirement of negative construction could be satisfied by diverting the surplus of some communities to others. Hence the actual construction of the country would exactly reproduce the presumptive construction—that is, the algebraic sum of the presumptive construction in the individual communities. The theoretical requirement of negative construction in some of the communities would influence neither the correspondence of actual construction to presumptive construction nor the relation of construction to changes in national population; both would be the same as in the case when presumptive construction is invariably positive. Only if the presumptive construction for the country occasionally fell below zero would the curve of actual construction differ from the curve of presumptive construction; and even this could not happen if the mobility of residential units extended to nonresidential uses.

Under conditions of immobility, however, the theoretical requirement of negative construction in any year can be satisfied only through failure to build in later years; and if the negative construction required is much larger than the average annual volume of construction, a surplus of residential units may continue for some years. Immobility is therefore likely to exert an influence on the character of the cycles in national construction whenever the presumptive construction is negative in any of the communities. Suppose that the population throughout the country has been stationary for some time, that there are as many residential units in each of the various communities as there are persons, and that replacements are unnecessary. Suddenly, in district 1 the population increases by 100 in community A and decreases by 100 in B, and in district 2 the population decreases by 100 in A and increases by 100 in B. There are three possible ways of restoring equilibrium without new construction. First, the surplus population of A in district 1 could move to residences of type A in district 2, and the surplus population of B in district 2 to residences of type B in district 1. Second, residential units of type A could be moved to district 1 and of type B to district 2. Third, in district 1 the surplus population of A could move to quarters of type B and in district 2 the surplus population of B to quarters of type A. But each of these possibilities is closed by the assumption of immobility contained in our original definitions of a residential district, a residential unit, and a community. Although the total population has remained unchanged in districts 1 and 2 and in the country as a whole, 100 residential units will have to be built in each of these districts.

In this example immobility has led to a fluctuation in construction when there was none in the changes of total population. Under conditions of mobility the movements of the two variables would be inexorably linked. It is clear, then, that immobility may serve to confuse the relation between national construction and changes of national population. However, we must not infer from the example that immobility will intensify the fluctuations of national construction whenever the presumptive construction is negative in any of the communities. Suppose, for instance, that there are two distinct groups of communities in the country and that replacements are nowhere required. Group I consists of communities that gain in numbers each year; the volume of construction of this group will therefore vary as the increases of its population vary. Group II consists of communities that experience periodic fluctuations in population but along horizontal or declining trends; the construction of this group will therefore be zero. The curve of national construction will reproduce with a one-year lag the curve of population changes in Group I. But the amplitude of population changes in Group I may be smaller or larger than the amplitude of population changes in the entire country, depending—roughly speaking—on whether the population-change curves of Groups I and II are positively or inversely correlated. Hence, immobility may dampen the fluctuations of national construction, magnify them, or leave them uninfluenced.

We may now take replacements into account and formulate more exactly the influence of immobility. Each year we can distribute the presumptive construction for the country between two groups. Let us define Group I as a quantity which equals each year the volume of national construction. By subtracting this quantity from the presumptive construction for the country we shall obtain Group II. The communities having a positive requirement for construction contribute to Group I. The communities having a negative or zero required construction contribute to Group II, as do those having a positive requirement for construction lower than the presumptive construction. There is some overlap between the communities in the two groups, but it will be negligible in a growing country. The composition of both groups will change from year to year.

Inasmuch as national construction reproduces the curve of Group I rather than the curve of presumptive construction for the entire country, immobility may result in an amplitude of construction that is larger or smaller than what would occur under conditions of mobility. The crucial factor is the character of the correlation between Groups I and II.[8] Let r represent the coefficient of correlation between Groups I and II, σ_I the amplitude of Group I, σ_{II} the amplitude of Group II, and σ_N the amplitude of the presumptive construction for the country.[9] Then, if $r=+1$,

$$\sigma_N = \sigma_I + \sigma_{II}$$

and if $r=0$,

$$\sigma^2_N = \sigma^2_I + \sigma^2_{II}$$

In either case $\sigma_I < \sigma_N$; that is to say, immobility will dampen the

[8] In this argument we assume implicitly that changes in the presumptive construction of the country are independent of immobility. We do not assume, however, that the presumptive construction of Groups I and II is independent of immobility. The reasonableness of the first assumption can hardly be questioned—particularly if it is observed that required replacements are determined by physical criteria, so that the assumption is simply that changes in national population are independent of immobility.

[9] Supra, notes 5 and 7.

amplitude of construction whether Groups I and II are uncorrelated or positively correlated. But if the two groups are inversely correlated immobility may intensify the amplitude of construction. Thus if $r = -1$, the amplitude will be intensified provided $\sigma_{II} < 2\sigma_{I}$. If $r = -0.8$, the amplitude will be intensified provided $\sigma_{II} < 1.6\sigma_{I}$. In general, $\sigma_{I} > \sigma_{N}$ if $\sigma_{II} < |2r\sigma_{I}|$. But the two groups may have both major and minor cycles, the major cycles being correlated in one manner and the minor cycles in another. If the major cycles are correlated positively and the minor ones inversely, immobility will dampen the major cycles in construction and may magnify the minor cycles; while if the major cycles are correlated inversely and the minor cycles positively, it may magnify the major cycles and will dampen the minor ones. The influence of immobility on the amplitude of national construction cannot therefore be known unless the data of Groups I and II are known.

The most we can do is to rely on reasoned expectations. We may anticipate that the communities of a growing country will tend to be subject to common influences on the side of natural increase and to random influences on the side of required replacements. But we may also expect that the rate of natural increase of some communities will depart from the national pattern; that net immigration will impinge chiefly on growing areas; and that internal migration will tend to produce an inverse relation between the population changes of the gaining and losing communities. Bearing in mind the composition of Groups I and II, it therefore seems probable that if the country experiences extensive internal migration the two groups will be inversely correlated. Immigration will tend to make the amplitude of Group I larger than that of Group II. Even if the amplitude of Group II were the same as that of Group I, a negative coefficient of correlation just greater than 0.5 would suffice to indicate that immobility had intensified the amplitude of national construction. All in all, therefore, it seems more reasonable to anticipate that immobility will magnify the building fluctuations of a progressive country than that it will dampen them.

We have proceeded on the assumption that the Council invariably adheres to the theoretical housing standard of one residential unit per person. Let us now drop this assumption. In practice the Council may occasionally find it desirable to suspend the standard. It will then make use of an instrument that has even greater cyclical power than fluctuations in the rate of population change. Suppose that there are 1,000 persons and 990 residential units in each community. To maintain the theoretical standard ten residential units will need to be built in each community. But if the standard is lowered by 0.5 per cent, only five units will be required; if it is lowered by 1 per cent, no construction at all will be required; if it is lowered by 5 per cent, a negative volume of forty units will be required. Thus, if the housing standard is reduced by a small percentage, the volume of building will be reduced by a much larger percentage from the level that would have been realized under a constant housing standard; the decline in building may readily reach 100 per cent and even then leave a surplus so large that all construction will need to cease for several years. In our example a 1 per cent drop in the housing standard has as much cyclical effect as would a 100 per cent drop in the sum of population change and required replacements. In other cases the disparity between the cyclical effects of the two factors may be larger or smaller; but it is nevertheless to be expected that occasional variations in the housing standard will tend to increase enormously the cyclical fluctuations in construction—even if the variations in the standard are correlated inversely with fluctuations in population changes. The great cyclical power of a fluctuating housing standard might, of course, be harnessed by the Council to counteract the impulses making for instability in construction that derive from a fluctuating rate of population change and of required replacements; but we must repeat that we "use collectivism merely as a vehicle for expressing the basic factors in the residential cycles of our business economy."

If the housing standard is at times reduced the occasions when negative construction is theoretically required will be multiplied. The cyclical role of immobility will therefore be larger; but it is difficult to say whether the role will be to dampen or to magnify the amplitude of construction. Much will depend on the frequency of the changes, their magnitude, and the degree of their uniformity in the various communities. We previously reached the conclusion that immobility is likely to magnify the building fluctuations of a growing country operating on a constant housing standard. This conclusion will still hold if the changes in housing conditions are infrequent but uniform over the country, while their influence on the volume of building is smaller than that of population changes. It will also hold under a variety of other conditions; but there can be little advantage from endowing our imaginary economy with special characteristics beyond the point that we have already gone. We need merely to recall that once the data of Groups I and II are known, the influence of immobility can be deduced from them.

Just as the cyclical power of fluctuations in the rate of population change derives from the durability of residential units, so does the cyclical power of inconstancy in the housing standard derive from the same source. A given reduction in the footwear standard, as previously defined, will produce merely a proportionate reduction in the output of shoes from the level that would have been attained under an unchanged standard. Thus, if the population of each community is 1,000 and the footwear standard is maintained the output of shoes will be 1,000 pairs for each community; otherwise it will be 995, 990, or 950, according as the standard is lowered by 0.5, 1, or 5 per cent. We may therefore say that durability is a necessary condition of the full release of the cyclical power of fluctuations in the housing standard; though durability can release only what is at its disposal—so that the cyclical power of durability will be zero if both the housing standard and population changes are constant. It is also true that the cyclical power of immobility derives from the durability of residential units. But we can no more say that durability—rather than inconstancy of the housing standard, or a fluctuating rate of population change, or immobility—is *the* basic factor in the fluctuations of residential construction, than we can say that "it is the upper" rather than "the under blade of a pair of scissors that cuts a piece of paper:"[10] they are all basic.

The large cyclical power of the basic factors in residential construction creates a presumption that long cycles will be produced through their joint action. The composition of the national construction curve changes. The incomers emerge from troughs of zero construction, the outgoers enter zero troughs. Any concentration of incomers or outgoers at certain dates will not fail to impress itself on the curve of construction. Temporary suspensions of the theoretical housing standard will also tend to produce sharp movements in the construction curve. If the housing standard is constant that curve, speaking roughly, is a composite of population changes and required replacements; but these variables may move in similar or in opposite directions. Over some years required replacements and population changes may tend upward quite generally, the movements of required replacements may be more violent than those of population changes, the housing stand-

[10] Alfred Marshall, *Principles of Economics* (8th edn., Macmillan, 1925), p. 348.

ard may move towards parity, and the incomers from zero troughs may greatly outnumber the outgoers. In other years other combinations will emerge. The combination of factors determining the volume of national construction will change over time; and the changing combination of factors of large cyclical power may easily produce long cycles in residential construction—all the more readily, of course, if there be long cycles in the increases of national population. In the absence of long cycles in population changes in the country as a whole, or in the areas gaining through internal migration, the minor cycles in construction may at times obscure the major cycles.

V. Intensifying Power of Uncertainty under Collectivism

Our analysis must now be extended to include the factor of uncertainty. We have abstracted from this factor by assuming that the Council sets building quotas according to known demand. But under this scheme there will rarely be a nice adjustment of the supply of residential units to the demand implied by the ruling housing standard. With the standard constant there will be a permanent undersupply of residential units in case the population increases steadily, and shortages will dominate over surpluses in case the population fluctuates but along a rising trend. Let us suppose that the Council normally seeks to attain a closer approximation to the theoretical standard of one residential unit per person. It will then be necessary to set the building quota for a year by estimating the new demand that will arise during the year and adjusting this estimate for any surplus or shortage that is known to exist. By assuming that the Council sets building quotas on the basis of only partial knowledge of demand, we shall take account of the factor of uncertainty and therefore approach more closely the conditions underlying the residential cycles of our business economy.

At the outset let us revert to a single community which gains in population each year and escapes the need for replacements. In this case the Council will need to estimate only the increases in population. Let P stand for the actual increase in population during a year, K for the estimated increase during the year, B for both the building quota and the number of residential units built during the year, S for the surplus (or shortage) of residential units at the beginning of the year, M for the size of population at the beginning of the year, H for the number of units available for residential use at the beginning of the year; and let subscripts refer to successive years. Then we have

$$B_n = K_n - S_n = K_n - H_n + M_n$$

when this quantity is positive; otherwise $B_n = 0$. If the negative construction required in any year could be realized in that year, the following relations would hold:

$$B_n = K_n - S_n = K_n - H_n + M_n = K_n - K_{n-1} + P_{n-1}$$

Actually, however, B_n may be zero when $(K_n - K_{n-1} + P_{n-1})$ is positive, because $(K_n - H_n + M_n)$ may be negative or zero. In conformity to earlier usage, $(K_n - H_n + M_n)$ measures the 'required construction' and $(K_n - K_{n-1} + P_{n-1})$ the 'presumptive construction.' Both are estimated quantities; $(K_n - P_n)$ measures the error of each. Since the increases of population will tend to fluctuate considerably, the estimates will be in error nearly always to some extent and at times to a great extent. These errors may serve to magnify the fluctuations in building; to make them larger than they would be if they were governed by population increases alone. We shall simplify the analysis by restricting it at first to the case where $(K_n - S_n)$ is invariably positive.

The Council will be faced with the task of forecasting population. Suppose that a constant is chosen in some fashion as the estimate of population increase. Assuming equilibrium between population and residences at the start, we have $B_1 = K_1$. Subsequently, however, we have $B_n = P_{n-1}$, since $K_n - K_{n-1} = 0$. Hence, no matter how large the errors of estimate may be, the building curve will be the same as if each year's output had been mechanically set at the level of increase in population during the preceding year. Unfortunately, the assumption of a constant estimate is likely to be inconsistent with the controlling assumption that the Council will attempt to approximate as closely as possible the theoretical housing standard. If an appreciable shortage or surplus continues for several years, the estimated constant will be abandoned. Given the purpose of the Council, the variable nature of population increase will almost certainly lead to inconstancy in the estimates of increase. In any case we shall assume that the estimates are of this character.

Suppose, next, that the Council resorts to 'rational' forecasts, making the best use it can of the knowledge at hand. In that case $(B_n - P_n)$ is likely to be uncorrelated with P_n. Hence the amplitude of B will tend to be larger than that of P; that is to say, the fluctuations of construction will tend to be magnified through errors of estimate.[11] Or else the Council may resort to 'mechanical' forecasts, using some simple formula that appears logical. It might, for example, take as an estimate of population increase in a given year, the actual increase during the preceding year; in this case,

$$B_n = 2P_{n-1} - P_{n-2}$$

Or it might estimate the population increase in a given year at the average increase during the two preceding years; in this case,

$$B_n = \tfrac{1}{2}(3P_{n-1} - P_{n-3})$$

In general, if the estimate is equal to the arithmetic mean of the actual increases during s preceding years,

$$B_n = 1/s[(s+1)P_{n-1} - P_{n-1-s}]$$

Clearly, any two-year combination of a large and small increase in population will produce an accentuated fluctuation in the curve of building; but the intensification will be largest when $s = 1$. As s increases in size the tendency will be for the fluctuations in building to approach the fluctuations in increases of population;[12] the smaller, therefore, will be the intensification of amplitude produced by errors of estimate.

Let us assume, for illustrative purposes, that the increase in population for a given year is estimated at the level of the preceding year; that is to say, that $s = 1$. The increases in population trace out fluctuations which, let us say, are irregular but clearly defined. The year following upon a cyclical peak in population increases will then witness a volume of building equal to twice the increase in population during the peak year minus the increase in population during the year preceding the peak. Hence, the peak in building will be sharper than the peak in population increases and is likely to follow it by one year. Similarly, the trough in building will be lower than the trough in population increases and is likely to lag by one year. During a cyclical rise in population increases the estimates are continually too low, which results in a shortage of residential units. To be sure, the shortage at the beginning of one year is corrected in that year, but underestimates of growth in population continue as long as the cyclical rise continues; a short-

11 Yule, op.cit., Chap. XI, paragraph 3.
12 If there is a strictly periodic cycle in the increases of population, the amplitudes of P and B will be the same whenever s is a multiple of the period of the cycle.

age therefore continues. Once a peak in population increases has been reached, the volume of construction in the following year not only corrects the shortage but also creates a surplus. The corrective movement in construction during the next year is therefore particularly pronounced, the recession being sharper than could be expected merely from a knowledge of the amplitude of population change. Similarly, there is a surplus of residential units during a cyclical decline in population increases; this becomes converted into a shortage after the trough in population has been passed; and the revivals in construction are peculiarly vigorous.

The intensification of cyclical fluctuations in construction will be more pronounced if we assume a somewhat different method of forecasting. Let us suppose that the estimate of population increase for a given year is fixed at the level of the actual population increase during the preceding year plus the excess of the actual increase during the preceding year over the increase during the next preceding year; that is,

$$K_n = 2\,P_{n-1} - P_{n-2}$$

The estimates of population increase will now bear exactly the same relation to the actual increases as the volume of building bears to the actual increases when the estimate for each year is fixed at the level of the actual increase during the preceding year. The estimates, therefore, now undergo fluctuations larger than those of the actual increases of population. They will tend to err on the side of 'optimism' or 'pessimism' according as the second differences of the curve of population increases happen to be negative or positive. The magnified fluctuations of the estimates will lead to still more magnified fluctuations in construction, so that the cycles in construction will be much more violent than in increases of population. How large the opportunities for magnification become, particularly just after the cyclical turning points in population increases are passed, is apparent from the construction formula which expresses the present method of making estimates:

$$B_n = 3\,P_{n-1} - 3\,P_{n-2} + P_{n-3}$$

The preceding description of the intensifying mechanism that may be contained in the technique of estimation is limited by the condition that the fluctuations in population increases are never so large as to make S_n exceed K_n. When this occurs a negative volume of construction is theoretically required. Since construction can drop to zero but not lower, it will be impossible to correct the surplus in one year and construction activity may therefore need to be suspended for some time. If the fluctuations in population increases are so large that $(K_n - S_n)$ is frequently negative, there may be little similarity between the cycles in construction and the cycles in population increases. Out of such conditions, however, temporal skeletons of long cycles in construction may be produced.

Let us illustrate by a numerical example the principle of magnification through errors of estimate, without reference to any specific method of estimation. We start with 10,000 persons and 10,000 residential units; that is, with equilibrium between the demand for the use of residential units and their supply. On the basis of recent experience and current prospects the Council anticipates an increase in population of 100; it therefore orders that 100 residential units be built during the year. If the increase in population is 10 instead of 100, there will be a surplus of 90 units. Let us suppose that the Council considers this year abnormal and again plans for an anticipated increase in population of 100. Since there is a surplus of 90 residential units, only 10 will be ordered built. But the population may again increase by only 10, and the surplus will therefore remain 90. It is likely that the Council will now lower drastically its estimate of population increase in the coming year. Suppose that the estimate is 10; in this case the surplus of residential units will be nine times as large as the number required by anticipated growth during the year. All construction will therefore cease; and, if the annual increases in population vary subsequently between 5 and 15, ten years may elapse before construction is again undertaken.

In this example errors of estimate reinforce variability of population increase, the original impulse making for fluctuations in construction. The amplitude of fluctuations is increased and a temporal framework for a long cycle is created. Quasi-cyclical forces are set in motion, in the sense that a given error leads to a corrective adjustment; but these forces have limited scope—the process of adjustment does not of itself breed fresh errors. The volume of building no longer lags passively after population increases, but anticipates them; it may therefore trace out fluctuations even when there are none in population increases. Thus, we could recast the preceding example by assuming that population actually grows at a stable rate, and that errors of estimate originating in inaccurate statistics lead to excessive construction, the errors being later detected through the improved data that accompany the introduction of building quotas.

But the most striking and significant feature of the example is that the magnified fluctuations in construction result from small errors in the forecasts of total population; or, what is the same thing for our purpose, from small errors in the forecasts of total demand for the use of residential units. The estimate of population for the end of the first year is 10,100, the second year 10,110, the third year 10,030. The actual population at the end of the first year is 10,010, the second 10,020, and the third anywhere from 10,025 to 10,035. Hence, there is an overestimate of only 0.9 per cent in the first and second years, and a maximum overestimate or underestimate of 0.05 per cent in the third year. But these small errors in the estimates of total demand mean enormous errors in the estimates of increase in demand: in each of the first two years the increase is overestimated by 900 per cent, and in the third year there is a maximum overestimate of 100 per cent or underestimate of 33 per cent. Under our assumptions the volume of construction in a year would equal the actual increase in demand if there were no errors in the estimates of demand. However, since small errors in estimates of demand mean large errors in estimates of increase in demand, they may produce fluctuations in construction that are vastly larger than the fluctuations in the increases of demand. Even a small overestimate of demand may result, as in the example, in a volume of construction that far exceeds the actual increase in demand; so that many years of inactivity in the construction industry will need to elapse before the error can be corrected.

This will be the case only when the commodity produced is highly durable. Let us suppose again that the theoretical footwear standard is one pair of shoes per person per year. Provision will now be made for the year-end population, so that estimates of this quantity will be identical with estimates of the total demand for shoes. The errors of the estimates of population assumed in the above example will lead also to errors in the production of shoes. But these errors are negligible in size; and, since the unadjusted quotas for the production of shoes vary as the estimates of population, not as the estimates of the increases in population, the errors in the actual production of shoes will also be negligible in size. Hence they will be subject to quick correction and their power to produce fluctuations will be insignificant. Thus the output of shoes in the first year will be 10,100, which is only 0.9 per cent in excess of what is actually required in that year; assuming, of course, that the population is homogeneous from the standpoint of footwear as well as residences. But the output of residential units will leave a surplus equal to 900 per cent of the actual need for new residential units in the year. In the second year the output of shoes will be 10,020, a decline of 0.8 per cent from the preceding year; and the surplus at the end of the year will be 0.9 per cent in excess of true demand. The output of residential units will decline by as much as 90 per cent; but the surplus will nevertheless continue to be nine times as large as the actual demand for new residential units during the year. In the third year the output of shoes will be 9,940, a decline of 0.8 per cent from the preceding year; this will mean a maximum surplus or shortage of 5 pairs of shoes, depending on whether the population is 10,025 or 10,035. However, although the output of residential units will decline by 100 per cent, the surplus of residential units will not be less than five times and may be seventeen times as large as the demand for new units during the year.

The contrast between dwellings and shoes will be even more pronounced if we posit that errors of estimate can cumulate. All along we have assumed that the volume of construction projected at the beginning of each year will correct fully for any error of estimate that may have been made at the beginning of the preceding year, provided, of course, that the correction does not require a negative quantity of construction. We have therefore proceeded on the assumption that errors cannot cumulate. Once the possibility of cumulation is admitted, the opportunities for magnifying building fluctuations through errors of forecast are indefinitely increased. We might assume, for example, that what is known when quotas are set is the surplus or shortage at the beginning of the preceding year rather than of the given year; that is to say, that B_n will be governed by $(K_n - H_{n-1} + M_{n-1})$. Thus, to return to the above example, if $H_0 = M_0$ and $P_0 = B_0$, B_1 will be 100 and B_2 will also be 100. The consequence of delay in the discovery of errors will be a larger surplus of residential units and therefore a longer cessation of building activity. But the effect on the production of shoes will again be negligible.

The preceding analysis is restricted to a community that experiences uninterrupted growth, requires no replacements, and attempts to adhere closely to a standard of one residential unit per person. These restrictions can be removed by writing the equation for B_n in more general form. In addition to the symbols already defined, let R_n be the number of residential units retired during any year, L_n the estimate of this quantity, and C_n the housing standard during the year. If we assume again that errors cannot cumulate, then

$$B_n = C_n K_n + L_n - H_n + C_n M_n$$

when this quantity is positive; otherwise $B_n = 0$. The preceding analysis, therefore, requires little elaboration. Since population changes may now be negative, there may be zero troughs of construction even when there are no errors of estimate. The task of estimation will consist of two parts, one estimate being of population change and the other of required replacements. The errors of these estimates will at times be cumulative, at others compensatory. When they are cumulative and positive, a larger surplus will arise than if the zone of errors had been confined to population change. The larger surpluses will tend to promote longer cessations of building activity; but this tendency will be counteracted by the decline in the useful stock of residential units through failure to make replacements. However, if even a slight reduction of the housing standard should be concurrent with, or follow shortly, a sizable overestimate of required construction, building might need to be suspended for many years.

Errors of estimate are likely to magnify the fluctuations of national construction as well as of the construction of a single community. This would tend to be the case even under conditions of mobility, since the errors for individual communities will not be entirely self-canceling. Immobility, however, may reinforce the amplifying stimulus of errors of estimate; for the errors will tend powerfully to multiply the occasions when negative construction is theoretically required, and in this way to enlarge the zone within which immobility can exercise its cyclical influence. If the housing standard is constant our earlier conclusion that immobility is likely to intensify the amplitude of national construction will probably still be valid—particularly if estimates for the various communities are made by the same mechanical formula. But if there are occasional departures from the standard of one residential unit per person the outcome is more uncertain. In any case once the data of Groups I and II are known, the influence of immobility can be deduced from them. Group I is now the sum for each year of the quantities $(C_n K_n + L_n - H_n + C_n M_n)$ wherever they are positive; while Group II is the quantity we get for each year by subtracting Group I from the algebraic sum of the quantities $[C_n (K_n + M_n)$

$+L_n-C_{n-1}(K_{n-1}+M_{n-1})-L_{n-1}+R_{n-1}]$ for all communities[13]—this being the construction that would take place under conditions of mobility.

With uncertainty at free play the cyclical power of the several basic factors in residential construction will be at a maximum. The troughs will last longer and be more numerous than when quotas were set by the method of known demand. Some tendency towards direct correlation of errors will arise if the same forecasting method is applied to the communities of a country whose population growth is fairly well diffused geographically. This will promote a clustering of zero troughs, which in turn will promote the formation of long cycles. But chance alone will be almost certain to produce some degree of clustering; thus the errors will be generally positive if some unexpected factor acts to diminish the growth of communities throughout the country. Hence the presumption is that when uncertainty reinforces the cyclical power of the other basic factors, the curve of actual construction will show long cycles with clearly defined contours.

VI. Long Construction Cycles in a Business Economy

We have shown that long cycles in residential construction may easily come into existence in a collectivist economy that adumbrates our business economy. But these long cycles are mechanical in character; and the process of their formation differs in important respects from that of the long cycles in our business economy. We must now extend and adapt the analysis, so that it may apply to the pecuniary organization of our economy. For our purpose the essence of pecuniary organization is economic freedom, which resolves itself into independent action on the part of individuals or groups with a view, mainly, to private advantage.

The touch of rigor in the preceding pages has exposed the power of the basic factors in the cycles of residential construction. But it is important to note that under collectivism, as we have sketched it, these factors are related only in the sense that a certain state of some factor or factors is a necessary condition of the expression of the cyclical power of other factors. In the actual economy, these integrative ties are maintained, but in addition strong geographic and temporal ties are established through the impact of pecuniary forces. Thus pecuniary forces tend to exercise similar sway over

---

[13] This expression is derived from the preceding expression by substituting for H_n the following quantity: $C_{n-1}(M_{n-1}+K_{n-1})+L_{n-1}-R_{n-1}$.

the various regions of the country, which leads to a fair degree of correlation in the fluctuations of construction of the various regions. Further, the common impress of pecuniary forces on the basic factors results in a sharp increase in their effective cyclical power—particularly during periods of extreme expansion or depression in general business. For example, a vigorous and sustained improvement in business conditions will ordinarily stimulate immigration, increase the demand for housing on the part of the average person or family, hasten the retirement of obsolete residential units, and lead to exaggerated forecasts of the real-estate market. In our analysis of collectivism we showed that such changes have large cyclical power in the case of the construction industry. Now, they will tend cumulatively to increase the volume of building once vacancies are at a relatively low level; and the impossibility of transferring dwellings from places or uses of declining demand to places or uses of rising demand, without incurring heavy sacrifices, will promote exaggerated forecasts and therefore work in the same direction. Sooner or later a condition of overbuilding will be discovered; and, as our previous analysis suggests, the durability of dwellings may enforce many years of comparative idleness on the construction industry.

Uncertainty is but one factor in the mechanism of long residential cycles. However, given durable dwellings and the institutional framework of the building and real-estate industries, it is a strategic factor in the prolongation of construction cycles. Let us therefore consider how pecuniary organization, by creating uncertainty at almost every turn, increases the difficulty of adjusting the supply of dwellings to the demand for their use. The current state of the residential market is never a matter of exact knowledge, because dwellings are heterogeneous and realized rentals cannot be ascertained precisely. The volume of current construction is influenced by prospective demand as well as by current demand. Prospective demand may be interpreted in the sense of gross income. This depends on the level of rentals, the size of population, and its housing standard; but these factors are interrelated, and the future state of each is uncertain—partly because it depends to some extent on the volume of future construction. The volume of current construction is governed also by conditions of cost; but land values and construction costs in the present or in the proximate future are only less uncertain than maintenance costs in the distant future. A speculative builder cannot appraise the prospective net income from a certain class of dwellings without taking account of the prospective supply of all classes of dwellings in the same residential district. He must therefore make due allowance for the actions of his fellow builders, who are not in the habit of consulting with him; many of whom, he knows, are more deficient than he in balancing nicely estimates of future income against estimates of present and future costs; and some of whom, he anticipates, have as yet not 'discovered' that deed-searching and house-painting are less profitable than house-building.

The opportunities for producing maladjustment between supply and demand in the market for dwellings are clearly ample. They are enhanced by lax methods of financing construction and by the existence of a double market for dwellings—one for the use of dwellings, another for the dwellings themselves. Excessive liberality in the extension of credit promotes speculation; for it may enable a builder to put up houses without risking much of his own capital. The double market for dwellings also promotes speculation; for, in the first place, it permits the investing public to participate with building operatives in appraising the future state of the rental market, and in the second place, it permits both builders and the public to devote their energies for a time to traffic in real estate with little heed to the rate of interest at which prospective incomes are being capitalized in prices. If a building operative put up houses with a view to rental rather than sale and if he could borrow only a small fraction of his outlays on construction, he would curtail his operations in case he considered the prospects of the rental market unfavorable. But this will not happen if he firmly believes that the outlook of the generality of real-estate traders, or the public who have turned traders, is genuinely optimistic. Nor will it happen if he firmly believes that traders have only a vague notion, if any, concerning the prospective market for the use of dwellings, but nevertheless entertain extremely optimistic notions concerning the prospective market for dwellings. In either case, if costs are not prohibitive, he will build more energetically than ever in the hope of making quick sales. And he will act in the same way, no matter what others may think about real estate, if only his banker is optimistic enough, or expects the public that buys real-estate bonds to be gullible enough, to be willing to lend on the security of what is proposed to be built as much as or more than it will cost to build it.[14] If the disaster envisaged by the building operative actually eventu-

[14] See F. F. French, *Financing Private Construction*, an address at the Fifteenth Convention of the Associated General Contractors of America, January 30, 1934.

ates, but not before he has succeeded in closing his operations at a profit, his private rationality will have contributed to the collapse of the real-estate market largely produced by mass irrationality.

With disequilibrium between demand and supply as the normal condition in the market for dwellings, corrective forces are constantly being set in motion by the profit motive. But the progress of corrective forces is slow in the case of dwellings, partly because of their durability, partly because of methods of financing and of transferring title, and partly because the profit motive often works blindly. Once a corrective adjustment gets firmly under way, it tends to be carried too far, so that errors are produced which in turn require correction. Hence long cycles operating on the reaction principle are likely to occur in residential construction, no matter what the period of the cycles in the changes in the demand for the use of dwellings may be; though the fluctuations of changes in demand will in actual fact be influenced by the long cycles in construction.[15]

Let us assume that after construction activity has been declining some eight or ten years, a vigorous revival in general business gets under way.[16] There will then be a sharp increase in the demand for the use of dwellings. Families that have 'doubled up' will seek separate quarters; marriages that have been postponed will be consummated; urban families that have sought refuge on farms will return to the cities; the normal flow of rural population to the cities will be resumed; and immigration will again set in. The number of vacancies will therefore diminish quickly, and

[15] The statistical indications are that annual increases in the population of the United States have traced out long cycles; that these cycles are largely, but not entirely, attributable to long cycles in immigration; that major depressions in this country have been followed by sharp and protracted declines in immigration and that this factor has played a dominant role in the formation of long cycles in immigration; and, finally, that the long cycles in the increases of national population have corresponded fairly closely, except for the eighties, to the long cycles in the construction of buildings.

[16] Some aspects of the mechanism of long cycles in construction are discussed ably and documented statistically by H. Hoyt in his *One Hundred Years of Land Values in Chicago* (University of Chicago Press, 1933), particularly in Chap. VII. A few suggestive hints are given by Clark, *op.cit.*, passim. For an elaborate statistical inquiry into the major factors in the long cycles of real-estate 'activity,' as exemplified by St. Louis, see R. Wenzlick, "The Problem of Analyzing Local Real Estate Cycles," *Proceedings of the American Statistical Association*, March 1933, and D. S. Wenzlick, "What about Rents," *Journal of the American Institute of Real Estate Appraisers*, January 1933. For illustrative data on fluctuations of real-estate prices, see J. G. Clark, "The Real Estate Cycle in San Diego, California, 1900 to 1932," *ibid.*, April 1933.

rentals may move slowly upward. Hence the gross income from real estate will rise; and the net income will rise faster, since the costs of maintenance are not likely to change appreciably. The pressure on owners of real estate will diminish; foreclosures will decline rapidly; and while there may as yet be little trading in real estate, prices will be higher than in the days when foreclosures were rampant. Conditions in the loan market for both new and old buildings will be improved. Construction costs are likely to be higher; but rising costs will be no bar to construction if the present value of the prospective income from dwellings is reckoned to be larger than their cost. As trading in real estate is revived, and the speculative public again enters the market, the prices of real estate will advance faster than costs of construction. Hence the incentive to new building will be increased.

Once the level of rentals and the rate of occupancy have reached a stage that is generally recognized as profitable, new capital will be increasingly attracted into building. For some time, however, as the demand for the use of dwellings increases, the stock of usable dwellings will increase more slowly. Builders proceed cautiously, fearing that the increase in demand may prove evanescent; much time needs to be expended in choosing sites, formulating plans, arranging loans, letting contracts, and so on; the process of physical construction requires a few months or longer; and the increase in the stock of dwellings is smaller than the volume of new construction, chiefly because of the replacement of obsolete units. But as vacancies tend to disappear, the incentive to build grows stronger; and within a few years the volume of construction will be perhaps several times as large as at the trough of the construction cycle.

There may now occur a depression in general business. This will be reflected in a reduced volume of residential construction. But the level of building activity will continue to be high, since a considerable volume of construction is in process and the condition of the rental market is still sufficiently favorable to stimulate a goodly number of new projects. The continuance of residential construction at a relatively high level will tend to check both the severity and the duration of the depression, while the close of the depression will give a new fillip to both the rental market and the market for houses. Easy credit and speculative zeal will now sharply advance the prices of real estate, and with little regard to the rate of interest at which prospective incomes are being capitalized. As the margin between construction costs and comparable real-estate prices continues to be wide, the volume of building will rise swiftly, particularly since the ranks of builders, no less than of traders, will be swollen by accessions from the public. With speculation rife the adjustment of the supply of dwellings to the increase in demand will be carried too far; and it is only a matter of time before a condition of overbuilding will be generally recognized to exist. At this stage much real estate, both old and new, will be in the hands of owners who have but a thin equity in their property and who will therefore find themselves in difficulty as soon as any decline takes place in rentals or in other sources of income.

A condition of overbuilding is slowly and reluctantly admitted; for what is merely the rising wave of a long cycle is generally mistaken for the underlying trend. The true state of the rental market is screened by the high rate of mobility of occupants of dwellings and by the double demand exercised for some months by families contemplating to vacate rented premises as soon as their new homes are completed. But two sets of forces gather momentum and conspire to bring the boom in residential construction to a halt. In the first place, the rental market becomes strained. It is more and more difficult to rent new dwellings at prices the expectation of which evoked the construction. Renting conditions are still worse in older houses which are also burdened by fairly numerous vacancies. Should a decline in general business occur at this stage, it will sharply intensify the tension in the rental market. In the second place, construction costs creep up on prices of comparable real estate. The competition among builders tends to raise the prices of labor and materials, and the frantic activity tends to diminish the efficiency of labor and management. Hence construction costs rise more sharply than the familiar index numbers may suggest. What is perhaps of even greater importance is that the rise in costs is very uneven, being highest for the inexperienced builders, who have only recently entered the trade. The pressure of rising costs, particularly on inexperienced builders, and of rentals that are barely maintained if not actually declining, will eventually be precipitated in a recognition that a state of overbuilding exists.

A condition of overbuilding cannot be corrected quickly. For a time, the difficulties on the supply side are even likely to increase. Some builders, or else their bankers, may find that the type of dwelling which they construct or the district which they serve still enjoys a favorable market; and this type of construction may continue unabated. Some building projects have been carried too far to be abandoned, and will add to the volume of construction activity for many months. And a demand for specially designed dwellings to be erected on certain preferred sites keeps recurring. Hence, although the volume of building declines, it lingers at a relatively high level at a time when a complete cessation of new construction for several years might be no more than sufficient to bring the supply of dwellings into adjustment with even an increased demand. As the new buildings are completed they enter into competition with the older stock and therefore help to depress rentals.

Therefore, the incentives to new construction progressively diminish. Owners find that their net income from real estate drops much faster than rentals, since costs of maintenance do not decline appreciably and may even rise. Cash sales of real estate are few; and while there may be a semblance of stable values, in actual fact real estate can now be sold at only sharply reduced prices. For a time owners make all sorts of sacrifices to preserve their equities, by drawing upon their savings and business incomes to meet interest on mortgages, amortization payments, and taxes. But if a decline in general business did not set in contemporaneously with the decline in residential construction, it will make its appearance not more than two or three years later. A reduction of the housing standard will take place; and we have already seen that a slight reduction of the housing standard may dispense with the need for new construction even in the face of an increasing population. Nominal rentals will fall considerably and realized rentals even more, at a time when the ability of owners of real estate to draw upon outside sources of income is declining. Hence the transfer of property from owners to creditors will commence on a large scale. The process of liquidation will extend over several years, partly because the period elapsing between the time of default and the end of foreclosure proceedings is normally a half year or longer, partly because mortgages have a term of several years and expire in but small quantities at any one time, and partly because some owners continue to resist stubbornly the loss of their equities at a time when they would do better financially to cut themselves loose from their heavily indebted property. As mortgagees acquire real estate, they are frequently glad to dispose of it for the face value of the mortgage or less, if only because they do not relish the function of real-estate management. There are also distress sales by persons seeking to realize some cash to protect other investments or to meet urgent household needs. Buyers bid cautiously, and many are excluded from the market because transfers cannot be adequately financed. The prices of real estate therefore drop precipitously, and since construction costs do not decline nearly so much, the prices at which dwellings only recently built change hands are considerably lower than it would now cost to build them. Hence the volume of residential construction is negligible, most of it being attributable to demand of a specialized character.

The severe drop in residential construction may help to bring about a deep and protracted depression in general business—one lasting from four to six years, such as that from 1837 to 1842, from 1873 to 1879, or from 1929 to 1933. But if conditions other than the state of the residential market are favorable, the depression will be short-lived. Improvement in general business will be accompanied by improvement in renting conditions. There will also be a revival in residential construction, though most of it will be in regions that have gained by population shifts and much of the rest will be initiated by owners, scattered through the country, who contemplate occupancy. But in spite of the revival the absolute volume of construction will continue at a low level, and will therefore promote an early recession in general business. For, with foreclosures at a high rate and vacancies in most places still numerous, the liquidation in the real-estate market will be uncompleted. So long as foreclosures are active and financial institutions hold title to property that they do not care to manage or to exhibit in their statements, the prices of real estate will continue at levels that imply high capitalization rates of even current incomes. The trend of residential construction will therefore be downward; though its course may be marked by two or three minor waves corresponding to the business cycles that are in the meantime undergoing their swing. We must note that the downward 'trend' of construction is but the declining phase of a long cycle.

Gradually, secular and cyclical forces change the face of the residential market. While the volume of construction has been declining, the trend of population in most cities has been rising; so that the condition of the rental market is bettered. New transportation facilities have become available, or old ones extended; so that residence in the suburbs has become more feasible. At the same time the technique of construction has been improving, and promising innovations in residential facilities have been multiplying. The prices of materials and of labor have, in all likelihood, fallen; and, what is of equal importance on the side of costs, the contractors now bidding for jobs are the more efficient builders who have survived the long depression in residential construction and they can command efficient labor. Finally, foreclosures and distress sales eventually turn downward. The gap between construction costs and comparable real-estate prices will therefore be narrowed, especially in the case of those types of dwellings that have won special favor. For a time, however, little money will be available for financing construction, lenders now tending to be as timorous as some eight or ten years ago they were venturesome.

Nevertheless, the volume of building will slowly rise. Of the many who have long postponed building a home, some will decide that it is not worth risking further hesitation. Some speculative builders, well equipped with capital, will build on a modest scale in anticipation of demand, devoting their resources primarily to houses of the sort that have lately gained most in esteem, but which are better, or more conspicuously, equipped. The revival in building may be one of the agencies that will usher in a revival in general business. Or, what is more likely, the revival in construction will reinforce the revival in other branches of industry, which occurred earlier and itself stimulated the improvement in construction; and it is only as readjustments spread from industry to industry that a general revival in business will get under way. But no matter what the sequence of factors may be, and whatever the role of the ever-disturbing random forces—from which we have abstracted completely in our brief and schematic description—a vigorous revival in business will sooner or later get under way. From this point the long construction cycle will repeat itself. It will not, of course, be a replica of its predecessor; but its general features will be the same and it will belong to the same class of economic movements.

The secular, cyclical, and random forces that combine to terminate the downward movement in the long construction cycle do not appear in exactly the same guise throughout the country. Hence the revival in construction is not synchronous in the various regions of the country, and some districts may entirely escape it. The timing of recessions is no more uniform than the timing of revivals. Only a moderate degree of synchronism in the long construction cycles of the various residential districts is to be expected, and just this is to be found. Since the differences among residential districts are less prominent than the similarities, we can justifiably speak of a long cycle in national construction. But the differences among the districts cannot be set aside, especially if our view extends beyond urban areas. We must therefore revert to the question of the influence of immobility on the amplitude of fluctuations in the national construction of dwellings.

We have already suggested that immobility is one of the channels through which pecuniary forces breed errors and thereby help to bring about, as the case may be, a condition of overbuilding or underbuilding. This might be interpreted as creating a presumption that immobility serves to intensify the fluctuations in national construction, but it does not prove the point. Nor can an analysis of Groups I and II, along the lines earlier suggested, yield a strict proof in the case of a business economy. For, quite apart from the considerations that the unit is now the owner of a dwelling instead of a community and that the data on presumptive construction for Group II are psychic facts, we may no longer assume that the presumptive construction of the country is independent of immobility. Only rough methods and correspondingly uncertain results seem possible. For the period since 1920 we have annual estimates of the increases of the urban and farm population of the United States. If we accepted the increases in urban population as a rough index of Group I and the increases in national population as an index of the presumptive construction of the country, we would infer from their amplitudes that immobility has definitely served to increase the amplitude of national construction. This conclusion is plausible; but it rests on so many dubious assumptions that even the figures involved in the comparison are not worth presenting.

Appendixes

APPENDIX ONE

Notes on Series in Table 1 of "Economic Research and the Keynesian Thinking of Our Times"

[These notes pertain to the annual data, 1923-1939, on which the relatives in Table 1 are based. The data are in the *Twenty-sixth Annual Report of the National Bureau of Economic Research*, pp. 30-35.]

1. July 1 estimates for continental United States, by the Bureau of the Census. Based on statistics of births, deaths, civilian immigration and emigration, in conjunction with the decennial census. *Statistical Abstract of the United States, 1943*, p. 3.

2. Year-to-year differences computed from series 1 before rounding, centered by a two-year moving average.

3-13. In 1929 prices. Simon Kuznets, *National Product since 1869* (National Bureau, 1946), Part I. In the breakdown of gross capital formation presented in our table two components are omitted: net changes in inventories, and net changes in claims against foreign countries.

14. 1923-1929: National Industrial Conference Board, *The Management Almanac, 1945*, pp. 18, 27. (Employment plus unemployment.) 1929-1939: U.S. Bureau of Labor Statistics, *Technical Memorandum No. 20* (July 4, 1945), Table 1.

15. Includes armed forces. Sources same as 14.

16. 1923-1929: Omits employment in agriculture, armed forces, and public employees in service industries. Public employees classified in other industries are included. Computed from data by the National Industrial Conference Board, given in part in their work above, p. 18. 1929-1939: Omits employment in agriculture, armed forces, and employees of federal, state, and local governments. Computed from data in U.S. Bureau of Labor Statistics, *Technical Memorandum No. 16* (July 13, 1944), and *Technical Memorandum No. 20* (July 4, 1945).

17. Series 14 minus series 15, before rounding.

18. Harold Barger and Hans H. Landsberg, *American Agriculture, 1899-1939* (National Bureau, 1942), p. 42.

19. Gainfully occupied. Unpublished revisions by Solomon Fabricant of estimates prepared by Barger and Landsberg.

20. Based on series 18 and 19.

21. Harold Barger and Sam H. Schurr, *The Mining Industries, 1899-1939* (National Bureau, 1944), Table A-5. (Indexes for total mining, including oil and gas wells, 1923-1939, are available for output but not for employment, hours, or hourly earnings. Hence series 21-24 and 50 are restricted to coal mining.)

22. All employees except office workers. *ibid.*, Table A-3, and p. 67.

23. Based on aggregate man-hours and number employed. *ibid.*, Table A-3.

24. Based on series 21, 22, and 23. *ibid.*, Table A-5.

25. Solomon Fabricant, "Labor Savings in American Industry," *Occasional Paper 23* (National Bureau, 1945), p. 46.

26. Wage earners. *ibid.*, p. 46.

27. U.S. Bureau of Labor Statistics, *Bulletin No. 694* (Handbook of Labor Statistics, 1941 edn., Vol. II), p. 16.

28. Based on series 25, 26, and 27. See Fabricant, *op.cit.*, p. 46.

29. Weighted index of freight traffic (ton-miles) and passenger traffic (passenger-miles). Unpublished data compiled by Harold Barger and Jacob M. Gould. See Fabricant, *op.cit.*, p. 50.

30. Wage earners and salaried employees. *ibid.*

31. Unpublished data compiled by Harold Barger and Jacob M. Gould.

32. Based on series 29, 30, and 31.

33. Estimates prepared by Jacob M. Gould for a National Bureau monograph, *Output and Productivity in the Electric and Gas Utilities, 1899-1942* (1946). The figures for 1927-1939 in our table are comparable with employment, i.e., series 34. The figures for 1923-1926 are not; the indexes of output comparable with employment for successive years during this period are 47, 53, 62, 73.

34. Wage earners and salaried employees. *ibid.*

35. *ibid.*

36. Based on series 33, 34, and 35. For 1923-1926 the output figures used are those cited in the note on series 33. *ibid.*

37-40. 1923-1938: Simon Kuznets, *National Income and Its Composition, 1919-1938* (National Bureau, 1941), pp. 322-323. 1939: Extrapolated by use of Department of Commerce data. Series 38 includes wages, salaries, and other compensation of employees.

41-42. Before federal income taxes. Preliminary estimates prepared by Simon Kuznets for a National Bureau monograph on the distribution of income by size.

43-48. Computations based on income tax forms and synopses of regulations in U.S. Bureau of Internal Revenue, *Statistics of Income*, on the assumption (a) that the taxpayer is married and living with spouse, (b) that he has two dependents, (c) that he claims all family exemptions, (d) that his capital gains or losses are nil, (e) that his income from partially tax-exempt interest on government obligations is nil, (f) that this income from dividends before 1936 was taxed on the same principle as in 1936 and later, and (g) that his 'earned net income' is equal to his total net income (i.e., the $5,000, $10,000, etc., in the table) or not less than the statutory maximum earned net income, according as his total net income is smaller or larger than the statutory maximum earned net income. Total net income is net of all deductions except personal exemption and credit for dependents.

The computations refer, obviously, to hypothetical families. The assumptions used blink differences in source of income (capital gains and losses, tax-exempt income, and 'unearned income' generally), differences in family composition, differences in respect of filing joint or separate returns, and changes in these factors and in the regulations affecting them. The actual (unaudited) returns for comparable income classes as given in *Statistics of Income* indicate, first, that the hypothetical figures portray rather faithfully the major changes in the federal personal income tax structure; second, that actual taxes of the upper income brackets relative to the low brackets are somewhat less than our computations may suggest.

49. 1923-1931: Obtained directly from U.S. Bureau of Labor Statistics. 1932-1939: Mimeographed releases by the Bureau of Labor Statistics, *LS44-3259* (March 1944) and *LS46-555* (September 1945).

50. Weighted average, bituminous and anthracite coal. Computed from data in U.S. Bureau of Labor Statistics, *Bulletin No. 694, op.cit.*, p. 13, and *Bulletin No. 697* ("Hours and Earnings in the United States, 1932-40"), p. 122, using man-hour weights from Barger and Schurr, *op.cit.*, p. 312.

51. U.S. Bureau of Labor Statistics, *Bulletin No. 694, op.cit.*, p. 10.

52. Without board. U.S. Bureau of Agricultural Economics, *Farm Labor*, January 12, 1945, p. 9.

53. Unpublished estimates for the United States by Leo Wolman. Data for 1923-1934, including Canadian membership, which is roughly 4 or 5 per cent of the total, are given in Leo Wolman, *Ebb and Flow in Trade Unionism* (National Bureau, 1936), p. 16.

54. Includes workers involved in lockouts as well as in strikes. *Monthly Labor Review*, May 1945, p. 958.

55-59. U.S. Bureau of Labor Statistics indexes. *Survey of Current Business*, 1942 Supplement, p. 18.

60. 1923-1935: Solomon Fabricant, *Capital Consumption and Adjustment* (National Bureau, 1938), Table 32. 1936-1939: Unpublished data by Fabricant.

61. U.S. Bureau of Labor Statistics, *Bulletin No. 699* ("Changes in Cost of Living in Large Cities in the United States, 1913-41"), Table 2.

62. Active corporations, including subsidiaries, filing federal income tax returns. 1923-1926: Reported number active and inactive, multiplied by 0.896 (ratio of active to total number of corporations in 1927), multiplied by 1.066 (ratio of number active including subsidiaries to number active excluding subsidiaries in 1929). 1927-1928: Reported number active multiplied by 1.066. 1929-1939: Reported number active plus reported number of subsidiaries. U.S. Bureau of Internal Revenue, *Statistics of Income for 1940*, Part 2, pp. 282 and 305.

63. Unpublished index based on data from six to eight states (New York is one of them), compiled for a National Bureau monograph on incorporations of business enterprises [*Business Incorporations in the United States, 1800-1943*], by G. Heberton Evans, Jr. Figures for New

York State do not go back of 1924. Indexes for 1923 and 1924 based on six states excluding New York are 99 and 90, respectively [1925:100].

64-66. Total profits and retained income are adjusted to eliminate effects of capital gains and losses, inventory revaluations, and the use of a historical cost rather than reproduction cost basis for depreciation charges. 1923-1938: Simon Kuznets, *National Income and Its Composition, 1919-1938* (National Bureau, 1941), pp. 216 and 316. 1939: Estimates based on Department of Commerce data.

67. Unpublished estimates by Simon Kuznets, based on *Statistics of Income* data, adjusted to reflect reproduction cost instead of historical cost.

68-71. Standard and Poor's Corporation, *Trade and Securities Statistics: Long Term Security Price Index Record*, pp. 5-11. (The issue cited is Vol. 96, No. 9, Sec. 2 of the Corporation's publications.)

72. Number of shares traded in round lots, as reported by the New York Stock Exchange. Successive issues of *Commercial and Financial Chronicle*.

73. New and refunding; Canadian and foreign issues included. *ibid.*

74. At New York City. 1923-1936: Frederick R. Macaulay, *Interest Rates, Bond Yields and Stock Prices in the United States since 1856* (National Bureau, 1938), Appendix A, Table 10. 1937-1939: Successive issues of the *Bank and Quotation Record*.

75-76. Weighted average of prevailing rates charged by banks to their customers on commercial and other loans. 1923-1929: *Banking and Monetary Statistics* (Board of Governors of the Federal Reserve System, 1943), p. 463. 1930-1938: Successive issues of the *Federal Reserve Bulletin*. The number of cities in the Southern and Western group is sixteen in 1923-1924, twenty-five in 1925-1928, and twenty-seven in 1929-1938.

These series were discontinued in February 1939, when a new method of compiling the rates was instituted. The new series are not strictly comparable with the old. See *Banking and Monetary Statistics*, pp. 426-427. Other data suggest that there was little or no difference between the rates prevailing in 1938 and 1939.

78-79. *ibid.*, p. 468. For description of series, see *ibid.*, pp. 429-430.

81. Annual averages derived from end-of-month figures estimated by Anna Jacobson Schwartz and Elma Oliver, National Bureau of Economic Research. The year-end figures were weighted one-half each in deriving the calendar-year averages.

82. Annual averages derived from semiannual call-date figures (December and June) of total demand and time deposits in all banks, reported in *ibid.*, pp. 34-35. Collection items and interbank and U.S. government deposits are excluded. The year-end figures receive a weight of one-half each in the calendar-year averages. A figure for December 29, 1922 was estimated by Anna Jacobson Schwartz.

83. Estimated debits at all commercial banks divided by total de-

mand and time deposits, excluding collection items and interbank deposits (but not U.S. government deposits). *ibid.*, p. 254.

84-86. Estimates for all commercial banks. Series 84: *ibid.* Series 85: supplied by the Federal Reserve Board. Series 86 is series 84 minus series 85.

87. General imports. U.S. Bureau of Foreign and Domestic Commerce, *Foreign Commerce and Navigation of the United States for the Calendar Year 1940*, p. XII.

88. Including reexports. *ibid.*

89-90. Calendar-year totals computed from monthly data, on basis of unrevised Daily Treasury Statements. 1923-1931: Successive issues of the *Annual Report of the Secretary of the Treasury*, 1926-1932. 1932: Supplied by George C. Haas, U.S. Treasury Department. 1933-1939: *Treasury Bulletin*, January 1943, March 1946. Trust accounts are included in 1931 and prior years, excluded thereafter. Estimates excluding trust accounts, on which to base relatives for 1937 and 1939 in Table 1, were computed for 1929 (receipts, $4,115 million; expenditures, $3,202 million). Expenditures exclude public debt retirements. Receipts are net of amounts transferred to the federal old-age and survivors insurance trust fund.

91. Annual averages computed from end-of-month data based on revised Daily Treasury Statements, presented in successive issues of the *Annual Report of the Secretary of the Treasury*, 1936-1940. The year-end figures receive a weight of one-half each in the average for a calendar year.

Notes on the Charts and Table in "New Facts on Business Cycles"

General Note

Only a relatively small fraction of the series summarized in this paper were used in deriving the National Bureau's chronology of business cycles. For the chronology, see A. F. Burns and W. C. Mitchell, *Measuring Business Cycles* (National Bureau, 1946), pp. 78-79. Note the revisions made since the publication of that volume: the trough in 1921 shifted from September to July, the trough in 1927 from December to November, and the trough in 1938 from May to June. Concerning the methods used in dating specific and business cycles, see the source cited, Chap. 4.

Except when otherwise noted, all the series in the following charts are monthly.

Chart 1

The sample is an extension of Moore's sample of well-conforming series, briefly described in the note to Chart 5. The present sample includes series that conform poorly or slightly as well as those that conform well to business cycles. New series analyzed by the National Bureau since Moore's compilation was made (autumn 1948) are not included in Chart 1 or in any of the subgroups in later charts.

Except for the first year and a half of the period, the number of series in the comprehensive sample exceeds 600 every month. The average number is 656 for the twenty-one years 1919-1939 and 665 for 1921-1939. From 642 in January 1921, the number rises to more than 680 throughout 1922-1928, after which it declines gradually to 635 in 1939.

The comparatively small number of series in the beginning of the period is due to the fact that many series in the National Bureau's collection begin in 1919, together with our practice of counting such series as additions to the sample only from the month of their first cyclical turn. A better practice would have been to introduce such series into the tabulations from the month of their first observation; and we have in fact adjusted this way the tabulations of the subgroups shown in later charts. These corrections proved to be so slight in the subgroups that we have not deemed it essential to make them in the full sample. After 1921 the effects produced by the corrections are not at all significant; they are not carried in the subgroups beyond 1922. A comparable inexactitude attends our practice of treating series that terminate during the period 1919-1939 as if they ended in the month following their last observed cyclical turn; but the number of series affected thereby is negligible throughout the period.

To take account of the fact that some series characteristically behave invertedly (falling during business cycle expansions and rising during contractions), the peaks of such series are counted as troughs and the troughs as peaks. For a precise definition of inverted behavior, see *Measuring Business Cycles*, Chap. 5, Secs. I and x. Concerning duplications and weighting, see notes to Charts 4 and 6.

Chart 2

The basic data used are the same as in Chart 1. As noted, the sample changes somewhat during the period covered; but the meaning of curves A, B, and C may be conveyed most readily by assuming a fixed number of series.

Let t represent the number of series reaching troughs in a given month, let p represent the number reaching peaks, let e and c represent the number expanding and contracting respectively, and let subscripts identify the month. Then

$$e_n = e_{n-1} + t_{n-1} - p_{n-1}$$

Thus curve A is essentially derived from the bottom curve in Chart 1.

Curve B, in principle, is defined as follows:

$$e_n - c_n = e_{n-1} - c_{n-1} + 2(t_{n-1} - p_{n-1})$$

Of course, when e and c are percentages,

$$e_n - c_n = 2e_n - 100$$

Let $e_0 - c_0$ be 0; in other words, fix the origin where $e = c$. Also, let T_n stand for $(t_n - p_n)$. Then the ordinate of curve C in month n is defined, in principle, as follows: $K + (e_1 - c_1) + (e_2 - c_2) + \cdots + (e_n - c_n)$, where K is an unknown constant. The indicated sum equals $K + 2[nT_0 + (n-1)T_1 + (n-2)T_2 + \cdots + T_{n-1}]$; the expression in brackets is a cumulative of the cumulative of T.

The meaning of curve C may be grasped without going through the preceding steps. Take a monthly time series, mark off its specific cycles, and discard all information pertaining to it except the dates of its cyclical turns. Draw a straight line with a slope of unity from the date of the first trough to the date of the succeeding peak, connect this peak and the following trough by a straight line with a slope of unity, and so on. Repeat these operations on every series in the group; that is, convert each series into a 'triangular curve.' The arithmetic sum of such converted series will be curve C. That is why it is briefly described in the text and in later charts as a 'simple aggregate of specific cycles.' That is why, also, the scale of the curve is expressed in an abstract unit. (Curve C is described on the chart as the cumulative of B, which is expressed in percentages. From the viewpoint of curve C the precentages serve merely the function of splicing segments based on varying numbers of series.)

Curve C has interesting properties. Assume that its shape is as follows: the curve is continuous, it moves in cycles, the tops and bottoms of the cycles are rounded (first derivative zero), and there is just one point of inflection between the peak and trough. Let the trough come at date a, the point of inflection at i, the peak at s. Then $e_a = c_a$; $e_s = c_s$; $e_n > c_n$ between a and s; e_n increases between a and i; e_n decreases between i and s; $t_n > p_n$ between a and i; $t_n < p_n$ between i and s; and $\Sigma t_n = \Sigma p_n$ between a and s.

Chart 3

The specific time series on this chart are so well known that brief identification will suffice.

1. Index of industrial production: Federal Reserve Board, 1943 revision.

2. Index of factory employment: Bureau of Labor Statistics.

3. Freight car loadings: Association of American Railroads, Car Service Division.

The series are seasonally adjusted: (1) by the compiler, (2) by Federal Reserve Board, (3) by National Bureau.

Chart 4

The total number of series included in the production group during some part of the period 1919-1939 is 115; the average number in any month is over 100, and in no month is the number less than 97.

The total number of series in the employment sample is 41; the average number in any month is 40, and the number is never less than 38.

Like the 'all-inclusive' sample in Chart 1, both the production and the employment subsamples contain duplications. These arise chiefly because comprehensive series as well as some of their components are included. Another reason is that some processes are represented by different series, as when records are compiled by different investigators. We have also studied nonduplicating groups consisting of 58 production and 21 employment series, and these give results that are almost indistinguishable from those yielded by the 115 production and 41 employment series, respectively. For the list of 21 employment series, see the National Bureau's *Twenty-sixth Annual Report*, p. 24 [reprinted on pp. 3-25, above]. Experiments with weighting, apart from those implicit in duplications, have not been made.

The subgroup samples are handled differently than the all-inclusive sample, in that peaks and troughs of 'inverted series' are not interchanged, but are tabulated as they come.

See notes to Charts 1 and 2.

Chart 5

For a full description of how this sample of well-conforming series was selected, see Geoffrey H. Moore, "Statistical Indicators of Cyclical Revivals and Recessions," *Occasional Paper 31* (National Bureau, 1950).

The number of series in a particular month changes steadily from 75 in January 1885 to 233 in January 1919, through a maximum of 366 in

June 1922, to 330 in December 1939. By quinquennial dates, in June, the numbers in (A) Moore's sample and (B) our 'all-inclusive' sample in Chart 1 are as follows:

	A	B
1920	336	602
1925	360	686
1930	356	674
1935	340	648

For the treatment of 'inverted series,' see note to Chart 1.

Chart 6

The number of series included in the group of new orders for investment goods during some part of the period 1919-1939 is 70; the average number in any month is over 65, and the number is never less than 63.

The group on income payments consists predominantly of payroll series, the only exceptions being (1) dividend payments and (2) total income payments to individuals. There are 33 payroll series in all, some of which are aggregates that overlap other series included in the sample. The average number of series in the group on income payments in any month is 35, and in no month is the number less than 34. Analysis of a nonduplicating sample for this group yielded results very similar to those shown on the chart; cf. note to Chart 4.

For the group on industrial production (excluding foods), see note to Chart 4. See that note also for the treatment of inverted series. For other details or interpretations, see notes to Charts 1 and 2.

Not all of the cyclical turning points can be easily made out in this chart. They are as follows:

Cyclical Turn	Orders For Investment Goods	Industrial Production (Excluding Foods)	Income Payments
Trough	Jan. 1919[a]	Mar. 1919[b]	Mar. 1919[b]
Peak	Dec. 1919	Feb. 1920	June 1920
Trough	Jan. 1921	Apr. 1921	July 1921
Peak	Mar. 1923	May 1923	June 1923
Trough	Sept. 1923	July 1924	July 1924
Peak	May 1926	Nov. 1926	July 1927
Trough	May 1927	Nov. 1927	Apr. 1928
Peak	Jan. 1929	July 1929	July 1929
Trough	Mar. 1933	Oct. 1932	Mar. 1933
Peak	Mar. 1937	May 1937	May 1937
Trough	Feb. 1938	May 1938	June 1938

[a] Or earlier.　　[b] Uncertain.

Chart 7

Industrial production: See note to Chart 3.

Net corporate profits: Series is quarterly, seasonally adjusted, and comes from Harold Barger, *Outlay and Income in the United States, 1921-38* (National Bureau, 1942), pp. 297-299.

Per cent of companies undergoing cyclical expansion of profits: Series is quarterly and comes from Thor Hultgren, "Cyclical Diversities in the Fortunes of Industrial Corporations," *Occasional Paper 32* of the National Bureau. Breaks in the series are due to expansion of the sample of companies. In each segment the number of companies is constant, being as follows in successive intervals:

Period	Number of Companies	Period	Number of Companies
1920-1921	17	1926-1927	153
1921-1923	31	1927-1929	155
1923-1924	71	1929-1933	185
1924-1926	101	1933-1938	244

None of these profits series enters the 'all-inclusive' sample of Chart 1. Further details on the composition and coverage of the profits sample will be found in the work cited.

Chart 8

The twenty-one series on which this chart is based are listed below. The first seven constitute the group with longest average leads at revivals; the remainder comprise the group with shorter average leads or with lags at revivals.

1. Dow-Jones index of industrial stock prices
2. Liabilities of business failures (inverted)
3. Inner tube production
4. Railway operating income
5. Paper production
6. Bank clearings outside New York City
7. Residential building contracts, floor space
8. Passenger car production
9. Steel ingot production
10. Industrial building contracts, floor space
11. Pig iron production
12. Index of wholesale prices, Bradstreet's and B.L.S.
13. Ton-miles of freight hauled by railroads
14. Truck production
15. Index of industrial production, Federal Reserve Board
16. Average hours per week, manufacturing
17. Index of business activity, A.T.&T.
18. Index of production, Standard Statistics Co.
19. Factory employment, total
20. Department store sales
21. Factory employment, machinery

For sources and brief descriptions of the behavior of these series, see W. C. Mitchell and A. F. Burns, "Statistical Indicators of Cyclical Revivals," *Bulletin 69* of the National Bureau, May 28, 1938. Readers who consult that bulletin will discover, however, that the top seven series in the present listing are not the same as the top seven presented there, nor are the ranges of the average timing measures the same in the bulletin and the present paper. These discrepancies are the result of revisions of the analyses on which *Bulletin 69* was based, and reflect changes either in the basic data or of the seasonal adjustments, or both. Though the ranking of series has been altered, the changes in average timing measures are slight.

For another analysis along the lines of Chart 8, see Geoffrey H. Moore, *op.cit.*, Table 2 and Appendix A. The appendix presents a method of utilizing current monthly observations in a framework similar to that based on specific cycle units but not requiring the prior identification of specific cycles.

See note to Chart 1 for the treatment of the inverted series, and note to Chart 2 for the interpretation of the curves.

Table 1

The rise in series 26 and the fall in series 2 might have been treated as extending through midcontraction. See *Measuring Business Cycles*, pp. 192-193, 195.

In series 2, 17, and 24, the number of expansions covered is greater by one than the number of full cycles. In series 4, 7, 10, 19, 21, and 26, the number of contractions covered is greater by one than the number of full cycles. In series 17, there are two additional contractions (they arise from a gap in the series).

Most series in this table are identified in the source cited. See *ibid.*, Appendix C, notes to Table 21, for series 1, 3, 4, 8, 9, 11-13, 17, 22, 25; notes to Chart 9, for series 6; notes to Chart 3, for series 14; and notes to Chart 8 and Tables 18-19, for series 19. Concerning series 2, 5, 16, 26, see *ibid.*, Chap. 6, note 7.

To identify series 7, 18, 20, see Appendix 1 of *Historical Statistics of the United States, 1789-1945* (a supplement to the *Statistical Abstract of the United States*).

Series 10: G. Heberton Evans, Jr., *Business Incorporations in the United States, 1800-1943* (National Bureau, 1948), pp. 80-81.

Series 15: Computed by National Bureau by compiling a weighted aggregate of seasonally adjusted production data for anthracite coal, bituminous coal, crude petroleum, and electric power. The weight for each is the average value of a unit of output during 1922-1931, except that the unit value for electric power is net of the cost of fuel consumed and of current purchased.

Series 21: Barger, *op.cit.*, pp. 297-299.

Series 23: Dollar volume of sales adjusted for price changes. Seasonally adjusted dollar sales from *Federal Reserve Bulletin*, August 1936, p. 631, and subsequent issues. Deflating index supplied by Federal Reserve Bank of New York.

Series 24: Federal Reserve Board index; seasonally adjusted by compiler. *Federal Reserve Bulletin*, December 1927, pp. 26-27, and subsequent issues.

Index

NATIONAL BUREAU OF ECONOMIC RESEARCH PUBLICATIONS IN REPRINT

An Arno Press Series

Barger, Harold. **The Transportation Industries, 1889-1946:** A Study of Output, Employment, and Productivity. 1951

Barger, Harold and Hans H. Landsberg. **American Agriculture, 1899-1939:** A Study of Output, Employment, and Productivity. 1942

Barger, Harold and Sam H. Schurr. **The Mining Industries, 1899-1939:** A Study of Output, Employment, and Productivity. 1944

Burns, Arthur F. **The Frontiers of Economic Knowledge.** 1954

Committee of the President's Conference on Unemployment. **Business Cycles and Unemployment.** 1923

Conference of the Universities-National Bureau Committee for Economic Research. **Aspects of Labor Economics.** 1962

Conference of the Universities-National Bureau Committee for Economic Research. **Business Concentration and Price Policy.** 1955

Conference of the Universities-National Bureau Committee for Economic Research. **Capital Formation and Economic Growth.** 1955

Conference of the Universities-National Bureau Committee for Economic Research. **Policies to Combat Depression.** 1956

Conference of the Universities-National Bureau Committee for Economic Research. **The State of Monetary Economics.** [1963]

Conference of the Universities-National Bureau Committee for Economic Research and the Committee on Economic Growth of the Social Science Research Council. **The Rate and Direction of Inventive Activity:** Economic and Social Factors. 1962

Conference on Research in Income and Wealth. **Input-Output Analysis:** An Appraisal. 1955

Conference on Research in Income and Wealth. **Problems of Capital Formation:** Concepts, Measurement, and Controlling Factors. 1957

Conference on Research in Income and Wealth. **Trends in the American Economy in the Nineteenth Century.** 1960

Conference on Research in National Income and Wealth. **Studies in Income and Wealth.** 1937

Copeland, Morris A. **Trends in Government Financing.** 1961

Fabricant, Solomon. **Employment in Manufacturing, 1899-1939:** An Analysis of Its Relation to the Volume of Production. 1942

Fabricant, Solomon. **The Output of Manufacturing Industries, 1899-1937.** 1940

Goldsmith, Raymond W. **Financial Intermediaries in the American Economy Since 1900.** 1958

Goldsmith, Raymond W. **The National Wealth of the United States in the Postwar Period.** 1962

Kendrick, John W. **Productivity Trends in the United States.** 1961

Kuznets, Simon. **Capital in the American Economy:** Its Formation and Financing. 1961

Kuznets, Simon. **Commodity Flow and Capital Formation.** Vol. One. 1938

Kuznets, Simon. **National Income:** A Summary of Findings. 1946

Kuznets, Simon. **National Income and Capital Formation, 1919-1935:** A Preliminary Report. 1937

Kuznets, Simon. **National Product in Wartime.** 1945

Kuznets, Simon. **National Product Since 1869.** 1946

Kuznets, Simon. **Seasonal Variations in Industry and Trade.** 1933

Long, Clarence D. **Wages and Earnings in the United States, 1860-1890.** 1960

Mendershausen, Horst. **Changes in Income Distribution During the Great Depression.** 1946

Mills, Frederick C. **Economic Tendencies in the United States:** Aspects of Pre-War and Post-War Changes. 1932

Mills, Frederick C. **Price-Quantity Interactions in Business Cycles.** 1946

Mills, Frederick C. **The Behavior of Prices.** 1927

Mitchell, Wesley C. **Business Cycles:** The Problem and Its Setting. [1927]

Mitchell, Wesley C., et al. **Income in the United States:** Its Amount and Distribution 1909-1919. Volume One, Summary. [1921]

Mitchell, Wesley C., editor. **Income in the United States:** Its Amount and Distribution 1909-1919. Volume Two, Detailed Report. 1922

National Accounts Review Committee of the National Bureau of Economic Research. **The National Economic Accounts of the United States.** 1958

Rees, Albert. **Real Wages in Manufacturing, 1890-1914.** 1961

Stigler, George J. **Capital and Rates of Return in Manufacturing Industries.** 1963

Wealth Inventory Planning Study, The George Washington University. **Measuring the Nation's Wealth.** 1964

Williams, Pierce. **The Purchase of Medical Care Through Fixed Periodic Payment.** 1932

Wolman, Leo. **The Growth of American Trade Unions, 1880-1923.** 1924

Woolley, Herbert B. **Measuring Transactions Between World Areas.** 1966